Third Edition

Real-Time Digital Signal Processing from MATLAB® to C with the TMS320C6x DSPs

Third Edition

Real-Time Digital Signal Processing from MATLAB® to C with the TMS320C6x DSPs

Thad B. Welch
Boise State University, Boise, ID, USA

Cameron H.G. Wright
University of Wyoming, Laramie, WY, USA

Michael G. Morrow
University of Wisconsin, Madison, USA

CRC Press
Taylor & Francis Group
Boca Raton London New York

CRC Press is an imprint of the
Taylor & Francis Group, an **informa** business

CRC Press
Taylor & Francis Group
6000 Broken Sound Parkway NW, Suite 300
Boca Raton, FL 33487-2742

First issued in paperback 2020

ISBN-13: 978-1-4987-8101-5 (hbk)
ISBN-13: 978-0-367-73645-3 (pbk)

Library of Congress Cataloging-in-Publication Data

Names: Welch, Thad B., author. | Wright, Cameron H. G., author. | Morrow, Michael G., author.
Title: Real-time digital signal processing from MATLAB to C with the TMS320C6x DSPs / Thad B. Welch, Cameron H. G. Wright, Michael G. Morrow.
Description: Third edition. | Boca Raton : Taylor & Francis, 2017. | Includes bibliographical references and index.
Identifiers: LCCN 2016033212| ISBN 9781498781015 (hardback) | ISBN 9781315365688 (ebook)
Subjects: LCSH: Signal processing--Digital techniques. | Texas Instruments TMS320 series microprocessors.
Classification: LCC TK5102.9 .W44 2017 | DDC 621.382/2--dc23
LC record available at https://lccn.loc.gov/2016033212

Visit the Taylor & Francis Web site at
http://www.taylorandfrancis.com

and the CRC Press Web site at
http://www.crcpress.com

To Donna...

To my young son Jacob and the memory of my beloved wife Robin...

To all those people whose friendship, counsel, and criticism have helped us along the way...

Foreword

Digital signal processing is at the "heart" of most technologies that we use today. Our cell phones use digital signal processing to generate the DTMF (dual tone multi-frequency) tones that are used to communicate with wireless networks. Our noise-canceling headphones use adaptive digital signal processing to cancel the noise in the environment around us. Digital cameras use digital signal processing to compress images into JPEG formats for efficient storage so that we can store many thousands of images in a single memory card. It is digital signal processing that allows us to play compressed music stored in our cellphones and iPods. Digital signal processing controls even the anti-lock brakes in our cars today. And these are just a few examples of real-time signal processing in the world around us.

There are many good textbooks today to teach digital signal processing—but most of them are content to teach the theory, and perhaps some MATLAB® simulations. This book has taken a bold step forward. It not only presents the theory, it reinforces it with simulations, and then it shows us how to actually use the results in real-time applications. This last step is not a trivial step, and that is why so many books, and courses, present only theory and simulations. With the combined expertise of the three authors of this text—Thad Welch, Cam Wright, and Mike Morrow—the reader can step into the real-time world of applications with a text that presents an accessible path. This Third Edition continues to support the C6713 DSK and the multi-core OMAP-L138 board from Texas Instruments. The multi-core OMAP-138 chip includes both a C6784 DSP core and an ARM9 GPP core, making it very powerful and attractive to a wide variety of users. The new addition also supports the TI LCDK (low cost development kit). New project chapters covering adaptive filtering and second-order sections (sos) have been added to the existing project chapters that include QPSK and QAM transmitters and receivers. All code has been updated to run on CCS version 6.1 and all m-files have been updated to run on MATLAB 2016a.

I have been fortunate to co-author several papers with the authors of this text, and can speak from first-hand experiences of their dedication to engineering education. They go the extra mile to continue to expand their understanding and their abilities to present complex material in a logical, straightforward manner. They attend conferences on engineering education; they chair sessions on engineering education; they write papers on engineering education; they live engineering education! (One of the co-authors, Thad Welch, was recently selected as the first Signal Processing Engineering Network Fellow to recognize his leadership and contributions.). I am delighted to be able to have an opportunity to tell the readers of this text that they are in for, in the authors' own words, "a ride...".

Delores M. Etter
Caruth Chair in Electrical Engineering
Distinguished Fellow, Darwin Deason Institute for Cyber Security
Lyle School of Engineering
Southern Methodist University
Dallas, Texas

(Dr. Etter is a member of the National Academy of Engineering and is a Fellow of both the IEEE and the American Society of Engineering Education. She served as the Assistant Secretary of the Navy for Research, Development and Acquisitions from 2005–2007, and as the Deputy Under Secretary of Defense for Science and Technology from 1998–2001. She is also the author of a number of engineering textbooks, including several on MATLAB.)

About the Authors

Thad B. Welch, Ph.D., P.E., is a Professor and past Chair of the Department of Electrical and Computer Engineering at Boise State University. He previously taught in the Department of Electrical and Computer Engineering at both the U.S. Naval Academy (USNA) and the U.S. Air Force Academy (USAFA). A retired Commander in the U.S. Navy, he was the inaugural 2011 SPEN Fellow, won the 2001 ECE Outstanding Educator Award, the 2002 Raouf Award for Excellence in the Teaching of Engineering, the John A. Curtis Lecture Award from the Computers in Education Division of ASEE in 1998, 2005, and 2010, the 2003 ECE Outstanding Researcher Award at USNA, and the 1997 Clements Outstanding Educator Award at USAFA. Dr. Welch is the former Chair and a founding member of the Technical Committee on Signal Processing Education for the Institute of Electrical and Electronic Engineers (IEEE) Signal Processing Society. He is a senior member of the IEEE and a member of the American Society for Engineering Education (ASEE), Tau Beta Pi (the engineering honor society), and Eta Kappa Nu (the electrical engineering honor society).

Cameron H. G. Wright, Ph.D., P.E., is a Professor in the Department of Electrical and Computer Engineering at the University of Wyoming. He previously taught at the U.S. Air Force Academy (USAFA) in the Department of Electrical Engineering where he was Professor and Deputy Department Head. A retired Lieutenant Colonel in the U.S. Air Force, he won the Brigadier General R. E. Thomas Award for Outstanding Contributions to Cadet Education in 1992 and 1993. In 2005 and 2008, he won the IEEE Student Choice Award for Outstanding Professor of the Year, the Mortar Board "Top Prof" Award at the University of Wyoming in 2005, 2007, and 2015, the Outstanding Teaching Award from the ASEE Rocky Mountain Section in 2007, the John A. Curtis Lecture Award from the Computers in Education Division of ASEE in 1998, 2005, and 2010, the Tau Beta Pi WY-A chapter Undergraduate Teaching Award in 2011, and the University of Wyoming Ellbogen Meritorious Classroom Teaching Award in 2012. Dr. Wright is a founding member of the Technical Committee on Signal Processing Education for the IEEE Signal Processing Society, a senior member of the IEEE, and a member of ASEE, the National Society of Professional Engineers, the Biomedical Engineering Society, SPIE–The International Society of Optical Engineering, Tau Beta Pi, and Eta Kappa Nu.

Michael G. Morrow, M.Eng.E.E., P.E., is a Faculty Associate in the Department of Electrical and Computer Engineering at the University of Wisconsin–Madison. A retired Lieutenant Commander in the U.S. Navy, he previously taught in the Electrical and Computer Engineering Department at the U.S. Naval Academy and in the Department of Electrical and Computer Engineering at Boise State University. Mr. Morrow won both the 2002 Department of Electrical and Computer Engineering Outstanding Educator Award and the 2003 Gerald Holdridge Teaching Excellence Award at the University of Wisconsin–Madison. He is the founder and president of Educational DSP (eDSP), LLC, a company devoted to the development of affordable DSP solutions for educators and students worldwide. He is a member of the Technical Committee on Signal Processing Education for the Institute of Electrical and Electronic Engineers (IEEE) Signal Processing Society, a senior member of the IEEE, and a member of the American Society for Engineering Education (ASEE).

Contents

List of Figures

List of Tables

Program Listings

Preface

THIS book is intended to be used by students, educators, and working engineers who need a straightforward, practical background in real-time digital signal processing (DSP). In the past, there has been a formidable "gap" between theory and practice with regard to real-time DSP. This book bridges that gap using methods proven by the authors. The book is organized into three sections: Enduring Fundamentals (9 chapters), Projects (12 chapters), and Appendices (10 chapters). The software that accompanies this book includes all necessary source code, along with additional information and tutorial material to help the reader master real-time DSP (see Chapter 1 for instructions to access the software). There is also a website that supports the book (see http://www.rt-dsp.com/), where the reader can find the latest news, tips, tutorials, errata, extra material, and software.

We anticipate that the reader will use this book in conjunction with a more traditional, theoretical signal processing text if this is their first exposure to DSP. *The book you are now reading is* **not** *intended to teach basic DSP theory*; we assume you already know or are in the process of learning the theory of DSP. Instead of teaching theory, this book uses a highly practical, step-by-step framework that provides hands-on experience in real-time DSP and, in so doing, reinforces such basic DSP theory (what the authors refer to as *enduring fundamentals*).[1] This framework utilizes a series of demonstrations, exercises, and hands-on projects in each chapter that begins with a quick overview of the applicable theory, progresses to applying the concepts using MATLAB®, and ultimately running applicable programs in real-time on some of the latest high-performance DSP hardware. For the projects, the readers are coached into creating for themselves various interesting real-time DSP programs. Be sure to check out the appendices of this book—some readers have commented that they are worth the price of the book all by themselves! Each of the *enduring fundamentals* chapters includes at the end of the chapter a number of problems, for homework or self-study, that probe the reader's understanding of key DSP concepts important to that particular chapter. These key concepts are typically only briefly covered in this text, as mentioned above; more depth is expected to come from the more traditional and theoretical text that the reader has already read or uses now in conjunction with this book. This is intentional. If the solutions to the end of chapter problems prove elusive to the reader, then a review of the theory is most likely warranted for the reader to get the most out of this text.

Ideally, the reader should either be enrolled in, or have already taken, an introductory DSP (or discrete-time signals and systems) course. However, we have had success using various parts of this book with students who have not yet had a DSP class, using a "just in time" approach to supplemental theory. The topic coverage of this book is broad enough to accommodate both undergraduate and graduate level courses. A *basic* familiarity with MATLAB and the C programming language is expected—but you don't have to be an expert

---

[1] It would be highly impractical for a book of reasonable size to teach both theory and hands-on practice in an effective manner.

in either. To take full advantage of this book, the reader should have access to a relatively modest collection of hardware and software tools. In particular, some recommended items include a standard PC running a fairly recent version of Microsoft Windows® (e.g., Windows 7 SP1, 8.1, or 10), a copy of MATLAB and its Signal Processing Toolbox, and one of the inexpensive Texas Instruments DSP boards (with software) described below. Some other miscellaneous items, such as a signal source (any device capable of digital music playback such as an iPod, smartphone, or even a CD player works well); speakers (the powered type typically attached to a PC works well), headphones, or earbuds; and 3.5 mm stereo patch cables (sometimes called 1/8th inch stereo phono plug cables) will all be useful. For processing the input and output signals with the greatest flexibility, several different codecs for the DSP boards are supported (see Chapter 1). Access to some common test equipment such as an oscilloscope, a spectrum analyzer, and a signal generator allows even more flexibility, but we show how a second inexpensive DSP board or even a PC's soundcard can be used as an inexpensive substitute for such test equipment if desired.

The real-time software explained in and provided with this book supports several of the relatively inexpensive DSP boards that are or were available from Texas Instruments (TI). These boards include the OMAP-L138 version of the TI Low Cost Development Kit (LCDK), the LogicPD Zoom OMAP-L138 Experimenter Kit, and the still available TMS320C6713 DSK.[2] There is limited backward compatibility with the TMS320C6711 DSK as well, but there is no explicit coverage in the text of this discontinued board. The currently available boards all come standard with (or have available for free download) a powerful set of software development tools (Code Composer Studio™), of which we make considerable use in the following chapters.

The first edition of this book was written in response to the many requests by both students and faculty at a variety of universities. When the authors presented some of the concepts and code that appear in this book at various conferences, we were besieged by an audience trying to "bridge the gap" from theory to practice (using real-time hardware) on their own. This book collects in a single source our unified step-by-step transition to get across that "gap," and the first edition proved to be quite popular.

The second edition updated the book to include support for a more powerful DSP development board that was then available from Texas Instruments, the LogicPD Zoom OMAP-L138 Experimenter Kit. This board is no longer being manufactured, but is still in use at many universities. The second edition also added some additional topics (e.g., PN sequences) and some more advanced real-time DSP projects (e.g., higher-order digital communications projects such as QPSK and QAM for transmitters and receivers) that were requested by readers of the first edition.

This third edition provides support for the most recent and powerful of the inexpensive DSP development boards currently available from Texas Instruments, the OMAP-L138[3] LCDK. This complicated but extremely versatile board is a good example of why our book is used by so many engineers, educators, and students: we make it easy to begin using this board for real-time DSP and save the reader many hours of frustration. A more detailed description of the DSP boards supported by this book is included in Chapter 1. The third edition also includes two new real-time DSP projects (exploring the use of second-order sections and the design of adaptive filters) as requested by readers of the earlier edition. We have also added three new appendices: an introduction to the Code Generation tools

---

[2]The acronym "DSK" stands for "**D**SP **S**tarter **K**it." While the LCDK and the Experimenter Kit boards discussed in this book are not officially called a "DSK" by TI, we choose to simplify the discussion and often call all the boards DSKs. The boards can be purchased from authorized TI distributors or directly from TI (see Section 1.3.1). Note that significant academic discounts and donations from TI are available (also discussed in Section 1.3.1).

[3]The OMAP-L138 contains both a C6748 processor core and an ARM processor core; we use both.

available with MATLAB, a guide on how to turn the LCDK into a portable battery-operated device, and a comparison of the three DSP boards directly supported by this edition. With the publisher's addition of color reproduction to this edition, we regenerated most of the figures in the book to take advantage of that. We also checked and ran (on each of the three boards) all the software that accompanies the book. As with previous editions, we have incorporated all the valuable and highly appreciated feedback and suggestions from many users of the earlier editions, resulting in what we hope is an even better book.

Note that any errata, updates, additional software, and other pertinent material will be posted on the book's website maintained by the authors at `http://www.rt-dsp.com`. Since DSP hardware updates are made faster than we can publish a new addition of the book, this website will provide a means for the authors to provide support even for selected new DSP boards that are introduced after this current edition is published. For your convenience, the QR code at the end of this preface will also take you to this website. The publisher, CRC Press (part of the Taylor & Francis Group), also provides a secure webpage for access to material such as the Solutions Manual for this text, to which they allow access by professors who adopt this text for one or more of their courses. Contact the publisher for details.

The path from DSP theory to real-time implementation is filled with many potential potholes, roadblocks, and other impediments that have historically created the well-known "gap" between theory and practice. This book provides a proven method to smooth out the path, clear the obstacles, and avoid the usual frustrations to get you across the gap. We hope you enjoy the ride...

T.B.W., C.H.G.W., M.G.M.

Scan the QR code below to access `http://www.rt-dsp.com`.

MATLAB® is a trademark of The MathWorks, Inc. For product information, please contact:
The MathWorks, Inc.
3 Apple Hill Drive
Natick, MA 01760-2098 USA
Tel: 508-647-7000
Fax: 508-647-7001
Email: `info@mathworks.com`
Web: `www.mathworks.com`

Acknowledgments

THIS book would not have been possible without the support and assistance of Texas Instruments (TI), Inc. In particular, the authors would like to extend a sincere thank you to Cathy Wicks, whose tireless efforts in directing TI's worldwide University Program has helped make DSP affordable for countless students and professors. Cathy's predecessors Christina Peterson, Maria Ho, and Torrence Robinson also contributed to our efforts that eventually resulted in this book. TI's support of DSP education is unsurpassed in the industry, and the authors greatly appreciate such a forward-looking corporate vision.

We would also like to thank Nora Konopka and Kyra Lindholm of CRC Press (part of the Taylor & Francis Group), who helped guide this third edition to completion. Their ready help, quick responses, and never-failing sense of humor should be the model to which other publishers aspire. Note that we provided the manuscript to the publisher fully formatted in "camera-ready" form, so any typos are the fault of the authors, not the publisher.

The authors would like to acknowledge Robert W. Conant for his valuable contributions to the chapter on QPSK digital receivers, and Brian L. Evans for his helpful suggestions regarding coverage of PN sequences in the text. Robert F. Kubichek, at the University of Wyoming, also provided many excellent suggestions and feedback.

This book was certainly improved because of the input of both anonymous reviewers and the experiences of the many users of the first and second editions, who gave us valuable feedback and many excellent suggestions.

We would be remiss if, in these brief acknowledgments, we omitted a "plug" related to the mechanics of writing the text: this book was typeset using LATEX, a wonderfully capable document preparation system developed by Leslie Lamport as a special collection of macros for Donald Knuth's TEX program (specifically, we used the pdfLATEX variant of pdfTEX created by Han The Thanh to directly produce output as a PDF file). LATEX is ideally suited to technical writing, and is well supported by the worldwide members of the TEX Users Group (TUG); investigate http://www.tug.org/ for details. TEX, LATEX, and pdfLATEX are *freely available* in the public domain (the name TEX is a trademark of the American Mathematical Society). We used the excellent TeXstudio freeware editor (see http://texstudio.sourceforge.net/) as a front-end to the comprehensive TeX Live distribution of LATEX freely provided by the TEX Users Group. For maintaining the database of bibliographic references in the standard BIBTEX syntax, we used the freely available and highly capable JabRef program (see http://jabref.sourceforge.net/). All these programs are not only free, but also available for a variety of operating systems. Figures in this book were created mainly with one of two programs: Canvas and MATLAB. Canvas is a high-end technical drawing package by ACD Systems of America, Inc.; it can create and manipulate both vector and bit-mapped graphics in the same figure, providing a capability similar to both Adobe Illustrator and Adobe Photoshop combined all in one package. MATLAB, by The MathWorks, Inc., is an incredibly powerful numerical computing environment and a fourth-generation programming language, with many Toolbox extensions available for various specialized fields.

Section I:
Enduring Fundamentals

Chapter 1

Introduction and Organization

1.1 Why Do You Need This Book?

IF you want to learn about real-time[1] digital signal processing (DSP), this book can save you many hours of frustration and help you avoid countless dead ends. In the past, "bridging the gap" from theory to practice in this area has been challenging. We wrote this book to eliminate the impediments that were preventing our own and our colleagues' students from learning about this fascinating subject. When these barriers are removed, as this book will do for you, we believe that you will find real-time DSP to be an exciting field that is relatively straightforward to understand. The expected background of the reader and the tools needed to get the most out of this book are listed in the Preface.

Real-time DSP can be one of the "trickiest" topics to master in the field of signal processing. Even if your algorithm is perfectly valid, the actual implementation in real-time may suffer from problems that have more to do with computer engineering and software engineering principles than anything related to signal processing theory. While becoming an *expert* in real-time DSP typically requires many years of experience and learning, such skills are in very high demand. This book was written to start you on the path toward becoming such an expert.

1.1.1 Other DSP Books

There are dozens of books that eloquently discuss and explain the various theoretical aspects of digital signal processing. Texts such as [1–7], written primarily for electrical engineering students, are all excellent. For a less mathematical treatment, [8,9] are good choices. It has been shown that computer-based demonstrations help students grasp various DSP concepts much more easily [10–26]. To take advantage of this fact, a number of books also include software programs that help the student more clearly understand the underlying concepts or mathematical principles that the author is trying to relate. In recent years, as MATLAB® has become an integral part of engineering education at most institutions, this software has increasingly been provided as MATLAB programs (often called *m-files*) delivered via enclosed CD-ROMs, DVDs, or the World Wide Web. Textbooks such as [1,4,27] are popular examples of comprehensive theoretical DSP texts that include MATLAB software. Some books are less theoretical but provide many MATLAB demonstrations [9,28–30]. These are often used along with one of the more in-depth texts listed previously. Finally, there are

---

[1]The phrase *real-time* means that the system is responding "fast enough" to some external event or signal to allow proper functioning. DVD players, digital cellular telephones, automobile anti-lock brake systems, and aircraft digital flight controls are common examples that rely on real-time DSP.

books that are aimed at helping the reader learn to make the best use of MATLAB for DSP and other technical pursuits [31–33].

1.1.2   Demos and DSP Hardware

Static demonstrations using MATLAB are extremely valuable, and we use them extensively in our own courses. However, they typically use previously stored signal files and cannot be considered "real-time" demonstrations. Some MATLAB programs, using a PC sound card or data acquisition card, have a fairly limited ability to bring signals in from the "real world" and perform some processing using the general purpose CPU of the PC, but we have found this to be inadequate for teaching real-time DSP. Students need to be introduced to some of the more common aspects of specialized hardware used for real-time DSP, but in a way that minimizes the many frustrations that past students and faculty have encountered.

While there are other books available that include discussions of using real-time DSP hardware (e.g., [34–36]), we found that these other books don't really meet our students' needs. These other books just don't provide a smooth transition for a reader unfamiliar with real-time DSP or specialized programming concepts, and many require fairly expensive DSP hardware to run the included programs. In response to that need, we created a set of tools that could be used to learn real-time DSP in a series of reasonable steps, beginning with the easy-to-use winDSK8 program, progressing to the familiar MATLAB environment, and finally making the transition to actual real-time hardware using inexpensive DSP Starter Kits (DSKs). When these tools became known [20, 21, 37–56] to our colleagues at various universities, we were inundated with requests to consolidate these tools into a book, which became the first edition of this book. The second edition benefited from many helpful suggestions by readers, and this third edition represents the result of over a decade of constructive feedback from users worldwide, combined with our own continuing work in the field of engineering education.

1.1.3   Philosophy of This Book

This book is designed to be used alone or with any of the previously mentioned DSP texts. What sets this book apart is that it allows the reader to take the next step in mastering DSP: we take a concept and show the reader how to easily progress from a demonstration in MATLAB to running a similar demonstration in real-time code on actual high-performance DSP hardware. Until this book was published, the learning curve in moving to real-time DSP hardware had been too steep for most students and too time-intensive for most faculty. This book overcomes these problems in a methodical and practical way.

The reader is guided through examples and exercises which demonstrate various DSP principles. Whenever possible, we begin with demonstrations that are easy to run and require no programming by using the functionality built into winDSK8, which can run seamlessly on any of the three DSP boards supported by this book, and does not require Code Composer Studio. We then transition to a familiar interface via MATLAB, introducing the needed programming ideas one concept at a time. After the concepts have been explained, we lead the reader in a step-by-step fashion to the point where the DSP algorithms first developed in MATLAB are converted to the C language, and are running in real-time on industry-standard DSP hardware. It's important to note that unlike most other DSP hardware-related books, the software for this book allows the transition to DSP hardware without requiring the reader to first learn assembly language or obscure C code libraries to implement the examples and exercises in real-time. Some examples don't even require a knowledge of MATLAB or C.

Some activity has been reported recently at engineering education conferences where very inexpensive, general-purpose processor-based solutions (e.g., Arduino, Raspberry Pi, etc.) have been used to teach some basic DSP concepts. While these efforts are very low-cost, using platforms that were originally intended for the hobbyist market, rather than using professional-grade DSP processors and development tools (as we do in this text), puts a significant limitation on the kinds of programs that can be run in real-time, and doesn't provide the student with important "industry-grade" experience.

1.2 Real-Time DSP

An underlying assumption of most digital signal processing operations is that we have a sampled signal, our *digital signal*, that we wish to process. In an educational environment, these signals are often stored for subsequent retrieval or synthesized when needed. While this storage or synthesis method is very convenient for classroom demonstrations, computer-based assignments, or homework exercises, it does not allow for real-time processing of a signal. Our students get much more excited about DSP when we incorporate real-time signal processing into our classroom presentations and the associated laboratory exercises. This increased excitement leads to greatly increased learning opportunities for our students.

We use the term *real-time processing* to mean that the processing of a particular sample must occur within a given time period or the system will not operate properly. In a *hard real-time* system, the system will fail if the processing is not done in a timely manner. For example, in a gasoline engine control system, the calculations of fuel injection and spark timing must be completed in time for the next cycle or the engine will not operate. In a *soft real-time* system, the system will tolerate some failures to meet real-time targets and still continue to operate, but with some degradation in performance. For example, in a portable digital audio player, if the decoding for the next output sample of the song being played is not completed in time, the system could simply repeat the previous sample instead. As long as this happened infrequently, it would be imperceptible to the user. Although general purpose microprocessors can be employed in many situations, the performance demands and power constraints of real-time systems often mandate specialized hardware. This may include specialized microprocessors optimized for signal processing (digital signal processors or DSPs), programmable logic devices (e.g., CPLDs or FPGAs), application specific integrated circuits (ASICs), or a combination of any or all of them as required to meet system constraints. *Please note that we have now used the acronym "DSP" in two different ways*—a very common occurrence in the digital signal processing field! In the first case, "DSP" meant "digital signal process*ing*." In the second case, "DSP" referred to a "digital signal process*or*." The intended use of the acronym DSP should be clear from the context in which it is used.

1.3 How to Use This Book

This book is designed to allow someone with a basic understanding of DSP theory to rapidly transition from the familiar MATLAB environment to performing DSP operations on a realistic hardware target. Our DSP target of choice is a member of the high-performance Texas Instruments (TI) C6000™ DSP family. Specifically, we chose the TMS320C67xx digital signal processor series, which supports both floating-point and fixed-point operation. The C67xx DSK target was selected because of its relatively inexpensive purchase price, widespread utilization and compatibility with designs used in industry, and a feature-rich software development tool set (called Code Composer Studio™) that is freely provided for this target.

1.3.1 Supported Boards

Three very affordable development boards are supported by this book, which all use C67xx processors. They are: the OMAP-L138 LCDK, the Zoom OMAP-L138 Experimenter Kit, and the TMS320C6713 DSK (often just called the C6713 DSK).[2] **Note:** TI makes two variants of the LCDK, the OMAP-L138 version and the C6748 version. They are the same price, but the OMAP version is a multi-core design. To make best use of this text, use the OMAP-L138 LCDK. The Zoom OMAP-L138 Experimenter Kit is no longer being manufactured, but is still in use at many universities. The LCDK and the C6713 DSK are both still available and can be purchased from authorized TI distributors or directly from TI (see `http://www.ti.com/tool/TMDSLCDK138` or `http://www.ti.com/tool/tmdsdsk6713`, respectively).[3] Academic discounts and donations are available through the TI University Program (go to `http://e2e.ti.com/group/universityprogram/`). Both boards come standard with (or have available free downloads of) the powerful software development suite called Code Composer Studio (CCS) of which we make considerable use in the following chapters (note that this book assumes the use of CCS version 6.1 or higher, but earlier versions of CCS will generally work just as well with little or no changes needed). Tutorial material for current and for many earlier versions of CCS can be found on the book's website at `http://www.rt-dsp.com`. See Figures 1.1 to 1.4 for photos of the three supported boards.

While the first edition of this book contained some explicit support of the older, no longer available C6711 and C6211 DSKs, we will not discuss them in this edition (although there is some limited backward compatibility with these older boards).

The OMAP-L138 is a multi-core processor that contains both a C6748 VLIW digital signal processor core and an ARM926EJ-S RISC general purpose processor core. On the LCDK, the processor runs at 456 MHz with 128 MB of DDR2 RAM available; this board also requires a JTAG emulator pod that provides communication via USB between the CCS

---

[2]As mentioned in the Preface, the acronym "DSK" stands for "**D**SP **S**tarter **K**it." To simplify the discussion, we sometimes choose to use the term "DSK" for all the boards.

[3]At the time of this writing the list prices on the TI website were $195 for the OMAP-L138 LCDK (plus $79 for the XDS-100 emulator), and $395 for the older but still very useful C6713 DSK.

Figure 1.1: The OMAP-L138 LCDK, shown with the XDS-100 emulator pod attached.

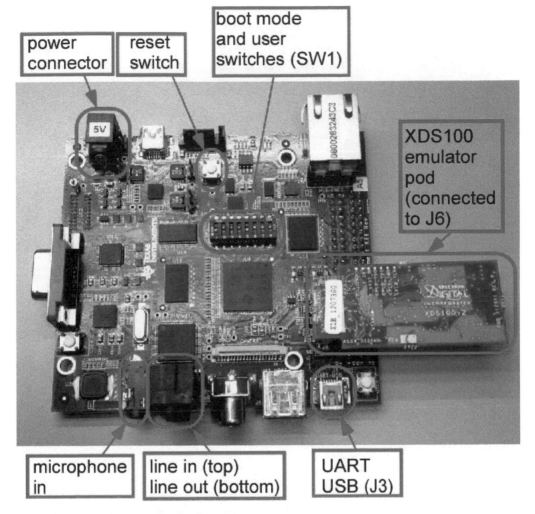

Figure 1.2: An annotated picture of the OMAP-L138 LCDK. The parts of the LCDK that need to be located most often by readers of this text are labeled.

program on the PC and the processor on the DSP board.[4] The most inexpensive JTAG emulator pod is the XDS-100v2 from TI; unless you are developing for other target processors or boards, there is no need to buy a higher priced emulator pod. In the Experimenter Kit configuration, the multi-core processor runs at 375 MHz and is located on a replaceable system-on-chip (SoC) module along with 128 MB of DDR RAM and a wide variety of I/O capabilities; a JTAG emulator is part of this board. The C6713 DSK uses a single-core TMS320C6713 VLIW digital signal processor running at 225 MHz, with 16 MB of RAM; a JTAG emulator is part of this board. See Appendix I for a more detailed comparison of the three boards, and Appendix D for more detail on certain computer architecture aspects of the C6713 and C6748 processors.

Typically, real-time DSP hardware has to communicate with the "outside" world. This is usually accomplished on the input side with an analog-to-digital converter (ADC) and on

---

[4]JTAG refers to a specialized interface originally developed for testing and debugging by the "Joint Test Action Group." The interface can also be used for general data transfer. Since 1990, it's been codified as IEEE Standard 1149.1, and is widely used in industry.

Figure 1.3: The OMAP-L138 Experimenter Kit, previously manufactured by Logic PD for Texas Instruments.

Figure 1.4: The C6713 DSK, manufactured by Spectrum Digital for Texas Instruments.

the output side with a digital-to-analog converter (DAC). Integrated circuit (IC) chips that combine the ADC and DAC functions in one device package are often called *codec* chips, which is an acronym for "*co*der and *dec*oder." This book supports several different codecs for the supported boards. We primarily support the codec that is included on each board, along with some optional plug-in codecs for specialized applications. Both the LCDK and the OMAP-L138 Experimenter Kit include a high-quality stereo codec (TLV320AIC3106) that is capable of up to 32-bits per sample and a maximum sample frequency of 96 kHz. The C6713 DSK's built-in stereo codec (TLV320AIC23) is capable of up to 24-bits per sample and a maximum sample frequency of 96 kHz. Most of the examples in this book configure these codecs to use 16-bits per sample at a sample frequency of 48 kHz (for reasons that will become evident), but we include all the necessary code to reconfigure the codecs as desired.

1.3.2   Host Computer to DSP Board Communication

Many demonstrations, examples, and projects in this book need to transfer data at high speed between the host PC and the memory space of the DSP, bypassing the codecs. This can be accomplished with the two OMAP-L138 boards through careful use of a serial port that is included on the board. The C6713 DSK, on the other hand, does not include any way to transfer data to and from the host computer except through the JTAG debugger interface, which is extremely limited in bandwidth (and therefore is slow); using the JTAG interface also requires that the TI Code Composer Studio (CCS) software tools be available. This means that the existing suite of winDSK8 [42, 57–59] demonstration software and other software tools cannot run on the "out of the box" C6713 DSK, denying educators a valuable teaching and classroom demonstration resource. Also, there is no way to interface an application on the host PC directly to the C6713 DSK, limiting the ability of students to create stand-alone, interactive projects using this DSK. To solve this problem, the authors created a small, inexpensive add-on interface board for the TMS320C6713 DSK that uses the Host Port Interface (HPI) to provide both a means for a PC host application to boot software onto the DSK, and to permit the transfer of data between the DSK and the host PC application [56]. Figure 1.5 shows this interface board installed on the C6713 DSK. We also created a software package that makes it possible for students to create stand-alone Microsoft Windows®applications that communicate directly with the OMAP-L138 boards or with the C6713 DSK (if the C6713 DSK has the HPI interface board installed).

While the two OMAP-L138 boards have many built-in I/O options, the C6713 DSK does not. To rectify this, the HPI interface board for the C6713 DSK provides parallel port communication, USB, RS-232, and digital input/output ports as user-selectable resources available to the DSK software (as shown in Figure 1.5(b); see the eDSP website [60] for more information). Using the HPI interface board on the C6713 DSK permits full use of all the winDSK8 features that appear throughout this book; this add-on board is not needed for the OMAP-L138 boards.

As mentioned above, the OMAP-L138 boards have many built-in I/O options. In addition to a number of specialized connections, these boards include multiple USB ports, an RJ-45 (Ethernet), and an RS-232 (serial port) connector. When using Code Composer Studio to run C programs on the C6748 core of the LCDK, use the USB port on the XDS100v2 emulator pod (see Figure 1.2); on the OMAP-L138 Experimenter Kit use the USB "mini-B" receptacle located closest to the DB-9 RS-232 connector. Note that these are *not* the same connectors to use when running winDSK8 with either of the two OMAP-L138 boards. When using the LCDK with the winDSK8 program, winDSK8 communicates with the DSP board using the USB "mini-B" receptacle designated as J3 (see Figure 1.2), which connects to a UART port on the board. When using the OMAP-L138 Experimenter Kit with the

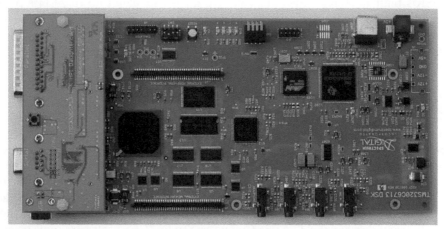

(a) Top view of the HPI interface board on the C6713 DSK.

(b) Side view of the HPI interface board on the C6713 DSK.

Figure 1.5: The HPI interface board on the C6713 DSK.

winDSK8 program, winDSK8 communicates with the DSP board using the DB-9 receptacle, which connects to the RS-232 UART port on the board. You will need to use a null modem cable or null modem adapter along with the connection to the DB-9 receptacle, and perhaps a USB-to-serial converter (see the book website for more details regarding this).

It's important to know that winDSK8 will not run on either of the two OMAP-L138 boards without a simple "do once and forget" procedure. To prepare either one of the OMAP-L138 boards for use with winDSK8, the user must first load some software code into the flash memory for the OMAP-L138, using a simple-to-use free flash programming utility. Complete and detailed instructions are given on the book website (look for the "Reflashing" instructions appropriate for the board you are using). This reflashing operation needs to be done only once (unless the user needs to reprogram the flash memory for some other purpose later). Power-on program execution for the two OMAP-L138 boards is determined by each board's DIP switches. With the DIP switches in the correct position (again, see the instructions on the book website), the ARM9 GPU core of the OMAP-L138 processor will load the stored winDSK8 code from the flash memory upon power up, and the ARM9 then takes control of the C6748 DSP core with communication to the host computer accomplished via the appropriate port. In this way, the ARM9 is acting in much the same way that the host port interface (HPI) board acts on the older C6713 DSK, but accomplishes these communication functions locally without the need for an additional interface board. In this configuration, both the ARM9 core and the C6748 core are being used.

If you are an OMAP-L138 Experimenter Kit user, you may be concerned that many newer computers, particularly laptops, don't come with serial ports anymore, since the ubiquitous USB interface has taken over many of the I/O needs of users. If the particular host computer to be used with the OMAP-L138 Experimenter Kit and winDSK8 has no serial port, an inexpensive USB-to-serial adapter works quite well. We have achieved transfer rates of over 900 kBaud using these adapters (but be aware that some older USB-to-serial adapters do not support such high rates).

When using winDSK8 with a C6713 DSK, clicking on a button in the graphical user interface (GUI) on the host computer initiates a download of the appropriate code from the host to the DSK, and starts the code running on the DSK. When using winDSK8 with the OMAP-L138 boards, clicking on a button in the GUI on the host computer sends a short message to the ARM9 core on the OMAP-L138, telling the ARM9 core to load the appropriate winDSK8 code from the on-board flash memory into the C6748 core and start it running. From the user's perspective, the primary difference between running winDSK8 on the C6713 DSK and running winDSK8 on one of the OMAP-L138 boards is that the former uses the USB connection on the HPI interface board, whereas the latter uses a connection directly on the main OMAP-L138 board. The "user experience" is very similar, regardless of the DSP hardware being used.

In a course-based laboratory setting, a mix of C6713 and OMAP-L138 boards could be used as desired for nearly all aspects of this book, including winDSK8 demonstrations and C programs using Code Composer Studio. The authors have gone to great lengths to maintain compatibility and similar operation for all three of these boards throughout the book.

1.3.3 Transition to Real-Time

For each DSP concept in this book, we will typically take a four-step approach. Specifically, we will follow the approach listed below.

- Briefly review the relevant DSP theory.

- Demonstrate the concept with an easy-to-use tool called winDSK8. With winDSK8, you can program and manipulate the real-time hardware *without* having to write a program.

- Explain and demonstrate how MATLAB techniques can be used to implement the concept (not necessarily in real-time, but in a way most students find easy to understand).

- Provide and explain the C code necessary for you to implement your own real-time program using a DSK and its software development tools.

For most readers of this book, the first step should serve only as a refresher and to set in context the overall discussion.[5] The second step permits the reader to further explore the concept and facilitates "what if" experimentation unencumbered by the need to program any code. The third step, using MATLAB examples, helps to reinforce your understanding of the underlying DSP theories. These examples use standard MATLAB commands that occasionally require the Signal Processing Toolbox.[6] Our well-commented MATLAB code is written such that the algorithm is clearly evident; optimizations that may obscure the underlying concept are avoided. Once the reader has worked through this non-real-time DSP experience, the final step is the key to "bridging the gap" to real-time operation. From the discussion in the book, the reader will be able to confidently implement the same algorithms in C using state-of-the-art real-time DSP hardware. Each chapter ends with a list of follow-on challenges that the reader should now be prepared to implement as desired. Section I (Enduring Fundamentals) chapters also include end-of-chapter problems for homework or self-study.

A cautionary note: some of our students have tried to "save time" by skipping the MATLAB step and jumping right into the C code. Don't do it! It's been demonstrated time and time again that the students who first work with the algorithms in MATLAB consistently get the C version to work correctly. Those who skip the MATLAB step have a much harder time, and often can't get their code to work properly at all. Don't say we didn't try to warn you!

1.3.4   Chapter Coverage

The first nine chapters of this book cover topics that we believe are a significant part of the *enduring fundamentals* of DSP, presented in the context of real-time operation. The experience you gain while studying these chapters is crucial to being ready for the real-time DSP projects that are presented in the chapters of Section II (Projects). A special mention needs to be made here regarding the appendices in Section III. While most other DSP books force you to track down and look up various key pieces of information that you need for real-time DSP from a plethora of sources, the appendices at the end of this book (with supplemental information provided on the book website) collect in a single location a distilled and simplified version of all the important topics that are needed to work effectively with DSP hardware such as the C67xx DSK. The appendices by themselves are probably worth the price of this book!

---

[5]As mentioned in the Preface, we anticipate that the reader will use this book in conjunction with a more traditional, theoretical signal processing text if this is their first exposure to DSP. *The book you are now reading is not intended to teach basic DSP theory.*

[6]The Signal Processing Toolbox is an optional product for MATLAB, also available from The Math-Works. You may also want to explore graphical programming environments suitable for DSP (i.e., Simulink from The MathWorks and LabVIEW from National Instruments).

Table 1.1: Top-level directory organization of the software that supports the book. CCS stands for Code Composer Studio, the software development environment for Texas Instruments DSPs.

File or Directory	Comment
`code`	contains subdirectories with source code for each chapter
`code\chapter_xx\matlab`	contains MATLAB files for Chapter xx
`code\chapter_xx\ccs`	contains CCS files for Chapter xx
`code\appendix_x`	contains files related to Appendix x
`code\common_code`	contains files related to all CCS projects
`code\target_configuration`	contains board setup for all CCS projects
`docs`	contains supplemental information
`test_signals`	contains test signals for exercises and projects
`pc_apps`	contains winDSK8 software

1.3.5 Hardware and Software Installation

The software that accompanies this book, available on the book website (at `http://www.rt-dsp.com`), contains a great deal of useful software (see Table 1.1 for the directory organization). This software is an integral part of the book, and the remaining chapters assume that you have already downloaded it, and installed it all properly, in addition to having already installed the DSK itself and the software that accompanies the DSK. To install the DSK hardware and software, complete the "Hardware Getting Started" guide and the "Software Getting Started" guide that come with your DSK. To install the software that accompanies this book, follow the procedure outlined below.

1. Set your web browser to `http://www.rt-dsp.com`.

2. Go to the Third Edition section of the website and find the instruction file, located at `http://www.rt-dsp.com/3rd_ed/3e_software.html`. Note that this file is not visible by a link; type the URL manually as needed for your browser. This file contains the specific instructions that will lead you through the process of downloading and installing the software for the book.

3. Follow the instructions in the file.

Following the instructions will result in the software for the book being installed on your computer in the correct directory structure. This directory structure is important for proper use of the software.

After you have completed the hardware and software installation discussed above, launch winDSK8. **Important:** Ensure the correct selections have been made in the "DSP Board" and "Host Interface" configuration panels of winDSK8 for each parameter[7] *prior* to initiating the DSK Confidence Test. A successfully completed DSK confidence test will be one of your best indicators that you have properly installed the DSK. You can also use the winDSK8 confidence test in the future to easily verify the proper operation of your DSK.

---

[7]You may want to experiment with communication port parameters, as more than one speed or configuration may work. In general, try to use the fastest mode that works with your computer and winDSK8. See the winDSK8 "Help" button for more information.

To help you avoid frustration, we repeat some information here. Note that when using the LCDK, the USB connector on the board labeled as J3 is used when running winDSK8, but the USB port located on the XDS-100v2 JTAG emulator pod is used when running C code with Code Composer Studio (see Figure 1.2). When using the OMAP-L138 Experimenter Kit, the RS-232 serial connector is used when running winDSK8, but the USB port located next to the RS-232 connector is used when running C code with Code Composer Studio. Both of these connectors on the OMAP-L138 Experimenter Kit are shown at the upper left of the board in Figure 1.3. When using a C6713 DSK, the USB port on the HPI interface card, shown in Figure 1.5(b), is used when running winDSK8, but the USB port on the DSK itself is used when running C code with Code Composer Studio. This important difference regarding which one of the connectors to use has been a common point of confusion in the past.

A minor point: where the text shows figures depicting various screen shots of winDSK8, MATLAB, Code Composer Studio, or other software tools, keep in mind that later versions of these tools may have slightly different screen representations for the user interface. It should be fairly obvious to the reader how a given figure as shown in the text relates to a possible newer version of the same software tool.

1.3.6   Reading Program Listings

Important: Some of the code listings in this book include lines that, despite our best efforts, are too long to fit within the book's margins and yet still use meaningful variable and function names. So be watchful when reading program listings for those instances where a line wrap occurred in the listing due only to page margins. In that case, the wrapped part of the line is indented, and the characters "[+]" show up to identify the beginning of the wrapped part of the line. The "[+]" characters are *not* part of the program, which you'll confirm if you compare the listing as printed in the book to the actual program file from the downloaded software archive. Note that the line numbers shown at the left edge of the listings do not increment for the wrapped part of a line.

A minor point: a particular code listing shown in the text may not always match exactly the associated code listing you'll find in the downloaded software archive (but should be very similar). This is because the manuscript for the book must be "frozen" before the code must be, and there may be slight improvements in the code before the software archive is created. There may also be later improvements and updates to the code on the textbook website, as mentioned in the Preface.

1.4   Get Started

Once the hardware and software are installed and you begin reading the remainder of this book, we encourage you to stop frequently and try out various programs and examples as they are mentioned. As Sophocles once said, "One must learn by doing the thing; for though you think you know it, you have no certainty until you try it." Real-time DSP can be tremendous fun; we hope this book helps you find it as much fun as we do ...

1.5   Problems

1. Describe the difference between real-time DSP and non-real-time DSP. Give an example of each.

2. Describe the difference between a hard real-time system and a soft real-time system. Give an example of each.

3. What are the two definitions of the acronym "DSP" used in this chapter? Give an example of each.

Chapter 2

Sampling and Reconstruction

2.1 Theory

WHENEVER we wish to obtain a real world signal in order to process it digitally, we must first convert it from its natural analog form to the more easily manipulated digital form.[1] This involves grabbing, or "sampling," the signal at certain instants in time. We assume the sampling instants are equally spaced in time (T_s), so that the *sampling frequency* (F_s) is equal to $1/T_s$. Each individual sample represents the amplitude of the signal at that instant in time, and the *number of bits* per sample that we use to store this amplitude determines how accurately we can represent it. More bits means better fidelity, but it also means greater storage and processing requirements. The effect of changing the number of bits will be discussed later in the chapter.

2.1.1 Choosing a Sampling Frequency

One potential problem that can occur during sampling is called *aliasing*, which results in samples that do not properly represent the original signal. Once aliasing has crept into your data, no processing in the world can "fix" your samples so that the original signal can be recovered. To prevent aliasing, the sample frequency, F_s, of the ADC (analog to digital converter) must be equal to or greater than twice the maximum frequency f_h contained in the analog input signal.[2] Often the sample frequency is considerably higher than $2f_h$. Typically, some form of input signal conditioning (such as an analog lowpass filter) ensures that the maximum frequency contained in the analog input signal is less than $F_s/2$. The effect of changing the sample frequency will be discussed later in the chapter.

2.1.2 Input/Output Issues: Samples or Frames?

While it is easier to understand DSP theory and operations on a sample-by-sample basis, in reality this is often an inefficient way to configure the actual input and output of data. Just as a computer hard disk transfers data in blocks of many bytes rather than one byte or word at a time, many DSP systems transfer data in "blocks" known as *frames*. We will discuss both methods in this book, beginning with sample-by-sample processing. Chapter 6 discusses frame-based processing in more detail.

---

[1]There is also an increasing number of signals that are "born digital." That is, they are created inside a computer. For these signals, each data point is considered a "sample."

[2]This assumes a lowpass, or baseband, signal. For a bandpass signal having bandwidth BW, we find $F_s \geq 2BW$ but F_s must also satisfy other conditions. See [5] for more detail.

Figure 2.1: A generic DSP system.

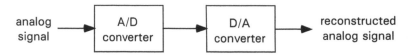

Figure 2.2: A talk-through system.

2.1.3   The Talk-Through Concept

A block diagram of a generic DSP system is shown in Figure 2.1. While this figure shows a highly simplified block diagram of a DSP system, for this discussion we can simplify the diagram even more. Our goal at this point in the text is simply to pass the signal entering the ADC directly to the DAC (digital to analog converter), with no actual processing being performed. This process is routinely called *talk-through*, and is often used as the first test of a DSP system to determine if it is working, if the input and output connections are correct, and to familiarize the user with the system and its software tools. Talk-through is also invaluable for showing the user what the underlying limitations of the ADC and DAC process will impose on more complicated applications. The DSP algorithm for talk-through is simply to pass the sample from the ADC directly to the DAC. A block diagram of this very basic operation is just a simplified version of Figure 2.1, and is shown in Figure 2.2. Note that the DSP talk-through algorithm is so simple that the entire DSP algorithm block can be omitted.

Our goal is for the reconstructed analog signal coming out of the DAC to be nearly identical to the analog input signal that went into the ADC. Once we have implemented a talk-through system similar to Figure 2.2, we can explore some of the capabilities and limitations of the hardware we are using. This may seem like a trivial step, but having a more detailed understanding of this process is very helpful before we move on to incorporating more complicated DSP algorithms into the system.

2.2   winDSK Demonstration

2.2.1   Starting winDSK

If you start the winDSK8 program, a window similar to Figure 2.3 will appear. In later discussions, we won't show the main interface screen for winDSK8. The secondary interface screens we show in this and in later chapters will be of more interest to the reader.

Ensure the correct selections have been made in the "DSP Board" and "Host Interface" configuration panels of winDSK8 for each parameter before proceeding. These selections are "sticky," such that the next time you run winDSK8, the choices you made will still be selected.

2.2.2   Talk-Thru Application

Clicking on the winDSK8 Talk-Thru button will start the Talk-Thru (talk-through) program in the attached DSK, and a window similar to Figure 2.4 will appear. If you have an audio source (e.g., an MP3 player or a CD player) connected to the DSK's audio input, and a

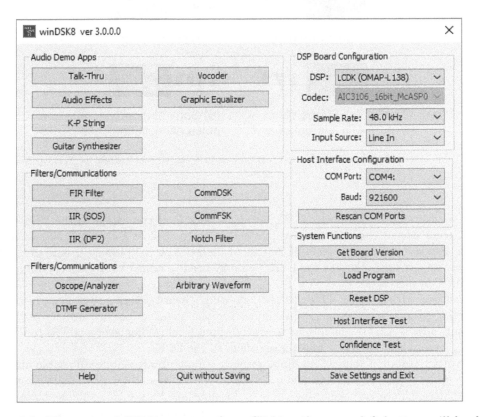

Figure 2.3: The main winDSK8 user interface. Clicking the upper left button will load the Talk-Thru application.

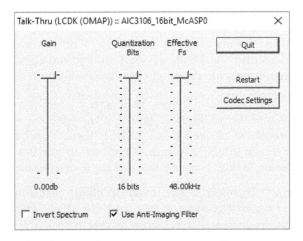

Figure 2.4: winDSK8 running the Talk-Thru application.

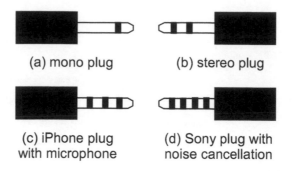

(a) mono plug   (b) stereo plug

(c) iPhone plug   (d) Sony plug with
with microphone   noise cancellation

Figure 2.5: Various types of audio mini-plugs used with devices such as MP3 players and CD players.

pair of speakers (common powered PC speakers work fine) connected to the DSK's audio output, then whatever music you are playing on your MP3 or CD player should now be audible. If you are using the headphone jack of the MP3 or CD player (instead of the "line out" jack) to send the signal to the DSK, you may need to adjust your player's volume level to obtain a proper result.

If you are experiencing difficulty (i.e., no audio heard), verify that your player and speakers are functioning properly by connecting the speakers directly to the player. At this point, adjust the system volume to your desired level. When everything is functioning properly, reconnect the player and the speakers to the DSK.

One other common cause of no signal is using a monaural (mono) audio cable instead of a stereo audio cable. Most small audio devices use 3.5 mm stereo patch cables (sometimes called 1/8th inch stereo phono plug cables). As shown in Figure 2.5, a mono cable's mini-plug has 2 metal segments while a stereo cable's mini-plug has 3 metal segments. Some devices use proprietary variations on the mini-plug, also shown in Figure 2.5. The DSK input and output connectors are intended to be used with the type of mini-plug shown in Figure 2.5(b); using any other type of mini-plug may cause problems.

If your output signal sounds fuzzy, distorted, or clipped (basically, not as you expected), you may be overdriving the ADC. For example, the TLV320AIC3106 codec used on the OMAP-L138 boards has a maximum input voltage of about ±1 volt. If you input a signal that exceeds this allowed range, your signal will sound fuzzy, distorted, or clipped.[3]

When using a multichannel Analog Interface Circuit (AIC), such as the native stereo codec found on the OMAP-L138 boards or the C6713 DSK board, the Talk-Thru demonstration application is executed independently on both left and right channels.

The application permits demonstration of three basic effects:

1. Quantization — The effect of different bit-length conversions can be shown by the variable truncation of the audio data, reducing the effective resolution of the codec converters to a minimum of one bit. From DSP theory, we know that the signal to quantization noise ratio (SQNR) is proportional to the number of bits used (approximately 6 dB increase in SQNR for each added bit of resolution).

2. Spectral Inversion — By selecting the Invert Spectrum checkbox, the sign bit of every other sample is changed (the same as having every other sample multiplied by −1). This is equivalent to modulating the input signal with a frequency of one-half the sample frequency. The effect is that the frequency spectrum is flipped around a

---

[3]How your ADC deals with this overdriven condition depends on how it was designed. The most common results are saturation or wraparound. Some ADCs can be programmed to either saturate or wraparound, depending upon the user's desires.

frequency equal to the sample frequency divided by four, effectively "scrambling" the signal as it would be heard by a listener. If the resulting signal is then passed through a second DSK performing the same operation, the original signal will be recovered.

3. Aliasing — The *effective* sample rate (or sample frequency F_s) can be varied by using a variable decimation factor.[4] A single input sample is repeatedly transmitted for an integral number of output samples, which reduces the effective sample rate of the converter by that integral number. In this way, aliasing can be easily demonstrated even when using a sigma-delta converter. When operating with a reduced effective sample rate, the Invert Spectrum effect is modified to give inversion about the effective F_s, not the actual codec F_s.

2.3 Talk-Through Using Windows

If you have a personal computer (PC), you almost certainly have the ability to record, store, and play back sound files. For PCs running Microsoft Windows,[5] the recorded files typically have file names that end with extensions such as .wav, .wma, .mp3, .m4a, and so on (depending on your input source, your hardware, and your version of Windows). There are many other audio file formats we don't have time or space to discuss. The *.wma file format, for example, is a proprietary Microsoft standard for compressed audio files created to compete with the *.mp3 file format. The *.m4a file format is an open standard for compressed audio files intended to be the successor to the *.mp3 file format. The older, but simpler, *.wav file format is a free and open standard that most commonly contains uncompressed linear pulse code modulation (LPCM) audio data, similar to the audio encoded on CDs. We prefer to deal with *.wav files for our purposes here. Even though the *.wav file sizes are larger, the uncompressed sound quality is higher, which allows better comparison of DSP results (e.g., is signal degradation due to your algorithm or is it related to the lossy compression of the file format?). It's also very easy to import *.wav files directly into MATLAB®, which will be handy when using this text.

If you haven't worked with wav-files before, you may be surprised to learn that even the latest versions of Windows include many such *.wav files. For example, all the little sounds your PC makes when Windows wants to alert the user to various events or errors are typically stored as *.wav files. For most recent versions of Windows, you can find many of them in the subdirectory C:\WINDOWS\MEDIA. Double-clicking on a *.wav file name will play back the wav-file through the PC's sound system. Note that this is really only the DAC half of the talk-through operation; the ADC has already been performed, and the resulting samples were stored in the wav-file.

In order to create your own wav-files, you'll need an input source (such as a microphone or a digital audio player) that can be connected to your PC's sound input. Note that some computers have separate sound cards, while others (lower-priced PCs and most laptop computers) have the sound card circuitry integrated on the main board (motherboard) of the computer; however, the connectors and operation should be similar. There are usually at least three sound connectors on a typical PC: "microphone in," "line out," and "speaker out." PCs with higher-end sound cards may have additional connectors, such as "line in." Most laptop computers have only two sound connectors: "microphone in," and "headphones out." The "microphone in" jack is typically where you connect your input source.

Different sound cards (or integrated sound circuits on motherboards) are shipped with different software to support them; use the appropriate program to ensure that the mi-

---

[4]All of the supported codecs use sigma-delta conversion, which internally oversamples the signal. This means that simply changing the basic sample frequency won't necessarily result in the expected aliasing.

[5]Microsoft Windows is a registered trademark of Microsoft Corporation.

(a) Included with Windows XP

(b) Included with Windows Vista, 7, 8, 8.1

Figure 2.6: The Sound Recorder program included in various versions of Windows.

crophone input setting is not muted, or no signal will be sent to the ADC. Be sure to also adjust the input levels so that while you are recording the system does not saturate (overdrive the input). The status of the input level is usually indicated by some type of colored bar or bars with an adjustable slider control nearby. A common implementation used is such that as the input level increases, a green bar grows in length. As the input increases further, the bar continues to grow in length, but the color changes to yellow (a warning), then to red (saturation or clipping is occurring). You will need to adjust your system using trial and error. While you do not want saturation (red bar) to occur (resulting in a distorted signal), you also don't want the system gain set so low that little or no green is displayed while you are recording (which would result in a low signal-to-noise ratio, and thus a "noisy" recording).

Past versions of the Windows operating system shipped with a rudimentary sound recording program, typically found under the "Accessories" category. The Sound Recorder program included with Windows XP is simple but useful, and is shown in Figure 2.6(a). The Sound Recorder program included with Windows Vista, Windows 7, Windows 8, and Windows 8.1, shown in Figure 2.6(b), is not very useful for our purposes, as it can only save files in the *.wma compressed file format. Windows 10 does not ship with even the rudimentary recording program of Figure 2.6(b). There is a "replacement" available as a free app from the Windows Store called Voice Recorder, but it is also unsuited to our purposes for this book.

Luckily, there are many freely available programs that can be used for recording your own wav-files (and for doing many other audio-related tasks such as mixing and editing). An outstanding example, shown in Figure 2.7, is called Audacity® (for more details, see http://www.audacityteam.org/). While Audacity can save recorded audio in over a dozen file formats, for our purposes here we recommend staying with simple *.wav files.

To actually record a wav-file, determine the sequence needed for the particular program you are using, provide an input source, and start the recording. Once you have recorded a wav-file, you can play back the file either in the program you used to record the file or by double clicking the file name (after it has been saved) from Windows Explorer.

You now have explored the ability to record, save, and playback a wav-file using only your PC. Playback using some sound recording programs can also incorporate various special effects such as changing the playback speed, adding an echo, or playing the file

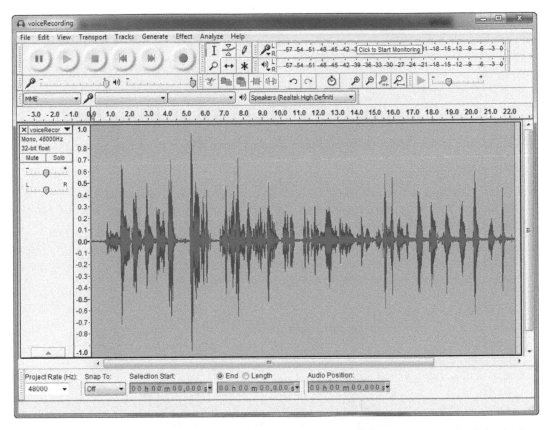

Figure 2.7: A freely available sound recorder, mixer, and editing program called Audacity.

backward.[6] Options within most sound recording programs also allow you to vary the sample rate, the number of bits used to represent each sample, and whether the recording is stereo or monaural. A few typical combinations of these settings, along with a subjective label regarding the sound quality, are shown below for uncompressed audio.

Telephone quality	8 bits/sample	mono	8,000 samples/sec
AM radio quality	8 bits/sample	mono	22,050 samples/sec
FM radio quality	16 bits/sample	stereo	32,000 samples/sec
CD quality	16 bits/sample	stereo	44,100 samples/sec
Studio quality A	16 bits/sample	stereo	48,000 samples/sec
Studio quality B	24 bits/sample	+stereo+	96,000 samples/sec

The term "+stereo+" means at least two channels of recording but often more. In many parts of this book, the audio format we use for real-time DSP operation is uncompressed LPCM (linear pulse code modulation), 16 bits/sample stereo at 48,000 samples/sec, which is the "studio quality A" listed above. These settings are convenient for reasons that will become more obvious later in the text, but the software supplied with this book allows the user to easily change to other settings if desired. Most audio software and sound systems also allow for other recording specifications and for encoding formats other than the default Pulse Code Modulation (PCM).

---

[6]For example, the free program Audacity mentioned in this chapter includes 42 built-in special effects.

While the sound recording programs greatly simplify the basic tasks of recording, storing, and playing back wav-files, you are limited to the features built into the program and by the ADC and DAC specifications of your PC's sound card. Obviously, this is not a real-time operation.

2.4   Talk-Through Using MATLAB and Windows

MATLAB has a number of data manipulation functions [61]. Executing the command

```
help audiovideo
```

will display the functions associated with audio and video data manipulation.[7] For the PC platform, the following edited results of the help command above are of interest for the talk-through operation:

```
Audio input/output objects.
   audioplayer   - Audio player object.
   audiorecorder - Audio recorder object.

Audio hardware drivers.
   sound         - Play vector as sound.
   soundsc       - Autoscale and play vector as sound.

Audio file import and export.
   audioread     - Read audio samples from an audio file.
   audiowrite    - Write audio samples to an audio file.
   audioinfo     - Return information about an audio file.
```

Help on these or any of the individual MATLAB functions can be accessed, as before, by typing the command

```
help functionname
```

where `functionname` is the name of the MATLAB function for which you desire help, or by clicking on the functionname in the workspace screen if it is highlighted. Additionally, you can access a number of help options using the pull-down help menu directly from the MATLAB menu bar (see Figure 2.8).

Given these audio file related MATLAB functions, we will now discuss a solution to the talk-through problem. We can import an existing wav-file using the `audioread` command,[8] then play the file back using the sound command. Example code to do this would be

Listing 2.1: Reading and playing back a wav-file using MATLAB.

```
[Y,Fs] = audioread('c:\windows\media\tada.wav');
sound(Y,Fs)
```

The first command reads a wav-file named `tada.wav`, which is located in the `c:\windows\media` directory. The outputs Y and Fs of the `audioread` command represent the file data and sample frequency, respectively. Finally, the `sound` command plays back the vector Y at a sample frequency of Fs through the PC's sound card.

If you wish to find out other details about the data file, use the the `audioinfo` command, as shown below.

---

[7]You may need to use `help audio` for earlier versions of MATLAB. For other audio/video file formats, free converters such as `mmread` and `mmwrite` can be found at http://www.mathworks.com/matlabcentral/fileexchange/.

[8]The `audioread` function is intended to replace the older `wavread` function in MATLAB.

Figure 2.8: MATLAB command window with the help pull-down menu open.

Listing 2.2: Obtaining details about a wav-file using MATLAB.

```
myFile = audioinfo('c:\windows\media\tada.wav');
```

The `audioinfo` command, as used here, outputs a structure we chose to name `myFile` that contains various details about the data file `tada.wav`. To see what is contained in the structure `myFile`, you can double-click on the structure name in the "Workspace" subwindow (by default in the upper right of the MATLAB command window). If you don't use the "Workspace" subwindow, you can type `myFile` at the MATLAB command line, for which you'll see a screen output similar to

```
myFile =

            Filename: 'c:\windows\media\tada.wav'
   CompressionMethod: 'Uncompressed'
         NumChannels: 2
          SampleRate: 44100
        TotalSamples: 71296
            Duration: 1.6167
               Title: []
             Comment: []
              Artist: []
        BitsPerSample: 16
```

This allows you to determine details about `tada.wav`, such as the sample frequency is 44,100 Hz, the number of bits per sample is 16 bits/sample, the file is stereo (2 channels), the file consists of 71,296 samples for each channel, the file lasts for 1.6167 seconds, and the data in the file is not compressed.[9] If all you want to do is just play back the audio file, only the sample frequency must be known, which can be obtained as shown previously with

---

[9]These values may differ somewhat depending upon your version of Windows.

the `audioread` command. The `audioinfo` command is used only when you want to know more about how the signal was recorded.

While not recommended, you could read and play the audio file by executing the commands shown below.

```
1  Y = audioread('c:\windows\media\tada.wav');
   sound(Y)
```

If you execute these two commands, the wav-file will not sound as it did before. This is because the `sound` command's default sample frequency is 8192 Hz. The reduction of the playback sample frequency from 44100 Hz to 8192 Hz results in a significantly increased playback time, and the subsequent distortion (to much lower frequencies) of the intended information within the wav-file.[10] This playback speed problem can be corrected by using the command

```
sound(Y,44100)
```

While this solution seems straightforward, it is much easier to obtain the correct sample frequency using the `audioread` command, and include this value in the sound playback command. This Windows and MATLAB technique has the added advantage that a wav-file can be created using a sound recording program and then either played back unmodified, or processed off-line and played back later. The results, after MATLAB processing, can be stored in the *.mat format by using the `save` command or in the *.wav format by using the `audiowrite` command.[11] As with any computer file, it can also be stored on removable media such as a USB memory stick or on a CD-R disk.

2.4.1   Talk-Through Using MATLAB Only

There are several ways that will allow a simple talk-through operation to be performed using only MATLAB and the PC sound card. Since our goal is to easily transition to DSP hardware implementation of this and other DSP algorithms, we will limit our discussion to MATLAB's built-in `audiorecorder` function and the Simulink® program (also from The MathWorks).

MATLAB's `audiorecorder.m` function

Recent versions of MATLAB provide the `audiorecorder.m` function. This function allows for sound recording and playback using the PC's soundcard *without* the need for MATLAB's DAQ (data acquisition) toolbox. Figure 2.9 depicts MATLAB interfacing to the sound card. An excerpt of the MATLAB help associated with the `audiorecorder` is provided next. Included in this help is a complete example related to sound recording and playback.

```
>> help audiorecorder

 audiorecorder Audio recorder object.
     audiorecorder creates an 8000 Hz, 8-bit, 1 channel audiorecorder object.
     A handle to the object is returned.

     audiorecorder(Fs, NBITS, NCHANS) creates an audiorecorder object with
     sample rate Fs in Hertz, number of bits NBITS, and number of channels
```

---

[10]The change from the correct value of 44,100 Hz to the default of 8,192 Hz results in frequencies being almost 5.4 times lower. This may be difficult to hear on some PC or laptop speakers.

[11]The `audiowrite` function is intended to replace the older `wavwrite` function in MATLAB.

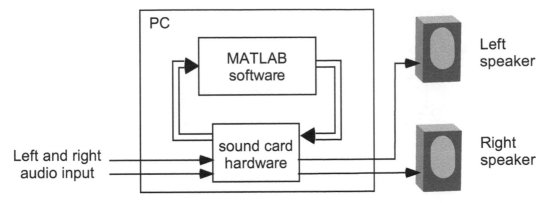

Figure 2.9: MATLAB interface to the PC sound card.

NCHANS. Common sample rates are 8000, 11025, 22050, 44100, 48000, and
96000 Hz. The number of bits must be 8, 16, or 24. The number of
channels must be 1 or 2 (mono or stereo).

audiorecorder(Fs, NBITS, NCHANS, ID) creates an audiorecorder object
using audio device identifier ID for input. If ID equals -1 the
default input device will be used.

    ...

Example:
    Record your voice on-the-fly. Use a sample rate of 22050 Hz,
    16 bits, and one channel. Speak into the microphone, then
    pause the recording. Play back what you've recorded so far.
    Record some more, then stop the recording. Finally, return
    the recorded data to MATLAB as an int16 array.

```
r = audiorecorder(22050, 16, 1);
record(r);      % speak into microphone...
pause(r);
p = play(r);    % listen
resume(r);      % speak again
stop(r);
p = play(r);    % listen to complete recording
mySpeech = getaudiodata(r, 'int16'); % get data as int16 array
```

See also audioplayer, audiodevinfo, audiorecorder/get, audiorecorder/set.

Simulink

Simulink is a graphical programming and simulation tool that complements the capabilities
of MATLAB.[12] It contains a huge variety of modeling and simulation environment tools
and blocksets (similar to toolboxes) for use with MATLAB. The example here uses the
Signal Processing Blockset for Simulink. As shown in Figure 2.10, the diagrams can look

---

[12]Another very popular graphical programming, simulation, and data acquisition tool that is useful for
DSP applications is LabVIEW from National Instruments.

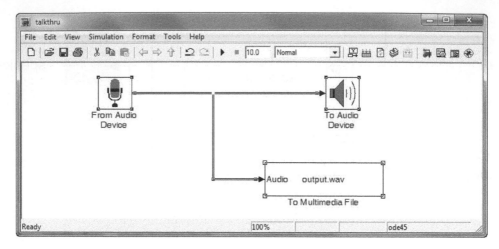

Figure 2.10: Simulink model of a PC-based talk-through system.

Figure 2.11: Block parameters from the wave device in Figure 2.10.

quite simple but still provide remarkable flexibility and versatility.

By double clicking on the *From Audio Device* Simulink block, all of the user adjustable parameters for that block are available for viewing and modification. This can be seen in Figure 2.11. To start the simulation, click on the start simulation button, as shown in Figure 2.12. This example is talk-through with the added feature of performing a recording to a wav-file. The wav file, `data.wav`, can be read back into MATLAB using the `wavread` function at any time.

2.4.2   Talk-Through Using MATLAB and the DSK

Controlling a DSK from within MATLAB is not a trivial task, so we've provided a support library for you. The files necessary to run this application are included in the software that accompanies this book in the `matlab` directory related to Appendix E. Using this MATLAB-to-DSK interface software (see details in Appendix E), a single MATLAB m-file allows a simple talk-through program to be constructed which uses the DSK rather than the

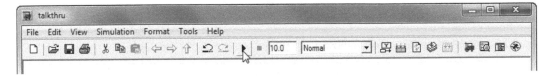

Figure 2.12: Click on the start simulation icon on the Simulink toolbar.

PC sound card. In this instance, we are reading frames (groups of samples) from the DSK into a MATLAB variable, then writing that same data back out to the DSK. The frame size in this example is 500 samples each. As shown below, the m-file consists of an initial setup phase (lines 1–8), then reads a single frame of data (line 10) before entering a forever loop (lines 12–15) where the "SwapFrame" function is used to do the actual talk-through operation. This is your first actual *real-time* operation! The code shown below is written for a C6713 DSK connected to the PC via the USB port on the HPI interface board port; to use a different DSK (such as one of the OMAP-L138 boards) and/or different configuration, see Section E.4 of Appendix E.

Listing 2.3: A simple MATLAB m-file for DSK talk-through.

```matlab
1  c6x_daq('Init', '6713_AIC23.OUT', 'DSK6713_USB_COM4');
   c6x_daq('FrameSize', 500);
3  c6x_daq('QueueSize', 2000);
   Fs = c6x_daq('SampleRate', 8000);
5  numChannels = c6x_daq('NumChannels', '1');
   c6x_daq('TriggerMode', 'Immediate'); % disables triggering
7  c6x_daq('LoopbackOff'); % turn off the direct DSK loopback
   c6x_daq('FlushQueues'); % flush the DSK's queues
9
   data = c6x_daq('GetFrame'); % read frame to prime for SwapFrame
11
   while 1 % begin forever loop
13    c6x_daq('SwapFrame', data); % send/receive data
      % data = data * 10; % add gain
15 end
```

To keep the number of samples acquired down, this demonstration uses a relatively low 8 kHz sample frequency for the DSK's onboard codec (TLV320AIC23), even though the codec itself is capable of much higher speeds. Most other programs in this book use a sample frequency of 48 kHz.

To verify that the data stream is actually being transferred through MATLAB, you can activate line 14 in the forever loop by removing the comment symbol (%). This adds a gain multiplicative factor of 10 to the signal.

2.5 DSK Implementation in C

The previous talk-through examples may be easy to understand, but we need to switch gears a bit. It's now time to move up in performance and capability by using C code to run talk-through in real time. The files necessary to run this application are in the ccs\MyTalkThrough directory of Chapter 2 in the software that accompanies this book. The primary file of interest is ISRs.c, which contains the interrupt service routines. This file includes the necessary variable declarations and performs a swap of the left and right channel data. This swap of left and right channel data is used so that you actually have a few lines of code to view.

The code listings are given below.

Listing 2.4: Talk-through declarations.

```
1 #define LEFT   0
  #define RIGHT  1
3
  float temp;
```

An explanation of Listing 2.4 follows.

1. (Lines 1–2): Define LEFT and RIGHT for user convenience.

2. (Line 4): Declares a temporary variable that is used to allow for channel swapping.

Listing 2.5: Talk-through code to swap left and right channels.

```
  /* I added my routine here  */
2
  temp=CodecData.channel[RIGHT];                          // R to temp
4 CodecData.channel[RIGHT]=CodecData.channel[LEFT];  // L to R
  CodecData.channel[LEFT]=temp;                           // temp to L
6
  /* end of my routine  */
```

An explanation of Listing 2.5 follows.

1. (Line 3): Assigns the right channel data to the variable temp.

2. (Line 4): Assigns the left channel data to the right channel.

3. (Line 5): Assigns temp to the left channel.

Note that if you are using a C6713 DSK, the board's input circuitry contains a voltage divider that reduces the input voltage level by a factor of 2 (i.e., a −6 dB change in voltage). To counteract this signal level decrease, the DSK_Support.c file (in the common_ code directory of the book's software) automatically inserts +6 dB of input gain whenever the C6713 DSK is selected. This voltage divider is not present on the OMAP-L138 boards.

Now that you understand the code...

Go ahead and copy all of the files into a separate directory to preserve the originals. Open the project in Code Composer Studio (CCS) and select "Rebuild All." Once the build is complete, select "Load Program" to load the binary code into the DSK and then click on "Run." Your talk-through system should now be running on the DSK. Remember, the codecs for the DSKs do not contain audio power amplifiers to drive the connected loads. For the best results, use amplified speakers with your DSK (e.g., powered speakers used with PCs), headphones, or earbuds to hear the audio output.[13]

---

[13]The OMAP-L138 boards provide only a line output, not a separate headphone output. Since impedance and efficiency of headphones (and earbuds) varies, the performance using a line output with these devices will also vary.

2.6 Follow-On Challenges

Consider extending what you have learned, using the C compiler and the DSK.

1. Experiment with scaling the output values (multiplying the input value, e.g., by 0.3, 1.6, and so on...) that you pass to the DAC. Are there limits associated with this scaling?

2. Implement your own program for spectral inversion on the DSK.

3. Change the sign bit of every sample that you pass to the DACs. Describe the effect of this sign bit change on how the output signal sounds.

4. Modify your talk-through code to output *only* the left or right channel value.

5. Modify your talk-through code to combine the left and right channel inputs and send the result to *both* the left and right channel outputs. Are there any limitations associated with combining the left and right channels?

6. Reduce the number of bits used by the DAC by using only the 8 most significant bits (MSBs). Can you hear the difference when only the 8 MSBs are used?

7. Reduce the number of bits used by the DAC by using only the 4 most significant bits (MSBs). Can you hear the difference when only the 4 MSBs are used?

8. Reduce the number of bits used by the DAC by using only the 2 most significant bits (MSBs). Can you hear the difference when only the 2 MSBs are used?

9. Reduce the number of bits used by the DAC by using only the most significant bit (MSB). Can you hear the difference when only the MSB is used?

2.7 Problems

1. Given a sample frequency of $F_s = 48$ kHz, what is the highest input frequency that, in theory, can be sampled without aliasing?

2. Suppose an input signal with a significant frequency component at 30 kHz was sampled at a frequency of $F_s = 48$ kHz, in a simple "talk-through" configuration. Assume no anti-aliasing filter is present. At what frequency would the original 30 kHz component appear at the output of the "talk-through" configuration?

3. An input signal ranges in amplitude from $+1$ V to -1 V, which matches the dynamic range of the ADC being used. No clipping of the input signal occurs. If each sample is uniformly quantized to 16 bits, what is the approximate resolution (also called the LSB voltage), in volts, of this ADC?

4. An input signal ranges in amplitude from $+1$ V to -1 V, which matches the dynamic range of the ADC being used. No clipping of the input signal occurs, and the signal amplitude is equally likely across the full dynamic range of the ADC. If each sample is uniformly quantized to 16 bits, what is the approximate signal to quantization noise ratio (SQNR) in dB? Assume no noise shaping or other advanced techniques are being used in the ADC design.

5. It was mentioned earlier in the chapter that changing the sign of every other sample of an input signal is equivalent to modulating the input signal by a sinusoid with a frequency of one-half the sample frequency. Explain why this is true.

Chapter 3

FIR Digital Filters

3.1 Theory

FILTERING is one of the most common DSP operations. Filtering can be used for noise suppression, signal enhancement, removal or attenuation of a specific frequency, or to perform a special operation such as differentiation, integration, or the Hilbert transform [1]. While this is not a complete list of all of the possible applications of filters, it may serve to remind us of the importance of filtering.

Filters can be thought of, designed, and implemented in either the sample domain or the frequency domain. This chapter, however, will only deal with sample domain filter implementation on a sample-by-sample basis. Frame-based processing and frequency domain filter implementation are discussed in Chapters 6 and 7, respectively.

3.1.1 Traditional Notation

The notation used in many continuous-time signals and systems texts[1] is to label the input signal as $x(t)$, the output signal as $y(t)$, and the impulse response of the system as $h(t)$. These time domain descriptions have frequency domain equivalents; they are obtained using the Fourier transform, which is shown as $\mathcal{F}\{\ \}$. The Fourier transform of $x(t)$ is $\mathcal{F}\{x(t)\} = X(j\omega)$; similarly the Fourier transform of $y(t)$ is $Y(j\omega)$ and that of $h(t)$ is $H(j\omega)$. $H(j\omega)$ is also called the frequency response of the system. These Fourier transform pairs are summarized below.

$$x(t) \xleftrightarrow{\mathcal{F}} X(j\omega)$$

$$y(t) \xleftrightarrow{\mathcal{F}} Y(j\omega)$$

$$h(t) \xleftrightarrow{\mathcal{F}} H(j\omega)$$

The most common notation used in discrete-time signals and systems texts is to label the input signal samples as $x[n]$, the output signal samples as $y[n]$, and the impulse response as $h[n]$. Note that the discrete-time impulse response $h[n]$ is called the *unit sample response* in some texts. In this book, parentheses "( )" will be used to denote continuous-time, while square brackets "[ ]" will be used to denote discrete-time. Discrete-time descriptions (such as $x[n]$, $y[n]$, and $h[n]$) have frequency domain equivalents that are obtained using the

---

[1]As in essentially all subject areas covered by engineering and science texts, there is *no* universally agreed upon standard notation. We use the notation of the majority here, but your favorite book may be different.

discrete-time Fourier transform (DTFT), which we will also abbreviate as $\mathcal{F}\{\}$. The DTFT of $x[n]$ is $\mathcal{F}\{x[n]\} = X\left(e^{j\omega}\right)$, of $y[n]$ is $Y\left(e^{j\omega}\right)$, and of $h[n]$ is $H\left(e^{j\omega}\right)$. $H\left(e^{j\omega}\right)$ is also called the frequency response of the system. These discrete-time Fourier transform pairs are summarized below.

$$x[n] \xleftrightarrow{\mathcal{F}} X\left(e^{j\omega}\right)$$
$$y[n] \xleftrightarrow{\mathcal{F}} Y\left(e^{j\omega}\right)$$
$$h[n] \xleftrightarrow{\mathcal{F}} H\left(e^{j\omega}\right)$$

Notice that the abbreviation used for the continuous-time Fourier transform and the DTFT are the same because the context should make it clear which transform is used. For example, if the signal or system being transformed is a discrete-time signal or system, it will be implied by the square bracket notation and thus the DTFT should be inferred. Also of interest is the fact that the DTFT of a discrete-time signal, e.g., $x[n]$, results in a continuous-frequency function, $X\left(e^{j\omega}\right)$, since ω is a continuous variable. A summary of the continuous-time and discrete-time notation is provided in Figure 3.1.

3.1.2   FIR Filters Compared to IIR Filters

The title of this chapter contains the acronym FIR, which stands for **F**inite **I**mpulse **R**esponse. All FIR filters are, by definition, discrete-time filters (there is no such thing as a continuous-time FIR filter). If we excite an FIR filter with a unit sample (a sample of value one) followed by an infinite number of zero-valued samples, we will have excited the system with the discrete-time version of an impulse function (sometimes called a unit sample function). Exciting an Nth order FIR filter with an impulse will result in $N+1$ output terms before all the remaining terms will have a value of exactly zero (since the filter has $N+1$ coefficients). Thus, the impulse response is finite.

Another type of filter, called an IIR filter, has an **I**nfinite **I**mpulse **R**esponse. If you have ever designed analog (i.e., continuous-time) filters, you have designed IIR filters. Think about the output of an analog filter that has an impulse for its input. Mathematically, the output of the system never fully decays to (and remains at) the exact value of zero. IIR filters can be either continuous-time or discrete-time, and are discussed in more detail in Chapter 4.

3.1.3   Calculating the Output of a Filter

We assume that our filter system is linear time invariant (LTI), which allows us to use some powerful linear analysis tools. To calculate the output of a continuous-time system that has been given a continuous-time input signal, we need to convolve the input signal with the system's impulse response. Since this involves continuous signals, we use integration

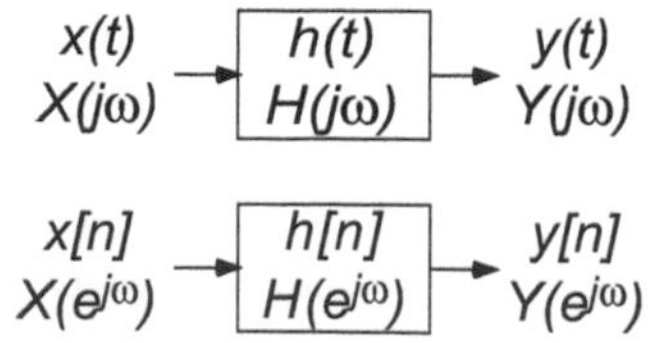

Figure 3.1: A summary of the continuous-time and discrete-time notation.

(discrete signals use summation instead of integration). Thus, to calculate the output, we need to evaluate the convolution integral. This is an operation that many beginning students find to be mysterious and intimidating (but get used to convolution—it comes up over and over again). The general form of the convolution integral is

$$y(t) = \int_{-\infty}^{\infty} h(\tau)x(t-\tau)\, d\tau.$$

If we restrict our discussion to realizable signals and systems, then, because of causality (i.e., we can't calculate the output based on an input that hasn't arrived yet), the convolution integral becomes

$$y(t) = \int_{0}^{\infty} h(\tau)x(t-\tau)\, d\tau.$$

Similarly, to calculate the output of a discrete-time system that has a discrete-time input signal, we use the convolution sum. The general form of the convolution sum is

$$y[n] = \sum_{k=-\infty}^{\infty} h[k]x[n-k].$$

If we again restrict our discussion to realizable signals and systems, then, due to causality, the convolution sum becomes

$$y[n] = \sum_{k=0}^{\infty} h[k]x[n-k].$$

For an FIR system, the filter coefficients are the individual terms that make up the impulse response of the system. These FIR filter coefficients are commonly called the b coefficients. In MATLAB®, when all of the b coefficients are formed into a vector, it is called the B vector. Making this substitution (b for h) and remembering that an FIR filter of order N has $N+1$ coefficients, the convolution sum takes on the general form of the FIR difference equation, namely,

$$y[n] = \sum_{k=0}^{N} b[k]x[n-k].$$

This equation tells us that, in order to calculate a value for the current output, $y[0]$, we must perform the dot product of $B \cdot X$, where $B = \{b[0], b[1], \ldots, b[N]\}$ and X represents the current and past values of the input, $X = \{x[0], x[-1], \ldots, x[-N]\}$. That is,

$$y[0] = \sum_{k=0}^{N} b[k]x[-k] = b[0]x[0] + b[1]x[-1] + \cdots + b[N]x[-N].$$

The block diagram associated with implementing the FIR difference equation, which is another way of saying an FIR filter, is shown in Figure 3.2. The blocks containing z^{-1} are delay blocks that store the value in the block for one sample period. The delay blocks may be thought of as synchronous shift registers that have their clocks tied to the ADC and DAC's sample clock, but are typically just memory locations accessed by the DSP CPU.

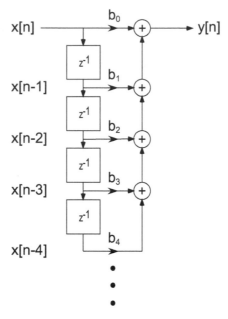

Figure 3.2: Block diagram associated with the implementation of an FIR filter.

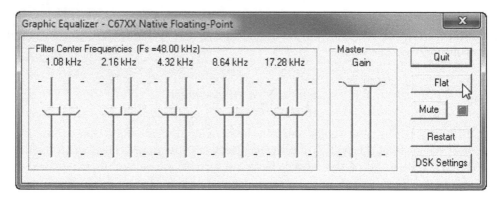

Figure 3.3: winDSK8 running the Graphic Equalizer application.

3.2   winDSK Demonstration

Start the winDSK8 application, and the main user interface window will appear. Ensure the correct selections have been made in the "DSP Board" and "Host Interface" configuration panels of winDSK8 for each parameter before proceeding. These selections are "sticky," such that the next time you run winDSK8, the choices you made will still be selected.

3.2.1   Graphic Equalizer Application

Clicking on the winDSK8 Graphic Equalizer button runs that program in the attached DSK, and a window similar to Figure 3.3 will appear. The Graphic Equalizer application implements a five-band audio equalizer, as shown in the signal flow shown in Figure 3.4. The DSK has a stereo codec, so an independently adjustable equalizer is active on both left and right channels.

The equalizer uses five FIR filters (a lowpass (LP) filter, three bandpass (BP) filters,

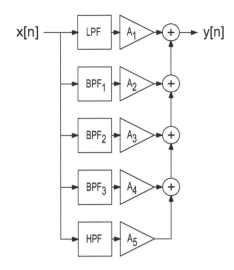

Figure 3.4: Block diagram associated with winDSK8's 5-band Graphic Equalizer application.

and a highpass (HP) filter) operating in parallel. The gain sliders (A_1 to A_5) in the dialog box operate on memory locations used to control the gains of each filter and the overall system gain. The five FIR filters are designed as high-order ($N = 128$) filters; the resulting steep roll-off of these filters can be seen in Figure 3.5.

There are a number of ways you can experience the effect of the graphic equalizer filtering. For example, you could connect the output of a CD player to the signal input of the DSK, and connect the DSK signal output to a set of powered speakers. Play some familiar music while you adjust the graphic equalizer slider controls and listen to the result. A more objective experiment would be to play the track of additive white Gaussian noise (AWGN) included with the software that accompanies this book (in directory `test_signals`

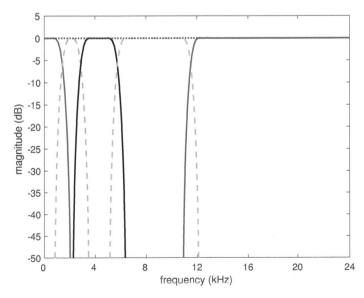

Figure 3.5: Frequency response of winDSK8's 5-band Graphic Equalizer application. The dotted straight line at 0 dB represents the sum of all five bands.

play file `awgn.wav`), which theoretically contains all frequencies. If the DSK signal output is then connected to a spectrum analyzer, you could observe which band of frequencies is affected, and how much it is affected, as you adjust the slider controls. If you don't have a spectrum analyzer available, a second DSK running winDSK8 can be used in its place (select the "Oscilloscope" button from the main screen, select "Spectrum Analyzer" from the next screen, and select "Log10" to display the result in decibels). Alternatively, you can use your computer's sound card to gather a portion of the DSK's output. This can be accomplished using the Windows sound recorder, MATLAB's data acquisition (DAQ) toolbox, or the audio recorder that is part of MATLAB (version 6.1 or later). This recorded data can be analyzed and displayed using MATLAB.

3.2.2   Notch Filter Application

The winDSK8 Notch Filter application actually implements a second-order IIR filter, but we can make it seem to be an FIR filter. Clicking on the Notch Filter button will run the program in the attached DSK, and a window similar to Figure 3.6 will appear. If you decrease the Q adjustment (r) until it reaches zero, you have put the poles of the filter at the origin of the z-plane and the system will behave just like an FIR filter (this concept will be discussed further in Chapter 4). This adjustment is shown on the bottom slider bar in Figure 3.6. Also notice that the "Filter Type" was changed from "Bandpass" to "Notch". The frequency responses associated with four different settings of the notch filter are overlaid and shown in Figure 3.7. Ideally, an infinite amount of attenuation is present at the notch frequency. This explains why a properly adjusted (tuned) notch filter can completely remove an interfering tone.

The effect of the Notch Filter application can be heard by adding a sinusoidal signal (tone) to a music signal. Most computer sound cards will perform this summing for you. You will need to experiment with your sound card's mixer controls to determine exactly how your particular system responds. Most systems are capable of summing an external audio signal (such as from a portable music player or a function generator) with an internal audio signal by playing a sound file or CD on the computer. In this example, one audio signal (typically the external source) is a tone and the other is music. Inject the external signal via the sound card "line input" or "microphone input" connector. The sound card "line output" or "headphone output" is then connected to the signal input of the DSK. As before, the DSK signal output is connected to a set of powered speakers. If a function generator isn't available, you can use one of the audio test tones (`*.wav`) in directory `test_signals` included with the software that accompanies this book and play them with

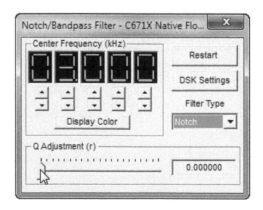

Figure 3.6: winDSK8 running the Notch Filter application with $r = 0$.

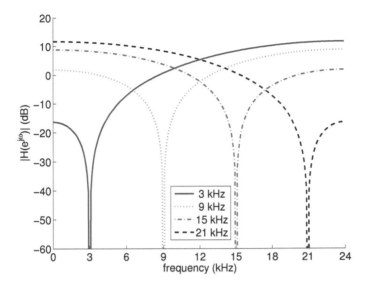

Figure 3.7: The frequency response of four different notch filters having notch frequencies of 3, 9, 15, and 21 kHz, respectively.

a second, external CD player or transfer the file to a portable music player. You can also easily create your own audio test tones in MATLAB, then save them as an audio file and play them in the same way on an external CD or music player (this concept will be discussed further in Chapter 5).

When the center frequency of the notch filter equals the frequency of the injected tone, you will hear the sound of the tone disappear from the speakers.

3.2.3 Audio Effects Application

The winDSK8 Audio Effects application contains a mixture of both FIR and IIR applications. Clicking on the Audio Effects button will load the program into the DSP core, and a window similar to Figure 3.8 will appear. The flanging and chorus effects are both implemented with FIR filters, so they provide good examples for this chapter.

The block diagram of the flanging effect is shown in Figure 3.9, where α is a scale factor and $\beta[n]$ is a periodically varying delay described by

$$\beta[n] = \frac{R}{2}\left(1 - \cos\left(\omega_0 n\right)\right).$$

R is the maximum number of sample delays and ω_0 is some low frequency. In winDSK8, you can adjust α with the Alpha slider, ω_0 with the Frequency slider, and R with the Delay slider enclosed in the Flanger portion of the winDSK8 Audio Effects window (see Figure 3.8). Thus, the delay time $\beta[n]$ varies sinusoidally from a minimum of 0 to a maximum of R. Flanging is a special sound effect often used by musicians (particularly guitarists); it sounds as if the musical instrument has taken on a sort of "whooshing" sound up and down the frequency scale. More about this and other special effects can be found in Chapter 10.

The block diagram of another musical special effect, the chorus effect, is shown in Figure 3.10. To generate the chorus effect, three separately flanged signals are summed with the original signal. For a proper chorus effect, each of the β's and α's should be independent.

Audio special effects such as flanging, chorus, reverb, etc. are described in more detail in Chapter 10.

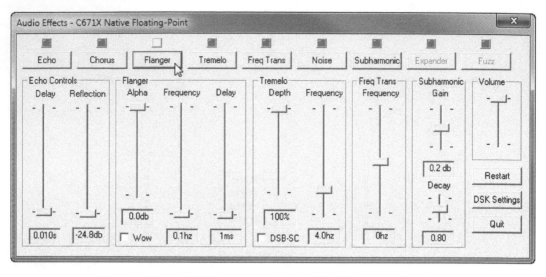

Figure 3.8: winDSK8 running the Audio Effects application.

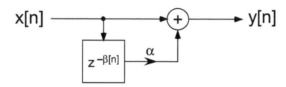

Figure 3.9: The block diagram of the flanging effect.

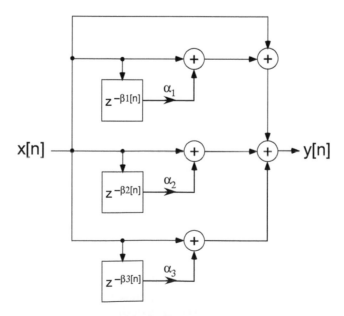

Figure 3.10: The block diagram of the chorus effect.

3.3 MATLAB Implementation

MATLAB has a number of ways of performing the filtering operation. In this chapter, we will only discuss two of them. The first is the built-in `filter` function, and the second is to build your own routine to perform the FIR filtering operation. The built-in function allows us to filter signals almost immediately, but does very little to prepare us for real-time filtering using DSP hardware.

3.3.1 Built-In Approach

As mentioned previously, MATLAB has a built-in function called `filter.m`. This function can be used to implement both an FIR filter (using only the numerator (B) coefficients) and an IIR filter (using both the denominator (A) and the numerator (B) coefficients). The first few lines of the online help associated with the `filter` command are provided below. This and any other MATLAB help is available from the command line by typing

```
help MATLAB function or command name
```

In the case of the `filter` command,

```
>> help filter

 FILTER One-dimensional digital filter.
    Y = FILTER(B,A,X) filters the data in vector X with the
    filter described by vectors A and B to create the filtered
    data Y.  The filter is a "Direct Form II Transposed"
    implementation of the standard difference equation:

    a(1)*y(n) = b(1)*x(n) + b(2)*x(n-1) + ... + b(nb+1)*x(n-nb)
                          - a(2)*y(n-1) - ... - a(na+1)*y(n-na)
```

Notice that in the difference equation discussion of the MATLAB `filter` command, the A and B coefficient vector indices start at 1 instead of at 0. MATLAB does not allow for an index value equal to zero. While this may seem like only a minor inconvenience, improper vector indices account for a significant number of the errors that occur during MATLAB algorithm development. In our classes, we typically create another vector, say n, which is composed of integers with the first element equal to zero (i.e., `n=0:15` creates $n = \{0, 1, 2, 3, \ldots, 15\}$), and use this n vector to "fool" MATLAB into counting from zero for things such as plot axes. See the code given below for an example of this technique.

The MATLAB code shown below will filter the input vector x using the FIR filter coefficients in vector B. Notice that the input vector x is zero padded (line 6) to flush the filter. This technique differs slightly from the direct implementation of the MATLAB `filter` command in which for M input values there will be M output values. Our technique assumes that the input vector is both preceded and followed by a large number of zeros. This implies that the filter is initially at rest (no initial conditions) and will relax or flush any remaining values at the end of the filtering operation.

Listing 3.1: Simple MATLAB FIR filter example.

```
1 % Simulation inputs
  x = [1 2 3 0 1 -3 4 1];              % input vector x
3 B = [0.25 0.25 0.25 0.25];          % FIR filter coefficients B
```

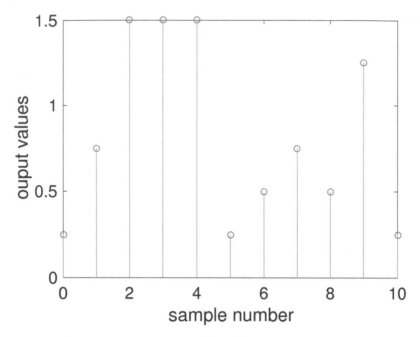

Figure 3.11: Stem plot of the filtering of x with B.

```
5 % Calculated terms
  PaddedX=[x zeros(1,length(B)−1)];  % zero pad x to flush filter
7 n=0:(length(x)+length(B)−2);        % plotting index for the output
  y=filter(B,1,PaddedX);              % performs the convolution
9
  % Simulation outputs
11 stem(n,y)                           % output plot generation
  ylabel('output values')
13 xlabel('sample number')
```

The output for this example follows.

```
y =
  Columns 1 through 8
    0.2500    0.7500    1.5000    1.5000    1.5000    0.2500    0.5000    0.7500
  Column 9
    0.5000    1.2500    0.2500
```

The stem plot from the example is shown in Figure 3.11.

In this example, eight input samples were filtered and the results were returned all at once. Notice that when an 8-element vector x is filtered by a 4-element vector B that 11 elements were returned ($8+4-1 = 11$). This is an example of the general result that states that the length L of the sequence resulting from the convolution (filtering) of x and B is $L = \text{length}(x) + \text{length}(B) - 1$.

The FIR filter coefficients associated with this filter were $B = [0.25\,0.25\,0.25\,0.25]$. Since there are four coefficients for the filter, this is a third-order filter (i.e., $N = 3$). The filtering effect in this case is an averaging of the most recent 4 input samples (i.e., the current sample and the previous three samples). This type of filter is called a moving average (MA) filter and is one type of lowpass FIR filter. Figure 3.12 shows the frequency response associated with MA filters of order $N = 3$, 7, 15, and 31, for a sample frequency of 48 kHz.

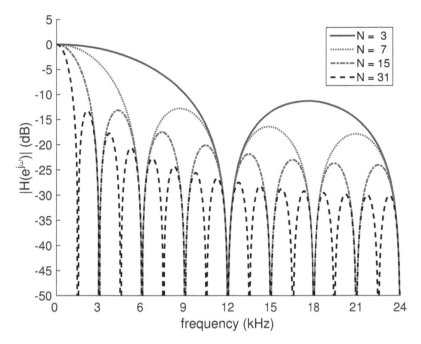

Figure 3.12: Magnitude of the frequency response for MA filters of order 3, 7, 15, and 31.

All of the MA filters shown in Figure 3.12 have a 0 Hz (DC) gain of 1 (which equals 0 dB). To ensure that any FIR filter has a DC gain of 0 dB, the impulse response $h[n]$ must sum to 1. The relationship between the DC response and the impulse response can be shown quickly by recalling the z-transform for a causal system described by $h[n]$,

$$H(z) = \sum_{n=0}^{\infty} h[n] z^{-n}.$$

To convert $H(z)$ into the frequency response $H(e^{j\omega})$, the variable substitution $z = e^{j\omega}$ is required.[2] Making this substitution,

$$H\left(e^{j\omega}\right) = \sum_{n=0}^{\infty} h[n] \left(e^{j\omega}\right)^{-n}.$$

To evaluate the DC response of an Nth order FIR filter, set $\omega = 0$ and the upper limit of summation equal to N. This results in

$$H\left(e^{j\omega}\right)\big|_{\omega=0} = H(1) = \sum_{n=0}^{N} h[n](1)^{-n} = \sum_{n=0}^{N} h[n].$$

This relationship explains why, for $N = 3$, each of the four $h[n]$ terms associated with the MA filter were defined as $1/4 = 0.25$. Similarly, for $N = 31$, each of the $h[n]$ terms would be $1/32 = 0.03125$ to ensure a DC response equal to 1 (i.e., 0 dB).

A Real-World Filtering Example

There are an unlimited number of data sets or processes that can be filtered. For example, what if we wanted to know the 4-day or 32-day average value of a stock market's closing

---

[2]The expression $e^{j\omega}$ can be thought of as a vector with a magnitude of 1 and an angle of ω.

value? If the closing values are filtered, much of the day-to-day market variations can be removed. The cutoff frequency[3] of the filter used to process the closing values would control the amount of the remaining variations. As shown in Figure 3.12 for an MA filter, the cutoff frequency is inversely related to the filter order. Figure 3.13 shows filtered and unfiltered closing values of the NASDAQ composite index for calendar year 2001.

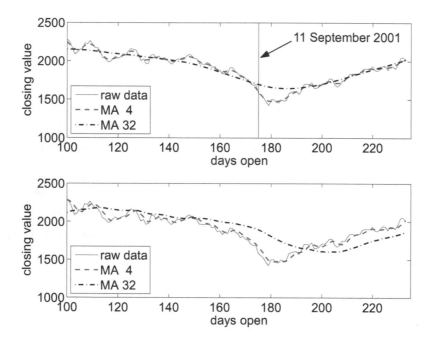

Figure 3.13: Filtered and unfiltered closing values of the NASDAQ composite index for calendar year 2001. The upper plot was generated with the MATLAB function `filtfilt`. The lower plot was generated with the MATLAB function `filter`.

The upper portion of the figure plots the raw data and the results of filtering the raw data with both a 4-term (3rd-order) and a 32-term (31st-order) MA filter. This subplot was created using the MATLAB function `filtfilt`. This function implements a zero-phase forward and reverse filter (that is, there is zero group delay). This forward/reverse technique to eliminate group delay *cannot* be used in real-time filtering, unless some frame-based "tricks" are employed (frame-based methods are discussed in a later chapter). For additional information on the MATLAB function `filtfilt`, type `help filtfilt` from the MATLAB command prompt.

The lower portion of the figure plots the raw data and the results of filtering the raw data with both a 4-term (3rd-order) and a 32-term (31st-order) MA filter using the MATLAB function `filter`. Since realizable MA filters have nonzero group delay, the filtered data lags the raw data by an amount of time equal to the group delay G_D multiplied by the sample period T_s. In non-real-time applications, this time lag due to filter group delay can be eliminated in postprocessing.

---

[3]A common definition of "cutoff frequency" for a filter is where the output power has dropped down to one-half (i.e., -3 dB) compared to the maximum output level. Note if power drops to 0.5, then voltage drops to 0.7071, all other things being equal. Additional characteristics, such as ripple in the passband, attenuation in the stopband, width of the transition bandwidth, and phase response, are also important in filter design but not mentioned for this simple example.

3.3.2 Creating Your Own Filter Algorithm

The previous example helped us with MATLAB-based filtering, but the built-in function filter.m is of little use to us in performing real-time FIR filtering with DSP hardware. The next MATLAB example more closely implements the algorithm needed for a real-time process. This code will calculate a single output value based on the current input value and the three previous input values.

Listing 3.2: MATLAB FIR filter adjusted for real-time processing.

```
1 %  This m-file is used to convolve x[n] and B[n] without
   %  using the MATLAB filter command.  This is one of the
3 %  first steps toward being able to implement a real-time
   %  FIR filter in DSP hardware.
5 %
   %  In sample-by-sample filtering, you are only trying to
7 %  accomplish two things,
   %
9 %  1.   Calculate the current output value, y(0), based on
   %       just having received a new input sample, x(0).
11 %  2.   Setup for the arrival of the next input sample.
   %
13 %  This is a BRUTE FORCE approach!
   %
15
   % Simulation inputs
17 x = [1  2  3  0];              % input x = [x(0) x(-1) x(-2) x(-3)]
   N = 3;                        % order of the filter = length(B) - 1
19 B = [0.25  0.25  0.25  0.25]; % FIR filter coefficients B

21 % Calculated terms
   y = 0;                        % initializes the output value y(0)
23 for i = 1:N+1                 % performs the dot product of B and x
       y = y + B(i)*x(i);
25 end

27 for i = N:-1:1                % shift stored x samples to the right so
       x(i+1) = x(i);           % the next x value, x(0), can be placed
29 end                          % in x(1)

31 % Simulation outputs
   x                            % notice that x(1) = x(2)
33 y                            % average of the last four input values
```

The input and output vectors from this FIR moving average filter program are shown below. Note the four input samples result in a single output sample, as expected of a third-order filter. Also, the displayed version of vector x shows the effect of shifting the values to the "right" to make room for the next sample, as discussed below.

```
x =
     1    1    2    3
y =
   1.5000
```

A few items need to be discussed concerning this example.

1. The filter order N was declared (line 18) despite the fact that MATLAB can determine the filter order based solely on the length of the vector B (that is, `N=length(B)-1`). Declaring both the filter order N and the FIR filter coefficients B (line 19) increases the portability of the C/C++ code we will derive from the MATLAB code. Increased code portability may also be thought of as decreased machine dependence, which is generally a sought-after code attribute.

2. Only four values of x were stored (line 17). FIR filtering involves the dot product of only $N+1$ terms. Since in this example $N=3$, only four x terms are required.

3. The example is called a "brute force" approach, which is based largely on the shifting of the stored x values within the x vector (lines 27–29), to make room for the next sample that would overwrite the value at $x(0)$. This unnecessary operation wastes resources which may be needed for other parts of the algorithm. Since our ultimate goal is efficient real-time implementation in DSP hardware, more elegant and efficient solutions to this problem will be discussed in the next section.

3.4 DSK Implementation in C

Several modifications of the MATLAB thought process are needed as we transition toward efficient real-time programming.

1. A semantic change is required since in MATLAB B is often called a vector, but in the C/C++ programming language, B is called an array.

2. The zero memory index value, which does not exist in a MATLAB vector, *does* exist in the C/C++ programming language, and it is routinely used in array notation.

3. The DSP hardware must process the data from the analog-to-digital converter (ADC) in real-time. Therefore, we cannot wait for all of the message samples to be received prior to beginning the algorithmic process.

4. Real-time DSP is inherently an interrupt-driven process and the input samples should only be processed using interrupt service routines (ISRs). Given this observation, it is incumbent upon the DSP programmer to ensure that the time requirements associated with periodic sampling are met. More bluntly, if you do not complete the algorithm's calculation before another input sample arrives, you have not met your real-time schedule, and your system will fail. This leads to the observation that, "the correct answer, if it arrives late, is wrong!"

5. Even though the DSP hardware has a phenomenal amount of processing power, this power should not be wasted.

6. The input and output ISRs are *not* magically linked! Nothing will come out of your DSP hardware unless you program the device to do so.

7. The digital portion of both an ADC and a digital-to-analog converter (DAC) are inherently *integer* in nature. No matter what the ADC's input range is, the analog input voltage is mapped to an integer value. For a 16-bit converter using two's complement signed representation, the possible integer values range from $+32,767$ to $-32,768$.

8. For clarity and understandability, declarations and assignments of variables (e.g., FIR filter coefficients) can be moved into `.c` and `.h` files.

3.4.1 Brute-Force FIR Filtering in C: Part 1

The first version we will examine of FIR filter implementation code in C continues with a brute-force approach, similar to the last MATLAB example. The purpose of this first approach is understandability, which comes at the expense of efficiency.

The files necessary to run this application are in the Chapter 3 ccs\FIRrevA directory. The primary file of interest is FIRmono_ISRs.c, which contains the interrupt service routines. This file includes the necessary variable declarations and performs the actual FIR filtering operation. To allow for the use of a stereo codec (e.g., the native codecs on the OMAP-L138 boards and the C6713 DSK), the program implements independent Left and Right channel filters if you use FIRstereo_ISRs.c. However, for clarity only the Left channel (as used in the mono mode) will be discussed below. In the code example, N is the filter order, the B array holds the FIR filter coefficients, the $xLeft$ array holds both the current input value ($x[0]$) and the past input values ($x[-1], x[-2]$, and $x[-3]$). The variable $yLeft$ is the current output value of the filter, $y[0]$. The integer i is used as an index counter in the for loops.[4]

Listing 3.3: Brute-force FIR filter declarations.

```
#define N 3

float B[N+1] = {0.25, 0.25, 0.25, 0.25};
float xLeft[N+1];
float yLeft;


Int32 i;
```

The code shown below, part of the interrupt service routine Codec_ISR, performs the actual filtering operation. The program instructions that move an incoming sample value from the appropriate ADC register to CodecDataIn.Channel[LEFT] and a processed sample from CodecDataOut.Channel[LEFT] to the appropriate DAC register are not shown here. The five main steps involved in the filtering operation will be discussed following the code listing.

Listing 3.4: Brute-force FIR filtering for real-time.

```
/* I added my routine here */
xLeft[0] = CodecDataIn.Channel[LEFT];   // current input value
yLeft = 0;                  // initialize the output value

for (i = 0; i <= N; i++) {  // x is length N+1
    yLeft += xLeft[i]*B[i]; // perform the dot-product
}

for (i = N; i > 0; i--) {
    xLeft[i] = xLeft[i-1];  // shift for the next input
}

CodecDataOut.Channel[LEFT] = yLeft; // output the value
/* end of my routine */
```

[4]**Note:** to help our code run as intended on this and future versions of CCS, and to gain some platform independence, we use specific declarations such as Int32 and Uint32 for signed and unsigned 32-bit integers, respectively. The meaning of other declarations, such as Int16 and Uint8 should be clear.

The five real-time steps involved in brute-force FIR filtering

An explanation of Listing 3.4 follows.

1. (Line 2): The most current sample from the ADC side of the codec is assigned to the current input array element, `xLeft[0]`.

2. (Line 3): The current output of this filter is given the name `yLeft`. Since this same variable will be used in the calculation of each output value of the filter, it must be reinitialized to zero before each dot product is performed.

3. (Lines 5–7): These 3 lines of code perform the dot product of x and B. The equivalent operation is,

$$yLeft = xLeft[0]B[0] + xLeft[-1]B[1] + xLeft[-2]B[2] + xLeft[-3]B[3].$$

4. (Lines 9–11): These 3 lines of code shift all of the values in the x array one element to the right. The equivalent operation is,

$$xLeft[2] \rightarrow xLeft[3]$$
$$xLeft[1] \rightarrow xLeft[2]$$
$$xLeft[0] \rightarrow xLeft[1].$$

After the shift to the right is complete, the next incoming sample, $x[0]$, can be written into the $xLeft[0]$ memory location without a loss of information. Also notice that $xLeft[3]$ was overwritten by $xLeft[2]$. You might expect the operation $xLeft[3] \rightarrow xLeft[4]$ and so on should be performed, but there is no $xLeft[4]$ or higher because $xLeft$ only contains four elements. In summary, the "old" $xLeft[3]$ is no longer needed and is therefore overwritten.

5. (Line 13): This line of code completes the filtering operation by transferring the result of the dot product, $yLeft$, to the `CodecDataOut.Channel[LEFT]` variable for transfer to the DAC side of the codec.

Now that you understand the code...

Go ahead and copy all of the files into a separate directory. Open the project in CCS and "Rebuild All." Once the build is complete, "Load Program" into the DSK and click on "Run." Your FIR LP filter is now running on the DSK. Remember this program would typically be used for audio filtering, so a good way to experience the effects of your filter is to listen to unfiltered and filtered music.[5] Figure 3.14 shows a method to listen to the original (unfiltered) music and the filtered music for comparison. This technique does require a second set of speakers, but it is a bit more convenient than using only one set of speakers and changing the connections back and forth. Remember, the DSKs do not contain audio power amplifiers to drive the connected loads. For the best results, use amplified speakers (e.g., powered speakers of the type used with PCs) or headphones with your DSK.

---

[5]You may need to increase the order of the filter to really hear a difference in the filtered output. Try a 31st-order MA filter by setting $N = 31$ and making all the values of B equal to $1/32 = 0.03125$.

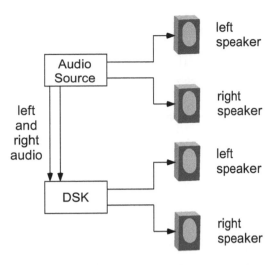

Figure 3.14: One method of listening to the unfiltered and filtered audio signals.

3.4.2 Brute-Force FIR Filtering in C: Part 2

The previous section introduced a *brute-force* approach to FIR filtering. While this implementation was straightforward and relatively easy to understand, it suffers from two major problems.

1. Routinely, FIR filters use a considerably higher order than the fourth-order filter discussed in the previous example. Most filters also require more than a few digits of numerical precision to accurately specify the B coefficients. These facts make manual entry of the B coefficients very inconvenient.

2. Step four in the five real-time steps involved in the brute-force FIR filtering section (that was discussed previously) shifted all of the values in the x array one element to the right after each dot product operation. This "manual" shifting is a very inefficient use of the DSK's computational resources.

These problems will be addressed in the sections that follow.

The declaration for array B[N+1] shown below represents just the first 12 lines required to initialize a 30th-order FIR filter (not a simple MA filter, obviously) that was designed with then exported from MATLAB's FDATool (see Figure 3.15 for a preview of this design tool). FDATool will be discussed in more detail in the next chapter.

```
float B[N+1] = {
{-0.031913481327},   /* h[0] */
{0.000000000000},    /* h[1] */
{-0.026040505746},   /* h[2] */
{-0.000000000000},   /* h[3] */
{-0.037325855883},   /* h[4] */
{0.000000000000},    /* h[5] */
{-0.053114839831},   /* h[6] */
{-0.000000000000},   /* h[7] */
{-0.076709627018},   /* h[8] */
{0.000000000000},    /* h[9] */
{-0.116853446730},   /* h[10]*/
```

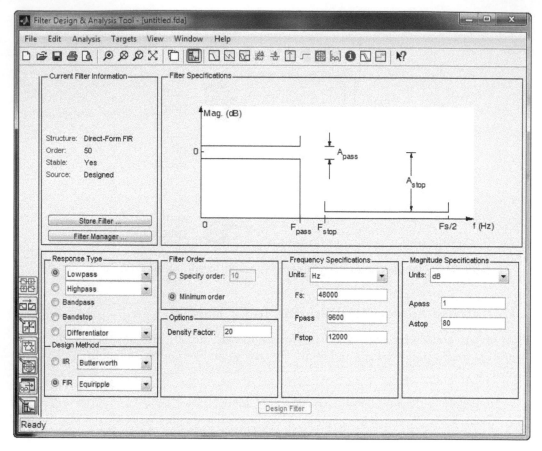

Figure 3.15: The MATLAB FDATool for designing digital filters.

Do you really want to enter all of these coefficient values manually? What about a 200th-order filter or an even higher-order filter? Supposing you had the time and inclination to do so, do you actually believe you could enter these coefficients without making a typographical error?

If you are designing your FIR filters using MATLAB, a solution to this problem could be copying and pasting coefficients from the MATLAB window to your C program editor screen.[6] An even better solution involves a single MATLAB script file that will create a coeff.h and a coeff.c file for use in your CCS project.[7] The script file is named FIR_DUMP2C.m and it can be found in the Appendix E \MatlabExports directory of the book's software. The MATLAB help associated with this file is shown below.

```
>> help FIR_dump2c

    function FIR_DUMP2C(filename, varname, coeffs, FIR_length)

    Dumps FIR filter coefficients to file in C language format in forward
    order. Then "cd" to the desired directory PRIOR to execution.
```

---

[6]This assumes you've used MATLAB tools such as firpm, fdatool, or sptool to design your filter. Use the help files in MATLAB to explore these commands; later chapters will discuss them further.

[7]Recent versions of the MATLAB Signal Processing Toolbox GUI FDATool include a similar capability via "Targets→Generate C header," but we feel it's not as easy to understand the result as with our technique.

This will provide for increased C code portability.

e.g., FIR_dump2c('coeff', 'B', filt1.tf.num, length(filt1.tf.num))

Arguments: filename   - File to write coefficients, no extension
           varname   - Name to be assigned to coefficient array
           coeffs   - Vector with FIR filter coefficients
           FIR_length - Length of array desired

This help output discusses the MATLAB cd function, which is an alternative to using the Current Directory field in the MATLAB desktop toolbar. Alternatively, you can allow the m-file FIR_dump2c to create the two files (coeff.h and coeff.c) in the current directory and then move the files to your CCS project using, for example, the Windows Explorer program. Once these files are in your CCS project directory you must add the files to your project. Note that Appendix A includes a short tutorial to help you get started with the basics of using CCS. In addition to adding the two files (coeff.h and coeff.c) to your project, the single line of C code,

#include coeff.h

must also be added to your FIRmono_ISRs.c or FIRstereo_ISRs.c file. An example of a coeff.h file is shown below.

Listing 3.5: An example coeff.h file.

```
1 /* coeff.h                              */
  /* FIR filter coefficients              */
3 /* exported by MATLAB using FIR_DUMP2C  */

5 #define N 30

7 extern float B[];
```

Within the coeff.h file, line 5 is used to define the filter order (not the filter length!) and line 7 allows the B coefficients to be defined in another file. In this case, the coefficients are defined in the file coeff.c.

Once you become familiar with these procedures and some of the MATLAB filter design techniques, FIR filters can be designed, implemented, and run in real-time very easily.

Now that you understand the code...

The files necessary to run this application are in the Chapter 3 ccs\FIRrevB directory. Go ahead and copy all of the files into a separate directory. Open the project in CCS and "Rebuild All." Once the build is complete, "Load Program" into the DSK and click on "Run." Your FIR filter is now running on the DSK.

3.4.3 Circular Buffered FIR Filtering

As previously stated, shifting all of the values in the x array one element to the right after each dot product operation is a very inefficient use of the DSK's computational resources. The need to perform this shift is based on the assumption that the physical memory is linear. Given linear memory, with the inherent static labeling of each memory location, this shifting of values would seem to be an absolute requirement.

Figure 3.16: The linear memory concept with static memory location labeling.

Figure 3.16 shows a linear memory model for the input to the filter x. As expected, to buffer the $N+1$ elements in the x array, there are memory locations labeled $x[0]$, $x[-1]$, $\cdots$, $x[-N]$, but there is also an $x[-(N+1)]$. While this location was not declared, it does physically exist, and any attempt to access the x array beyond its declared bounds will result in *something* being retrieved and used in any subsequent calculations. The results of this indexing error may be catastrophic (e.g., a run-time error), or more subtle (e.g., the program runs, but gives inaccurate results). Either way, this type of indexing error must be avoided at all costs.

An alternative to the linear memory paradigm is to think of an array as circular memory. As shown in Figure 3.17, the circular memory concept wraps the next memory location "beyond" the one labeled $x[-N]$ back to the memory location labeled $x[0]$. Since the purpose of this circular memory is to store or buffer x, this concept is routinely referred to as circular buffering.

If instead of using static memory location labels, a pointer can be used to point to and insert the newest sample that just arrived, $x[0]$, into the memory location containing the oldest sample, $x[-N]$, that is no longer needed, then a circular buffer has been created. No physical shifting of the x values is required since the pointer will always point to the most recent sample value. As the pointer advances, the oldest sample in the buffer is replaced by the most recent sample. This process can be continued indefinitely. The result of inserting the next sample into the buffer is shown in Figure 3.18.

To implement the circular buffer, a pointer must be established that points to the array xLeft. The required C code to create this pointer is shown below.

```
float xLeft[N+1], *pLeft = xLeft;
```

The remainder of the circular buffered FIR filter code is shown below, with explanatory comments. Note that the proper use of pre- or post-increment and -decrement commands as shown in the code is very important to obtain correct operation.

Listing 3.6: FIR filter using a circular buffer.

```
*pLeft = CodecDataIn.Channel[LEFT];      // store LEFT input value

output = 0;                    // set up for LEFT channel
p = pLeft;                     // save current sample pointer
if(++pLeft > &xLeft[N])        // update pointer, wrap if necessary
    pLeft = xLeft;            // and store
for (i = 0; i <= N; i++) {    // do LEFT channel FIR
    output += (*p--) * B[i];  // multiply and accumulate
    if(p < &xLeft[0])         // check for pointer wrap around
        p = &xLeft[N];
}
CodecDataOut.Channel[LEFT] = output; // store filtered value
```

The files necessary to run this application are in the Chapter 3 ccs\FIRrevD directory.[8] Go ahead and copy all of the files into a separate directory. Open the project in CCS and

---

[8]We haven't mentioned the code in ccs\FIRrevC for Chapter 3. Consider it a bonus.

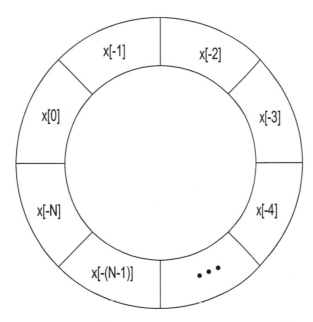

Figure 3.17: The circular buffer concept with static memory location labeling.

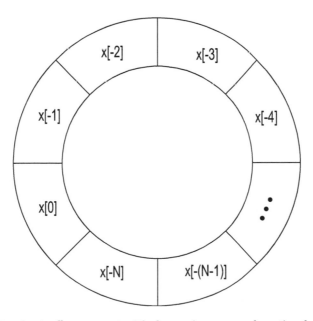

Figure 3.18: The circular buffer concept with dynamic memory location labeling, one sample time after Figure 3.17.

"Rebuild All." Once the build is complete, "Load Program" into the DSK and click on "Run." Your FIR filter is now running on the DSK.

3.5 Follow-On Challenges

Consider extending what you have learned.

1. Change the B coefficients associated with the `FIRrevA` code and verify that as additional terms are added to the moving average filter, the LP filter cutoff frequency decreases (see Figure 3.12). As you increase the filter order, don't forget to scale each filter coefficient so that they all sum to 1 (i.e., the DC response equals 0 dB).

2. There are many different ways to implement an FIR filter. Most of the examples in this chapter have used only the direct-form one (DF-I) techniques. Investigate and implement other forms, e.g., direct-form two, direct-form two transpose, lattice structure, second-order sections (SOS), etc.

3. Routinely, FIR filter coefficients have even or odd symmetry. Develop an algorithm that takes advantage of this symmetry. This will result in lower storage requirements for the filter coefficients.

4. Some FIR filters, for example, a Hilbert transforming filter (bandpass filter) symmetrically centered around $\frac{F_s}{4}$, contain a significant number of zeros in the filter coefficients. Develop an algorithm that takes advantage of the fact that you don't need to calculate the terms that involve multiplication by zero.

5. Explore some of the FIR filter design tools that are available in MATLAB (e.g., `firpm`, `SPTool`, and `FDATool`). A complete listing of the functional capabilities included in the signal processing toolbox can be found by typing `help signal`. The toolbox functions are grouped by category. You are looking for the `FIR filter design` heading (which in recent versions is found by clicking on the higher-level heading `Digital Filters`). Use the `FIR_dump2c` function from the book's software to export the filter coefficients. Implement your design using the `FIRrevB` code.

6. There is a limit to the number of calculations that the DSK can complete before the next input sample arrives. Design and implement an increasingly higher-order lowpass filter using the `FIRrevB` code (compiled as a DEBUG build) until the output of the filter sounds either distorts or no longer can be heard at all. These are two of the possible indications that you are no longer meeting your real-time schedule. Is the `FIRrevD` code (circular buffering) able to implement a higher-order filter compared to the `FIRrevB` code (brute force) before it fails?

7. Repeat the previous challenge, but compile your code as a RELEASE build. You should be able to use a higher filter order before the real-time schedule fails, since a greater number of optimizations are used by the compiler.

3.6 Problems

1. In terms of a z-plane plot of the poles and zeros, what are the conditions required for an FIR filter to be stable?

2. How many filter coefficients are there for a 41st-order FIR filter?

3. How many poles and zeros are there in the transfer function of a 10th-order FIR filter?

4. Only an FIR filter can exhibit truly linear phase, but not all FIR filters have linear phase. What is the specific requirement for an FIR filter to have a linear phase response?

5. What is meant by the term "group delay" and why is it particularly important for applications such as audio signal processing and phase-sensitive demodulation of communication signals?

6. What is the relationship between group delay and phase response?

7. What is the group delay, in seconds, of a 20th-order linear phase FIR filter when the sampling frequency is $F_s = 48$ kHz?

Chapter 4

IIR Digital Filters

4.1 Theory

GIVEN the simplicity and stability of the FIR filter, why would you ever want to consider using an IIR filter? This issue has been debated over the years in numerous articles, papers, and book chapters in the DSP literature. The short answer to the FIR versus IIR question can be distilled down to two brief points.

1. There is a tremendous amount of analog filter design knowledge available and, as mentioned in Chapter 3, these analog filters are all IIR in nature. There are times when we should take advantage of this wealth of design information.

2. To meet certain filter design specifications, very high-order FIR filters may be needed. Yet we can usually implement a lower-order (sometimes *much* lower-order) IIR filter that can meet such filter specifications.

Discrete-time IIR filter design takes advantage of decades of analog (continuous-time) filter design discoveries and advances and provides implementations usually requiring considerably less complexity (lower order) than an equivalently performing FIR filter. With this realization that IIR filters can play a vital role in some real-time DSP systems, we provide below a brief reminder of how IIR digital filters are typically designed.

Analog filters are, in most cases, the basis on which digital (i.e., discrete-time) IIR filters are created. As an example of why analog filters are IIR, let's examine a simple RC analog filter. A first-order analog filter can be built using a single resistor R and capacitor C. If the output of the circuit is taken to be the voltage across the capacitor, then a lowpass (LP) filter has been created. Figure 4.1 shows the schematic diagram of this circuit. Similarly, if the output is taken to be the voltage across the resistor, then the circuit implements a highpass (HP) filter.

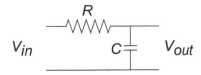

Figure 4.1: Schematic for a continuous-time (analog) first-order RC filter. The configuration of the inputs and outputs results in a lowpass filter.

Using voltage division and the fact that the impedance of a capacitor is $Z_c = 1/sC$, the transfer function of this first-order RC LP filter is

$$H(s) = \frac{\frac{1}{sC}}{R + \frac{1}{sC}} = \frac{1}{sRC + 1} = \frac{\frac{1}{RC}}{s + \frac{1}{RC}}.$$

Since the impulse response and the transfer function of a continuous-time system are a Laplace transfer pair,

$$h(t) \overset{\mathcal{L}}{\longleftrightarrow} H(s),$$

the impulse response of this filter, $h(t)$, can be obtained by taking the inverse Laplace transform of $H(s)$; that is, $h(t) = \mathcal{L}^{-1}\{H(s)\}$. This results in

$$h(t) = \frac{1}{RC}\, e^{-\frac{t}{RC}} u(t),$$

where $u(t)$ is the unit step function. For this system, as t gets very, very large (i.e., as $t \to \infty$), the impulse response $h(t)$ gets very, very small—but it would still take an *infinite amount of time* for $h(t)$ to actually reach and remain at zero. For this reason, this first-order LP filter is an example of an IIR filter, because its impulse response lasts an infinite amount of time. An example of this behavior can be seen in Figure 4.2. In this example, the RC time constant ($\tau = RC$) is 1 ms; an engineering rule of thumb states that, after approximately five time constants, the system has reached its final or steady-state value. Notice in Figure 4.2 that the impulse response value at 5 ms *appears* to be approximately zero. But Figure 4.3 plots the same impulse response on a semilog plot all the way out to 500 ms. Looking at this new figure, it now becomes clear that the impulse response of the system *never* actually reaches and remains at a zero value—so it must be categorized as an IIR filter. We hasten to say that, practically speaking, the impulse response decays to a low enough value (usually below the noise floor of our measurement equipment) shortly after five time constants, so the engineering rule of thumb is useful.

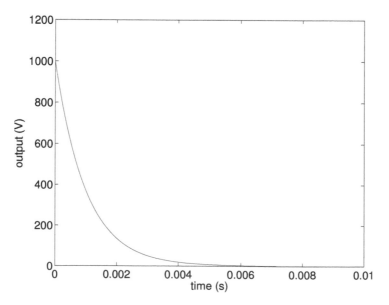

Figure 4.2: Linear plot of the impulse response associated with the first-order analog lowpass filter of Figure 4.1 with $R = 1000\ \Omega$ and $C = 1\ \mu F$.

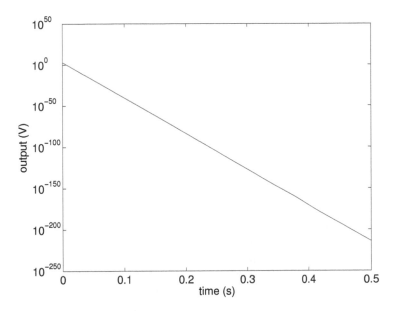

Figure 4.3: Semilog plot of the impulse response shown in Figure 4.2.

Enough about analog filters—this is a DSP book! IIR digital filters are routinely created by adapting well-proven analog filter designs using one of three major techniques listed below.

Impulse invariance methods These methods are based on the idea that we can design a discrete-time filter with an impulse response $h[n]$ that is a scaled and sampled version of $h_c(t)$, the analog (continuous-time) filter's impulse response [2]. Using these techniques, the impulse response of the discrete-time filter becomes

$$h[n] = T_s h_c[nT_s]$$

where T_s is the sample period and $h_c[nT_s]$ is the sampled (i.e., discrete-time) version of the continuous-time impulse response associated with the original analog filter. Since reality forces us to only a finite duration $h[n]$, we can never truly sample the entire infinite duration of $h_c(t)$.

Bilinear transformation methods These methods take a continuous-time transfer function, $H_c(s)$, and replace its independent variable, s, with a discrete-time, independent transform variable, z, to produce a discrete-time transfer function, $H(z)$. This transformation can be accomplished using the variable substitution,

$$s = \frac{2}{T_s}\left(\frac{1-z^{-1}}{1+z^{-1}}\right),$$

which results in the transfer function

$$H(z) = H_c\left(\frac{2}{T_s}\left(\frac{1-z^{-1}}{1+z^{-1}}\right)\right),$$

where T_s is the sample period and H_c is the continuous-time transfer function. Note that, even though z is used as the transform variable for discrete-time functions, the variable z itself is continuous across the entire z-plane.

Optimization methods These methods are based on optimizing filter performance using iterative numerical techniques that converge (we hope!) to a design that is close to the stated filter specifications.

In this book, we assume you are designing your digital filters with the help of software tools such as SPTool or FDATool in MATLAB®. The fact that the software arrives at the IIR digital filter coefficients using one of the previously mentioned methods may or may not be of interest to you. See the appropriate chapter of a more theoretical DSP text for more detail about filter design, if needed.

As is almost always the case in engineering design, systems that perform well in some areas routinely perform poorly in other areas. With IIR filters, we are particularly concerned about two issues:

- Stability: Since feedback is always involved in an IIR design, the system may become unstable. For real-time (causal) systems, we can mathematically ensure stability by keeping the poles inside the unit circle (magnitude of the poles < 1) as plotted on the z-plane. As a reminder, the poles are the roots of the denominator polynomial and the zeros are the roots of the numerator polynomial of the system transfer function, $H(z)$. The transfer function normally takes the form

$$H\left(z\right) = \frac{Y(z)}{X(z)} = \frac{b_0 + b_1 z^{-1} + b_2 z^{-2} + b_3 z^{-3} + \cdots}{1 + a_1 z^{-1} + a_2 z^{-2} + a_3 z^{-3} + \cdots}.$$

- Phase response: A symmetric (or antisymmetric) FIR filter exhibits a linear phase response, while an IIR filter does not (cannot!) exhibit true linear phase. Different IIR filter design techniques can result in varying approximations to a linear phase response, but can never achieve it completely. Depending on the application, having linear phase (i.e., constant group delay) may be crucial to the proper operation of the DSP-based filtering operation. If so, symmetric (or antisymmetric) FIR filters are recommended.

In summary, IIR filters can take advantage of known analog filter designs and can meet steep requirements (particularly for the magnitude response) at a lower order than FIR filters. But IIR filters are subject to instability if the designer is not careful, and their phase response can never be truly linear. There are times when an IIR filter is exactly what you want for your DSP application, so let's explore them further.

4.2   winDSK Demonstration: Notch Filter Application

Start the winDSK8 application, and the main user interface window will appear. Ensure the correct selections have been made in the "DSP Board" and "Host Interface" configuration panels of winDSK8 for each parameter before proceeding. The winDSK8 Notch Filter application implements a second-order IIR filter. Clicking on the Notch Filter button will run the program in the attached DSK, and a window similar to Figure 4.4 will appear.

In Chapter 3, we decreased the Q adjustment (determined by the value of variable r in the filter's transfer function) until it reached zero. This put the poles of the filter at the origin of the z-plane and the DSK behaved as if it was running an FIR filter. In this section, we will increase the Q adjustment (by increasing $|r|$), which causes the poles to move away from the origin and approach the unit circle. This adjustment (via the slider control at the bottom of the Notch/Bandpass Filter window) is shown in Figure 4.4. Also notice that the "Filter Type" was selected to be "Notch" rather than "Bandpass" for this demonstration;

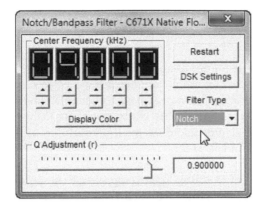

Figure 4.4: winDSK8 running the Notch Filter application with $r = 0.9$.

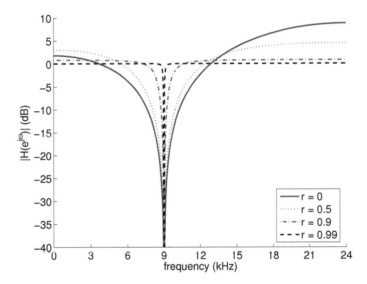

Figure 4.5: The frequency responses of four different notch filters having a notch frequency of 9 kHz and r values of 0, 0.5, 0.9, and 0.99.

a notch filter may also be called a bandreject filter. As the poles of the notch filter get closer to the unit circle (i.e., as $|r| \to 1.0$), they progressively increase the "steepness" of the notch. But, as with all IIR filters, stability is an issue: if $|r| = 1.0$, then the poles are *on* the unit circle and the filter will not be stable (i.e., it will tend to break into oscillation).[1]

To show you the effect on the notch filter's magnitude response caused by moving the poles, we keep a constant notch frequency and change only $|r|$. Theoretically, an infinite amount of attenuation is present at the exact notch frequency (in practice it's a very large yet finite amount of attenuation, but it's so large that we can treat it as if it's infinite attenuation). This explains why a properly adjusted (tuned) notch filter can completely remove an interfering tone for all practical purposes. The frequency responses associated with four different settings of $|r|$ for the notch filter are overlaid and shown in Figure 4.5.

---

[1] Actually, the notch filter application in winDSK8 is a special case, where poles on the unit circle (caused by setting $r = 1.0$) are canceled by zeros on the unit circle in exactly the same location, so no oscillation will result (assuming coefficient quantization hasn't "moved" the poles or zeros slightly). However, if the poles move outside the unit circle, the filter will not be stable.

Comparing the frequency responses shown in this figure demonstrates two ramifications of moving the poles of an IIR filter close to the unit circle.

1. As $|r| \to 1.0$, the maximum gain of the filter (without scaling) approaches 1 (0 dB). For any value of $|r|$, the maximum gain may always be *forced* to 1 (0 dB) by including a multiplicative scale factor that would have to be multiplied by *all* of the b coefficients, but we would prefer to avoid this extra step. Remember, excess gain in a DSP algorithm can cause significant problems if it results in an output value that exceeds the numerical range of the DAC.

2. As $|r| \to 1.0$, the Q of the filter (i.e., steepness of the notch) increases dramatically. At the same time, as the poles approach the unit circle, that portion of the impulse response of the filter with significant non-zero values increases in length.[2] This indicates that more time will be needed for the filter to effectively reach a steady-state condition (that's right, there's no free lunch!). And, as mentioned earlier, if we ever allow $|r| = 1.0$ (or more precisely $|r| \geq 1.0$), then the filter would be unstable.

To hear the effect of the Notch Filter application, add a sinusoidal signal (tone) to a music signal in a similar fashion as we described in Chapter 3. Most software programs that support computer sound cards will perform this summing for you. You will need to experiment with your audio mixer program controls to determine exactly how your particular system responds. Most systems are capable of summing an external audio signal (such as from a portable music player or a function generator) with an internal audio signal by playing a sound file or CD on the computer. In this example, one audio signal (typically the external source) is a tone and the other is music. Inject the external signal via the sound card "line input" or "microphone input" connector. The sound card "line output" or "headphone output" is then connected to the signal input of the DSK. As before, the DSK signal output is connected to a set of powered speakers. If a function generator isn't available, you can use one of the audio test tones (`*.wav`) in directory `test_signals` of the software that accompanies this book and play them with a second, external CD player or transfer the file to a portable music player. You can also easily create your own audio test tones in MATLAB, then save them as an audio file and play them in the same way on an external CD or music player (this concept will be discussed further in Chapter 5).

When the center frequency of the notch filter equals the frequency of the injected tone, you should hear the sound of the tone disappear from the speakers.

4.3   MATLAB Implementation

4.3.1   Filter Design and Analysis

After designing a filter in MATLAB, the discrete-time difference equation is routinely available in the form of two vectors: B (numerator coefficients) and A (denominator coefficients). Given these two vectors, MATLAB can rapidly analyze and plot your filter's performance using several different toolbox functions. To find help on the MATLAB Signal Processing Toolbox, type `help signal`. Then click on "Digital Filters" to see more information on that subtopic. An edited version of the results associated with entering this command and mouse click are shown below.

---

[2]Recall that while the impulse response of an FIR filter is equal to the filter coefficients, this is *not* the case for an IIR filter. In this example, the number of non-trivial impulse response values of a second-order IIR filter can be quite large if the poles are close to the unit circle.

```
>> help signal

  Signal Processing Toolbox
     . . .
  Filter analysis
    abs        - Magnitude
    angle      - Phase angle
    filternorm - Compute the 2-norm or inf-norm of a digital filter
    freqz      - Z-transform frequency response
    fvtool     - Filter Visualization Tool
    grpdelay   - Group delay
    impz       - Discrete impulse response
    phasedelay - Phase delay of a digital filter
    phasez     - Digital filter phase response (unwrapped)
    stepz      - Digital filter step response
    unwrap     - Unwrap phase angle
    zerophase  - Zero-phase response of a real filter
    zplane     - Discrete pole-zero plot
```

Of particular interest are the frequency response, impulse response, pole-zero, and group delay plots.

Creating an Impulse Response Plot

Unlike an FIR filter, the filter coefficients of the IIR filter are *not* the individual terms that make up the impulse response of the system. The impulse response of an IIR filter must be calculated iteratively. The MATLAB command `impz` can greatly simplify this process. For example, if we design our filter using the **butter** command (for Butterworth filters) and wish to examine the impulse response, we will need to use commands similar to

```
[B,A] = butter(4,0.25);
impz(B,A,10,48000);
```

to create the impulse response plot. In line 1, we design a fourth-order Butterworth lowpass filter with a cutoff frequency of $0.25F_s/2$. In the second line of code, we use the four argument variation of `impz` to determine the impulse response of the filter, where B and A are the numerator and denominator coefficient vectors (respectively), 10 is the desired number of points of the impulse response to be calculated and plotted, and 48000 is the sample frequency to be used with the filter. Since we included the sample frequency (the fourth input argument), the horizontal axis of the resulting plot will have units of time. If we leave off the fourth argument (sample frequency), the horizontal axis will have units of samples (i.e., sample number n). If we further leave off the third argument (number of points to be calculated), the algorithm will determine for you the number of samples to be evaluated and plotted. Try it and see!

Instead of using the command line execution of **butter**, we could have used the command SPTool (Signal Processing Tool), which brings up a graphical user interface (GUI), as shown in Figure 4.6 that, among other things, allows us to design digital filters.[3] To design a new digital filter, click the "New" button in the center column of the SPTool GUI. This will result in the FDATool GUI that is shown in Figure 4.7, where we show the Butterworth filter

---

[3]The descriptions we provide here for using particular MATLAB tools may require modification with later versions of MATLAB, but the overall techniques should be similar.

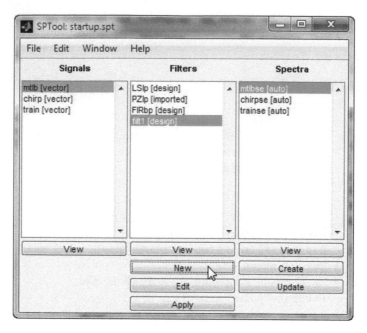

Figure 4.6: The GUI associated with SPTool.

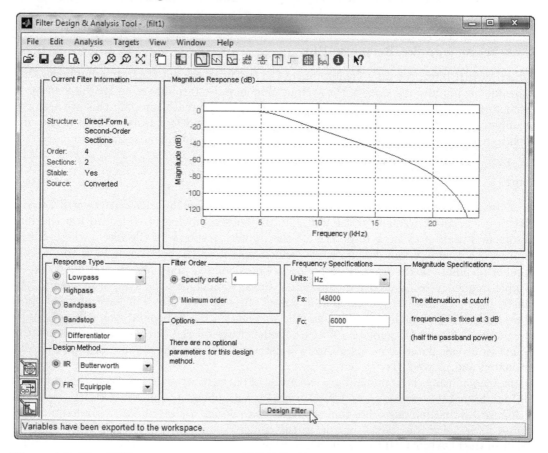

Figure 4.7: The GUI associated with MATLAB's FDATool showing the magnitude response of a Butterworth LPF.

already having been designed using this GUI.[4] Note that this tool defaults to designing this particular filter in a form called "second-order sections" that is discussed in more detail later in this chapter. To use the `impz` program, we would need to use FDATool to convert to a single section ("Edit, Convert to Single Section"), export the filter coefficients to the workspace ("File, Export"), and then call `impz(Num,Den)`, assuming you kept the default names for the numerator and denominator coefficient vectors instead of B and A that we used above.[5] Using this version of the `impz` command will result in the plot shown in Figure 4.8(a).

While the command line use of tools such as `impz` is still quite useful, the same information can be obtained directly from the FDATool GUI. Once the filter has been designed, you can use the "Analysis" drop-down menu or click on the desired icon near the top of the GUI. Clicking on the "Impulse response" icon in FDATool results in Figure 4.8(b). Compare the two figures. In a similar, one-click fashion, FDATool can show plots of the filter's magnitude, phase, group delay, phase delay, step response, pole-zero plot, and other useful information. Explore the capabilities of this versatile tool.

We will show a few more examples of using the individual command line tools, but if you prefer you can accomplish similar tasks directly from FDATool. Advantages of command line tools include more direct control over the resulting plots (font size, line thickness, etc.) and the ease of incorporating the various operations into your own m-files.[6] Therefore, time invested to learn the command line tools is well spent. If all you desire is a bit more control over figures but prefer to stay with FDATool, use "View, Filter Visualization Tool" to call up another GUI from which you can export just the plots.

Creating a Frequency Response Plot

Plotting the frequency response can be accomplished using the MATLAB command `freqz`. An example of using this command follows.

```
freqz(B,A);
```

The resulting frequency response plot is shown in Figure 4.9. Without specifying the sample frequency as an additional argument to `freqz`, the frequency axis of the plot is shown as normalized radian frequency in π units, so the far right value shown as 1 on the x-axis is where the normalized radian frequency equals π. This is equivalent to where the frequency equals $F_s/2$. Where the normalized axis equals 0.25 is where $f = 0.25F_s/2$; this is the cutoff frequency (where the filter magnitude response is down by 3 dB) that we specified earlier when we designed the filter. Note the nonlinear phase response of this IIR filter (although just in the passband, the deviation from linear phase is not too egregious).

Creating a Pole/Zero Plot

Plotting the locations of the poles and zeros on the z-plane can be accomplished using the MATLAB command `zplane`. An example using this command follows.

```
1  zplane(B,A);
```

The resulting pole/zero plot is shown in Figure 4.10. In filter design, the location of poles and zeros with respect to the unit circle is very important, and the designer may rely quite a bit on plots such as those produced by `zplane`. But there instances when such plots can be misleading. The MATLAB command `zplane` calls another function called `zplaneplot`

---

[4]Note that you can call up FDATool directly by typing `fdatool` at the MATLAB command line.

[5]You could also export the second-order sections and then use `sos2tf` or a related conversion command in MATLAB.

[6]FDATool is simply a GUI shell that calls these very same command line tools for you.

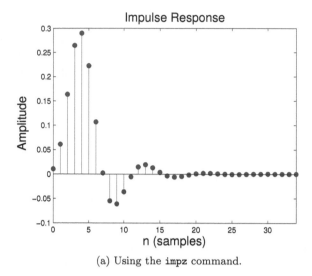

(a) Using the `impz` command.

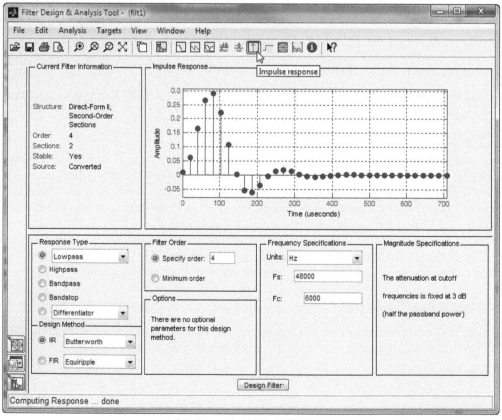

(b) Using the GUI of **FDATool**.

Figure 4.8: The impulse response associated with a fourth-order Butterworth lowpass filter having a cutoff frequency of $0.25F_s/2$.

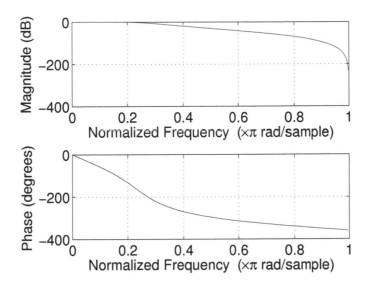

Figure 4.9: The frequency response diagram associated with a fourth-order Butterworth lowpass filter having a cutoff frequency of $0.25F_s/2$.

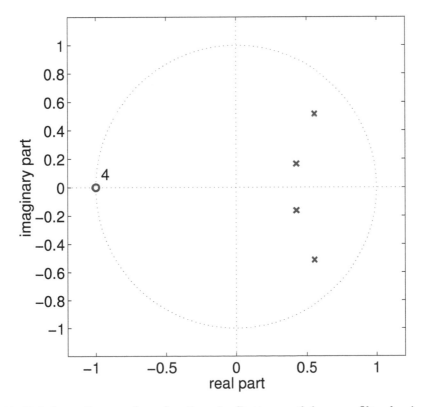

Figure 4.10: Pole/zero diagram for a fourth-order Butterworth lowpass filter having a cutoff frequency of $0.25F_s/2$.

which actually creates the pole/zero plot, including plotting the unit circle on the z-plane. This is also how the pole/zero plot is created for FDATool. At this point in our discussion, it may be useful to many readers if we briefly digress from IIR filter design and turn to a short side discussion about zplaneplot.

The original version of zplaneplot used only 70 points to form the unit circle. Since MATLAB plots are largely straight lines drawn between points, this leads to a 69-sided polygon. This very *faceted* approach to plotting a circle or arc may be inadequate if your poles and/or zeros are very close to the unit circle. After feedback to The MathWorks from the authors of this text (and perhaps others), a modified version of zplaneplot tests to see how close the poles and zeros are to the unit circle and uses more points than 70 if needed. This version of zplaneplot can use a maximum of 50,000 points to construct the unit circle, which might seem to be enough. Unfortunately, the problem of plotting poles and zeros very close to the unit circle continues to exist for versions up through MATLAB 2010b. For MATLAB 2011a and later, The MathWorks modified zplaneplot again and has resolved the issue. We've also noticed, looking at MATLAB 2016a, that zplaneplot has been refined in this regard even more.

For the benefit of those readers who are using a version of MATLAB earlier than 2011a, we discuss a simple fix. Suppose, for example, that the location of poles for a particular filter design included the conjugate pair described by $0.998446047456247 \pm j0.045491015143694$. This is obviously very close to the unit circle, and if the poles are on or outside the unit circle, our filter design would be unstable. We can manually calculate the magnitude (using MATLAB's abs() command, for example), which we would find to be 0.999481836823364, so the filter should be stable (ignoring possible coefficient quantization issues, discussed later in this chapter). But most people would just look at the pole/zero plot, and zoom in to see if the pole was beyond the unit circle. An enhanced pole/zero plot for this conjugate pole pair is shown in Figure 4.11. In particular, note the bottom zoomed-in plot. The dashed line to the left of the "X" is supposedly the unit circle as would be plotted by the zplaneplot routine, and the solid line to the right of the "X" is a more accurate plot of the unit circle (as would be plotted by our own ucf routine) by using 100,000 points for the entire circle. In this situation, the designer could be misled by zplaneplot into thinking a stable filter was unstable.

There are two easy solutions to this problem.

- **RECOMMENDED** Use the ucf function provided with the book software (in the Chapter 4 matlab directory) to correct the problem. Basically, ucf erases the original unit circle by overwriting it with a white line and then plots a more accurate unit circle. The name ucf stands for "unit circle fixer," and can be updated to your own specifications without causing problems with any MATLAB toolbox functions.

- **NOT RECOMMENDED** Edit the MATLAB m-file zplaneplot where the number of points is determined. Originally, the lines that do this are in the range of line numbers 85–94; look at your own version for the exact line numbers. The code in this section of zplaneplot.m is shown below.

```
   closest = min(1-[abs(z(:)); abs(p(:))]);
86 points = 1/2e8/closest;
   if points < 70
88    points = 70;
   elseif points > 50000
90    points = 50000;
   elseif isempty(points)
92    points = 70;
```

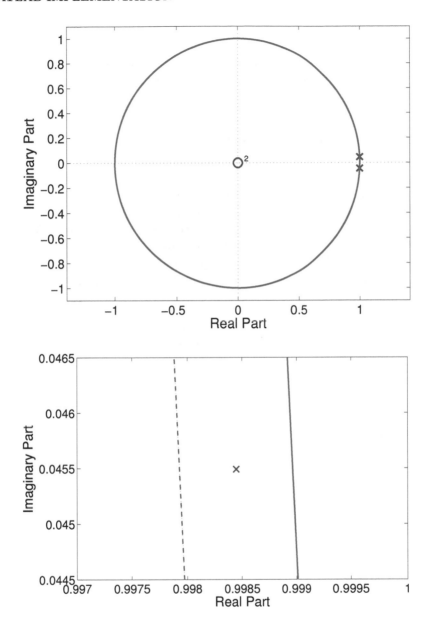

Figure 4.11: Pole/zero diagram for poles at $0.998446047456247 \pm j0.045491015143694$. Top: entire plot. Bottom: zoomed in to the upper pole.

```
   end
94 theta = linspace(0,2*pi,points);
```

Line 85 determines how close the poles and zeros are to the unit circle. Lines 86–93 determine how many points to use to plot the unit circle. The linspace command on line 94 creates a variable, theta, which consists of the value of points elements that are uniformly spaced between 0 and 2π. Changing the value of points to a much larger integer (for example, 100,000), will result in more points being used to plot the unit circle. More points allow the plotted polygon to much more closely approximate a circle. However, this approach is *not recommended* because it modifies a MATLAB toolbox function that was provided to you by The MathWorks. Modifying this and other code that you have paid money to other people to develop and maintain is a bad idea for at least four different reasons.

1. If you believe production code is in error, you should submit a formal request to have the code corrected. This may allow others to benefit from your efforts.

2. If you do modify the MATLAB code, the next update of the toolbox that you receive and install will invariably overwrite the updated function that you have created and all of your modifications will be lost.

3. The chance that you will remember what you have done in the distant future is very small, and you will need to rediscover the entire unit circle plotting problem after installing a new version of the toolbox.

4. You may break the toolbox function so that it no longer works or even worse: you think that the function is working, but it is actually returning inaccurate results.

If you remember these ideas each time that you inevitably encounter a problem with someone else's software, you will have fewer problems in the long run. Now we return to the discussion of IIR filter design.

Creating a Group Delay Plot

Plotting the group delay can be accomplished using the MATLAB command `grpdelay`. An example using this command follows.

```
grpdelay(B,A);
```

The resulting plot is shown in Figure 4.12. Note that the group delay is *not* constant, which is due to the nonlinear phase response of this filter.

Using FDATool and FVTool

As we've already implied, the MATLAB environment and its Signal Processing Toolbox provides even more tools for designing digital filters. For example, you can use MATLAB's FDATool (Filter Design and Analysis Tool) to design your filter. As shown earlier in Figure 4.7 and Figure 4.8(b), there are several software pushbuttons in FDATool that are available to allow you to not only specify and design your filter, but also to view a number of filter analysis plots. The filter coefficients exported from FDATool are just vectors (by default).

Finally, regardless of how you design your filter, you can analyze your filter by using MATLAB's FVTool (Filter Visualization Tool) either by using the "View" drop-down menu of FDATool or by calling FVTool directly:

```
1  fvtool(B,A);
```

As shown in Figure 4.13, several software pushbuttons are available in FVTool that will allow you to view a number of filter analysis plots, which we've annotated with labels and arrows on the figure. In that figure, the group delay of the filter has been selected (compare Figure 4.13 to Figure 4.12).

While all the MATLAB commands and tools were discussed here in the context of IIR filters, they can all just as easily be used for FIR filters. The primary difference is that the "vector" A for all FIR filters is equal to the scalar value of 1.

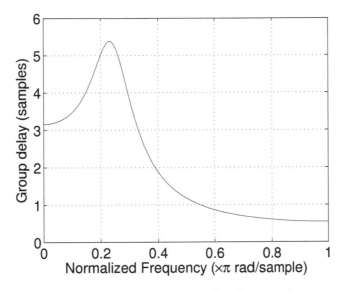

Figure 4.12: The group delay associated with a fourth-order Butterworth lowpass filter having a cutoff frequency of $0.25F_s/2$.

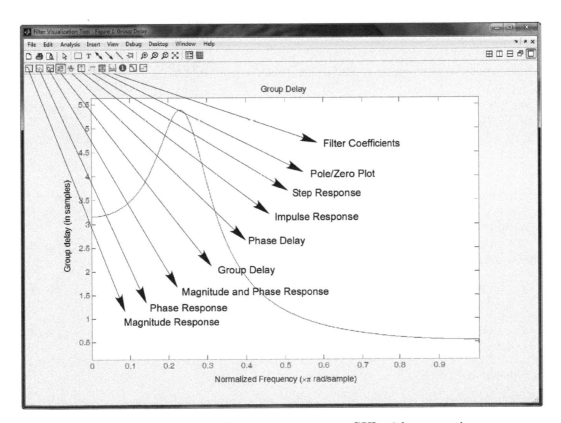

Figure 4.13: The FVTool filter viewer program GUI, with annotations.

4.3.2   IIR Filter Notation

IIR filters are more complicated than FIR filters, and there are various choices the designer must make when implementing them. The remainder of this chapter will focus primarily on implementation issues associated with IIR filters. Recall that the generalized difference equation associated with a causal IIR filter is

$$\sum_{k=0}^{M} a[k]y[n-k] = \sum_{k=0}^{N} b[k]x[n-k]$$

or in output variable form,

$$a[0]y[n] = -\sum_{k=1}^{M} a[k]y[n-k] + \sum_{k=0}^{N} b[k]x[n-k].$$

The $a[0]$ term, the coefficient of $y[n]$, is usually normalized to 1. In fact, MATLAB normalizes the $a[0]$ coefficient prior to almost all of its calculations. This normalization results in

$$y[n] = -\sum_{k=1}^{M} a[k]y[n-k] + \sum_{k=0}^{N} b[k]x[n-k],$$

where each of the remaining $a[k]$ and $b[k]$ terms are scaled by $a[0]$. We have chosen not to rename this normalized version of the coefficients in the equation above, as this form is how most DSP books depict the difference equation of an IIR filter.

Alternatively, the IIR filter's difference equation can be converted to a transfer function in the z-domain:

$$H\left(z\right) = \frac{b_0 + b_1 z^{-1} + b_2 z^{-2} + \cdots + b_N z^{-N}}{1 + a_1 z^{-1} + a_2 z^{-2} + \cdots + a_M z^{-M}}.$$

If we use a similar notation for filter implementation as we did in Chapter 3, the transfer function becomes

$$H\left(z\right) = \frac{b\left[0\right] + b\left[1\right] z^{-1} + b\left[2\right] z^{-2} + \cdots + b\left[N\right] z^{-N}}{1 + a\left[1\right] z^{-1} + a\left[2\right] z^{-2} + \cdots + a\left[M\right] z^{-M}}.$$

Notice that the number of a terms $(M+1)$ and the number of b terms $(N+1)$ are often not equal. That is the reason for using M for the order of the denominator and N for the order of the numerator in the transfer function polynomial.

To calculate $y[0]$ (the current output value of the IIR filter), we must perform two operations:

1. the dot product $\mathbf{B} \cdot \mathbf{x}$, where $\mathbf{B} = \{b[0], b[1], \ldots, b[N]\}$ and $\mathbf{x} = \{x[0], x[-1], \ldots, x[-N]\}$ (the current and past values of the input signal), and

2. a dot product of $\mathbf{A} \cdot \mathbf{y}$, where $\mathbf{A} = \{1, a[1], \ldots, a[M]\}$ and $\mathbf{y} = \{y[0], y[-1], \ldots, y[-M]\}$ (the current and past values of the output signal).

Specifically,

$$y[0] = -a[1]y[-1] - a[2]y[-2] - \cdots - a[M]y[-M] + b[0]x[0] + b[1]x[-1] + \cdots + b[N]x[-N].$$

Notice that the $\mathbf{A} \cdot \mathbf{y}$ term is really only a partial dot product because the $a[0]y[0]$ term is not needed and is therefore not calculated.

4.3.3   Block Diagrams

Routinely, engineers use block diagrams to help understand implementation issues and signal flow. One of the standard block diagram forms associated with implementing this IIR filter is shown in Figure 4.14. The blocks containing z^{-1} are delay blocks that store the input into the block for one sample period. The delay blocks may be thought of as synchronous shift registers that have their clocks tied to the ADC and DAC's sample clock, but are typically just memory locations accessed by the DSP CPU. This form is called direct form I (DF-I) and is the most straightforward implementation of the standard difference equation. Alternatively, a single summing node can be used to more accurately implement the difference equation as a single equation. This can be seen in Figure 4.15.

Another variant is shown in Figure 4.16. It is called direct form II (DF-II) and is achieved by reversing the order of the feed forward and feedback terms and combining the delay elements. This form only requires half the DF-I memory elements, and thus would be a more efficient implementation. A slight variation of the direct form II that is shown in Figure 4.16 is called the direct form II transpose (DF-IIt); it is shown in Figure 4.17. The transpose, which comes from the theory of linear signal flow graphs, provides exactly the same output, but in general can use fewer addition operations and therefore is slightly more efficient than the DF-II version. In MATLAB, if you type `help filter`, you'll see that the filter function implements the direct form II transpose version by default.

Figure 4.18 is called a cascade of two second-order sections (SOS), where each SOS is implemented as a DF-II. Second-order sections are also called "biquads" or "biquadratic sections" by some authors. Higher-order filters can be divided into a number of first- or second-order terms that can then be multiplied (cascaded) together. Second-order terms are preferred over higher-order terms since real coefficients can be used to accurately describe the locations of complex conjugate pairs. This often forgotten fact is a result of the fundamental theorem of algebra. Coefficient quantization effects are also far less problematic using cascaded SOS compared to other implementations. MATLAB does provide a wide

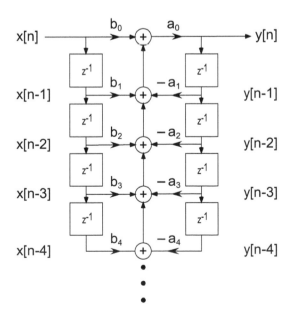

Figure 4.14: Block diagram associated with the DF-I implementation of an IIR filter. The coefficient a_0 is typically normalized to 1.0.

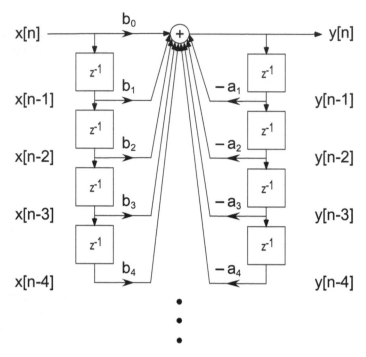

Figure 4.15: Block diagram associated with the direct form I (DF-I) implementation of an IIR filter using only one summing node. Coefficient a_0 is not shown (assumed to be 1.0).

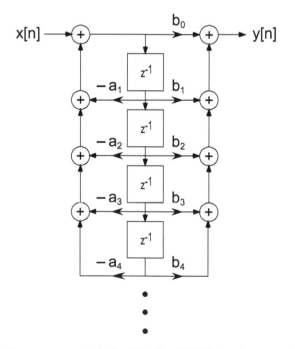

Figure 4.16: Block diagram associated with the DF-II implementation of an IIR filter. Coefficient a_0 is not shown (assumed to be 1.0).

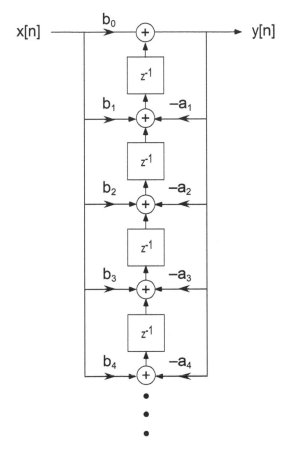

Figure 4.17: Block diagram associated with the DF-II transpose implementation of an IIR filter. Coefficient a_0 is not shown (assumed to be 1.0).

variety of conversion m-files for various implementations. Of particular interest is **tf2sos** (transfer function to second-order section) and **zp2sos** (zero/pole to second-order section). A complete listing of the MATLAB conversion routines can be found using **help signal**; click on the **Linear Systems** heading and see the functions listed under **Linear systems transformations**.

The final block diagram we will mention is the parallel form, which is shown in Figure 4.19. We have shown only first-order numerator (b) terms in this figure because that is

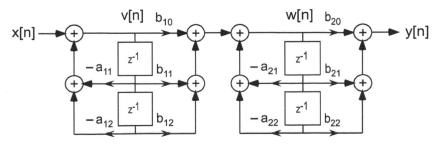

Figure 4.18: Block diagram associated with the second-order section (SOS) implementation of an IIR filter, showing two SOS stages. Each SOS is a DF-II form.

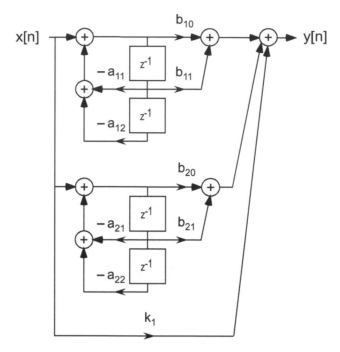

Figure 4.19: Block diagram associated with the parallel implementation of an IIR filter. Coefficient k_1 is an overall gain factor.

routinely the result after the parallel decomposition is complete. MATLAB's Signal Processing Toolbox does not currently have an m-file that converts to parallel form. We have written such an m-file and included it in the `matlab` directory for Chapter 4. Conforming to the MATLAB naming convention, our m-file is named `filt2par`. This m-file converts numerator and denominator vectors of filter coefficients to parallel form.

There are dozens of implementation block diagrams, and we have selected only a few of the most common forms for discussion here. Each form has advantages and disadvantages, and we will not dwell on this topic; however, a design example will be used to help explain a few of these issues. The MATLAB code associated with this example can also be found in the `matlab` directory for Chapter 4. The m-file is called `ellipticExample` and, as its name implies, it designs and implements an elliptic filter. The `ellipticExample` m-file generates the filter coefficients, pole/zero diagrams, and frequency responses associated with DF-I/DF-II, SOS, and parallel implementation. This fourth-order filter was carefully selected to cause the filter to become unstable if it is implemented using single precision DF-I or DF-II techniques. Instability in IIR filters is often caused by the result of finite precision arithmetic (i.e., coefficient quantization) causing the poles to move outside the unit circle. This can be seen in Figure 4.20, where the smaller circles (zeros) and x's (poles) represent the correct location of the filter's poles and zeros. The larger circles and x's are where the poles and zeros end up when direct form arithmetic is used, and the coefficients are represented as 16-bit fixed-point integers. Because one of the larger x poles is outside the unit circle, this filter will be unstable if implemented as a direct form I or direct form II using 16-bits to represent each coefficient. Any attempt to implement such a filter in either MATLAB or real-time code will produce an undesirable result. Simply changing to an SOS implementation fixes the problem. Of course *zeros* outside the unit circle do not affect stability in any way.

A useful MATLAB-based tool to help evaluate the implementation effects associated

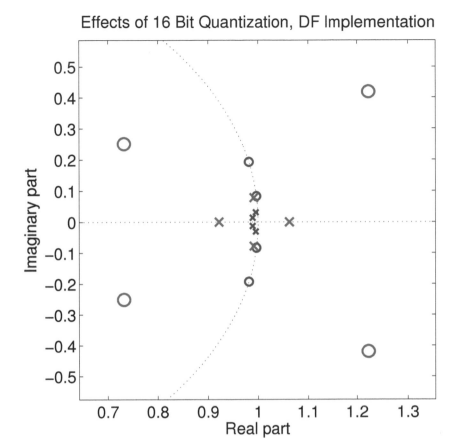

Figure 4.20: Pole/zero plot (zoomed in) associated with a fourth-order elliptic filter implementation using direct form techniques.

with DF-I, DF-II, and SOS is included with the software for this book. The tool is a collection of MATLAB m-files that are controlled through the `qfilt` GUI, seen in Figure 4.21. This GUI was written not only to evaluate finite precision arithmetic effects but to implement the quantized coefficient FIR or IIR filter on a TI TMS320C31 DSK. Not having a C31 DSK attached to the host PC will only prevent you from loading and running the displayed filter on the DSK. You will be able to use all the other features of the program. Years after we introduced the `qfilt` program, The MathWorks released a number of tools and toolboxes (e.g., FDATool in the Signal Processing Toolbox, when used with the Fixed Point Toolbox) to deal with the same finite precision effects. They have also introduced a series of toolboxes and blocksets that allow some of your work to be run in Simulink via CCS on selected TI hardware targets. You may want to investigate these recent tools from The MathWorks on your own.

Should you implement an unstable filter, it may sound similar to audio feedback (getting the microphone too close to the speakers). But most of the time it sounds as if the speakers are not plugged in, since the output of the DSP algorithm grows rapidly to the point that the numbers can no longer be represented in the DSP hardware. Using a CCS watch window to troubleshoot this and other logical programming errors can be a very effective technique. Evaluating and plotting the frequency response of an unstable system, although allowed by MATLAB, is meaningless, since the DFT operation upon which the `freqz` command is

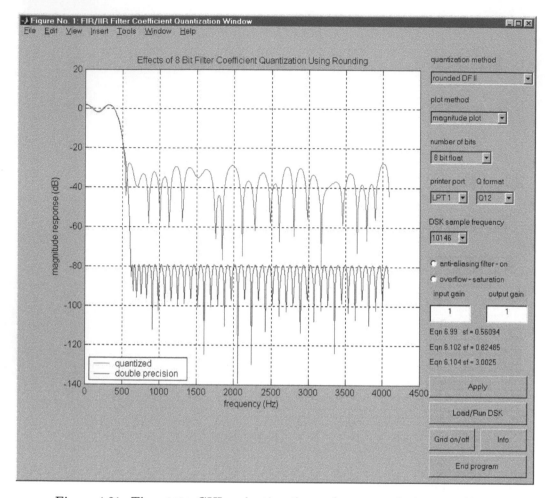

Figure 4.21: The `qfilt` GUI evaluating the performance of a lowpass filter.

based is undefined for unstable systems.

If you run the `ellipticExample` m-file, the filter coefficients will be available in the MATLAB workspace. The resulting transfer functions (rounded) are shown below.

$$H_{DF}(z) = \frac{0.000996 - 0.0039z^{-1} + 0.0059z^{-2} - 0.0039z^{-3} + 0.000996z^{-4}}{1 - 3.97z^{-1} + 5.909z^{-2} - 3.911z^{-3} + 0.971z^{-4}}$$

$$H_{sos}(z) = \frac{0.00101 - 0.00195z^{-1} + 0.00101z^{-2}}{1 - 1.99z^{-1} + z^{-2}} \cdot \frac{1 - 1.98z^{-1} + 0.978z^{-2}}{1 - 1.99z^{-1} + 0.992z^{-2}}$$

$$H_{parallel}(z) = \frac{-0.00385 + 0.00360z^{-1}}{1 - 1.99z^{-1} + 0.992z^{-2}} + \frac{0.00382 - 0.00348z^{-1}}{1 - 1.98z^{-1} + 0.978z^{-2}}$$

In Figures 4.22, 4.23, 4.24, and 4.25, we show the DF-I, DF-II, SOS, and parallel implementation block diagrams, respectively, with the filter coefficients.   The coefficient values in the figures are also rounded to three significant digits in the block diagrams for compactness. In each figure the same filter is implemented, but each implementation has its own advantages and disadvantages.

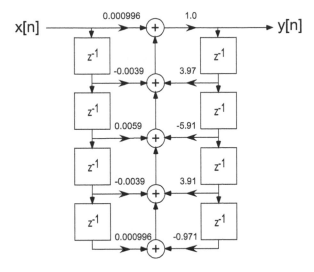

Figure 4.22: Block diagram of direct form I (DF-I) fourth-order elliptic filter.

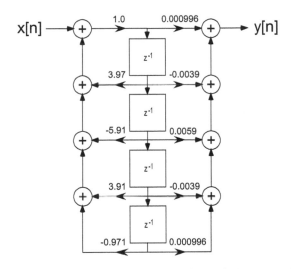

Figure 4.23: Block diagram of a direct form II (DF-II) fourth-order elliptic filter.

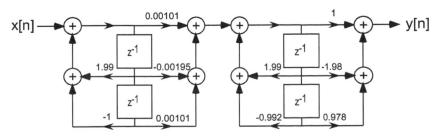

Figure 4.24: Block diagram of a the second-order section (SOS) implementation of a fourth-order elliptic filter.

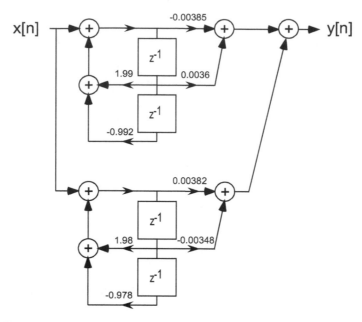

Figure 4.25: Block diagram of a parallel implementation of a fourth-order elliptic filter.

4.3.4 Built-In Approach

As mentioned in Chapter 3, MATLAB has a built-in function called `filter.m`. It can be used to implement FIR filters (using only the numerator (B) coefficients and setting $A = 1$) and IIR filters (using both the numerator (B) and the denominator (A) coefficients). The first few lines of the online help associated with the `filter` command are provided next.

```
>> help filter

 FILTER One-dimensional digital filter.
    Y = FILTER(B,A,X) filters the data in vector X with the
    filter described by vectors A and B to create the filtered
    data Y.  The filter is a "Direct Form II Transposed"
    implementation of the standard difference equation:

    a(1)*y(n) = b(1)*x(n) + b(2)*x(n-1) + ... + b(nb+1)*x(n-nb)
                          - a(2)*y(n-1) - ... - a(na+1)*y(n-na)
```

This function is useful for quickly implementing a filter with minimal programming on your part.

4.3.5 Creating Your Own Filter Algorithm

In this next MATLAB example, we are trying to implement a first-order IIR notch filter (this is *not* the same notch filter implemented in winDSK8). We desire the filter to have a zero at $z = 1$ and a pole at $z = 0.9$. The transfer function associated with this pole/zero diagram is

$$H(z) = \frac{1 - z^{-1}}{1 - 0.9z^{-1}}$$

and the difference equation is

$$y[n] = 0.9y[n-1] + x[n] - x[n-1].$$

We will use a unit impulse as the input to the system. If we calculate an infinite number of output terms, we will have determined the system's impulse response. Manually calculating a few terms from the difference equation is very helpful in understanding this process.

1. Label the columns as shown below.

$$n \quad y[n] \quad y[n-1] \quad x[n] \quad x[n-1]$$

2. Fill in the $n = 0$ row information.

n	$y[n]$	$y[n-1]$	$x[n]$	$x[n-1]$
0		0	1	0

3. Calculate the $y[0]$ term.

n	$y[n]$	$y[n-1]$	$x[n]$	$x[n-1]$
0	1	0	1	0

4. Fill in the $n = 1$ row information. Notice the "down and to the right" flow of the stored values.

n	$y[n]$	$y[n-1]$	$x[n]$	$x[n-1]$
0	1	0	1	0
1		1	0	1

5. Calculate the $y[1]$ term.

n	$y[n]$	$y[n-1]$	$x[n]$	$x[n-1]$
0	1	0	1	0
1	−0.1	1	0	1

6. Continue this process until you have calculated all of the terms that you need.

The MATLAB code shown in the listing below will only calculate the $y[1]$ term. This code more closely implements the algorithm required for the real-time process. While it may seem strange to calculate only a single term, you must remember that this is *exactly* how sample-by-sample processing works.

Listing 4.1: Simple MATLAB IIR filter example.

```
1 % begin simulation

3 % Simulation inputs
  x = [0 1];        % input vector x = x[0] x[-1]
5 y = [1 1];        % output vector y = y[0] y[-1]
  B = [1 -1];       % numerator coefficients
7 A = [1 -0.9];     % denominator coefficients

9 % Calculated terms
  y(1) = -A(2)*y(2) + B(1)*x(1) + B(2)*x(2);
```

```
11 x(2) = x(1);      % shift x[0] into x[-1]
   y(2) = y(1);      % shift y[0] into y[-1]
13
   % Simulation outputs
15 x                 % notice that x(1) = x(2)
   y                 % notice that y(1) = y(2)
17
   % end simulation
```

As in the manual calculations, you should find that the output value is −0.1. In summary, the input (receive) ISR provides a new sample to the algorithm, the algorithm calculates the new output value, the algorithm prepares for the arrival of the next sample, and finally, the algorithm gives the new output value to the output (transmit) ISR, so that it may be converted back into an analog value. Notice that, for low-order filters, the actual calculation of the output value may be a *single* line of code!

4.4   DSK Implementation in C

4.4.1   Brute-Force IIR Filtering

This version of the IIR implementation code, similar to the last MATLAB example, takes a brute-force approach. The intention of this approach is understandability, which comes at the expense of efficiency.

The files necessary to run this application are in the **ccs\IIRrevA** directory of Chapter 4. The primary file of interest is the **IIR_mono_ISRs.c** interrupt service routine. This file contains the necessary variable declarations and performs the actual IIR filtering operation. To allow for the use of a stereo codec (e.g., the native codecs on the OMAP-L138 boards and the C6713 DSK), the program can easily implement independent Left and Right channel filters (see the difference between **FIRmono_ISRs.c** and **FIRstereo_ISRs.c** in Chapter 3). For clarity, however, only the Left channel mono version will be discussed below. In the code shown below, N is the filter order, the B array holds the filter's numerator coefficients, the A array holds the filter's denominator coefficients, the x array holds the current input value $x[0]$, and past values of x (namely, $x[-1]$ for this filter), and the y array contains the current output value of the filter, $y[0]$, and past values of y (namely, $y[-1]$ for this filter).

Listing 4.2: Brute-force IIR filter declarations.

```
#define N 1                           // filter order
2
   float B[N+1] = {1.0, -1.0};        // numerator filter coefficients
4  float A[N+1] = {1.0, -0.9};        // denominator filter coefficients
   float x[N+1];                      // input values
6  float y[N+1];                      // output values
```

The code shown below performs the actual filtering operation. The four main steps involved in this operation will be discussed following the code listing.

Listing 4.3: Brute-force IIR filtering for real-time.

```
/* I added my routine here */
2 x[0] = CodecDataIn.Channel[LEFT]; // current input value
4 y[0] = -A[1]*y[1] + B[0]*x[0] + B[1]x[1]; // calc. the output
```

```
6  x[1] = x[0];   // setup for the next input
   y[1] = y[0];   // setup for the next input
8
   CodecDataOut.Channel[LEFT] = y[0]; // output the result
10 /* end of my routine */
```

The four real-time steps involved in brute-force IIR filtering

An explanation of Listing 4.3 follows.

1. (Line 2): This code receives the next sample from the receive ISR and assigns it to the current input array element, x[0].

2. (Line 4): This code calculates a single value of the difference equation's output, y[0].

3. (Lines 6–7): These 2 lines of code shift the values in the x and y arrays one element to the right. The equivalent operation is

$$x[0] \rightarrow x[1]$$
$$y[0] \rightarrow y[1].$$

After the shift to the right is complete, the next incoming sample, $x[0]$ can be written into the $x[0]$ memory location without a loss of information.

4. (Line 9): This line of code completes the filtering operation by transferring the result of the filtering operation, $y[0]$, to the **CodecDataOut.Channel[LEFT]** variable for transfer to the DAC side of the codec via the transmit ISR.

Now that you understand the code. . .

Go ahead and copy all of the files into a separate directory. Open the project in CCS and "Rebuild All." Once the build is complete, "Load Program" into the DSK and click on "Run." Your IIR HP filter (actually a DC blocking filter) is now running on the DSK. Remember this program would typically be used for audio filtering, so a good way to experience the effects of your filter is to listen to unfiltered and filtered music.[7]

4.4.2 More Efficient IIR Filtering

Making the processor physically shift the location of the x and y values to make room for the next sample (lines 6 and 7 above) is very inefficient. For the particular example above that has such a low filter order, it doesn't take much time to do it that way. But for larger-order filters, this would be a bad idea. Looking back at Section 3.4.3, review how the idea of a circular buffer was implemented for an FIR filter; that same idea, using the same technique with pointers, can be applied to IIR filters. Rather than just give you the code, this is left as one of the Follow-On Challenges below.

---

[7]You may need to adjust the value of $A[1]$ from -0.9 to a value such as -0.7 or even -0.5 to hear the effect well.

4.5   Follow-On Challenges

Consider extending what you have learned.

1. We have discussed only the brute-force approach to IIR filtering. Similar to the Chapter 3 discussion, investigate and implement a version of the code that will work with MATLAB exported coefficient files (`coeff.c` and `coeff.h`). Put your solution in a directory called `IIRrevB`. Use the `IIR_dump2c` function from the text software to export the filter coefficients for this program.

2. There are dozens of different ways to implement an IIR filter. Most of the examples in this chapter have used only the direct-form one (DF-I) techniques. Investigate and implement other forms, e.g., DF-II, DF-II transposed, lattice structure, parallel form, second-order sections, etc.

3. Explore the IIR filter design tools that are available in MATLAB (e.g., `butter`, `cheby1`, `cheby2`, SPTool, and FDATool). A complete listing of the functional capabilities included in the Signal Processing Toolbox can be found by typing `help signal`. The toolbox functions are grouped by category. You are looking for the `IIR filter design` heading. Use the `IIR_dump2c` function from the text software to export the filter coefficients. Implement your design using the `IIRrevB` code that you created as part of Challenge 1 above.

4. Create an IIR filter routine using circular buffers. You may want to review the discussion related to the `FIRrevD` code in Chapter 3 (see Section 3.4.3).

4.6   Problems

1. In terms of a z-plane plot of the poles and zeros, what are the conditions required for an IIR filter to be stable?

2. Can an IIR filter exhibit truly linear phase? Why or why not?

3. Some traditional designs from analog filters commonly adapted for digital filters include Butterworth, Chebychev, Elliptic, and Bessel. Compare these four in terms of phase linearity, sharpness of cutoff for a given filter order, and ripple in the passband.

4. When implementing an IIR filter with a 16-bit fixed-point processor, to what does the designer need to pay close attention, as compared to using a floating-point processor?

5. With regard to filter coefficient quantization (primarily due to the use of a fixed-point processor), what is the general effect on the IIR filter response?

6. With regard to filter coefficient quantization (primarily due to the use of a fixed-point processor), which implementation is generally best: direct form I, direct form II, or cascaded second-order sections? Explain why.

Chapter 5

Periodic Signal Generation

5.1 Theory

$\mathbf{M}$ANY interesting and useful signals can be generated using a DSP. Applications of some DSP-generated signals include, but are not limited to,

alerting signals such as different telephone rings, beeper message alerts, the call waiting tone, and the emergency alert system, which is the replacement for the emergency broadcast system tones;

system signaling such as telephone dialing tones (DTMF) and caller ID tones;

oscillators such as a sine and/or cosine waveform that are routinely used to generate a wide variety of communications signals; and

pseudonoise such as the special signals used for spread spectrum methods (e.g., satellite communication, Wi-Fi, etc.) and other uses.

To keep the length of this chapter reasonable, we will only discuss periodic signal generation. We first review how periodic signals are represented as discrete-time signals, then transition to how such signals can be generated by a DSP. Pseudonoise (PN) sequences are a special class of periodic signals that are used for many purposes, but because they are so different, they are covered in a separate section toward the end of this chapter.

5.1.1 Periodic Signals in DSP

Periodic signals have a fundamental period that is usually just called the period. During the period the entire signal is defined, and the signal repeats for every period that follows. For a continuous-time signal the fundamental period T_0 is the least amount of time required to completely define the signal; we shall see that the associated fundamental frequency is $f_0 = 1/T_0$. A periodic signal may contain many frequencies but only a single fundamental frequency. The simplest periodic signal is a sinusoid because it contains only a single frequency. Using the sine wave as an example, the concept of the fundamental period means that the sine must satisfy the equation

$$\sin\left(2\pi f_0 t + \phi\right) = \sin\left(2\pi f_0 t + 2\pi f_0 T_0 + \phi\right) = \sin\left(2\pi f_0(t + T_0) + \phi\right),$$

where f_0 is the frequency (Hz) of the sine, t is the time (s) variable, ϕ is some arbitrary phase (rad), and T_0 is the period.[1] For T_0 to be one full period of 2π radians, $2\pi f_0 T_0 \equiv 2\pi$.

---

[1] If you prefer to work with angular frequency, simply substitute ω_0 for $2\pi f_0$.

This means that, as we mentioned earlier, $f_0 = 1/T_0$. Notice that T_0 must be both positive and real. While this seems to be a trivial discussion, it proves useful when changing from continuous-time to discrete-time representations.

For a discrete-time version of our sine wave, we sample every T_s seconds (recall $T_s = 1/F_s$), and thus we replace the variable t with nT_s for $n = 0, 1, 2, \ldots$ for however many samples we obtain. The period N of a discrete-time signal will be expressed in units of *samples* and in the case of our sine wave example must satisfy the equation

$$\sin\left[2\pi f_0 n T_s + \phi\right] = \sin\left[2\pi \frac{f_0}{F_s} n + \phi\right]$$

$$= \sin\left[2\pi \frac{f_0}{F_s} n + 2\pi \frac{f_0}{F_s} N + \phi\right]$$

$$= \sin\left[2\pi \frac{f_0}{F_s}(n + N) + \phi\right],$$

where the value $2\pi(f_0/F_s)$ is the normalized discrete angular frequency (radians/sample). If the discrete-time signal is periodic, then the value at sample n must be equal to the value at sample $n + N$ for some integer N. This implies that $2\pi(f_0/F_s)N \equiv 2\pi k$, where k is another arbitrary integer. Rearranging this equation results in

$$\frac{N}{k} = \frac{F_s}{f_0}.$$

Since both N and k must be integers, the ratio F_s/f_0 must be rational for the discrete-time signal to be periodic. In this case, k represents the number of periods of the continuous-time signal spanned by the N samples of the periodic discrete-time signal. If there are no integer values of N and k that solve the equality $N/k = F_s/f_0$, then the sampled version of the signal is *not* periodic. This result of the sampling process is why many continuous-time signals that are periodic do *not* result in periodic discrete-time signals.

The information that defines a discrete-time signal is not necessarily unique; we can define one period of the signal starting at any point. To help understand this concept, Figure 5.1 shows portions of both a continuous- and discrete-time 1 kHz sinusoid. Part (a) shows the continuous-time sinusoid with the horizontal axis (time axis) labeling on top of the figure. Additionally, the period ($T = 1$ ms) is also shown. To calculate the period of the sampled, discrete-time version of this signal, we must solve

$$\frac{N}{k} = \frac{F_s}{f_0} = \frac{48000}{1000}.$$

The obvious solution is $N = 48$ and $k = 1$. Part (b) shows the first 48 samples (i.e., for $n = 0, 1, 2, \ldots, 47$) of a discrete-time (sampled) version of the 1 kHz sinusoid ($F_s = 48$ kHz) starting at $t = 0$. It is *very* important to realize that the last sample in part (b), where $n = 47$, does *not* equal the value at $n = 0$. Rather, the *next* sample (at $n = 48$) would equal the value at $n = 0$. If a complete discrete-time period is provided, the signal can be "continued" by replicating the information in the selected period. This concept is demonstrated in part (c) where 48 consecutive samples are replicated and concatenated together for two full periods. Repeating this concatenation process will allow you to generate arbitrary length versions of the signal. Parts (d–f) are examples of the same signal where the signal was defined by starting the sampling process at $n = 20$, 30, and 40 samples, respectively, and providing the next $N = 48$ samples of the signal.

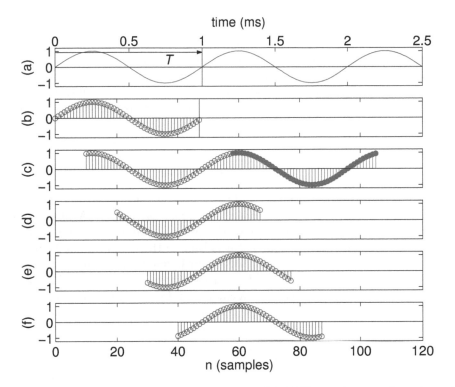

Figure 5.1: Continuous and discrete-time sinusoids. (a) 1 kHz continuous-time sinusoid. (b–f) 1 kHz sinusoid sampled at 48 kHz. (b) One period starting at $n = 0$. (c) Demonstration of the periodic nature of a sampled sinusoid. (d–f) Sampling/display commencing at $n = 20$, 30, and 40 samples, respectively.

5.1.2 Signal Generation

In order to limit the discussion to a reasonable length, we will only discuss the following techniques to generate a sinusoid:

direct digital synthesizer (DDS): these techniques can use a phase accumulator with a sin() or cos() trigonometric function call or use a table lookup system.

special cases: this includes sine and cosines with $f = F_s/2$, $f = F_s/4$, and other frequencies that result in reasonable values for N.

digital resonator: this technique uses an impulse-excited, second-order IIR filter, where the complex conjugate pole-pairs are placed *on* the unit circle.

impulse modulator (IM): this technique is based on using scaled impulses to periodically excite an FIR filter. Impulse modulation is commonly used in digital communications transmitters and is discussed further in Chapter 18.

We will discuss the theory of these signal generation techniques before proceeding to examples.

Direct Digital Synthesizer Case

You are probably familiar with plotting deterministic waveforms such as

$$w(t) = A \sin(2\pi f t)$$

in many of your math, physics, and engineering classes. In the equation above, A is the waveform's amplitude, f is the desired output frequency, and t represents the time variable.

The DDS idea, as it is implemented in real-time hardware, starts by converting $w(t)$ to a discrete-time process. This conversion is accomplished by replacing t by nT_s, where n is an integer and T_s is the sample period. Therefore, $w(t)$ becomes $w[nT_s]$, which is equal to $A\sin[2\pi f nT_s]$. Remembering that $T_s = 1/F_s$, where F_s is the sample frequency, and rearranging the argument of the sine function, we arrive at

$$w[n] = A\sin[2\pi f nT_s] = A\sin\left[n\left(2\pi\frac{f}{F_s}\right)\right] = A\sin\left[n\phi_{inc}\right],$$

where we have used the common notation of using $w[n]$ in place of $w[nT_s]$ since T_s is tacitly assumed. The value $\phi_{inc} = 2\pi f/F_s$ is called the *phase increment*. A phase accumulator can be used to add the phase increment to the previous value of the phase accumulator every sample period. The phase accumulator is kept in the interval 0 to 2π by a modulus operator. Since real-time processes can run for an indefinite amount of time, a modulus operation is required to prevent an overflow of the phase accumulator. Finally, the sin() of the phase accumulator's value can be calculated and the value provided as the system's output. The block diagram for this process is shown in Figure 5.2. Notice that since ϕ_{inc} is added to the phase accumulator each time the input ISR is called (which is every $T_s = 1/F_s$ seconds or 48,000 times/sec in this example), the value n never appears in the algorithm.

The argument of the sin() operator, $n\phi_{inc}$, is a linearly increasing function whose slope depends on the desired output frequency. To illustrate this point, Figure 5.3 plots the accumulated phase as a function of time for four different frequencies. Figure 5.4 plots the sampled ($F_s = 48$ kHz) version of Figure 5.3 for only the 1000 Hz case. Figure 5.5 expands a portion of Figure 5.4 and adds additional labeling. To prevent aliasing, a minimum of

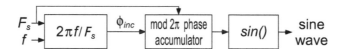

Figure 5.2: Block diagram associated with sinusoid generation.

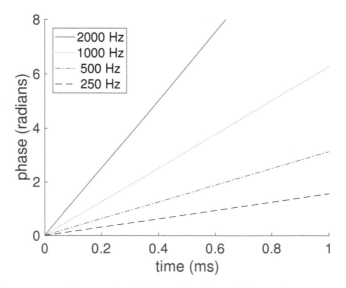

Figure 5.3: Accumulated phase for four different frequencies.

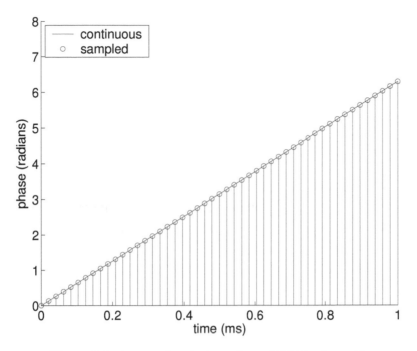

Figure 5.4: Accumulated phase for a 1000 Hz sinusoid.

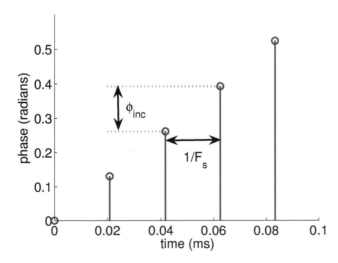

Figure 5.5: Accumulated phase for a 1000 Hz sinusoid (zoomed in from Figure 5.4).

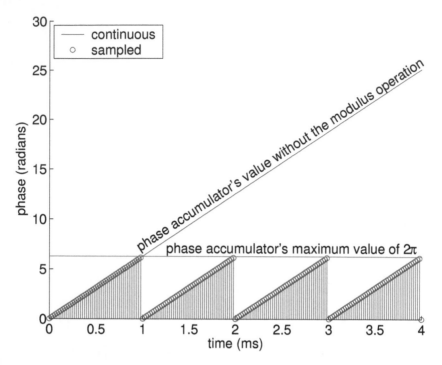

Figure 5.6: Accumulated phase for a 1000 Hz sinusoid with modulus 2π applied.

two samples per period are required. This limit requires that $\phi_{inc} \leq \pi$. Finally, Figure 5.6 demonstrates the effect of the modulus operation on the phase accumulator's value.

Special Cases

If the characteristics (frequency and phase) of the signal that you need to generate will not change with time, then you may not need a phase accumulator at all. A few special cases follow.

1. Sine and cosine with $f = \frac{F_s}{2}$. Substituting $f = \frac{F_s}{2}$ into the ϕ_{inc} equations results in

$$\phi_{inc} = 2\pi \left(\frac{f}{F_s} \right) \Bigg|_{f=\frac{F_s}{2}} = \pi.$$

This is the aliasing limit for ϕ_{inc} and results in

$$w\,[n] = A \sin\left(n\phi_{inc}\right)\big|_{(\phi_{inc}=\pi)} = A \sin\left(n\pi\right) = 0.$$

A signal generator that always has an output $= 0$ is of little use. However, the cosine version results in

$$w\,[n] = A \cos\left(n\phi_{inc}\right)\big|_{(\phi_{inc}=\pi)} = A \cos\left(n\pi\right) = A, -A, A, -A \dots$$

This implies that a cosine waveform of frequency $F_s/2$ can be created by simply generating $A, -A, \dots$ for however long you need the signal. The CPU resources required to generate these or other alternating values are inconsequential. Notice that for $f = F_s/2$, $N = 2$ (2 samples per period).

Table 5.1: Some special case frequencies of direct digital synthesis (DDS). The frequency values shown in the right column assume $F_s = 48$ kHz.

F_s ratio	N	frequency (Hz)
$F_s/2$	2	24,000
$F_s/3$	3	16,000
$F_s/4$	4	12,000
$F_s/5$	5	9,600
$F_s/6$	6	8,000
$F_s/8$	8	6,000
$F_s/10$	10	4,800
$F_s/12$	12	4,000
$F_s/15$	15	3,200
$F_s/16$	16	3,000
$F_s/20$	20	2,400
$\vdots$	$\vdots$	$\vdots$
F_s/N	N	$48,000/N$

2. Sine and cosine with $f = \frac{F_s}{4}$. Substituting $f = \frac{F_s}{4}$ into the ϕ_{inc} equations results in

$$\phi_{inc} = 2\pi \left(\frac{f}{F_s}\right)\Bigg|_{f=\frac{F_s}{4}} = \frac{\pi}{2}.$$

This yields

$$w[n] = A\sin(n\phi_{inc})|_{\left(\phi_{inc}=\frac{\pi}{2}\right)} = A\sin\left(n\frac{\pi}{2}\right) = 0, A, 0, -A, \ldots$$

and

$$w[n] = A\cos(n\phi_{inc})|_{\left(\phi_{inc}=\frac{\pi}{2}\right)} = A\cos\left(n\frac{\pi}{2}\right) = A, 0, -A, 0, \ldots$$

This implies that a sine or cosine waveform of frequency $\frac{F_s}{4}$ can be created by simply generating $0, A, 0, -A, \ldots$ or $A, 0, -A, 0, \ldots$, respectively. As in the $\frac{F_s}{2}$ case, the CPU resources required to generate these or other repeating values are inconsequential. Notice that for $f = \frac{F_s}{4}$, $N = 4$ (4 samples per period).

3. Sines and cosines with other frequencies that result in reasonable values for N. Assuming from our discussion in Section 5.1 that $k = 1$, we simply divide F_s by the desired frequency f to find N. Table 5.1 shows several possible frequencies and the corresponding values of N.

All of the table entries in the right column are based on $F_s = 48$ kHz. For example, to generate a 4,800 Hz cosine waveform, we would only need to calculate the first 10 values of the sequence. These values are based on $N = 10$ and $\phi_{inc} = \frac{\pi}{5}$. Specifically, we would need to evaluate

$$w[n] = A\cos\left(\frac{\pi}{5}n\right), \quad \text{for } n = 0, 1, \ldots, 9.$$

These values can be calculated once by the real-time program (i.e., in StartUp.
c) or off-line using tools such as a handheld calculator, spreadsheet program, or
MATLAB®. Continuously repeating all 10 values (in the proper order), with one
value every sample time of $T_s = \frac{1}{48,000}$ seconds, will result in the desired 4,800 Hz
signal.

Digital Resonator

The digital resonator technique is based on the idea that, if you refer to any z-transform
table, you will find an entry similar to,

$$[r^n \sin(\omega_0 n)]\, u\,[n] \xleftrightarrow{Z} \frac{r \sin(\omega_0)\, z^{-1}}{1 - [2r \cos(\omega_0)]\, z^{-1} + r^2 z^{-2}}.$$

Letting $r = 1$ (equivalent to placing the poles on the unit circle), this equation simplifies to

$$[\sin(\omega_0 n)]\, u\,[n] \xleftrightarrow{Z} \frac{\sin(\omega_0)\, z^{-1}}{1 - [2 \cos(\omega_0)]\, z^{-1} + z^{-2}}.$$

This transform pair implies that, if you excite this system with an impulse, the system's
output will be a sine wave. The system's difference equation can be determined from the
transfer function

$$H(z) = \frac{Y(z)}{X(z)} = \frac{\sin(\omega_0)\, z^{-1}}{1 - [2 \cos(\omega_0)]\, z^{-1} + z^{-2}}.$$

Cross multiplying, taking the inverse z-transform, and rearranging the terms into the standard form results in the difference equation

$$\boxed{y[n] = \sin(\omega_0)x[n-1] + 2\cos(\omega_0)y[n-1] - y[n-2]}.$$

Thus, to create a sine wave of digital frequency $\omega_0 = 2\pi f_0/F_s$, we need to excite this
second-order IIR filter with an impulse. To find out where the poles and zeros are located,
we convert the transfer function to positive powers of z, then factor the transfer function.
This leads to

$$\frac{\sin(\omega_0)\, z^{-1}}{1 - [2 \cos(\omega_0)]\, z^{-1} + z^{-2}} = \frac{\sin(\omega_0)\, z^{-1}}{1 - [2 \cos(\omega_0)]\, z^{-1} + z^{-2}} \cdot \frac{z^2}{z^2} = \frac{\sin(\omega_0)\, z}{z^2 - [2 \cos(\omega_0)]\, z + 1}.$$

The numerator term reveals a single zero at the origin. For the denominator, we apply the
quadratic equation

$$\frac{2\cos(\omega_0) \pm \sqrt{(2\cos(\omega_0))^2 - 4(1)(1)}}{2(1)} = \cos(\omega_0) \pm \sqrt{\cos^2(\omega_0) - 1},$$

which, using the trigonometric identity

$$\sin^2(\omega_0) + \cos^2(\omega_0) = 1 \;\therefore\; \cos^2(\omega_0) - 1 = -\sin^2(\omega_0),$$

can be simplified to

$$\cos(\omega_0) \pm \sqrt{-\sin^2(\omega_0)} = \boxed{\cos(\omega_0) \pm j\sin(\omega_0) = e^{\pm j\omega_0}}.$$

This result, shown above in both rectangular and polar forms, should be recognized as
indicating that the complex conjugate poles are located *on* the unit circle at the frequency

$\pm\omega_0$. This is at best a marginally stable system (in that it oscillates at a constant frequency of ω_0), and some authors would call this system unstable. Actually, it is "intentionally unstable." Oscillators and resonators are definitely on a fine line between systems that are clearly stable and those that are clearly unstable. While the system is unstable in the sense that the output does not change regardless of the input, it is stable in the sense that the output frequency remains the same.

We will now use a unit impulse as the input to the system and calculate the first few output terms. Manually calculating a few terms for the difference equation is very helpful, not only in understanding this process, but it will greatly assist our real-time algorithm development. Remember that the difference equation is

$$y[n] = \sin(\omega_0)x[n-1] + 2\cos(\omega_0)y[n-1] - y[n-2].$$

1. Label the columns as shown below.

n	$y[n]$	$y[n-1]$	$y[n-2]$	$x[n]$	$x[n-1]$

2. Fill in the $n = 0$ *at rest* row information.

n	$y[n]$	$y[n-1]$	$y[n-2]$	$x[n]$	$x[n-1]$
0		0	0	1	0

3. Calculate the $y[0]$ term.

n	$y[n]$	$y[n-1]$	$y[n-2]$	$x[n]$	$x[n-1]$
0	0	0	0	1	0

4. Fill in the $n = 1$ row information. Notice the "down and to the right" flow of the stored y values and the stored x values.

n	$y[n]$	$y[n-1]$	$y[n-2]$	$x[n]$	$x[n-1]$
1		0	0	0	1

5. Calculate the $y[1]$ term.

n	$y[n]$	$y[n-1]$	$y[n-2]$	$x[n]$	$x[n-1]$
1	$\sin(\omega_0)$	0	0	0	1

6. Fill in the $n = 2$ row information.

n	$y[n]$	$y[n-1]$	$y[n-2]$	$x[n]$	$x[n-1]$
2		$\sin(\omega_0)$	0	0	0

We stop here with the $n = 2$ initial conditions loaded and ready to calculate $y[2]$. This is an excellent place for us to pause and pick the idea up again for our real-time C digital resonator discussed later in this chapter. The difference equation for the rest of time (i.e., where $n \geq 2$) now simplifies to

$$y[n] = 2\cos(\omega_0)y[n-1] - y[n-2]$$

since, from this point on, all of the $x[n-1]$ terms will equal zero.

Note that the impulse modulator (IM) technique is commonly used in digital communications transmitters. We therefore postpone its discussion until Chapter 18, which includes a digital transmitter project.

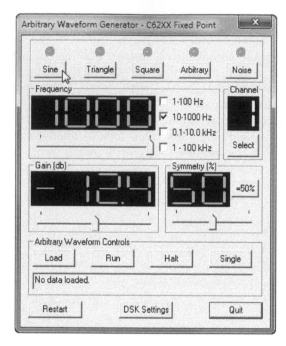

Figure 5.7: winDSK8 running the Arbitrary Waveform application.

5.2   winDSK Demonstration

Start the winDSK8 application, and the main user interface window will appear. Ensure the correct selections have been made in the "DSP Board" and "Host Interface" configuration panels of winDSK8 for each parameter before proceeding.

5.2.1   Arbitrary Waveform

Clicking on the winDSK8 Arbitrary Waveform button will run that program in the attached DSK, and a window similar to Figure 5.7 will appear. The arbitrary waveform program generates sine, square, and triangle waves at frequencies between 1 Hz and the upper limit of the codec in use. For multichannel codecs, each output channel is capable of simultaneous independent operation. The displays show the settings for the currently selected channel, as indicated by the channel number display. The frequency displays will turn red if the selected frequency exceeds the capabilities of the codec, and the DSK frequency will not be updated. As an arbitrary waveform generator, the program can load up to 2,000,000 sample values (depending on the DSK version) per channel from a text file. In this mode, the sample values in the file are repeatedly used as the system output. The values will be automatically scaled to fit within the ADC range. A sample waveform file called `chirp.asc` is included in the winDSK8 installation. This file contains a 2,500 sample chirp waveform that can be played through the application.[2] The arbitrary waveform generator can also function as a noise generator. Finally, one-shot operation is also supported.

Selecting the arbitrary waveform generator in the "sine" mode will run a program in the DSK that is most similar to the examples given in the preceding discussion regarding periodic signal generation. Of course square and triangle waves are also periodic signals.

---

[2]A *chirp* is typically a short duration signal in which the frequency sweeps monotonically (up or down) with time. Chirps can have linear sweeps or logarithmic sweeps, and are used in a variety of radar, sonar, and communications applications.

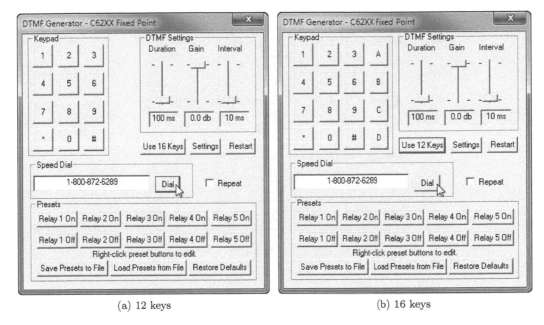

(a) 12 keys   (b) 16 keys

Figure 5.8: winDSK8 running the DTMF application.

5.2.2 DTMF

Signals can also be created using winDSK8 that consist of two pre-defined sinusoids mixed together.

Clicking on the winDSK8 DTMF button will load and run that program into the attached DSK, and a 12-keypad window similar to Figure 5.8(a) will appear by default. Clicking on the "Use 16 keys" button will add a fourth column to the keypad display, as shown in Figure 5.8(b).

This application generates standard Dual-Tone, Multiple-Frequency (DTMF) signals as defined by telephone companies. These are signals that consist of two sinusoids of different frequencies that are added together. Any time you dial a modern telephone, DTMF tones are generated that correspond to the buttons you pressed on the telephone's keypad (or correspond to a telephone number that was stored as an autodial selection). The DTMF standard specifies that tones must persist for at least 40 ms and have at least 50 ms of "quiet time" between tones. Additionally, DTMF tones must not occur at a faster rate than 10 characters/sec [62].

A speed-dial feature is available on the DTMF application of winDSK8 by clicking the "Dial" button; it provides automatic generation of DTMF sequences based on the number you type into the "Speed Dial" entry window. For this option, only the standard 12-key tone pairs are generated by the characters 0–9, #, *. Any other characters are ignored. The duration and volume (i.e., gain) of a tone, as well as the interval of silence between tones, may be adjusted by using the slider controls in the upper right of the DTMF application window.

If you're using a stereo codec on the DSK, both channels are driven with the same signal. As mentioned above, a 12-key or 16-key keypad can be selected. In 16-key mode, all 16 standardized tone pairs can be generated. The two frequencies that are generated for any given key press can be determined by inspecting Figure 5.9.

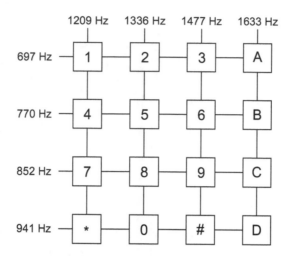

Figure 5.9: The DTMF frequencies.

5.3   MATLAB Implementation

MATLAB has a number of ways of generating sinusoids. However, we will focus on three of the techniques that can help prepare us for the realities of real-time signal generation using DSP hardware.

5.3.1   Direct Digital Synthesizer Technique

In this technique, MATLAB is used to implement the phase accumulator process. A listing demonstrating this technique is shown below.

Listing 5.1: MATLAB implementation of phase accumulator signal generation.

```
% Simulation inputs
A = 32000;                      % signal's amplitude
f = 1000;                       % signal's frequency
phaseAccumulator = 0;           % signal's initial phase
Fs = 48000;                     % system's sample frequency
numberOfTerms = 50;             % calculate this number of terms

% Calculated and output terms
phaseIncrement = 2*pi*f/Fs; % calculate the phase increment

for i = 1:numberOfTerms
    % ISR's algorithm begins here
        phaseAccumulator = phaseAccumulator + phaseIncrement;
        phaseAccumulator = mod(phaseAccumulator, 2*pi);
        output = A*sin(phaseAccumulator)
    % ISR's algorithm ends here
end
```

A few items need to be discussed concerning this listing.

1. Variable initialization section (lines 2–6). Remembering that the sine and cosine functions are constrained to the range ±1 requires an amplitude scale factor, A, or the DAC's output will only use a tiny portion of the full range of +32767 to –32768.

2. For a constant output frequency, the calculation of the phase increment (line 9) need only be accomplished once. The calculated value of the phase increment *must* be $\leq \pi$ or signal aliasing will occur.

3. The actual algorithm to generate the sinusoidal signal requires only three lines of code (lines 13–15), inside a "for" loop that simulates the execution of an ISR in C that is called each time a new sample arrives. These lines of code accomplish the following three tasks each time the "ISR" is called:

    (a) line 13: add the phase increment's value to the phase accumulator.

    (b) line 14: perform a modulus 2π operation to keep the phase accumulator in the range 0 to 2π.

    (c) line 15: calculate the system's output value by scaling the sine of the phase accumulator's value by A.

These three lines of code could be combined, but that would result in less understandable code.

5.3.2 Table Lookup Technique

This section demonstrates how MATLAB can be used to implement the table lookup technique, which is a very efficient method to generate a discrete-time signal. In this technique, we repeatedly cycle through a stored vector of predefined signal values. We will again simulate the execution of an ISR at the sample frequency by using a "for" loop. A new value of the signal is read from the table each time the "ISR" is called.

Listing 5.2: MATLAB implementation of the table lookup-based signal generation.

```
1  % Simulation inputs
   signal = [32000 0 −32000 0];   % cosine signal values (Fs/4 case)
3  index = 1;                     % used to lookup the signal value
   numberOfTerms = 20;            % calculate this number of terms

5
   % Calculated and output terms
7  N = length(signal);            % signal period

9  for i = 1:numberOfTerms
       % ISR's algorithm begins here
11         if (index >= (N + 1))
               index = 1;
13         end
           output = signal(index)
15         index = index + 1;
       % ISR's algorithm ends here
17 end
```

A few items need to be discussed concerning this listing.

1. Variable initialization section (lines 2–4). These lines of code establish the variable **signal** that stores the required values of the output signal and the integer variable **index** that is used to access the different storage locations of **signal**.

2. Period determination (line 7). This line of code determines the period of the signal based on the length of the variable **signal**.

3. The actual algorithm to generate the sinusoidal signal requires only five lines of code (lines 11–15). These lines of code accomplish the following three tasks each time the ISR is called:

   (a) line 11–13: performs a modulus N operation to keep **index** in the range 1 to N. Remember that, unlike C/C++, MATLAB array indices start at 1 instead of 0.

   (b) line 14: calculates the system's output value by selecting the appropriate **index** of **signal**.

   (c) line 15: increments the integer variable **index**.

5.4   DSK Implementation in C

Note that the examples in this section may require you to change the ISR file in a project to change the operation of the code. **Important:** you must have only *one* of these ISR files loaded as part of your project at any given time. To switch from using one ISR file to another, right click the current ISR file in the left project window and select "Remove from Project." At the top of the Code Composer Studio window click "Project," "Add Files to Project," and select the new ISR file. Then click "Rebuild All" (or "Incremental Build"). Once the build is complete, "Load Program" (or "Reload Program") into the DSK and click on "Run." You will then be using the new ISR file.

5.4.1   Direct Digital Synthesizer Technique

This version of the direct digital synthesizer technique is very similar to the DDS MATLAB example. The intention of this first approach is understandability, which often comes at the expense of efficiency.

The files necessary to run this application are in the **ccs\sigGen** directory of Chapter 5. The primary file of interest is the **sinGenerator_ISRs.c**, which contains interrupt service routines; ensure this is the only ISR file included in the project. This file contains the necessary variable declarations and performs the actual sinusoid generation. However, as with all the Code Composer Studio projects we include with this text, you should make a habit of inspecting other files in the project, such as **StartUp.c**, to be sure you understand the full workings of the program.

If you're using one of the stereo codecs on your DSK, the program could implement two independent sinusoid generators for the Left and Right channels. For clarity, this example program will contain only a single phase accumulator, but that phase will be used to generate a sine wave for the Left channel and a cosine wave for the Right channel.

In the code shown below, **A**, **fDesired**, and **phase** (lines 1–3) are the signal's amplitude, frequency, and phase, respectively. Remember that a 16-bit DAC has a range of +32767 to −32768. The variable **phase** sets not only the signal's initial phase, but will also serve as the phase accumulator. Having π (pi on line 5), and the system's sample frequency (**fs** on line 8), defined allows us to calculate the phase increment, which is declared on line 6.

Listing 5.3: Variable declaration associated with sinusoidal signal generation.

```
1  float A = 32000;         /* signal's amplitude */
   float fDesired = 1000;   /* signal's frequency */
3  float phase = 0;         /* signal's initial phase */

5  float pi = 3.1415927;    /* value of pi */
   float phaseIncrement;    /* incremental phase */

7
   Int32 fs = 48000;             /* sample frequency */
```

The code shown below performs the actual signal generation operation. The four main steps involved in this operation will be discussed below the code listing.

Listing 5.4: Algorithm associated with sinusoidal signal generation.

```
   /* algorithm begins here */
2  phaseIncrement = 2*pi*fDesired/fs;
   phase += phaseIncrement;        // calculate the next phase

4
   if (phase >= 2*pi) phase -= 2*pi;  // modulus 2*pi operation

6
   CodecDataOut.Channel[ LEFT] = A*sinf(phase); // scaled L output
8  CodecDataOut.Channel[RIGHT] = A*cosf(phase); // scaled R output
   /* algorithm ends here */
```

The four real-time steps involved in DDS-based signal generation

An explanation of Listing 5.4 follows.

1. (Line 2): This code calculates the phase increment each time the ISR is called. This will allow us to *change* the signal's frequency if desired during program execution.

2. (Line 3): This code adds the phase increment to the current value of the phase.

3. (Line 5): This code performs the equivalent of a modulus 2π operation. To prevent signal aliasing, the phase *increment* must be $\leq \pi$. With a maximum increment value of π, the modulus operation can be simplified to just a test and a subtraction of 2π. Subtracting 2π "starts over" by one full period. This method is far more efficient than using the modulus operation.

4. (Lines 7–8): These two lines of code calculate the sine and cosine values, scale these values by A, and write the results to the DAC.

You may want to refer Appendix H, in particular Section H.3, if you are unsure why the `math.h` header had to be included in the DDS code.

Now that you understand the code...

Go ahead and copy all of the files into a separate directory. Open the project in CCS and "Rebuild All." Once the build is complete, "Load Program" into the DSK and click on "Run." Your 1 kHz sine generator is now running on the DSK.

5.4.2   Table Lookup Technique

This version of the table lookup technique is very similar to the table lookup MATLAB example. The files necessary to run this application are in the same place as before, the ccs\sigGen directory of Chapter 5. The primary file of interest this time is sinGenerator_ISRs1.c, which contains the interrupt service routines; remove the previous ISR file from your project and add this one. This file contains the necessary variable declarations and performs the actual sinusoid generation.

To allow for the use of a stereo codec (e.g., the on-board codec on the C6713 or the OMAP-L138 boards), the program implements independent Left and Right channel sinusoid generators. For clarity, this example program will only generate $f = F_s/4 = 12$ kHz, but will output a sine wave to the Left channel and a cosine wave to the Right channel.

In the code shown below, N (line 1) is the signal's period, signalCos (line 3) and signalSin (line 4) store the table values for the cosine and sine waveforms, respectively, and index (line 5) is an integer used to cycle through the values stored in the table.

Listing 5.5: Variable declaration associated with sinusoidal signal generation.

```
1 #define N 4              // signal period for f = Fs/4

3 Int32 signalCos[N] = {32000, 0, -32000, 0}; // cos waveform
  Int32 signalSin[N] = {0, 32000, 0, -32000}; // sin waveform
5 Int32 index = 0;         /* signal's indexing variable */
```

The code shown below performs the actual signal generation operation. The three main steps involved in this operation will be discussed below the code listing.

Listing 5.6: Algorithm associated with sinusoidal signal generation.

```
1 /* algorithm begins here */
  if (index == N) index = 0;
3
  CodecDataOut.Channel[ LEFT] = signalCos[index]; // cos output
5 CodecDataOut.Channel[RIGHT] = signalSin[index]; // sin output
7 index++;
  /* algorithm ends here */
```

The three real-time steps involved in table lookup-based signal generation

An explanation of Listing 5.6 follows.

1. (Line 2): This code performs a modulus operation and keeps the variable index between 0 and 3.

2. (Line 4–5): This code outputs the next value from the cosine and sine tables. Notice that the signal's amplitude is included in the signalCos and signalSin array values.

3. (Line 7): This code increments (increases by 1) the value of index.

Now that you understand the code...

Go ahead and copy all of the files into a separate directory. Open the project in CCS and "Rebuild All." Once the build is complete, "Load Program" into the DSK and click on "Run." Your 12 kHz ($\frac{F_s}{4}$) cosine and sine generators are now running on the DSK.

5.4.3   Table Lookup Technique with Table Creation

This version of the table lookup technique adds a table creation routine. While this adds marginally to the code size, it frees you from needing a special table length or requiring a specific ratio between f_0 and F_s. Note that the table creation routine only needs to run once at startup, so the real-time operation is not affected. The files necessary to run this application are in the ccs\sigGenTable directory of Chapter 5. In the previous examples, we only looked at the ISR file in detail. For this example, there are two files of interest: StartUp.c and tableBasedSinGenerator_ISRs.c. The file StartUp.c contains code not tied to any interrupt, and so is the appropriate place for the code that runs just once to create the table values. The file tableBasedSinGenerator_ISRs.c contains the interrupt service routines. These files contain routines to generate and fill the table as well as the necessary variable declarations and routines to perform the actual sinusoid generation.

To allow for the use of a stereo codec (e.g., the on-board codec on the C6713 DSK or one of the OMAP-L138 boards), the program could implement independent Left and Right channel sinusoid generators. For clarity, this example program will only generate a 6 kHz sine wave, which will be heard on both the Left and Right channels.

In the code shown below, NumTableEntries (line 2) defines the size[3] of the table, desiredFreq (line 4) is the desired output frequency, and SineTable (line 5) is the array (i.e., table) that will be filled with sine values. The FillSineTable function (lines 7–13) is only called once by the StartUp.c file. This function call occurs just after the DSK finishes initializing. This one-time calculation prevents repeated calls of the computationally expensive trigonometric function sinf().

Listing 5.7: Variable declaration and table creation associated with table-based sinusoidal signal generation.

```
  /* declared at file scope for visibility */
2 #define NumTableEntries 100

4 float desiredFreq = 6000.0;
  float SineTable[NumTableEntries];

6
  void FillSineTable()
8 {
      Int32 i;

10
      for(i = 0; i < NumTableEntries; i++)  // fill table values
12        SineTable[i]=sinf(i*(float)(6.283185307/NumTableEntries));
  }
```

The code shown below performs the actual signal generation operation. The four main steps involved in this operation will be discussed below the code listing.

Listing 5.8: Algorithm associated with table-based sinusoidal signal generation.

```
1 /* ISR's algorithm begins here */
  index += desiredFreq;             // calculate the next phase
3 if (index >= GetSampleFreq())     // keep phase between 0-2*pi
      index -= GetSampleFreq();

5
  sine=SineTable[(Int32)(index/GetSampleFreq()*NumTableEntries)];
```

---

[3]Using a larger value of NumTableEntries produces a larger lookup table which, in general, produces a more "pure" sinusoid with less harmonic distortion. Experiment with various sizes of the lookup table.

```
7  CodecData.Channel[LEFT]  = 32767*sine; // scale the result
   CodecData.Channel[RIGHT] = CodecData.Channel[LEFT];
9  /* ISR's algorithm ends here */
```

The four real-time steps involved in table lookup-based signal generation with table creation

An explanation of Listing 5.8 follows.

1. (Line 2): This code is the equivalent operation of adding the phase increment to the phase accumulator.

2. (Lines 3–4): This code performs a modulus operation and maintains **index** between 0 and the sample frequency (typically, $F_s = 48$ kHz). Note the use of the function **GetSampleFreq()** in these lines and line 6. This is a very simple function call which returns a float value equal to the sample frequency you chose for the DSK. Using a function call instead of hard-coding a number makes the code a bit more portable.

3. (Line 6): This code calculates the next floating point value of the table index, converts this number to an integer, and then uses this to access the required table value's location in the **SineTable** array.

4. (Lines 7–8): This code scales the table's output (**sine**) and outputs the result to both the Left and Right channels.

Now that you understand the code ...

Go ahead and copy all of the files into a separate directory. Open the project in CCS and "Rebuild All." Once the build is complete, "Load Program" into the DSK and click on "Run." Your 6 kHz sine generator is now running on the DSK.

5.4.4   Digital Resonator Technique

The digital resonator technique implements a second-order IIR filter with very special initial conditions stored in the $y[n-1]$ and $y[n-2]$ memory locations. You may want to refer to the theoretical discussion of digital resonators given earlier in the chapter. The intention of the approach we use is understandability, which may come at the expense of efficiency.

The files necessary to run this application are in the same **ccs\sigGen** directory of Chapter 5 that contained the files for the first two C examples of this chapter. The primary file of interest this time is **resonator_ISRs.c**, which contains the interrupt service routines; remove any other ISR file from the project and add this one. This file contains the necessary variable declarations and performs the actual sinusoid generation.

If you're using one of the stereo codecs on your DSK, the program could implement independent Left and Right channel sinusoid generators. For clarity, this example program only generates one sine wave but outputs the sine wave to both the Left and Right channels.

In the code shown below, **fDesired** and **A** (lines 1–2) are the signal's frequency and amplitude, respectively. Remember that a 16-bit DAC has a range of +32767 to −32768. Having π (**pi** on line 4), and the system's sample frequency (**fs** on line 8), defined will allow us to calculate **theta**, the digital frequency, which is declared on line 5. Finally, **y[3]** declares the storage for the current and past output values. Only three terms are needed to implement the second-order difference equation.

Listing 5.9: Variable declaration associated with a digital resonator.

```
1  float fDesired = 1000;   // your desired signal frequency
   float A = 32000;         // your desired signal amplitude
3
   float pi = 3.1415927;    // value of pi
5  float theta;             // the digital frequency
   float y[3] = {0, 1, 0};  // the last 3 output values.
7
   Int32 fs = 48000;            // sample frequency
```

The code shown below performs the actual signal generation operation using the digital resonator techniques. The four main steps involved in this operation will be discussed below the code listing.

Listing 5.10: Algorithm associated with a digital resonator.

```
   /* algorithm begins here */
2  theta = 2*pi*fDesired/fs;    // calculate digital frequency

4  y[0] = 2*cosf(theta)*y[1] - y[2];   // calculate the output
   y[2] = y[1];                        // prepare for the next ISR
6  y[1] = y[0];                        // prepare for the next ISR

8  CodecDataOut.Channel[ LEFT] = A*sinf(theta)*y[0]; // scale
   CodecDataOut.Channel[RIGHT] = CodecDataOut.Channel[LEFT];
10 /* algorithm ends here */
```

The four real-time steps involved in digital resonator-based signal generation

An explanation of Listing 5.10 follows.

1. (Line 2): This code calculates the digital frequency. This term is needed as an input argument for both a scale factor and a filter coefficient.

2. (Line 4): This code calculates the current output value by implementing the system's difference equation.

3. (Lines 5–6): These two lines of code shift the values in the y arrays one element to the right. The equivalent operation is

$$y[1] \rightarrow y[2]$$
$$y[0] \rightarrow y[1].$$

4. (Lines 8–9): These two lines of code scale the filter's output to achieve an amplitude of A. The resulting value is then sent to both the Left and Right output channels.

Now that you understand the code...

Go ahead and copy all of the files into a separate directory. Open the project in CCS and "Rebuild All." Once the build is complete, "Load Program" into the DSK and click on "Run." Your 1 kHz sine generator is now running on the DSK.

5.5   Pseudonoise Sequences

There are many, many application areas today that use the special class of periodic signals called pseudonoise (PN) sequences.[4] For example, applications that depend on PN sequences include cellular (mobile) telephones and base stations, GPS navigation systems, wireless Internet (Wi-Fi) communications, Bluetooth communications protocol, satellite communications transmitters and receivers, deep space probes, satellite TV transmitters and receivers, garage door openers, wireless (residential) telephones, data scramblers, dither generators, timing recovery modules, system synchronization modules, noise generators, concert hall equalizers,... the list goes on and on. We hope you can appreciate that the topic of PN sequences is important!

All the applications listed above use some form of real-time DSP to generate, process, or otherwise manipulate PN sequences, which is why the topic shows up in this book. Because PN sequences are so different from other signals, they are covered here in a separate section in which we introduce just the main ideas. Space limitations won't allow us to cover this fascinating topic in detail, so we will refer you to some excellent texts. Use of PN sequences is central to a form of digital communications called "spread spectrum," so any good digital communications book, such as [63–67], will cover much more of the theoretical aspects of PN sequences than we can include here. For a very practical and extremely useful book that goes beyond the theory, we highly recommend Dixon [68]. While we are reluctant to recommend web pages as references (since they can change without warning), at the time of this writing the website of New Wave Instruments provides an excellent online resource regarding PN sequences [69]. Note that much of the following discussion assumes the primary application of the PN sequences is spread spectrum (SS) communications, but it is applicable to any use of these special periodic signals.

Why are they called PN sequences? While a PN sequence is just a sequence of symbols (typically called chips) that represent binary 1's and 0's, the sequence at first glance appears to be just random noise, and indeed has many of the characteristics of random noise. But if you know the "secret," each PN sequence is deterministic and can be generated, predicted, or extracted from a signal with relative ease. Note that by convention, we use the distinction in our terminology that data is made up of bits but that a PN sequence is made up of chips. The time duration of a chip is almost always much shorter than the time duration of a bit, so the bandwidth (i.e., the spectrum) of a PN sequence is much greater than the bandwidth of just the data.

In spread spectrum communications, a PN sequence is used in various ways to modulate the data, and thus "spreads" the spectrum of the data greatly. This has many advantages. For example, for a given transmitter output power, spreading out the bandwidth lowers the energy at any particular frequency, often near the apparent noise level, making SS signals hard to detect if you don't know they are there.[5] But by using a receiver that "knows" the correct PN sequence, the data from the SS signal can be easily "pulled out of the noise" and recovered. Other advantages of SS communication include greater resistance to jamming or interference, better performance in multipath environments, and the ability for multiple users (each having their "own" PN sequence) to simultaneously share the same frequency band (a technique called code division multiple access, or CDMA). PN sequences also enable precise ranging and timing measurements (such as with GPS), and allow robust synchronization of data in noisy environments. We hope the preceding discussion has piqued your interest, and stimulated your desire to learn more about PN sequences.

---

[4]Note that the term "PN code" is commonly used synonymously with the term "PN sequence."

[5]While spread spectrum techniques can provide a level of privacy from the casual observer, they are not, by themselves, a secure communications technique. For secure communications, other techniques such as data encryption must be used.

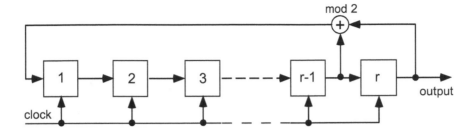

Figure 5.10: An r-stage simple shift register generator with one feedback tap shown.

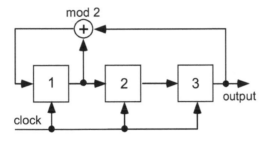

Figure 5.11: A 3-stage simple shift register generator with one feedback tap shown.

5.5.1   Theory

The easiest way to introduce PN sequences is in the context of a type of finite state machine called a shift register. Consider the generalized r-stage shift register generator (SRG), with feedback, shown in Figure 5.10. Each stage contains (or stores its state as) a 1 or 0, which we will call a chip.[6]

Each time the clock ticks, the contents of stage n moves "to the right" to stage $(n + 1)$. The new contents of stage 1 is determined by the feedback path, which in Figure 5.10 is the result of the modulo-2 addition (equivalent to the exclusive OR binary logic operation) of the contents of stage $(r - 1)$ and stage r. Since the operation in the feedback path is linear, this is sometimes called a Linear Feedback Shift Register (LFSR). Nonlinear feedback shift registers are interesting theoretically, but are not commonly used in practice. All shift registers discussed here are LFSRs. The final stage (i.e., stage r) is *always* fed back, and one or more other stages can be combined in modulo-2 addition to produce the new value for stage 1 each time the clock ticks. Connecting the output of a given stage in such a way is commonly called a "feedback tap." If the selection of the feedback taps is made carefully, then the output will have a period of $N = 2^r - 1$ clock cycles, and thus the output sequence will have a length of N. This PN sequence output is called a "maximal length sequence" (or more commonly, m-sequence) and it has special properties that make it very useful. Note that the "all zeros state" is a forbidden state for the SRG (why?). The remaining part of this discussion will be restricted to m-sequences unless otherwise noted, and when we write the phrase "PN sequence" here, we mean an m-sequence.

As an example of a specific SRG, see Figure 5.11. This SRG has only 3 stages, and has a feedback tap coming from stage 1. A compact way to describe this SRG configuration is

---

[6]**Important:** An r-stage shift register can be implemented in hardware (e.g., where each stage could be a D flip-flop), or in software (where each "stage" could be just a single memory location or more commonly where each "stage" is just one bit of a single r-bit wide memory location or CPU register).

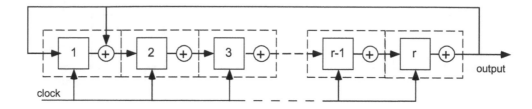

Figure 5.12: An r-stage modular shift register generator with one feedback tap shown.

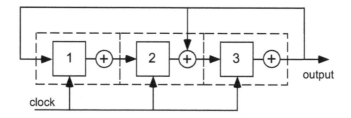

Figure 5.13: A 3-stage modular shift register generator with one feedback tap shown.

$[3,1]_s$ using the notation found in Dixon [68].[7] The first number is the number of stages, r, and the subsequent numbers define the stages from which the feedback taps are taken. The "s" subscript here denotes use of a "simple shift register generator," or SSRG (sometimes called a Fibonacci implementation), as opposed to another type called a "modular shift register generator," or MSRG (sometimes called a Galois implementation). Both figures 5.10 and 5.11 depict SSRGs.

Figure 5.12 shows a generalized r-stage modular shift register generator (MSRG), where in this case each "stage" includes both a storage location for one bit (or rather, one chip) and an exclusive OR gate for the modulo-2 addition. While the MSRG is better suited to hardware implementations, due to both the modular form of the stages and the elimination of logic gates in the main feedback path, the SSRG is simpler to understand and is more often the version discussed in textbooks. Figure 5.13 shows a 3-stage MSRG with a feedback tap entering stage 2. A compact way to describe this MSRG configuration, again using the notation found in Dixon, is $[3,2]_m$. The SSRG of Figure 5.11 (designated $[3,1]_s$) and the MSRG of Figure 5.13 (designated $[3,2]_m$) will output an identical PN sequence. This illustrates the relationship between a Fibonacci implementation (i.e., SSRG) and a Galois implementation (i.e., MSRG): $[r,n,p,q,\ldots]_s$ is equivalent to $[r, n-r, p-r, q-r, \ldots]_m$. Some reference authors choose to reverse the ordering of stage numbers for an SSRG from that shown in Figure 5.10, resulting in identical feedback listings for either Fibonacci or Galois implementations (for example, see [69]). We mention all this here to warn the reader to pay careful attention to the notation used in a given reference source regarding how the feedback taps are listed, especially if a particular PN sequence is desired. Reference sources such as [68, 69] provide extensive tables listing feedback taps for valid m-sequences using both SSRGs and MSRGs.[8]

As an example, let's follow the output for the $[3,1]_s$ SSRG shown in Figure 5.11. Recalling that the contents of each stage is a binary 1 or 0, and that the modulo-2 addition is

---

[7]Another compact method is a polynomial representation [63, 65].

[8]Finite (Galois) field mathematics can be used to derive feedback taps for m-sequences, but this can be tedious and is beyond the scope of this text.

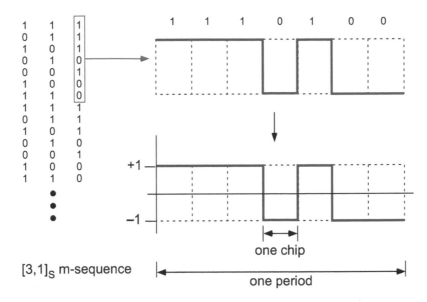

Figure 5.14: Output of a $[3,1]_s$ SSRG. Left: contents of all three stages. Top right: output chips. Bottom right: antipodal signal conversion of chips.

just the exclusive OR binary logic operation, start with the state where all stages contain a 1 (the "all ones state") and calculate the output until you see it repeat. You should find that the repeating output will be 1 1 1 0 1 0 0, as depicted in Figure 5.14. The output is taken from the 3rd stage, and it repeats after $N = 2^3 - 1 = 7$ clock cycles; thus the length of the PN sequence is $N = 7$ chips; this is a maximal length PN sequence. Note that the "all zeros state" never occurs, and as mentioned earlier is a forbidden state.[9] In practical use, the PN sequence is usually converted to ± 1 as shown at the bottom right of Figure 5.14. While this particular SRG has too few stages to be useful for nontrivial applications, its simplicity makes it well-suited for a first exposure to the concept.

As mentioned earlier, the SSRG of Figure 5.11 (designated $[3,1]_s$) and the MSRG of Figure 5.13 (designated $[3,2]_m$) will output an identical PN sequence. However, for the same initial state (often called the "seed" state), the sequence will start at a different point in the sequence. You should confirm that if you start with the "all ones state" as the seed state, the $[3,2]_m$ MSRG of Figure 5.13 will provide the repeating output of 1 0 1 0 0 1 1, which is the same output sequence, but shifted by two positions. To obtain the identical output shown at the right of Figure 5.14, you would need to begin $[3,2]_m$ with the seed state of 0 0 1.

Maximal length PN sequences have many valuable properties (see [64, p. 371] for a succinct summary), with one of the most important being their correlation properties. Recall that the normalized (by the length of the sequence) autocorrelation of a truly random process will have a single peak equal to 1.0 only at the zero offset point, and essentially zero everywhere else. The normalized autocorrelation of a maximal length PN sequence will also have a peak equal to 1.0 at the zero offset point, and will drop linearly to a very low constant value (equal to $-1/N$) at $\pm T_c$ on either side of that peak (where T_c is the time duration of one chip). Because the PN sequence is periodic, the normalized autocorrelation of a maximal length PN sequence will also have identical peaks equal to 1.0 spaced at offsets equal to NT_c. See Figure 5.15 for a plot of the normalized autocorrelation of a maximal

---

[9]For robust operation, real-world PN sequence generators include the ability to detect and recover from the "all zeros state."

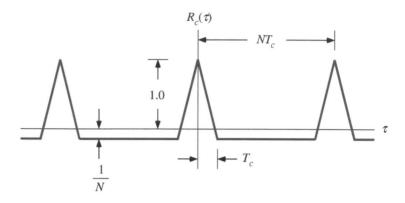

Figure 5.15: Normalized autocorrelation of a length $N = 7$ maximal length PN sequence.

length PN sequence. The fact that any timing offset more than $\pm 0.5 T_c$ from an integer value of T_c will result in a very low constant autocorrelation equal to $-1/N$ is a valuable property for CDMA, ranging, synchronization, and other applications. Note that for very long sequences, the $-1/N$ term is approximately zero, and the autocorrelation peaks are spaced so far apart that it appears to be very much like random noise. The IS-95 2G cellular telephone standard, for example, uses a 15-stage SRG, so the m-sequences used are 32,767 chips long.

We need to make a few comments about Figure 5.15. Essentially, all textbooks that explain maximal length PN sequences show a figure similar to Figure 5.15. However, well over half the textbooks we have seen fail to mention two assumptions behind the result shown in this figure. One assumption is that the values of the chips in the PN sequence are not 1 and 0 but rather the antipodal pair $+1$ and -1. Another key assumption is that the operation performed is circular correlation, not the more common linear correlation. The different result of circular versus linear correlation will be shown in a MATLAB demonstration later in the chapter. For now, just accept the result of Figure 5.15.

Since we have the autocorrelation $R_c(\tau)$, the Wiener-Khintchine theorem tells us that the power spectral density (PSD) of the PN sequence is simply $\mathcal{F}\{R_c(\tau)\}$, the Fourier transform of the autocorrelation output. Before showing the result, we should be able to predict certain aspects of the PSD. Since $R_c(\tau)$ is periodic, its spectrum should be discrete, with a fundamental frequency equal to the reciprocal of the period of $R_c(\tau)$. The envelope of the discrete components should follow the shape of the Fourier transform of the basic shape of one period of $R_c(\tau)$, which is a triangular pulse. The Fourier transform of a triangular pulse is a squared sinc. The PSD of $R_c(\tau)$, often designated $S_c(f)$, is shown in Figure 5.16.

Our predictions hold true for Figure 5.16, including the fact that for this $N = 7$ example, the fundamental frequency of the discrete components, $1/(NT_c)$, is 1/7 the frequency of the first zero of the envelope at $1/(T_c)$. This is because the period of the PN sequence is $N = 7$ times longer than the period of one chip.

Besides the autocorrelation properties of PN sequences, we are often interested in the crosscorrelation properties, which is when one PN sequence is correlated with a different PN sequence. Ideally, we would like the crosscorrelation to be as close to zero as possible. This is especially important, for example, in CDMA systems such as the IS-95 (2G) and CDMA2000 (3G) cellular telephone systems, where low crosscorrelation allows multiple users to simultaneously share the same frequency band without interfering with each other. But not all PN sequence pairs have low crosscorrelation, so great care must be taken when assigning the PN sequences for such applications. When appropriate m-sequences can't be found, engineers then turn to alternative sequences such as Gold codes (non-maximal length

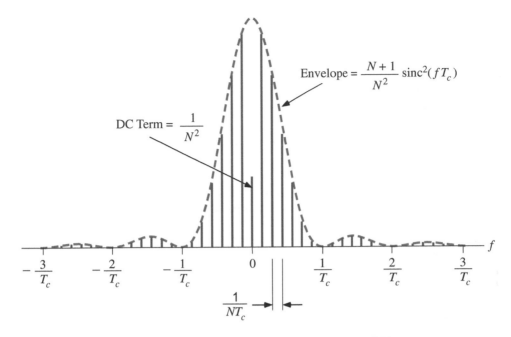

Figure 5.16: PSD of a length $N = 7$ maximal length PN sequence.

PN sequences formed from two or more m-sequences) or Barker codes (not PN sequences at all, but rather hard-coded sequences of length 2, 3, 4, 5, 7, 11, or 13; no other Barker codes are known to exist). Gold codes are widely used in applications from deep space probes to CDMA cellular telephone systems, and an $N = 11$ Barker code is part of the IEEE 802.11 wireless Internet (Wi-Fi) digital communications standard.

5.5.2 winDSK Demonstration

The winDSK8 program does not provide any functions which incorporate PN sequences.

5.5.3 MATLAB Implementation

Using MATLAB to explore various aspects of PN sequences and to generate PN sequences as desired is relatively easy, but there are a few potential pitfalls that we will point out at the appropriate place. Readers should note that there are PN sequence generators built into the Communications Toolbox (for MATLAB) and the Communications Blockset (for Simulink), but as we've indicated in earlier chapters, avoid such tools until you've written some of your own code and become familiar with the fundamentals of a given topic. The xor logic function is now built into MATLAB, which is handy for generating PN sequences. The programs pngen.m and pngen2.m are included with the software for the book; they generate PN sequences given the SSRG feedback specifications.

Let's explore the autocorrelation properties of some PN sequences. The MATLAB program pn_corr.m is included with the software for the book, and provides a handy way to do this. Multiple sequences are hard coded into the program, both valid and invalid m-sequences. Simply uncomment the pair of (equal length) sequences you want to use and run the program. Both autocorrelation and crosscorrelation can be easily performed, and the program illustrates the difference between circular and linear correlation. The key part of the pn_corr.m program is shown in Listing 5.11.

Listing 5.11: MATLAB implementation of circular and linear correlation for PN sequences.

```matlab
N=length(seq1);

% Convert to +/- 1
seqn1=(2*seq1)-1;
seqn2=(2*seq2)-1;

% Set up correlation with three periods of the PN sequence
tmp1=[seqn1 seqn1 seqn1];

% Time domain method for circular correlation of seq1 and seq2.
% Could also use frequency domain method with no zero padding
for index=1:2*N+1;
   tmp2=[zeros(1,index-1) seqn2 zeros(1,2*N-index+1)];
   cor(index)=sum(tmp1.*tmp2)/N;
end;
n=0:2*N;

%% frequency domain method of circular correlation
%% uncomment and use this instead if desired
% S1=fft(seqn1);
% S2=fft(seqn2);
% cor=ifft(S1.*conj(S2));

% standard linear correlation in MATLAB
lincor=xcorr(seqn1,seqn2)/N;
nn=0:2*N-2;
```

Note that the program shows both a time domain method (lines 12–15) and a frequency domain method (lines 20–22) of performing circular correlation, along with the linear correlation (line 25) using xcorr that is built into MATLAB's Signal Processing Toolbox. Figure 5.17 shows both methods of correlation for the autocorrelation of the PN sequence shown in Figure 5.14. Observe that the theoretical autocorrelation of Figure 5.15 is only obtained when circular autocorrelation is used. The chips of the PN sequence are shown in Figure 5.17 as a MATLAB bar plot for clarity; the actual PN sequence would be like that shown in Figure 5.14. If someone new to PN sequences just used the xcorr command in MATLAB expecting to get a result similar to Figure 5.15, they might be confused when they did not get that result. We hope this short example dispels any such confusion, and we won't waste space showing any further linear correlation results.

The crosscorrelation of $[3,1]_s$ (from Figure 5.14) and $[3,2]_s$ is shown in Figure 5.18. Notice there is no peak equal to 1.0 in this case. The autocorrelation of the 31-chip maximal length PN sequence specified by $[5,2]_s$ is shown in Figure 5.19. The crosscorrelation of maximal length PN sequences $[5,3]_s$ and $[5,4,3,2]_s$ is shown in Figure 5.20. As a last example of correlation properties, Figure 5.21 shows the autocorrelation of a sequence that is *not* a maximal length PN sequence. Note that while there is a peak of 1.0 at zero offset and at offsets equal to multiples of NT_c, similar to a maximal length PN sequence, the highly desirable low autocorrelation at other offsets does not exist. Compare Figure 5.21 with Figure 5.19.

Exploring the spectral properties of PN sequences using MATLAB presents some potential pitfalls as well.[10] Trying to observe the PSD by using traditional spectral analysis

---
[10]Spectral analysis is covered in more detail in Chapter 9.

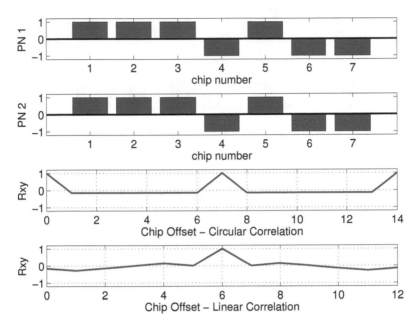

Figure 5.17: Autocorrelation using MATLAB of a length $N = 7$ maximal length PN sequence. Second from bottom: circular autocorrelation. Bottom: linear autocorrelation.

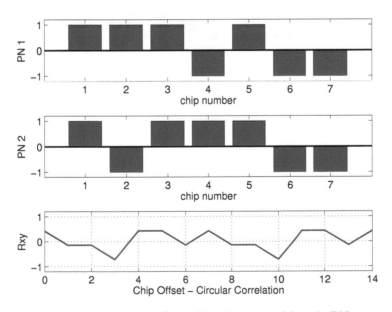

Figure 5.18: Crosscorrelation of two $N = 7$ maximal length PN sequences.

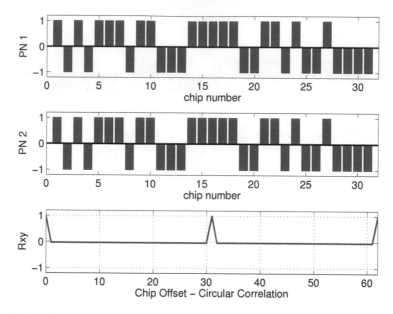

Figure 5.19: Autocorrelation of a length $N = 31$ maximal length PN sequence.

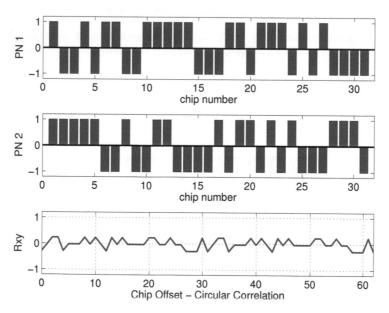

Figure 5.20: Crosscorrelation of two length $N = 31$ maximal length PN sequences.

tools such as the `psd` or `pwelch` commands in MATLAB on a PN sequence will typically not provide a satisfactory result, yielding a plot with little resemblance to Figure 5.16. The frequency resolution of the FFT, determined in part by the number of data points provided to the FFT, is partly to blame.[11] Trying to get around this problem by using many copies of the PN sequence strung together in a single row vector as input to the FFT doesn't provide much improvement.

One way around this problem is to "fool" MATLAB into "thinking" that the input is

---

[11]The FFT is covered in more detail in Chapter 8.

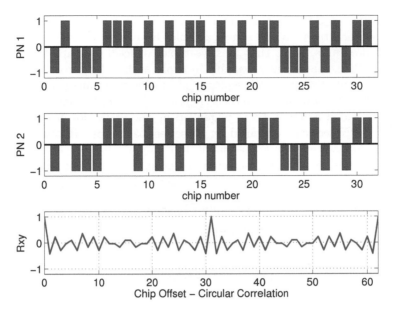

Figure 5.21: Autocorrelation of a length $N = 31$ sequence that is *not* a valid maximal length PN sequence.

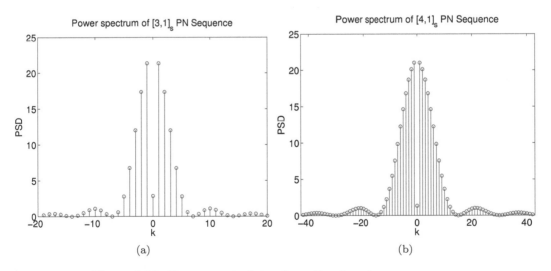

Figure 5.22: Power spectral density estimate using `pn_spec.m`.

a continuous waveform that follows the pattern of the desired PN sequence. We can do this by providing MATLAB with multiple data points per chip; a reasonable number that provides a very nice output is 20 data points per chip. This technique is exploited in the program `pn_spec.m` included with the software for the book; it generates a very nice plot of the PSD of a PN sequence. See Figure 5.22. In particular, compare Figure 5.22(a) to Figure 5.16. In this $N = 7$ example, both figures show that the fundamental frequency of the discrete components is $1/7$ the frequency of the first zero of the envelope. This is because the period of the PN sequence is $N = 7$ times longer than the period of one chip.

We have provided programs in MATLAB for exploring the correlation properties and spectral properties of PN sequences, and for generating any desired PN sequence for a given set of feedback taps. While some examples have been provided in the text and in the MATLAB programs, recall that massive tables of feedback taps for generating valid maximal length PN sequences are available in books such as [68] or online such as [69].

The more general of the two PN sequence generation programs is `pngen2.m`, and it can accept any number of feedback taps in the $[r, n, p, q, \ldots]_s$ format we have used in this chapter. The taps are provided as input `fb` to `pngen2.m` in row vector format, and the output of `pngen2.m` is the PN sequence specified by those feedback taps. If you're generating long codes, be sure to use a semicolon at the end of the command line on which you call `pngen2.m` to keep the output from filling the screen and slowing down the program execution. The key part of the code for `pngen2.m` is given in Listing 5.12.

Listing 5.12: MATLAB program to generate PN sequences for a given set of feedback taps.

```
   % perform one cycle of code generation
2  for i = 1:N
       output(i) = shift_reg(r);
4      if (ntaps > 2) % multiple feedback taps
           feedback = shift_reg(fb(2));
6          for j = 3:ntaps
               feedback = xor(shift_reg(fb(j)), feedback);
8          end
           feedback = xor(shift_reg(r), feedback);
10     else  % only one feeback tap
           feedback = xor(shift_reg(r), shift_reg(fb(2)));
12     end
       % perform brute force shift
14     shift_reg(2:r) = shift_reg(1:r-1);
       shift_reg(1) = feedback;
16 end
```

The number of stages is `r`, and the program uses the vector `fb` to determine from which stages to perform the exclusive OR operation. Note that one entire period of the PN sequence is generated before the program exits and provides output, so this code would need to be modified for a real-time approach. That is, a real-time approach would output a single chip of the desired PN sequence each "tick" of the clock, and keep running for however many periods were needed.

Before continuing, it should be noted that the PN sequence generation programs we have provided implement shift registers in a brute force way for simplicity of the code. For example, the `shift_reg` variable is a memory array of length r, which is very wasteful since each stage of the shift register only needs to store a single-bit binary value. There are certainly more elegant techniques that can be used.

5.5.4 DSK Implementation in C

This chapter is a rather long one, and space limitations restrict what we can show here for the real-time generation of PN sequences on the DSK. We will show only one method of generating a PN sequence in real-time on the DSK, and provide some basic suggestions for how you might use it.

One of the first questions to be answered would be, "Do you really need to generate the PN sequence in real time?" If the desired sequence is not long, it would be more efficient to just store it in memory (this method is really just a look-up table implementation). This is always true for Barker sequences, which are not generated by an SRG, and are always relatively short in length. But for longer-length PN sequences, storing them in memory becomes impractical, and it is more efficient to just generate them with a DSP software SRG implementation.

Real-Time Considerations

Following the same method we've used in previous chapters, you can carefully modify "de-vectorized" MATLAB code to get an initial version of C code that will run in real-time on the DSK. Looking at Listing 5.12, for example, you would first remove the outer `for` loop to convert to a sample-by-sample (or, in this case, chip-by-chip) approach. In an earlier part of the code, you would already have declared in memory an integer variable of sufficient size to hold `shift_reg` (that is, having at least r bits), and an appropriate variable for `fb`; only a single bit would be needed for `output` since each chip of the PN sequence would be output individually in real-time. Note that by using an appropriate size of unsigned integer variable (such as `Uint32` for an SRG up to 32 stages) in your C code for the shift register, you can take advantage of the highly efficient shift-right command. The basic approach from Listing 5.12 could then be used to output a given PN sequence (as determined by the feedback taps defined by `fb`) on a chip-by-chip basis. After getting such a "brute force" method to work, the next step would be to implement a more elegant technique.

If you intend to use the PN sequence as part of a real-time program using one or more DSKs where the input and output go through the codec(s), don't neglect the fact that the $F_s/2$ bandwidth limitation imposed by the sampling theorem also applies to the PN sequence if it (or data modulated by it) goes through the codec. For this reason, it may be prudent to include in your real-time PN sequence generation code a method of some kind for constraining the "chip rate" of $1/T_c$ to stay within the limits of the sampling theorem.

This brings up the question how to provide the output containing the real-time PN sequence. While the PN sequence can be used to modify (i.e., "spread" or "de-spread") input data as part of the desired DSP algorithm and output the result via the codec, we recognize that some users may want access to just the PN sequence itself. Therefore, we make the real-time PN sequence available as a digital output from the board, using the `WriteDigitalOutputs` function (see `LCDK_Support_DSP.c`, `OMAPL138_Support_DSP.c`, or `DSK6713_Support.c` in the `common_code` directory of the book's software). Note that the `WriteDigitalOutputs` function behaves a bit differently on the OMAP-L138 Experimenter Kit versus the LCDK or the C6713 DSK. On the LCDK and the C6713 DSK, `WriteDigitalOutputs` sends four bits 0–3 (where bit 0 is the LSB) to four user LEDs (LED 1 through LED 4, respectively) included on the board where the pins are easily accessible. On the OMAP-L138 Experimenter Kit, writing to the board's LEDs involves the relatively slow I²C interface. To avoid this slowdown, `WriteDigitalOutputs` for the OMAP-L138 Experimenter Kit sends signals to four digital output pins on the LCD connector J15. Specifically, four bits 0–3 (where bit 0 is the LSB) are sent to pins 6–9, respectively, of connector J15. Ground is available on that connector at pins 1, 5, and 10. For all three boards, `WriteDigitalOutputs` allows the user to connect (e.g., with a test probe clip) to the digital output signal as desired.

Generating a Real-Time PN sequence

We show an example of C code for real-time generation of a PN sequence using the DSK. The files necessary to run this application are provided in the `ccs\PN` directory of Chapter 5. The primary file of interest is `ISRs_LFSR.c`, which contains various declarations and the interrupt service routine to perform the PN sequence generation algorithm. As this program is written, the PN sequence that is generated does not modify the input data in any way.

Data samples are brought in from the codec and output to the codec with no modification (i.e., a simple "talk-through"). The PN sequence is sent as a digital output as described above. The reader is free to modify the input data with the PN sequence as desired.

An excerpt of the declaration section of the code is shown in Listing 5.13.

Listing 5.13: Declarations for the PN Generator code.

```
// implementing Galois 16-bit LFSR  x^16 + x^14 + x^13 + x^11 + 1
#define LFSR_LENGTH            16
#define LFSR_BIT_MASK          ((1 << LFSR_LENGTH) - 1)
#define LFSR_XOR_MASK          (((1 << 16) | (1 << 14) | (1 << 13) |
    [+] (1 << 11)) >> 1)
#define LFSR_SEED_VALUE        3

// reduce LFSR update rate to Fs/DIVIDE_BY_N
#define DIVIDE_BY_N            10

Uint32 LSFR_reg = LFSR_SEED_VALUE;
```

An explanation of Listing 5.13 follows.

1. (Line 1): Note the SRG will be a Galois implementation, which has implications for how the feedback taps should be specified.

2. (Line 2): Declares the SRG to have 16 stages.

3. (Line 3): This mask is used in the ISR to set the SRG to the number of stages specified by line 1.

4. (Line 4): This is where you specify the feedback taps for the PN sequence you wish to generate. In this case, the PN sequence to be generated will be $[16, 14, 13, 11]_m$, which produces a maximal-length sequence with a length of 65,535 chips. By simply changing this line and line 2, you can specify any PN sequence of up to 32 stages.

5. (Line 5): Determines the "seed state" for the SRG. It doesn't matter what value is used here, as long as it's not zero.

6. (Line 8): The factor by which the chip rate will be slowed compared to the sample frequency of the codec.

7. (Line 10): This 32-bit unsigned integer LFSR_reg is where the stages of the SRG are stored.

The algorithm section of the code is shown in Listing 5.14.

Listing 5.14: Algorithm for the PN Generator code.

```
interrupt void Codec_ISR()
{
    /* add any local variables here */
    Uint8 lsb;
    static Int32 divide_by_n = 0;     // used to slow PN rate

    if(CheckForOverrun())             // overrun error occurred
        return;                       // so serial port is reset
```

```
10    CodecDataIn.UINT = ReadCodecData();    // get input data

12    /* add your code starting here */

14    if(--divide_by_n <= 0) {         // wait for counter to expire
          divide_by_n = DIVIDE_BY_N;    // reset counter
16        LSFR_reg &= LFSR_BIT_MASK;  // mask LFSR to desired length
          lsb = LSFR_reg & 1;          // store state of LS bit
18        LSFR_reg >>= 1;              // shift LFSR right
          if(lsb)
20            LSFR_reg ^= LFSR_XOR_MASK; // XOR only if LSB was 1

22        WriteDigitalOutputs(LSFR_reg); // write LS four bits to
              [+]digital outputs
      }
24
      CodecDataOut.UINT  = CodecDataIn.UINT; // just do talk-
          [+]through
26
      /* end your code here */
28
      WriteCodecData(CodecDataOut.UINT);     // send output data
30 }
```

An explanation of Listing 5.14 follows.

1. (Line 4): Declares the lsb variable as an 8-bit unsigned integer. While this variable is used to store just a single bit (the least significant bit (LSB) of LFSR_reg), an 8-bit memory location is typically the smallest individually addressable unit. This might be a good time to remind readers that the Boolean variable type, bool, is *not* part of the C language but rather part of the C++ language. Note that we typically visualize a register in such a way that the MSB is on the far left and the LSB is on the far right; thus, the LSB of LFSR_reg is where stage r of the SRG is located and is where we take the output from the SRG.

2. (Line 5): Used in conjunction with line 8 of Listing 5.13 to implement the slowing of the chip rate compared to the sample frequency of the codec. This is needed if you must output the PN sequence (or data modified by the PN sequence) through the codec.

3. (Lines 7–8): Checks to see if the DSK halted due to an overrun of the McASP (on the OMAP) or McBSP (on the C6713) and if so resets the port as necessary.

4. (Line 10): Gets an input sample from the codec (both left and right channels together).

5. (Line 14): Pre-decrements the divide_by_n counter and only executes the PN sequence generation algorithm if the counter is "finished." This effectively slows down the chip rate of the PN sequence as desired.

6. (Line 15): Resets the divide_by_n counter.

7. (Line 16): Using a bit mask and the logical AND operation, keeps only the part of LFSR_reg, in particular the least significant part, needed to implement the desired number of stages for the SRG. This forces the unused "upper" bits of LFSR_reg to 0, which ensures a 0 will be shifted into the MSB of LFSR_reg by default.

8. (Line 17): Saves just the least significant bit of `LFSR_reg` in variable `lsb`.

9. (Line 18): Performs the shift-right operation on the SRG.

10. (Lines 19–20): Implements the equivalent of a Galois LFSR using the specified feedback taps.

11. (Line 22): Writes the least significant four bits to the digital output pins. While `LFSR_reg` is 32-bits long, the `WriteDigitalOutputs` function will only send the least significant four bits of the input argument as outputs. In most cases, the reader will only be interested in just one bit, the LSB, which by convention constitutes the output of the SRG. For the LCDK or C6713 DSK, the LSB will be found at LED 1. For the OMAP-L138 Experimenter Kit, the LSB will be found at connector J15 pin 6.

12. (Lines 25 and 29): Sends the input sample obtained in line 10 back out to the codec, in a "talk-through" operation.

Now that you understand the code...

Go ahead and copy all of the files into a separate directory. Open the project in CCS and "Rebuild All." Once the build is complete, "Load Program" into the DSK and click on "Run." Your PN sequence generator is now running in real-time on the DSK. Assuming the sample frequency is set to 48 kHz, then the divide by 10 will result in a chip rate of 4800 chips per second.

Example Results

Assuming your real-time PN sequence generation project is working, and you have access to appropriate test and measurement equipment,[12] you should be able to observe the resulting PN sequence in both the time domain and frequency domain. An example of the $[16, 14, 13, 11]_m$ PN sequence in the time domain is shown in Figure 5.23. For clarity, only 20 ms are shown, which for this 4800 chip per second PN sequence equates to 96 chips. If we tried to show one full cycle of all 65,535 chips (lasting just over 13.6 seconds) the chips would be so tightly packed together that the display would be meaningless. Note that this is a unipolar digital output; conversion to an antipodal chip sequence has not been implemented here.

An example of the PN sequence in the frequency domain is shown in Figure 5.24. Note the shape follows that of a sinc squared, and the first null of this 4800 chip per second PN sequence is located at 4.8 kHz, as expected.

The PN sequence we generated was slowed down by a factor of 10 to 4800 chips per second. If we set the `DIVIDE_BY_N` factor to 1, we would have obtained a 48,000 chip per second PN sequence. As long as we are taking the PN sequence directly from the digital outputs and not the codec DAC, this would still be acceptable. What if you needed an even faster chip rate? You could easily change the codec sample frequency to 96 kHz by changing which `#define SampleRateSetting` is uncommented in the `DSP_Config.h` file in your project, and obtain a 96,000 chip per second PN sequence with no other code modifications. What if you needed an even faster chip rate than this? Instead of using the codec interrupt, you could use a timer interrupt and easily get rates in the low MHz range. Alternatively, you could disable interrupts and put the PN sequence generation algorithm in the `main.c` loop and obtain chip rates in the tens of MHz.

---

[12]Alternatively, you could use a spare DSK running winDSK8 and select the oscilloscope function or the spectrum analyzer function.

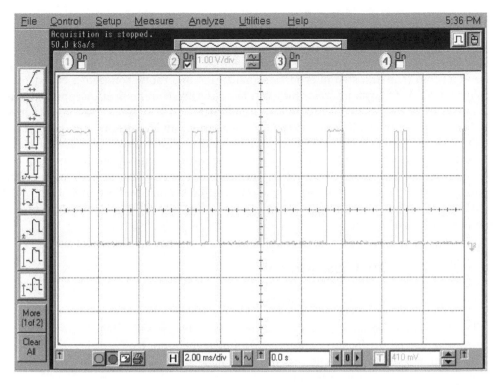

Figure 5.23: Time domain display from a DSK generating a 65,535-chip length PN sequence using a 16-stage SRG. For clarity, only 96 chips are shown.

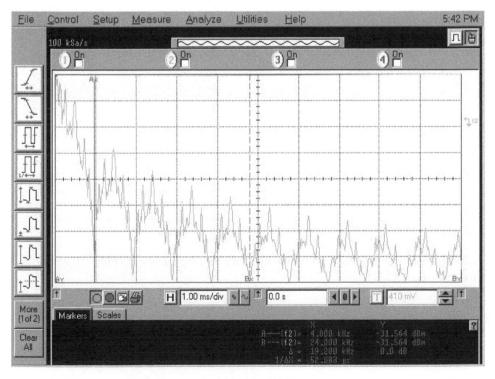

Figure 5.24: Frequency domain display from a DSK generating a 65,535-chip length PN sequence using a 16-stage SRG. Note the first null is located at 4.8 kHz.

Using the Real-Time PN sequence

The generation of PN sequences in real-time on a DSK could be used in many ways. For example, the DSK could provide the source signal for measuring the acoustic frequency response of a room (the first step in acoustic equalization of a room, sometimes called "digital room correction"). Or your interests may run more toward communications applications, in which case you may want to refer to digital communications books, such as [63–68] for some ideas. For example, the DSK could provide the spreading (and/or despreading) signal to another DSK acting as a BPSK or QPSK modulator or demodulator (see Chapters 18 through 21 for projects that implement these digital communication methods on the DSK) to create a spread spectrum communication system, although the bandwidth of such an application is a challenge if you restrict yourself to the onboard codec and audio frequencies. A DSK generating a PN sequence could provide the basis for a simple CDMA demonstration...Let your imagination guide you.

5.6   Follow-On Challenges

Consider extending what you have learned.

1. The trigonometric function call-based technique discussed in this chapter uses single precision variables (floats). Design and implement a double precision variable (doubles) version of the real-time program. What are the advantages and disadvantages of this higher-precision technique?

2. Create a DTMF signal generator that creates the tones associated with your phone number.

   (a) Consider starting the process by embedding the phone number in your ISR. You can always add more sophisticated coding techniques later.

   (b) Ensure that your system will work with any phone number.

   (c) Ensure that your system will handle parentheses, space, and dash characters.

   (d) Ensure that your system allows for user-defined tone durations and tone spacing.

   (e) Ensure that your system has the ability to repeat dial.

3. The table lookup technique actually only needs to define 1/4 of the table since the sine and cosine functions are symmetric functions (only 1/4 of a 0 to 2π table is unique). Design and implement a real-time program that takes advantage of this symmetry.

4. Modify your PN sequence generator to detect and recover from an accidental condition of the forbidden "all zeros state."

5. Modify your PN sequence generator to generate chip rates faster than the codec sample frequency.

5.7   Problems

1. If you use a trigonometric function call such as `sinf()` in your real-time C code, what will happen if the `math.h` header file is not included in your program?

2. Describe the effect of coefficient quantization (or just a low precision when specifying the coefficients) on the digital resonator form of sinusoid generation.

3. Compare and contrast DDS, digital resonator, and lookup table methods of sinusoid generation.

4. Which is more suitable for arbitrary waveform generation: DDS, digital resonator, or the lookup table method?

5. In what way would the topic of "harmonic distortion" be applicable to sinusoid generation?

6. In what way would the topic of "intermodulation distortion" be applicable to DTMF generation?

7. Why is the "all zeros state" forbidden for SRGs used to generate PN sequences?

8. Manually calculate the autocorrelation of a $[3, 1]_s$ PN sequence. Show both linear autocorrelation and circular autocorrelation, and compare the results.

Chapter 6

Frame-Based DSP

6.1   Theory

THE discussion up until this point in the book has usually assumed that the real-time
processing is accomplished on a sample-by-sample basis. That is, an input sample
$x(t)$ was converted to digital form $x[n]$ by the ADC part of the codec and transferred to
the DSK's CPU for whatever processing was desired. This processed sample $y[n]$ was then
transferred to the DAC part of the codec, converted back to analog form $y(t)$, and sent
to an output device (e.g., a speaker). Processing the data in this way has two distinct
advantages. First, this approach makes the DSP algorithms easier to understand and easier
to program. Second, sample-by-sample processing also minimizes the system latency by
acting on each sample as soon as it is available. However, sample-by-sample processing has
serious drawbacks, and is not commonly used for many types of commercial code.

6.1.1   Drawbacks of Sample-Based DSP

One of the implications of real-time sample-based DSP is that all processing must be completed in the time between samples. For many complex DSP algorithms, this becomes
difficult if not impossible, especially for fast sampling rates. For example, if we are using the sample frequency of $F_s = 48$ kHz that we often use in this text, we have only
$T_s = 1/(48 \times 10^3) = 20.83$ μs to process *both* the left and the right channel samples (assuming stereo operation), or 10.42 μs per sample. Given the 456 MHz clock frequency of
the LCDK (2.193 ns per clock cycle), this means we have approximately 4,752 clock cycles
per sample.[1] Note that we must also include in this time period all the "overhead" such
as that associated with codec transfers, memory access, instruction and data cache latency,
and other unavoidable factors when we assess the available clock cycles. While this many
clock cycles may seem to be plenty, a complex algorithm with many memory transfers could
easily exceed this number. Of course, if we are performing *non-real-time* DSP with previously stored data, then this limitation does not exist. But the emphasis of this book is how
to effectively perform real-time DSP.

Another implication of real-time sample-based DSP, which seems fairly obvious, is that
there is only one *new* sample available for processing at any given time (some number of
previous samples are often available as well). Certain classes of DSP algorithms, such as
many implementations that use the FFT (fast Fourier transform), require (or perform better

---

[1]The OMAP-L138 Experimenter Kit runs at a clock frequency of 300 MHz, or 3.333 ns per clock cycle.
The C6713 DSK runs at a clock frequency of 225 MHz, or 4.444 ns per clock cycle. A slower clock frequency
means fewer clock cycles available for processing each sample.

with) some contiguous range of *new* samples to be available at any given time, which is clearly impossible with sample-based DSP.[2] A second implication of real-time sample-based DSP is that the processor must respond to each interrupt from the devices that are data sources and sinks (such as a codec) in order to perform the required data transfers. Doing this means that the current processing is interrupted, the state of the processor preserved, control is transferred to the appropriate interrupt service routine and it is executed, then the processor state must be restored and execution restarted at the interrupted point. During this process, additional inefficiencies also occur, such as pipeline flushes and cache misses. This overhead represents lost processing time, and can significantly reduce the overall performance of the DSP. To remove this burden from the processor, specialized hardware components, referred to as direct memory access (DMA) controllers, are normally included as peripheral elements on the DSP device itself. Once the DMA controller is programmed to respond to a device that is sourcing or sinking data, it will automatically perform the required transfers to or from a memory buffer without processor intervention. When a buffer has been filled or emptied, the DMA controller then interrupts the DSP. This frees the DSP from the mundane task of repetitive data transfers, and allows its resources to be focused on the computationally-intense processing once a buffer of data is available. In order to make this process efficient, the buffers will typically be designed to contain hundreds or thousands of samples. For those instances where one or both of these situations occur, we need an alternative method of processing signals, which we shall call frame-based DSP.

6.1.2   What Is a Frame?

A frame is the name we will use to describe a group of consecutive samples. Some other texts may use the term "block" or "packet" instead of "frame," but they mean essentially the same thing. In order to implement frame-based DSP, we must collect N samples, and at that point initiate the processing of the frame. See Figure 6.1 for a pictorial comparison of sample-based versus frame-based processing.

How many samples constitute a frame? While frame sizes are common where the number of samples is some power of two (i.e., $N = 2^n$), there is no particular number that *must* be used. The frame size is selected based on several factors, such as the DSP algorithm to be used, the speed and efficiency of the ADC, the overhead required for memory transfers, other hardware limitations, and the performance of the DSP system. This last consideration is driven by the fact that, whatever result is obtained by the DSP, a new "updated" result cannot be obtained any faster than it takes to sample an entire frame of data.

For example, suppose we are graphically displaying the spectrum of a signal based on the FFT of that signal. The FFT requires a frame of data to be available at one time. If we assume a sample frequency of $F_s = 48$ kHz (thus, $T_s = 1/(48 \times 10^3) = 20.83$ μs) and a frame size of 2048 samples, then the spectrum display cannot be updated any faster than 2048×20.83 μs $= 42.66$ ms, which equates to 23.44 display updates per second. Around the world, standard definition television video (both older analog formats and newer digital formats) is updated either 25 or 30 frames per second (depending upon the country), and movies shown in theaters are typically updated 24 frames per second, so this might be satisfactory.[3] Note the implication in this example is that we now have 42.66 ms, or over

---

[2]Be aware that there are other classes of DSP algorithms, such as active noise cancelation, that typically require sample-by-sample processing to update the adaptive algorithm as quickly as possible.

[3]Various "tricks" are often used to increase the apparent screen update rate so the human visual system will not perceive a flickering image. Most television standards allow two interlaced fields per frame (although this has other drawbacks compared to progressive scan), some high-end television displays internally reformat the frame rate to a higher frequency, and movie projectors often use a light source chopper to provide the illusion of a higher frame rate.

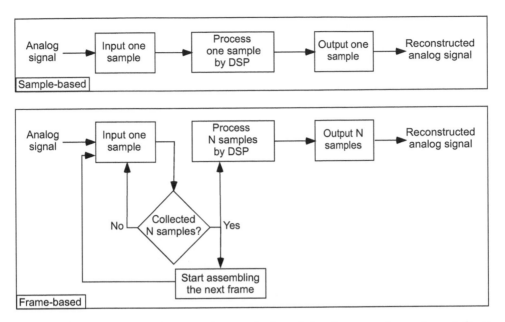

Figure 6.1: A comparison of a generic sample-based (top) versus frame-based (bottom) processing system. Note that some systems may not require the input or output conversions from/to analog as shown here.

19.4 *million* clock cycles of the LCDK to process the data! If we double the frame size, we get twice as much time to process the data, but we can only update the spectrum display half as fast, which may not be acceptable to the user. Thus, as the frame size increases we get more time to process the data, but the response time of the system output gets slower. Frame size is one of many engineering design tradeoffs that need to be made. If the system output frames are sent to the DAC, they will be converted to an analog signal on a sample-by-sample basis, at the given sample frequency F_s. For proper operation, the next frame for output must be available by the time the last sample of the current frame is converted. If, for example, we were performing audio processing, this ensures that from the listener's perspective there would be no "gap" in the music and the output would sound no different than if sample-based processing were being used. Of course there is a time lag, or latency, equal to the frame period, but it is imperceptible to the listener.

Most real-time DSP, such as CD and DVD players, the telephone system (both land-line and wireless cellular), internet communications, and digital television (such as HDTV) implement a form of frame-based processing. For example, CD players use a data frame that is made up of six sample periods (six left channel samples, six right channel samples, alternating) [70]. Each sample is 2 bytes (16 bits), so the initial frame size is 24 bytes in length.[4]

6.2 winDSK Demonstration

Most of the functions available in winDSK8 are implemented as sample-based programs to keep the code simple. However, one exception is the Oscilloscope function, which must transfer information to be displayed in real-time on the video screen of the PC via the I/O

---

[4]Additional DSP steps, including error correction and modulation, expand this to 73.5 bytes (588 bits) per frame that is actually stored on the CD.

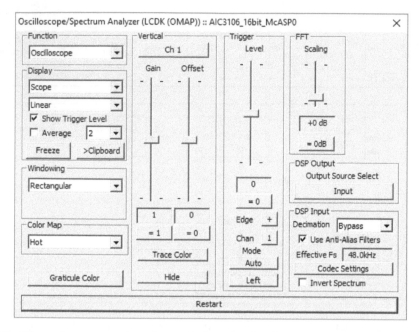

Figure 6.2: The primary user interface window for the Oscilloscope function of winDSK8.

port interface. Since there is significant timing overhead in both I/O port transfers and video screen rendering, frame-based processing is used. In fact, the overhead incurred just in writing to the video screen would make sample-by-sample video transfers impractical. The actual frame size used in this part of winDSK8 is 512 samples per channel.

If you haven't yet tried the Oscilloscope function of winDSK8, try it now by clicking on the "Oscope/Analyzer" button of the main winDSK8 interface. The primary user interface window for this function is shown in Figure 6.2. Note that in winDSK8, the word "Oscilloscope" is selected in the top left drop-down menu. This function can provide both time domain (i.e., Oscilloscope) or frequency domain (i.e., Spectrum Analyzer) displays. In some DSP texts, "time domain" is called "sample domain." A time domain example, using the Oscilloscope function, is shown in Figure 6.3.

When the Spectrum Analyzer function is selected, frequency domain values are calculated by performing the FFT on each 512 sample block of data. Using the Log10 units option instead of Linear often provides better results for the spectrum. Try the "waterfall" option as well, which adds a moving time-axis to the display. A waterfall spectral display is often called a *spectrogram*, which may seem familiar to you if you have tried the non-real-time spectrogram function (or the related specgramdemo) in MATLAB. In winDSK8, the most recent data is shown at the top of the waterfall display.[5]

6.3   MATLAB Implementation

Frame-based processing in MATLAB was demonstrated previously in Section 2.4.2, where frames of 500 samples each were transferred from the DSK to the PC and manipulated using MATLAB. Another MATLAB-related application where frame-based processing is typically used is Simulink, which was demonstrated in Section 2.4.1 where frames of 1024

---

[5]In case you're interested, this is similar to the type of readout provided by a typical sonar system on U.S. nuclear submarines.

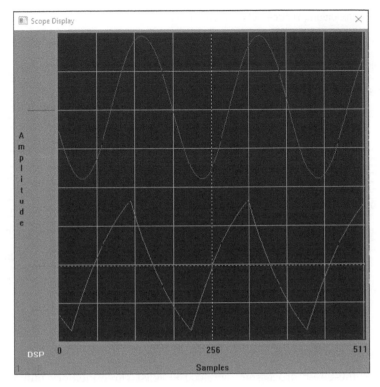

Figure 6.3: An example of a two-channel time domain display using the Oscilloscope function of winDSK8.

samples each were used. In fact, for those MATLAB Toolboxes that generate code for a C6x target DSP from Simulink models, we have found that the actual code generated uses a double buffering scheme for both input and output streams, or four buffers total. The triple-buffered frame-based approach we explain in the next section is actually a more efficient technique, as it requires only three buffers rather than four to achieve the same effect.

6.4 DSK Implementation in C

Important: As mentioned in Chapter 1, some of the code listings in this book (and particularly in this section) include lines that, despite our best efforts, are too long to fit within the book's margins and still allow us to use meaningful variable and function names. So we remind you that, in all program listings where a line wrap occurred in the listing due only to page margins, the characters "[+]" show up to identify the beginning of the wrapped part of the line. The line numbers shown at the left edge of the listings do not increment for the wrapped part of a line.

Note that, for a real-time process, the collection of samples by the ADC never stops as long as the system is in operation. When N samples have been collected, they are transferred for processing by the DSP and the collection of a new frame begins without interruption. As shown in Figure 6.1, frame-based processing requires some means to determine when we have acquired N samples. A common technique is to incorporate a counter and a flag in the associated ISR.

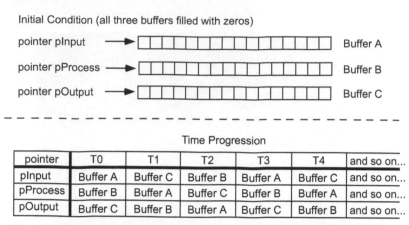

pointer	T0	T1	T2	T3	T4	and so on...
pInput	Buffer A	Buffer C	Buffer B	Buffer A	Buffer C	and so on...
pProcess	Buffer B	Buffer A	Buffer C	Buffer B	Buffer A	and so on...
pOutput	Buffer C	Buffer B	Buffer A	Buffer C	Buffer B	and so on...

Notes: 1. Each time block is the amount of time needed to fill one frame with samples.
2. Time T0: Buffer A is filling, Buffers B and C are still filled with zeros.
3. Time T1: Buffer C is filling, Buffer A is being processed, Buffer B is all zeros.
4. Time T2: the first actual output appears when Buffer A is sent to the DAC.
5. The same pattern repeats as shown above for as long as the program runs.

Figure 6.4: A pictorial representation of triple buffering.

6.4.1   Triple Buffering

For real-time frame-based processing, we need at least three memory buffers at any given time: one for filling a frame with new samples, one for processing a frame by the DSP, and one for sending a frame of processed samples to the output. Let's call them buffer A, buffer B, and buffer C, then follow a single frame through the system to illustrate the basic process. A brute force method would fill the input frame using buffer A to store samples from the ADC, then copy the contents of buffer A to buffer B for processing (freeing up buffer A for the next frame), then after processing the samples copy the contents of buffer B to buffer C, whereupon the contents of buffer C are sent to the DAC and so on... but this technique is *extremely* inefficient. All the memory transfers involved incur considerable overhead.

The most efficient way to implement frame-based processing in real-time is to use a technique known as "triple buffering." There is a related method called "ping pong buffers," which uses four buffers (two for input, two for output), but we focus here on the more efficient triple buffering method. In this technique, no copying of buffer contents is needed. All we do is define three pointers that will be used for the addresses of the input, processing, and output buffer memory locations. When the input buffer fills up, we just change the *pointers* instead of physically copying any of the buffer contents. The best way to visualize the process is with a picture; Figure 6.4 shows the typical sequence in which the pointers are updated. We could think of this as a variation on circular buffering (first discussed in Chapter 3), but which in this case rotates through *frames* instead of samples.

To implement triple buffering, we use a single ISR that performs both input and output of the data, and tracks the status of the frame filling and processing. The input part of the ISR brings samples in from the ADC and fills the input buffer, the output part of the ISR sends samples from the output buffer to the DAC, and the main program runs whatever algorithm is needed on the processing buffer when it isn't being interrupted by an ISR. The ISR must be responsible for keeping track of when a full frame has been gathered, and sets a flag so the main program can update the pointer assignments for the buffers. The ISR also checks if the buffer processing is "finished" in time, or else erroneous output may occur without the user's knowledge.

6.4.2 A Frame-Based DSP Example

We will keep the DSP algorithm very simple so we don't obscure the main point: to introduce you to frame-based processing. A more realistic example will be shown in Chapter 7. Since the primary purpose of this section is to show you how to input, process, and output data in "blocks" of samples called frames, the actual processing we do doesn't matter as long as it doesn't exceed the real-time schedule. Suppose we simply make the left channel output be the sum $(L + R)$ of the left and right channel inputs and make the right channel output be the difference $(L - R)$ of the left and right channel inputs. An example of this simple program implemented in frame-based code is given in the `ccs\Frame` directory of Chapter 6. Be sure to inspect the full code listings in this directory to understand the complete working of the program.[6] Here we simply point out some highlights. The main program (`main.c`) is very basic, as shown below.

Listing 6.1: Main program for simple frame-based processing using ISRs.

```
#include "DSK_Config.h"
#include "frames.h"

int main() {
    // initialize all buffers to 0
    ZeroBuffers();

    // initialize DSK for selected codec
    DSK_Init(CodecType, TimerDivider);

    // main loop here, process buffer when ready
    while(1) {
        if(IsBufferReady()) // process buffers in background
            ProcessBuffer();
    }
}
```

While this is similar in many respects to the main program used in previous examples that implemented sample-based processing, there are a few significant differences. For example, in line 6 we ensure that the contents of all three buffers are set to zero before the program proceeds.[7] In line 12, we enter a continuous `while` loop similar to what we did for sample-based processing, only in this instance the `while` loop isn't empty: we first test to see if the buffer is full in line 13, and when it is full we process the samples in the full buffer in line 14.

The real "meat" of the program is in the file `ISRs.c`, which contains the interrupt service routine. The first part of this file contains various declarations, as shown below.

Listing 6.2: Declarations from the "ISRs.c" file.

```
#define LEFT  0
#define RIGHT 1

volatile union {
    Uint32 UINT;
```

---

[6]Be sure to look also in the `DSK_Support.c` file in the `common_code` directory for initialization functions shared by multiple programs.

[7]While many modern compilers set the contents of a newly created buffer or variable to zero, it may not be wise to rely on that feature.

```
6      Int16 Channel[2];
    } CodecDataIn, CodecDataOut;
8

10 /* add any global variables here */
   // frame buffer declarations
12 #define BUFFER_LENGTH     96000 // buffer length in samples
   #define NUM_CHANNELS      2     // supports stereo audio
14 #define NUM_BUFFERS       3     // don't change
   #define INITIAL_FILL_INDEX 0    // start filling this buffer
16 #define INITIAL_DUMP_INDEX 1    // start dumping this buffer

18 // allocate buffers in external SDRAM
   #pragma DATA_SECTION(buffer, "CE0");
20 volatile float buffer[NUM_BUFFERS][2][BUFFER_LENGTH];
   // there are 3 buffers in use at all times, one being filled,
22 // one being operated on, and one being emptied
   // fill_index   --> buffer being filled by the ADC
24 // dump_index --> buffer being written to the DAC
   // ready_index --> buffer ready for processing
26 Uint8 buffer_ready = 0, over_run = 0, ready_index = 2;
```

Note that lines 4 to 7 continue our previous technique of efficiently bringing in both the left and right 16-bit samples as a single 32-bit unsigned integer, but still allowing separate manipulation of the left and right channels by declaring both `CodecDataIn` and `CodecDataOut` as a union. Lines 12 and 13 specify the dimensions of the buffers to be used for frames: in this example, each frame will be 192,000 samples long, consisting of 96,000 samples from the left channel and 96,000 samples from the right channel; line 14 specifies that there will be three identical buffers of this size. Lines 15 and 16 specify which of the three buffers will start out as the input buffer and which will start out as the output buffer. Line 20 is the actual declaration that allocates memory space for all three buffers, and the compiler pragma on line 19 ensures that the external SDRAM memory space is used for these buffers.[8] Line 26 establishes variables that will indicate when a buffer is full, whether or not there has been a buffer overrun (i.e., the DSP operation on the current processing buffer didn't complete before the current input buffer needed to become the new processing buffer), and an index value used to determine the next buffer to start filling with input samples.

The interrupt service routine `Codec_ISR` transfers input samples from the ADC to the proper input buffer. The input part of that routine is shown below.

Listing 6.3: The input part of the interrupt service routine from the "ISRs.c" file.

```
interrupt void Codec_ISR() {
2 static Uint8 fill_index = INITIAL_FILL_INDEX; // for fill buffer
  static Uint8 dump_index = INITIAL_DUMP_INDEX; // for dump buffer
4 static Uint32 sample_count = 0; // current sample count in buffer

6 if(CheckForOverrun()) // overrun error occurred (halted DSP)
    return;             // so serial port is reset to recover
8
  CodecDataIn.UINT = ReadCodecData();     // get input data samples
```

---

[8]Unless the buffers are rather small, they typically won't fit in the RAM space on the DSP chip itself. We'll see this again later.

```
10
    // store input in buffer
12  buffer[fill_index][ LEFT][sample_count] = CodecDataIn.Channel[
        [+]LEFT];
    buffer[fill_index][RIGHT][sample_count] = CodecDataIn.Channel[
        [+]RIGHT];
```

The variable `fill_index` in line 2 is used to select which buffer is the current input buffer, and the variable `sample_count` in line 4 is used as a counter to determine when the buffer is filled. As we saw in previous chapters, declaring these variables as `static` allows them to keep their values between calls of the ISR. Keep in mind that this ISR gets called many times (96,000 times in this implementation) before the input buffer is filled, and the processing routine `ProcessBuffer` has all this time (minus the brief times devoted to any other ISRs) to do its work. Line 9 brings the new sample in from the ADC. Lines 12 and 13 transfer the new sample into the appropriate location in the current input buffer.

Now that we've seen how the input buffer is filled, just what does the `ProcessBuffer` function look like? As stated earlier, we show a very simple example of forming the sum and difference of the left and right channels just to illustrate how the buffer values are manipulated.

Listing 6.4: Abbreviated version of `ProcessBuffer` from the "ISRs.c" file.

```
1  ProcessBuffer() {
       Uint32 i;
3      float *pL = buffer[ready_index][LEFT];
       float *pR = buffer[ready_index][RIGHT];
5      float temp;

7  /* addition and subtraction */
       for(i=0;i < BUFFER_LENGTH;i++){
9          temp = *pL;
           *pL = temp + *pR; // left = L+R
11         *pR = temp - *pR; // right = L-R
           pL++;
13         pR++;
       }
15
       buffer_ready = 0;
17 }
```

Two things in particular should be noticed about the `ProcessBuffer` function. First, all the values in the buffer (96,0000 samples of the left channel and 96,000 samples of the right channel) are processed before this function is completed (although it is interrupted many times by ISRs). Second, when the processing is completed, the variable `buffer_ready` is set to 0, so that the rest of the program will know that this function completed properly.

How do the processed samples get sent to the output? When the buffers change, the current processing buffer becomes the new output buffer, which is sent to the DAC by the part of the ISR `Codec_ISR` shown below.

Listing 6.5: The output part of the interrupt service routine from the "ISRs.c" file.

```
1  // bound output data before packing
   // use saturation of SPINT to limit to 16-bits
3  CodecDataOut.Channel[ LEFT] = _spint(buffer[dump_index][ LEFT][
       [+]sample_count] * 65536) >> 16;
```

```
   CodecDataOut.Channel[RIGHT] = _spint(buffer[dump_index][RIGHT][
      [+]sample_count] * 65536) >> 16;
 5
   // update sample count and swap buffers when filled
 7 if(++sample_count >= BUFFER_LENGTH) {
        sample_count = 0;
 9      ready_index = fill_index;
        if(++fill_index >= NUM_BUFFERS)
11          fill_index = 0;
        if(++dump_index >= NUM_BUFFERS)
13          dump_index = 0;
        if(buffer_ready == 1) // set a flag if buffer isn't
           [+]processed in time
15          over_run = 1;
        buffer_ready = 1;
17 }

19 WriteCodecData(CodecDataOut.UINT); // send output data to  port
   }
```

In lines 3 and 4, the processed sample is bounded to the allowable range of a signed 16-bit number by the compiler intrinsic function _spint, which is faster than a double comparison with the largest positive value and the smallest negative value as would otherwise have to be performed. Lines 3 and 4 also transfer the processed sample from the buffer to the appropriate CodecDataOut variable. Lines 7 to 17 contain the logic that changes to the next buffer when the current input buffer is full and determines if the processing buffer is ready to be switched as well. Note that if the processing buffer is *not* ready (indicated by buffer_ready[9] being equal to 1 in line 16) the program will still switch the buffers, but the over_run flag indicates that this error condition has occurred. A buffer overrun means you have not met the real-time schedule; this means the ProcessBuffer function must be made faster somehow. The actual DSP algorithm is implemented within the ProcessBuffer function.

Note that each time an ISR interrupts the CPU, some time is "lost" that might have been used for the main algorithm. If we can reduce the number and duration of these interruptions, we can gain even more programming efficiency and gain time for our main algorithm. One very elegant method of achieving this goal, briefly mentioned earlier in this chapter, is to take advantage of something called Direct Memory Access.

6.4.3 Using Direct Memory Access

Direct Memory Access (DMA) is a mechanism that transfers data from one memory location to another without any intervention or work required by the CPU. In essence, the DMA hardware contains a controller unit that can perform memory transfer operations, either one location at a time or in blocks, independent of the CPU. Once the DMA hardware has been configured with the initial source and destination memory locations, and the number of transfers to perform, it can run on its own without any need to "bother" the CPU. Since transferring data from a memory buffer to the codec (or vice versa) is essentially a memory transfer, we can cut the CPU interruptions dramatically by delegating these tasks to the DMA hardware instead of using the CPU to perform such memory transfers.

---

[9]Recall the buffer_ready flag is set to 0 at the end of the ProcessBuffer function, indicating that processing is completed.

In order to implement triple buffering with DMA, our program must first initialize and configure the DMA hardware. The C6x DSK documentation calls this hardware "EDMA," where the "E" stands for *enhanced* because it has more capabilities than typical DMA hardware. For a complete description of the C6x EDMA, see the *TMS320C6000 Peripherals Reference Guide* [71]. For our purposes here, we use only a subset of the EDMA capabilities.

One consideration we can't ignore when using DMA is the need to keep the input and output synchronized. While we gain the advantage of not needing the CPU to perform memory transfers, we must realize that the CPU will thus be unaware of when and how fast these transfers are taking place unless we include some type of code to ensure synchronization. Without such code, the three buffers may get "out of step" with each other, leading to unpredictable behavior. Luckily, the EDMA hardware has the ability to configure and monitor "events" that behave in many ways as interrupts do with the CPU. This gives us a flexible method of keeping the three buffers synchronized, and enables us to swap buffer pointers as needed to implement the triple buffering scheme, all with minimal interruption of the CPU. Thus, the CPU's time can be devoted almost entirely to whatever DSP algorithm is being performed. This technique represents one of the most efficient ways possible to implement a real-time DSP program.

In the next example program, we modified our previous example in only one significant aspect: we now get the input from the ADC side of the codec and send the output to the DAC side of the codec using the EDMA hardware instead of having the CPU do it inside of an ISR. This EDMA program is given in the ccs\Frame_EDMA_6713 subdirectory for Chapter 6. **All the code we show here is for the C6713 DSK;** the code for the OMAP-L138 boards is very similar and is provided in the ccs\Frame_EDMA_6748 directory. Use the code appropriate for your hardware. Be sure to inspect the full code listings in the appropriate directory to understand the complete working of the program. Here we simply point out some highlights. The main program (main.c) is once again very basic, as shown below, with only a few minor differences from Listing 6.1 (see lines 10 and 13).

Listing 6.6: Main program for frame-based processing using EDMA.

```
#include "DSP_Config.h"
#include "frames.h"

int main()
{
    // initialize all buffers to 0
    ZeroBuffers();

    // initialize EDMA controller
    EDMA_Init();

    // initialize DSP for EDMA operation
    DSP_Init_EDMA();

    // call to StartUp not needed here

    // main loop here, process buffer when ready
    while(1) {
        if(IsBufferReady()) // process buffers in background
            ProcessBuffer();
    }
}
```

The functions `ZeroBuffers` and `IsBufferReady` are unchanged from the non-EDMA versions presented earlier. However, the initialization routines, the single ISR routine (triggered by an EDMA "event"), and the `ProcessBuffer` function are all different from what we have presented before, so we need to examine these. Because we're changing the way the interrupts are assigned, we'll also use a different file that assigns the interrupt vectors; that is, instead of `vectors.asm` we'll use `vectors_EDMA.asm`. We'll also define a different buffer size just for variety. Note that, as with our previous Code Composer Studio projects, the EDMA version of the DSK initialization functions can be found in the file `DSK_Support.c`, which is in the `common_code` directory. This is also where the interrupt vector files are located. Other files for the EDMA version are located in the `ccs\Frame_EDMA_6713` subdirectory for Chapter 6.

We begin by listing the declarations in the EDMA version of the file `ISRs.c`, as they differ somewhat from the non-EDMA version.

Listing 6.7: Declarations from EDMA version of the "ISRs.c" file.

```
#include "DSP_Config.h"
#include "math.h"
#include "frames.h"


// frame buffer declarations
#define BUFFER_COUNT 1024              // buffer length per channel
#define BUFFER_LENGTH BUFFER_COUNT*2   // two channels
#define NUM_BUFFERS   3   // don't change this!

#pragma DATA_SECTION (buffer, "CE0"); // put buffers in SDRAM
Int16 buffer[NUM_BUFFERS][BUFFER_LENGTH];
// 3 buffers used at all times, one being filled from the McBSP,
// one being operated on, and one being emptied to the McBSP
// ready_index --> buffer ready for processing
volatile Int16 buffer_ready = 0, over_run = 0, ready_index = 0;
```

Note that in this EDMA version of the declarations the data buffers in line 11 are declared as type `Int16`, which we have defined as a 16-bit signed integer. In all our past code, we have used buffers of type `float` to take advantage of the ease and flexibility that floating point numbers provide. We will continue to do so here, and the values in these buffers will be converted to type `float` before processing. Why the extra conversion step? Recall that the samples coming in from the ADC (or going out to the DAC) of the codec are integers. In non-EDMA code, the transfer of values to or from the codec and the buffer is performed by the CPU, which takes care of the necessary conversion between floating point and integer data types. However, in the EDMA code the transfer to or from the codec and the buffer is performed without any participation of the CPU, so in effect this is a "brainless" transfer that cannot do any data type conversions. Such conversions require the CPU, so we move the necessary conversion from integer to floating point (and back to integer again) into the `ProcessBuffer` function as will be shown subsequently.

The frame size specified in lines 6 and 7 is 1024 samples per frame (1024 left channel samples and 1024 right channel samples). Previously, we efficiently moved both the left and right channel samples (each 16 bits) in a single 32-bit transfer operation, but by declaring a `union` we were able to individually manipulate the two channels. We accomplish a similar feat here by observing that the data type `Uint32` is twice the length of `Int16`, and you will see that the EDMA hardware is initialized to transfer `Uint32` data types.

We now discuss `EDMA_ISR`, which is the function that actually implements the triple buffering scheme (i.e., enabling the pointer addresses to change as necessary). In the non-

EDMA program, this task was performed by the function Codec_ISR in Listing 6.5. EDMA_ISR is contained in the ISRs.c file located in the ccs\Frame_EDMA_6713 subdirectory for Chapter 6 and is shown below. This code is simpler and faster than the code in Listing 6.5.

Listing 6.8: Function for implementing triple buffering using the EDMA hardware.

```
1  interrupt void EDMA_ISR()  {
       *(volatile Uint32 *)CIPR = 0xf000; // clear all McBSP events
3      if(++ready_index >= NUM_BUFFERS) // update buffer index
           ready_index = 0;
5      if(buffer_ready == 1) // if buffer isn't processed in time
           over_run = 1;
7      buffer_ready = 1; // mark buffer as ready for processing
   }
```

Note that, in the non-EDMA version, the ISR was triggered by an interrupt which was generated for every sample. In the EDMA version, the ISR-like "event" occurs only when the entire frame of samples has been transferred. This event triggers an interrupt which causes interrupt service routine EDMA_ISR to run. Thus, in this example, EDMA_ISR is called 1024 times *less often* than Codec_ISR would be in the non-EDMA program for a frame size (per channel) of 1024. Using the EDMA event allows us to keep all the buffers synchronized just as well as the non-EDMA version.

While we still use an interrupt service routine for the EDMA version shown here, EDMA_ISR is a very short and fast routine that minimizes the interruption of the CPU. It is important to reiterate here that in order to map the vector for the proper interrupt (INT8, triggered by an EDMA event) to the proper address of the EDMA_ISR function, the Code Composer Studio project for this program must include the file vectors_EDMA.asm (provided for you in the common_code directory) *not* the file vectors.asm as was the case in our previous programs that used CPU ISRs.

Because the DSK initialization is slightly different for this EDMA program compared to previous programs, we show the initialization function below.

Listing 6.9: Function for initializing the DSK when using EDMA.

```
   void DSP_Init_EDMA()  {
2      CSR=0x100;                  // disable all interrupts
       IER=0;

4
       Init_6713PLL();
6      Init_AIC23(CodecType);      // initialize codec using McBSP0

8      IER |= 0x0102;              // enable EDMA interrupt (INT8)
       ICR = 0xffff;              // clear all pending interrupts
10     CSR |= 1;                  // set GIE
   }
```

The primary difference in this version compared to the non-EDMA version used before is in line 8, where we enable interrupt 8 for the EDMA hardware (rather than using interrupts 11 and 12 as we did before for the McBSP interrupts). You may want to verify for yourself that vectors_EDMA.asm maps interrupt 8 to the EDMA_ISR function.

The next function we need to discuss, EDMA_Init, is quite a bit more involved. It is contained in the ISRs.c file located in the ccs\Frame_EDMA_6713 subdirectory for Chapter 6 and is shown next.

Listing 6.10: Function for initializing the EDMA hardware.

```
1  void EDMA_Init()   {
       EDMA_params* param;
3
       // McBSP tx event params
5      param = (EDMA_params*)(EVENTE_PARAMS);
       param->options = 0x211E0002;
7      param->source = (Uint32)(&buffer[2][0]);
       param->count = (0 << 16) + (BUFFER_COUNT);
9      param->dest = 0x34000000;
       param->reload_link = (BUFFER_COUNT << 16) + (EVENTN_PARAMS &
           [+]0xFFFF);
11
       // set up first tx link param
13     param = (EDMA_params*)EVENTN_PARAMS;
       param->options = 0x211E0002;
15     param->source = (Uint32)(&buffer[0][0]);
       param->count = (0 << 16) + (BUFFER_COUNT);
17     param->dest = 0x34000000;
       param->reload_link = (BUFFER_COUNT << 16) + (EVENTO_PARAMS &
           [+]0xFFFF);
19
       // set up second tx link param
21     param = (EDMA_params*)EVENTO_PARAMS;
       param->options = 0x211E0002;
23     param->source = (Uint32)(&buffer[1][0]);
       param->count = (0 << 16) + (BUFFER_COUNT);
25     param->dest = 0x34000000;
       param->reload_link = (BUFFER_COUNT << 16) + (EVENTP_PARAMS &
           [+]0xFFFF);
27
       // set up third tx link param
29     param = (EDMA_params*)EVENTP_PARAMS;
       param->options = 0x211E0002;
31     param->source = (Uint32)(&buffer[2][0]);
       param->count = (0 << 16) + (BUFFER_COUNT);
33     param->dest = 0x34000000;
       param->reload_link = (BUFFER_COUNT << 16) + (EVENTN_PARAMS &
           [+]0xFFFF);
35

37     // McBSP rx event params
       param = (EDMA_params*)(EVENTF_PARAMS);
39     param->options = 0x203F0002;
       param->source = 0x34000000;
41     param->count = (0 << 16) + (BUFFER_COUNT);
       param->dest = (Uint32)(&buffer[1][0]);
43     param->reload_link = (BUFFER_COUNT << 16) + (EVENTQ_PARAMS &
           [+]0xFFFF);
```

```
45    // set up first rx link param
      param = (EDMA_params*)EVENTQ_PARAMS;
47    param->options = 0x203F0002;
      param->source = 0x34000000;
49    param->count = (0 << 16) + (BUFFER_COUNT);
      param->dest = (Uint32)(&buffer[2][0]);
51    param->reload_link = (BUFFER_COUNT << 16) + (EVENTR_PARAMS &
         [+]0xFFFF);

53    // set up second rx link param
      param = (EDMA_params*)EVENTR_PARAMS;
55    param->options = 0x203F0002;
      param->source = 0x34000000;
57    param->count = (0 << 16) + (BUFFER_COUNT);
      param->dest = (Uint32)(&buffer[0][0]);
59    param->reload_link = (BUFFER_COUNT << 16) + (EVENTS_PARAMS &
         [+]0xFFFF);

61    // set up third rx link param
      param = (EDMA_params*)EVENTS_PARAMS;
63    param->options = 0x203F0002;
      param->source = 0x34000000;
65    param->count = (0 << 16) + (BUFFER_COUNT);
      param->dest = (Uint32)(&buffer[1][0]);
67    param->reload_link = (BUFFER_COUNT << 16) + (EVENTQ_PARAMS &
         [+]0xFFFF);

69    *(volatile Uint32 *)ECR = 0xf000; // clear all McBSP events
      *(volatile Uint32 *)EER = 0xC000;
71    *(volatile Uint32 *)CIER = 0x8000; // interrupt on rx reload
         [+]only
}
```

To fully understand what this EDMA_Init function does, you should read the TI documentation that describes how to use EDMA, *TMS320C6000 Peripherals Reference Guide* [71], and look at the header file c6x11dsk.h in common_code that contains the various defines for the DSK. If you're a bit rusty regarding structures and pointers in C, now might be a good time to refresh yourself! The EDMA_Init function runs only once, and it is where we specify various necessary parameters such as the source address, the destination address, and the number of elements for each DMA transfer. This function also sets up the links so that a triple buffering scheme is implemented. In the interest of brevity, only a synopsis of the transmit (i.e., output) function is described in any detail. The receive (i.e., input) function operates similarly.

Keep in mind we are still dealing with three buffers as before. The function EDMA_Init sets up two EDMA channels, one to service the McBSP transmitter and one for the McBSP receiver. Each channel of the EDMA has an "event" dedicated to it (as mentioned previously, this relationship is quite similar to that between the CPU and the interrupt lines). Each EDMA transfer is controlled by values set in a parameter RAM block; setting up these RAM blocks is the primary purpose of EDMA_Init. The first block of code (lines 5 to 10) sets the appropriate parameters. The parameter values given in the listing configure the event for the number of elements (which themselves are each 32-bit unsigned integers) specified by `BUFFER_COUNT` (defined in `ISRs.c`), and transfers them to buffer[2],[10] the initial buffer designated for output. The code is written such that when it finishes that transfer, it automatically reconfigures the channel with the information stored at `EVENTN_PARAMS` in the parameter RAM (this is accomplished by the `reload_link` field in line 10). `EVENTN` is set up in the next code block starting at line 13, which configures the EDMA to use buffer[0] and reconfigures the channel with the information stored at `EVENTO_PARAMS` when it finishes. `EVENTO_PARAMS` (starting on line 21) will then cause the EDMA transfer to use buffer[1], and reconfigures the channel with the information stored at `EVENTP_PARAMS` when it finishes. `EVENTP_PARAMS` (starting on line 29) will then cause the EDMA transfer to use buffer[2], and reconfigures the channel with the information stored at `EVENTN_PARAMS` when it finishes, which is effectively a loop back to the original buffer; this cycle of using the three buffers in sequence continues for as long as the program runs. This illustrates an important point: for essentially zero CPU overhead, we can get automatic n-way (in this case 3-way) buffering. The receive channel (see lines 37 to 67) operates in an identical fashion, but it begins with a different buffer (buffer[1]) so we can keep the input and output transfers working on different buffers.

The last few lines of `EDMA_Init` cannot be ignored. Line 69 clears all McBSP events (although we are using only two events—transmit and receive—we might as well clear them all). Line 70 sets the appropriate value in the event enable register. Finally, line 71 is a critical line in that it sets the channel interrupt enable register so that an EDMA "event" occurs when the particular EDMA channel serving the McBSP receive operation finishes transferring a frame, which means that an event is only triggered each time the input frame buffer is full.

Finally, we now show the function `ProcessBuffer` as modified for the EDMA version of the program. This function is where the actual DSP algorithm is implemented. The first thing you will notice is that this version of `ProcessBuffer` is much longer than the non-EDMA version from Listing 6.4. This is due to the need to perform type conversions on the data in the buffers (we also included in the listing other simple examples).

Listing 6.11: An abbreviated version of the `ProcessBuffer` function from the EDMA version of the "ISRs.c" file.

```
void ProcessBuffer()    {
    Int16 *pBuf = buffer[ready_index];
    static float Left[BUFFER_COUNT], Right[BUFFER_COUNT];
    float *pL = Left, *pR = Right;
    Int32 i;
    float temp;

    WriteDigitalOutputs(0); // set digital outputs low for time
        [+]measurement

    for(i = 0;i < BUFFER_COUNT;i++) { // extract data to float
        [+]buffers
        *pR++ = *pBuf++;
        *pL++ = *pBuf++;
    }

    pL = Left; // reinitialize pointers
    pR = Right;
```

---

[10]Recall that `&buffer[2][0]` is the address of the first element of `buffer[2]`.

```
18  /* gain
        for(i=0;i < BUFFER_COUNT;i++){
20          *pL++ *= 0.5;
            *pR++ *= 2.0;
22      }  */

24  /* zero out left channel
        for(i=0;i < BUFFER_COUNT;i++){
26          *pL = 0.0;
            pL++;
28      }  */

30  /* zero out right channel
        for(i=0;i < BUFFER_COUNT;i++){
32          *pR = 0.0;
            pR++;
34      }    */

36  /* reverb on right channel
        for(i=0;i < BUFFER_COUNT-4;i++){
38          *pR = *pR + (0.9 * pR[2]) + (0.45 * pR[4]);
            pR++;
40      }
    */

42
    /* addition and subtraction   */
44      for(i=0;i < BUFFER_COUNT;i++){
            temp = *pL;
46          *pL = temp + *pR; // left = L+R
            *pR = temp - *pR; // right = L-R
48          pL++;
            pR++;
50      }

52  /* add a sinusoid
        for(i=0;i < BUFFER_COUNT;i++){
54          *pL = *pL + 1024*sinf(0.5*i);
            pL++;
56      }
    */
58
    /* AM modulation
60      for(i=0;i < BUFFER_COUNT;i++){
            *pR = *pL * *pR * (1/32768.0); // right = L*R
62          *pL = *pL + *pR; // left = L*(1+R)
            pL++;
64          pR++;
        }
66  */
```

```
68      pBuf = buffer[ready_index];
        pL = Left;
70      pR = Right;

72      for(i = 0;i < BUFFER_COUNT;i++) { // pack into buffer after
            [+]bounding
            *pBuf++ = _spint(*pR++ * 65536) >> 16;
74          *pBuf++ = _spint(*pL++ * 65536) >> 16;
        }

76

        pBuf = buffer[ready_index];

78

        WriteDigitalOutputs(1); // set digital output bit 0 high for
            [+]time measurement

80

        buffer_ready = 0; // signal we are done
82 }
```

Many examples of simple DSP algorithms are included in this code; all but one have been commented out. You can see that the actual DSP algorithm, which is just the same example of adding and subtracting the left and right channels, is implemented in lines 44 to 50.

In line 2, a pointer is declared that is set to the address of the frame buffer of data type Int16 that was previously filled using EDMA and is now designated to be ready for processing. Line 3 declares two buffers of floats that will be used to contain the left and right frame data, after conversion to floating point. Line 4 declares pointers that will be used to manipulate individual samples (in floating point format) in the frames. Line 8 and line 79 are used only for testing and evaluation purposes during code development. The actual conversion from Int16 to float occurs in lines 10 to 13; the C compiler ensures that, when the CPU transfers the integer values pointed to by *pBuf into the floating point locations pointed to by *pR for the right channel and *pL for the left channel, the appropriate conversion takes place. Note the transfer and conversion alternates first right channel then left channel, which is the order in which the data was stored in the EDMA buffer in the first place. We could also have used a "cast" from Int16 to float here, but there is no advantage and we prefer this method. While it may seem inefficient to transfer from one buffer to another in this way, it is in fact very fast. The CPU savings realized by the EDMA transfers far outweigh the CPU time required for this buffer transfer.

Lines 15 and 16 set the appropriate pointers back to the first element of the arrays of floating point values for the left and right channels, and the actual DSP algorithm can then commence. Similarly, lines 68 to 70 reset the appropriate pointers after the DSP algorithm has completed. To convert the now "processed" floating point values back into integer values suitable for EDMA transfer to the codec, the code in lines 72 to 75 uses bounds checking (a good idea) via the intrinsic _spint function. Line 77 resets the *pBuf pointer after the packing operation performed in lines 72 to 75.

6.5   Summary of Frame-Based Processing

This chapter has introduced you to a new way of thinking about how to implement DSP programs. While the sample-by-sample processing of earlier chapters is typically easier to understand, there are many reasons to consider frame-based processing. First and foremost, the speed and efficiency of frame-based processing—especially when using EDMA transfers—cannot be matched using sample-by-sample processing. Second, certain DSP algorithms require that a contiguous block of "new" samples be available at once, which is not possible with sample-by-sample processing.

The disadvantages of frame-based processing are somewhat greater code complexity, and a time latency equal to NT_s where N is the frame size and $T_s = 1/F_s$ is the time between samples. While the latency is unavoidable, code complexity should not deter you. Most users can adapt the example code given in this chapter to create a "skeleton" of a frame-based program where they only need to adjust the frame size and the operations performed in the ProcessBuffer function to produce their own customized program. Keep in mind that nearly every DSP text discusses theory on a sample-by-sample basis, but that most production real-time DSP code is written on a frame-by-frame basis. Having an understanding of frame-based processing is therefore highly recommended.

The next chapter will introduce frame-based DSP programs that are more complicated (and more useful) than the simple $L + R$ and $L - R$ used in this chapter.

6.6   Follow-On Challenges

Consider extending what you have learned.

1. Replace the addition and subtraction of the left and right channels in ProcessBuffer with some other operation of your choosing. Try this with both the interrupt-driven and the EDMA versions of the program.

2. Making no other changes to the non-EDMA version of the triple buffer program, increase the size of the buffer until the process can no longer "keep up" with the real-time schedule.

3. Making no other changes to the EDMA version of the triple buffer program, increase the size of the buffer until the process can no longer "keep up" with the real-time schedule. Is there a difference with what you found for the non-EDMA version?

4. If you are (or are willing to become) familiar with the profiler capability of Code Composer Studio, you can use this to measure the increase in program speed of the EDMA version compared to the non-EDMA version of the program.

5. Some algorithms implement an "overlap and add" process where some portion of the processed frame is combined with some portion of the prior frame. How would you implement such a process with your own code?

6.7   Problems

1. Describe the difference between sample-based DSP and frame-based DSP.

2. What are some types of "overhead" that are reduced using frame-based processing compared to sample-based processing?

3. What are some of the practical considerations that help determine the frame size for a particular DSP algorithm?

4. Suppose frame-based processing is used to provide visual data to a video screen. Assume the sample frequency is $F_s = 48$ kHz, and the screen updates must occur at a minimum of 60 frames per second. Ignoring time lost to overhead, what is the maximum frame size that could be used to support the desired display rate?

5. What are the definitions of the acronyms "DMA" and "EDMA" used in this chapter?

6. Describe the difference between a non-DMA implementation of a DSP algorithm and a DSP implementation that uses DMA.

Chapter 7

Digital Filters Using Frames

7.1 Theory

AS discussed in Chapter 6, using frame-based processing greatly increases the efficiency of DSP programs. The CPU performing the signal processing algorithm is only interrupted at the end of a frame rather than at every sample. In this chapter, we will show how frames can be used for time-domain digital filtering similar to the filters we discussed in Chapter 3.

Recall that a time-domain implementation of a digital filter involves an iterative calculation of the filter's difference equation. The only change in this chapter is that we will be dealing with our samples a frame at a time rather than a sample at a time. For simplicity, we will restrict this discussion to FIR filters, but IIR filters can be implemented with frames in essentially the same manner.

7.2 winDSK Demonstration

The winDSK8 program does not provide an equivalent function; all the filtering in winDSK8 is accomplished sample by sample to keep the code very simple.

7.3 MATLAB Implementation

Frame-based filtering in MATLAB® can be accomplished using resources such as the Data Acquistion Toolbox or by using Simulink®, both available from The MathWorks, or by using the MATLAB-to-DSK interface software included with this book. See Section 2.4.1 and Section 2.4.2 for examples, and Appendix E for more details.

7.4 DSK Implementation in C

To demonstrate frame-based digital filtering on the DSK, we provide a C program that implements a filter similar to the FIR filters shown in Chapter 3. Before discussing the C code, however, it's important to understand the process required to implement an FIR filter in a frame-based manner.

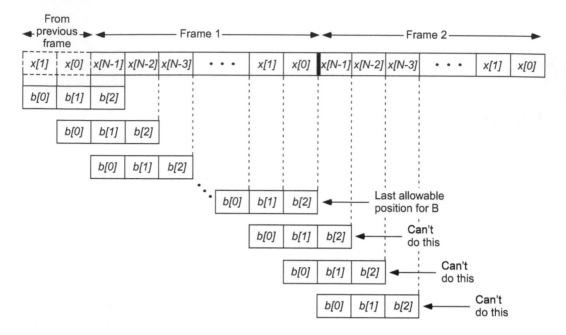

Figure 7.1: Implementing a second-order FIR filter with a frame-based approach. Note that the b coefficients can't "slide" past the edge of Frame 1 without some programming "tricks."

7.4.1   Understanding the FIR Process for Frames

Using triple-buffered EDMA-transferred frames for I/O will make the program far more efficient and faster than the sample-based versions discussed in Chapter 3. However, the program will have available to it a fixed-size frame of samples at any given time, which complicates the filter convolution at the "edges" of the frame. Recall from Chapter 3 that the output $y[n]$ of a digital filter is calculated by performing the discrete-time convolution of the input $x[n]$ with the filter's impulse response $h[n]$. When written as the difference equation for an FIR filter, the numerator values $b[n]$ are equivalent to the impulse response $h[n]$. Making this substitution (b for h) and remembering that an FIR filter of order K has $K+1$ coefficients, the convolution sum becomes the general form of the FIR difference equation, namely,

$$y[n] = \sum_{k=0}^{K} b[k]x[n-k] \quad \text{for} \quad n = 0, 1, 2, \ldots, N-1,$$

where N represents the length of $x[n]$ and $K+1$ is the length of $b[n]$.[1] This equation tells us that to calculate the values for an entire frame's worth of filter output, we will need to "slide" the filter coefficients "across" the entire frame of filter input, multiplying and summing point-by-point as indicated by the equation above. This process is depicted in Figure 7.1, where it can be seen that there is a potential problem at the "edges" of the frame.

There is only a single frame of input data available at any given time. In Figure 7.1, the values in Frame 2 aren't available yet, and the values from the previous frame shown to

---

[1]There is nothing magical about the letters K, N, M, and so on. Sometimes N is used to represent the length of the input data as we do here; another time N might represent the order of a filter. The context of the discussion should make clear what the letters represent.

the left of Frame 1 would be "gone" by now unless we use some programming "tricks" to keep those values around. If we ignore the "edges" of the frame, we would be ignoring the initial and final conditions of the filter for that frame of data, and we would not correctly implement the filter. For audio applications, the result of ignoring these "edge" problems would be heard as a distinctive "clicking" or "popping" noise in the output occurring at the frame rate.

7.4.2 How to Avoid the "Edge" Problems

How do we fix this problem? We create a buffer large enough to contain both the frame of current input data and also have room to hold the necessary edge values from the previous frame. In Figure 7.1 this would mean an array that includes both the values labeled "From previous frame" and the values labeled Frame 1. We "slide" the filter starting from the left most element (the first "From previous frame" element) until the right edge of the filter reaches the end of Frame 1, indicated in the figure by a thick, dark line. We can't go any farther than this because the data for Frame 2 isn't available yet. Before the current frame (Frame 1) is transferred out and the next frame (Frame 2) comes in to overwrite it, we copy the right edge values of Frame 1 into the locations labeled "From previous frame." The next frame values are stored in the remaining locations, so we have effectively "saved" the values from the previous frame. In this way, the edge effects are eliminated, as will be shown in the actual C code.

7.4.3 Explanation of the C Code

As an illustrative example, we will show you a program that implements a simple low-pass FIR filter that provides a similar output result to that of the FIR filters discussed in Chapter 3. But the method used to obtain our output will be to use frame-based processing, written in such a way that we avoid the "edge" problems discussed above. Thus, the associated "clicking" or "popping" noise in the output is avoided. Before you read the program listing, you may want to glance back at Figure 7.1.

The C program to implement this as frame-based code can be found in the ccs\ FiltFrame directory of Chapter 7. Be sure to inspect the full code listings in this directory to understand the complete working of the program.[2] Here we simply point out some highlights. The discussion which follows assumes you have read and are familiar with the explanation of frame-based processing given in Chapter 6.

Realistically, you would use MATLAB or some other filter design program to determine your filter coefficients. To easily use FIR filter coefficients generated by the filter design tools in MATLAB, you can use the script file named fir_dump2c.m that is located in the MatlabExports directory for Appendix E (there are other script files in the same directory for IIR filters). As discussed in Chapter 3, this script creates two files needed by your C program, typically named coeff.h and coeff.c. These files define N, representing the order of the filter, and $B[N + 1]$, the array of filter coefficients.

The program we provide makes use of the EDMA capabilities of the DSK. This C code is almost identical to the EDMA version of the frame-based C code described in Chapter 6. The only differences are the need to include coeff.h and coeff.c in your project, and the changes described below to the ProcessBuffer() routine in the ISRs.c file. The contents of coeff.h and coeff.c were discussed in Chapter 3. The code for the ProcessBuffer() routine is shown in Listing 7.1.

---

[2]Look also in the DSK_Support.c file in the common_code directory for initialization functions shared by multiple programs.

Listing 7.1: `ProcessBuffer()` routine for implementing a frame-based FIR filter.

```c
void ProcessBuffer()    {
    Int16 *pBuf = buffer[ready_index];
    // extra buffer room for convolution "edge effects"
    // N is filter order from coeff.h
    static float Left[BUFFER_COUNT+N]={0};
    static float Right[BUFFER_COUNT+N]={0};
    float *pL = Left, *pR = Right;
    float yLeft, yRight;
    Int32 i, j, k;

    // offset pointers to start filling after N elements
    pR += N;
    pL += N;

    // extract data to float buffers
    for(i = 0;i < BUFFER_COUNT;i++) {
    // order is important here: must go right first then left
        *pR++ = *pBuf++;
        *pL++ = *pBuf++;
    }

    // reinitialize pointer before FOR loop
    pBuf = buffer[ready_index];

//////////////////////////////////////////
// Implement FIR filter
// Ensure COEFF.C is part of project
//////////////////////////////////////////
    for(i=0;i < BUFFER_COUNT;i++){
        yLeft  = 0;                // initialize the L output value
        yRight = 0;                // initialize the R output value

        for(j=0,k=i+N;j <= N;j++,k--){
          yLeft  += Left[k] * B[j];    // perform the L dot-product
          yRight += Right[k] * B[j];   // perform the R dot-product
        }

        // pack into buffer after bounding (first right then left)
        *pBuf++ = _spint(yRight * 65536) >> 16;
        *pBuf++ = _spint(yLeft * 65536) >> 16;
    }

    // save end values at end of buffer array for next pass
    //  by placing at beginning of buffer array
    for(i=BUFFER_COUNT,j=0;i < BUFFER_COUNT+N;i++,j++){
        Left[j]=Left[i];
        Right[j]=Right[i];
    }
```

```
50 //////// end of FIR routine ///////////

52     // reinitialize pointer
       pBuf = buffer[ready_index];

54
       buffer_ready = 0; // signal we are done
56 }
```

The key parts of the code that differ from the EDMA code in Chapter 6 are:

- (lines 5–6) declaring the arrays to be BUFFER_COUNT+N, which leaves enough room for the edge values that need to be saved;

- (lines 12–13) advancing the pointers so that the incoming data doesn't overwrite the edge values from the previous frame;

- (lines 33–36) using different array index values to implement the convolution properly across the frame; and

- (lines 45–48) copying the edge values of the current frame to the beginning of the buffer so they will be available when the next frame comes in.

Now that you understand the code...

Go ahead and copy all of the files into a separate directory. If you wish to design your own FIR filter using MATLAB rather than using the provided filter (a simple low-pass filter), use the script file fir_dump2c.m that can be found in the **MatlabExports** directory of Appendix E and was first discussed in Chapter 3. Copy any new versions of coeff.h and coeff.c that you create into your project directory before proceeding. When ready, open the project in CCS and "Rebuild All." Once the build is complete, "Load Program" into the DSK and click on "Run." Your frame-based FIR filter is now running on the DSK.

7.5   Follow-On Challenges

Consider extending what you have learned.

1. Compare the sample-based FIR code to the frame-based FIR code. Which do you predict could handle the higher-order filter in real time? Try to get the sample-based FIR code to break the real-time schedule by using a large-order filter; try the same filter with the frame-based code.

2. Many FIR filters exhibit some form of symmetry in the coefficients to ensure linear phase response. For example, $b[0] = b[N-1]$, $b[1] = b[N-2]$, $b[2] = b[N-3]$, and so on. Modify the code provided in this chapter to take advantage of this symmetry.

3. In addition to symmetry, some FIR filters also exhibit a regular pattern of zero-valued coefficients (such as every other value). Modify the code provided in this chapter to take advantage of this fact.

4. This chapter demonstrated an FIR filter using frames. Implement an IIR filter using frames.

7.6 Problems

1. Suppose an FIR filter of order $N = 30$ is implemented using frames. Assume the sample frequency is $F_s = 48$ kHz, and the frame size is 1024 (per channel) as defined by BUFFER_COUNT in the C code. If the "edge effects" described in this chapter are not avoided by increasing the size of the Left and Right buffers, how many times per second would a "clicking" or "popping" noise (due to edge effects) be heard in the output?

2. Suppose an FIR filter of order $N = 30$ is implemented using frames. Assume the sample frequency is $F_s = 48$ kHz, and the frame size is 1024 (per channel) as defined by BUFFER_COUNT in the C code. Further assume that the "edge effects" described in this chapter are avoided by increasing the size of the Left and Right buffers as needed, but that the programmer neglected the step of copying the end values of the buffers to the beginning of the buffers before the new frame data arrives. How many times per second would the output be in error, and for how long would it be in error?

3. Assume the sample frequency is $F_s = 48$ kHz, and the frame size is 1024 (per channel) as defined by BUFFER_COUNT in the C code for the frame-based approach. Compare the time available to the DSP to implement an FIR filter (on both the left and right channels) using a frame-based approach versus a sample-by-sample approach. Neglect overhead in your answer.

Chapter 8

The Fast Fourier Transform

8.1 Theory

THE fast Fourier transform (FFT) is just what the name says it is: a fast way for computers to calculate the Fourier transform, specifically the discrete Fourier transform (DFT). The introduction of the FFT algorithm by Cooley and Tukey in 1965 revolutionized signal processing and has had an enormous effect on engineering and applied science in general [1]. This chapter is by no means a treatise on the FFT. Despite the fact that we will only cover a few of the major points, this is still a long chapter, but we encourage you to read it completely. For more details about the FFT, see [2, 4, 72].

Having a fast way to calculate the DFT has many advantages. We will see in Chapter 9 how it can be used for practical spectral analysis. In this chapter, we investigate how the FFT can be used for efficiently implementing digital filters.

8.1.1 Defining the FFT

Before proceeding with a discussion of this application of the FFT, we first need to briefly discuss the DFT and how the FFT is faster. The N-point DFT for $k = 0, 1, \ldots, N-1$ is defined as

$$X[k] = \sum_{n=0}^{N-1} x[n]e^{-j2\pi kn/N} \quad = \quad \sum_{n=0}^{N-1} x[n]W_N^{kn}$$

where the "twiddle factor" notation $W_N = \exp\left(-j\frac{2\pi}{N}\right)$ is often used for a more compact form. This equation is identical for the FFT; we simply use an efficient programming method to implement it. The inverse DFT or FFT is defined by

$$x[n] = \frac{1}{N}\sum_{n=0}^{N-1} X[k]e^{j2\pi kn/N} \quad = \quad \frac{1}{N}\sum_{n=0}^{N-1} X[k]W_N^{-kn} \ .$$

Some books may show the $1/N$ factor as part of the FFT definition rather than the inverse FFT definition, and some even show a $1/\sqrt{N}$ factor in *both* definitions. All three forms of the definition are correct, since $1/N$ is just a scale factor to ensure invertibility.

8.1.2 The Twiddle Factors

The only difference between the FFT and the inverse FFT (IFFT) is the division by N and the negative power of the twiddle factors; thus, the same basic algorithm can be used for

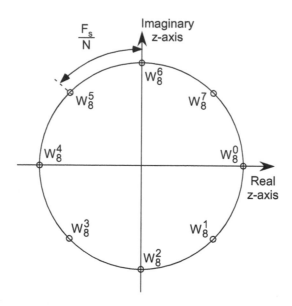

Figure 8.1: The placement of twiddle factor points for the DFT or FFT.

both. Note that the integer powers of W_N form a periodic sequence of numbers, having a period of N. That is, $W_N^n = W_N^{n+N}$. Since in the DFT and FFT definition both k and n in W_N^{kn} are always integers, the same set of twiddle factors appears over and over again. For example, in a 2-point FFT the only two twiddle factors for any of the positive k values are

$$W_2^0 = \exp\left(-j\frac{2\pi(0)}{2}\right) = 1,$$

$$W_2^1 = \exp\left(-j\frac{2\pi(1)}{2}\right) = -1.$$

Likewise, for a 4-point FFT the only four twiddle factors for all the positive values of k are $W_4^0 = 1$, $W_4^1 = -j$, $W_4^2 = -1$, $W_4^3 = j$. To visualize this, we can plot W_N^n on a circle (analogous to the unit circle on the z-plane). Figure 8.1 shows where all the twiddle factor points would be for an 8-point FFT given any positive value of k. This can be thought of as a vector rotating clockwise along the unit circle, and the spacing of the twiddle factors in real-world frequency is always F_s/N, where F_s is the sample frequency.[1] For W_N^{-kn} used in the IFFT, the vector would be rotating *counter*clockwise, and $W_8^{-1} = W_8^7$, $W_8^{-2} = W_8^6$, $\ldots$, $W_8^{-7} = W_8^1$. We take advantage of the periodicity of the twiddle factors to implement the FFT.

8.1.3   The FFT Process

The main idea behind the FFT developed by Cooley and Tukey is that when the length N of the DFT is not a prime number, the calculation can be decomposed into a number of shorter length DFTs. The total number of multiplications and additions required for all the shorter-length DFTs is fewer than the number required for the single full-length DFT. Each of these shorter-length DFTs can then be further decomposed into a number of even shorter DFTs, and so on, until the final DFTs are of a length that is a prime factor of N.

---

[1]Note that F_s/N is the best frequency resolution possible for the FFT or DFT.

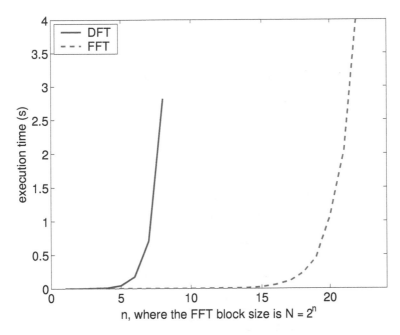

Figure 8.2: Relative calculation time for the "brute-force" DFT versus a commercially available radix-2 FFT routine. The data plotted is the averaged empirical timing results from a desktop workstation. The specific execution time isn't important, only the comparison between the DFT and FFT.

Then these shortest DFTs are calculated in the normal fashion. The opposite order can be used, starting with the smallest DFTs and building (recombining) into larger ones for an equivalent savings. For the radix-2 FFT (a common type), the length of the FFT must be a power of 2. If $N = 8$, for example, the FFT would decompose this into two 4-point FFTs, which are each decomposed into two 2-point FFTs (for a total of four 2-point FFTs), and the calculation is complete. Or it could perform four 2-point DFTs, using these results to compute two 4-point DFTs for the final result. The former method is called *decimation-in-frequency*, and the latter method is called *decimation-in-time*. With appropriate summing and reuse of intermediate results, as well as taking advantage of the periodicity of the twiddle factors, the FFT can be performed at a tremendous increase in efficiency compared to the "brute-force" DFT. The number of complex mathematical operations required to calculate an N-point DFT is proportional to N^2; for the same N-point radix-2 FFT, it would be proportional to $N \log_2 N$. Thus, for a 512-point example, the DFT would require on the order of 262,144 complex mathematical operations, while the FFT would require only 4,608 operations—which is more than 50 times faster than the DFT! For larger DFTs, the difference is even more dramatic. The empirical speedup provided by the FFT on a typical computer is shown graphically in Figure 8.2. Note from the figure that the FFT can perform the DFT on $N = 2^{20} = 1,048,576$ data points in the same amount of time that the "brute-force" DFT would take for $N = 2^7 = 128$ data points. That's a speedup factor of 8,192, which shows why the FFT is so widely used.

The traditional way to show the FFT algorithm is through the use of "butterfly diagrams," which depict the decomposition, intermediate summing, and application of the twiddle factors. These are shown in Figures 8.3, 8.4, and 8.5 for a 2-point, 4-point, and 8-point decimation-in-time FFT. It is *very* beneficial to manually trace your way through these small butterfly diagrams, until you get a feel for what is going on.

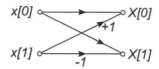

Figure 8.3: Butterfly diagram of a decimation-in-time radix-2 FFT for $N = 2$. Any branches not marked have a gain of $+1$.

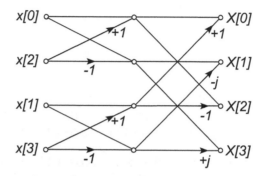

Figure 8.4: Butterfly diagram of a decimation-in-time radix-2 FFT for $N = 4$. Any branches not marked have a gain of $+1$.

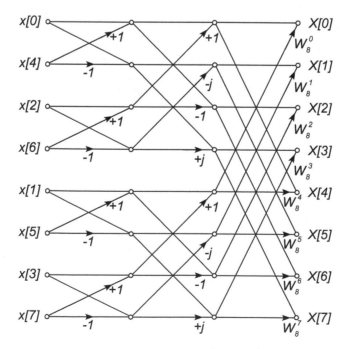

Figure 8.5: Butterfly diagram of a decimation-in-time radix-2 FFT for $N = 8$. Any branches not marked have a gain of $+1$.

8.1.4 Bit-Reversed Addressing

The ordering of the input values on the left side of the butterfly figures may seem strange to you. To account for the most efficient way to perform the butterfly operation by computer for a decimation-in-time FFT, the order of the input values must be rearranged into what is known as *bit-reversed* addressing. You know that to address (or index) N values for an $N = 2^n$ FFT input array requires n bits if the index is expressed in binary from. For bit-reversed addressing, the binary index number of the data array element at the input is reversed left to right. For example, in Figure 8.5, you might expect the second input element to be $x[1]$. With the index expressed as a 3-bit binary number this would be $x[001]$. Reversing the bits of the index yields $x[100]$, which in decimal notation is $x[4]$; this is the actual second input element in bit-reversed addressing. The dual of a decimation-in-time FFT is a decimation-in-frequency FFT. The only difference in the butterfly for a decimation-in-frequency FFT is that the order of the butterfly sections is reversed, the twiddle factors swap positions, and the output values rather than the input values appear in bit-reversed order. There is no intrinsic advantage of one over the other and the implementation choice is typically arbitrary.

When we use bit-reversed addressing on either the input or output side of a butterfly, we can perform what is called an "in-place" calculation, which means the same memory array that holds the input data is used to hold the output data. The bit-reversed addressing ensures that no input data element gets overwritten by an output value until it is no longer needed for any more calculations of the FFT.

8.1.5 Using the FFT for Filtering

As the order of a filter increases, the time required to calculate the output value associated with each input sample also increases. As we saw in Chapter 7, frame-based filtering helps increase the overall efficiency of the filtering operation by reducing the time required to pass samples to and from the DSP CPU. Yet we are still calculating a time domain convolution. If we can also take advantage of the FFT to perform the *equivalent* of convolution, then we can save even more time and thus implement even longer (higher-order) filters in real-time. Using the FFT in this way is generally referred to as *fast convolution*.

Frequency-domain techniques such as this extend the concepts first introduced in Chapter 3. We know the filtering equation is really just the convolution integral

$$y(t) = \int\limits_{0}^{\infty} h(\tau)x(t-\tau)\,d\tau.$$

If we take the Fourier transform of the convolution integral, we obtain

$$Y(j\omega) = H(j\omega)X(j\omega).$$

Notice that the original convolution operation in the time domain has been converted into a multiplication operation in the frequency domain. Similarly, the discrete-time version of the convolution integral (the convolution sum) is

$$y[n] = \sum_{m=0}^{M-1} h[m]x[n-m] \quad \text{for} \quad n = 0, 1, 2, \ldots, N-1,$$

where, in this context, M is the *length* of the filter (thus, the filter order is $M-1$) and N

is the length of the data.[2] The FFT of the convolution sum is

$$Y[k] = H[k]X[k].$$

Again notice that the convolution operation in the discrete-time domain has been converted into a multiplication operation in the discrete-frequency domain.

We might expect that to calculate the digital filter's output back in the time domain, we can use the IFFT and calculate

$$\begin{aligned} y[k] &= \text{IFFT}\{Y[k]\} \\ &= \text{IFFT}\{H[k]X[k]\} \\ &= \text{IFFT}\{\text{FFT}\{h[n]\}\text{FFT}\{x[n]\}\}. \end{aligned}$$

Using this approach, we would take the FFT of our filter's impulse response, $h[n]$, and multiply the result by the FFT of the input signal, $x[n]$. We would then take the inverse FFT of the product. As we shall see below, this approach requires a slight modification to avoid the effects of circular convolution but otherwise will work splendidly. As the lengths of $h[n]$ and $x[n]$ increase, there comes a point beyond which the frequency-domain transform technique of fast convolution will require fewer mathematical operations than the traditional time-domain convolution approach. For a constant coefficient filter (non-time varying), additional savings can be gained by realizing that the transform of the filter's impulse response need only be calculated once.

8.1.6   Avoiding Circular Convolution

Remembering that for discrete-time systems the transform-based approach results in *circular* convolution instead of *linear* convolution, we must zero pad both $h[n]$ and $x[n]$. When two sequences $h[n]$ and $x[n]$ are properly padded, the circular convolution of the two that is due to multiplication in the frequency domain provides the exact same result as would the linear convolution of $h[n]$ and $x[n]$ in the time domain. Without such padding, circular convolution is *not* equivalent to linear convolution. This can be seen in the MATLAB® listing shown below.

Listing 8.1: A MATLAB listing that compares linear and circular convolution.

```
  % Simulation inputs
2 h = [1  2  3  2  1];       % impulse response declaration
  x = [1  3  -2  4  -3];     % input term declaration

4
  % Calculated and output terms
6 y = conv(h, x)
  yLength = length(y)
8 circularConvolutionResult = ifft(fft(h).*fft(x))
  circularConvolutionResultLength=length(circularConvolutionResult)
```

In this listing, line 2 declares the impulse response, $h[n]$, of a fourth-order filter and line 3 declares the input sequence, $x[n]$, which will be "processed" by the filter. Line 6 performs the linear convolution with MATLAB's built-in conv() command, and line 7 determines the length of the convolution result. Line 8 performs the *circular* convolution (by using the FFT, point-by-point multiplication, and the IFFT), and line 9 determines the length of that resulting sequence. The MATLAB command window results are similar to

---

[2]As mentioned earlier, it is common practice in DSP texts to use letters such as N as the filter order in some contexts and as the filter length in other contexts. From the nature of the discussion, it should be clear to the reader which definition is being used.

```
y = 1  5  7  11  6  5  -3  -2  -3
yLength = 9
circularConvolutionResult = 6.0000  2.0000  5.0000  8.0000  6.0000
circularConvolutionResultLength = 5.
```

At this point, two very important observations are required.

1. The outputs of the two processes, y and `circularConvolutionResult`, are not the same sequence.

2. The resulting sequences, y and `circularConvolutionResult`, are not the same length.

As stated earlier, zero padding (sometimes just called padding), can turn circular convolution into the equivalent of linear convolution. To accomplish this task, we must

1. Ensure that the padded lengths of $h[n]$ and $x[n]$ are the same.

2. Adjust the padded lengths of $h[n]$ and $x[n]$ to be at least equal to the length of the resulting linear convolution of the sequences $h[n]$ and $x[n]$, given by

$$N + M - 1$$

where N is the unpadded length of $x[n]$ and M is the unpadded length of $h[n]$. In the previous MATLAB code listing output, $N = 5$ and $M = 5$. Therefore,

$$N + M - 1 = 5 + 5 - 1 = 9.$$

Notice that this result, 9, is the length of the linear convolution, yLength, calculated previously by MATLAB. So, to convert the circular convolution to the equivalent of linear convolution, we must pad $h[n]$ and $x[n]$ to at least a length of 9. The updated MATLAB code listing to accomplish this task is shown below.

Listing 8.2: A MATLAB listing that demonstrates how to convert circular convolution into the equivalent of linear convolution.

```
1  % Simulation inputs
   format short g         % set format to short g
3  h = [1 2 3 2 1];       % impulse response declaration
   x = [1 3 -2 4 -3];     % input term declaration
5
   hZeroPad = [h zeros(1, 4)];
7  xZeroPad = [x zeros(1, 4)];

9  % Calculated and output terms
   y = conv(h, x)
11 yLength = length(y)
   circularConvolutionResult=ifft(fft(hZeroPad).*fft(xZeroPad));
13 circularConvolutionResult=real(circularConvolutionResult)
   circularConvolutionResultLength=length(circularConvolutionResult)
```

In this listing, line 2 changes the display format to suppress trailing zeros while lines 6 and 7 pad $h[n]$ and $x[n]$ by appending 4 zeros onto the original sequences. The MATLAB command window results are similar to

```
y = 1  5  7  11  6  5  -3  -2  -3
yLength = 9
circularConvolutionResult = 1  5  7  11  6  5  -3  -2  -3
circularConvolutionResultLength = 9.
```

Notice that the results, and therefore the lengths of both techniques, are the same. Did you also notice that in line 13 of the listing the MATLAB command `real` was added to remove unwanted imaginary terms from the answer? Since we know that the convolution of two real-valued sequences, namely, $h[n]$ and $x[n]$, is another real valued sequence, these imaginary terms are the result of numerical "noise" that occurs due to limited numerical precision during the transform process. Since the imaginary part of the filter's output should be zero, the resulting imaginary noise should be ignored.

Note that the padding may also be driven by the requirements of the FFT. For a radix-2 FFT, the input array length must be a power of 2. In our example above, if we were using a radix-2 FFT, we would need to pad M and N so that their padded length L is the next higher power of two such that $L \geq (N + M - 1)$. In the above example, $N + M - 1 = 9$, so we would need to pad to $L = 16$. A time-domain convolution requires on the order of NM operations, but the fast convolution using an L-point radix-2 FFT requires on the order of $(8L \log_2(L) + 4L)$ operations [62].

8.1.7   Real-Time Fast Convolution

The techniques developed above work well for filtering short- or medium-length sequences, but what about filtering very long sequences? How about real-time systems, where nearly infinite length sequences (sequences where the input may persist for days or months) are common? We need to find a variation on the fast convolution described above to perform the filtering operation since we don't want to store all the input samples in memory before processing. Additionally, the wait or latency associated with gathering all the samples of a long sequence before we commence the actual filtering operation defeats the intent of real-time DSP.

To filter very long signal sequences, we must, therefore, partition the signal into shorter length sequences that we can filter individually and then recombine into a complete, filtered version of the original signal. A number of techniques have been developed to perform this operation, but we will limit our discussion to the two most common: overlap-add and overlap-save techniques. In our brief discussion of these two techniques we will use only short input sequences for both $h[n]$ and $x[n]$ in the hope that this will improve the understandability of the processes required, but the technique is intended for very long sequences of data.

Overlap-Add

In Figure 8.6, $x[n]$ is a 30-point sequence that is padded out to 36 points ($0 \leq n \leq 35$) to allow for a uniform x-axis labeling for all of the subplots. In this example, we wish to convolve $x[n]$ with the impulse response $h[n]$ of the sixth-order lowpass filter shown in Figure 8.7. Obviously, the length of $h[n]$ is $M = 7$. The second ($x_0[n]$), third ($x_1[n]$), and fourth ($x_2[n]$) subplots in Figure 8.6 partition $x[n]$ into 3 non-overlapping segments, each segment being 10 samples in length ($N = 10$). This partition length ($N = 10$ samples) was chosen based on the desire to use a 16-point FFT. Remember that the output of a convolution operation has a length equal to $L = N + M - 1$. For this example, the total length is $L = 16$, the filter length is $M = 7$, and therefore our data length is required to be $N = 10$ samples. The fifth ($y_0[n]$), sixth ($y_1[n]$), and seventh ($y_2[n]$) subplots in Figure 8.6 show the results of the transform-based filtering operation (fast convolution using the FFT

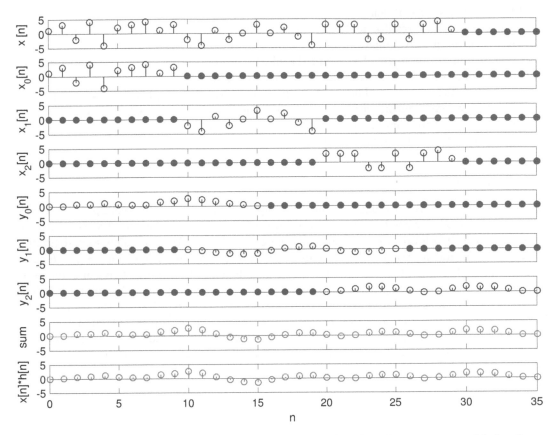

Figure 8.6: The overlap-add fast convolution process. Filled circles are zero padded values.

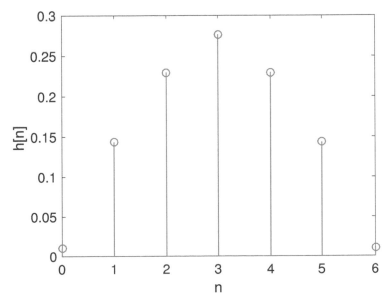

Figure 8.7: The impulse response associated with the lowpass filter used in the overlap-add fast convolution process.

and IFFT) of $x_0[n]$, $x_1[n]$, and $x_2[n]$ with $h[n]$. Notice that the filtering of $x_0[n]$, a 10 sample sequence, using $h[n]$, results in the 16 sample sequence $y_0[n]$. The last 6 samples of $y_0[n]$ overlap with the first 6 samples of $y_1[n]$. Similarly, the last 6 samples of $y_1[n]$ overlap with the first 6 samples of $y_2[n]$. To obtain the filter's proper output, the overlapping regions must be added *prior* to these samples being sent to the DSP system's output device (hence the name, "overlap-add"). The final subplot in Figure 8.6 is provided for comparison and is the system's output using traditional time-domain convolution. These last two subplots demonstrate that the transform-based technique and the traditional convolution sum technique return the same result.

Overlap-Save

In Figure 8.8, $x[n]$ is once again a 36-point input sequence. In this example, our desire is to convolve $x[n]$ with the impulse response of the same sixth-order lowpass filter as before, shown in Figure 8.7; therefore, the length of $h[n]$ is $M = 7$. The second ($x_0[n]$), third ($x_1[n]$), and fourth ($x_2[n]$) subplots in Figure 8.8 partition $x[n]$ into 3 *overlapping* segments, each segment being 16 samples in length, and the overlap being 6 samples in length. This partition length was chosen based on the desire to use a 16-point FFT. The fifth ($y_0[n]$), sixth ($y_1[n]$), and seventh ($y_2[n]$) subplots in Figure 8.8 show the results of the transform-based filtering operation of $x_0[n]$, $x_1[n]$, and $x_2[n]$ with $h[n]$. The first 6 samples ($M - 1 = 6$, which is the order of the LP filter) of $y_0[n]$, $y_1[n]$, and $y_0[n]$ are not accurate and are not used. To indicate this fact, these values have large X's drawn through them.

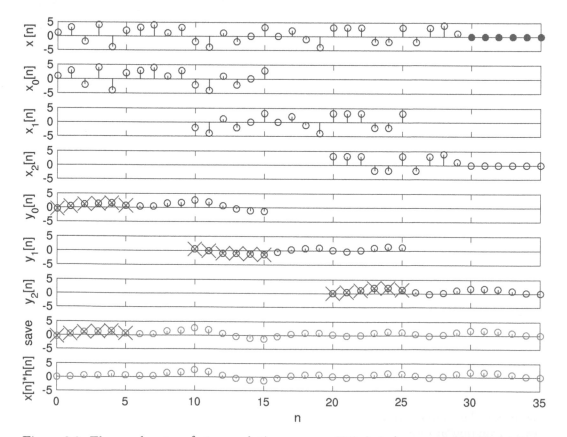

Figure 8.8: The overlap-save fast convolution process. Filled circles are zero padded values.

To obtain the filter's output, the portions of $y_0[n]$, $y_1[n]$, and $y_0[n]$ that do *not* have large X's drawn through them are concatenated. The final subplot in Figure 8.8 is provided for comparison and is the system's output using traditional time-domain convolution. These last two subplots demonstrate that, with the exception of the filter's initial transient, the transform-based technique and traditional convolution return the same result.

In summary, the *overlap and add* technique has no overlap of the inputs but must add the overlapped portions of the output segments for a correct result. The *overlap and save* technique overlaps the input segments, then throws away the resulting overlapped regions of the output segments and seamlessly "stitches together" the remaining portions. Either technique allows real-time filtering of long-duration input sequences even if you're using high-order filters.

8.2   winDSK Demonstration

There is no example of fast convolution in winDSK8.

8.3   MATLAB Implementation

There are many ways to demonstrate the FFT using MATLAB, and a basic example of fast convolution was shown on line 12 of Listing 8.2. The overlap techniques for real-time DSP can be simulated in MATLAB, but because this chapter is already rather lengthy, we prefer to move on to the C code.

8.4   Implementation in C

We are dealing with several new ideas in this chapter, namely, the FFT and its inverse, fast convolution in general, and the two overlap methods of real-time fast convolution. It would be unwise of us to attempt to cover them all in detail within a single chapter. We therefore choose to concentrate here on helping you become familiar with just the FFT algorithm. The other concepts, including real-time implementation, are left for follow-on exercises. If you understand the FFT code example that follows, they are not hard to implement on your own.

To ensure we understand and have implemented the FFT algorithm correctly, we can test it in non-real-time using the CPU of your workstation or laptop (i.e., the host PC you normally connect to the DSK) and compare the output to known correct values. The C program to implement this can be found in the `fft_example` directory of Chapter 8. It is by no means a fully optimized FFT routine, but is useful for understanding the concepts. Because it's intended to be compiled and run on your host PC and not the DSK, you won't use CCS this time as the compiler.

The code in `fft_example` is fairly straightforward C programming. We incorporate a common "trick" in the code: since the FFT must be able to handle complex numbers, and C does not support complex numbers directly, we use a structure.

Listing 8.3: A structure for implementing complex numbers in C.

```
typedef struct {
    float real, imag;
} COMPLEX;
```

The `float` datatype that we use above is typical for DSP CPUs to save memory and gain speed if we don't really need the full precision of the `double` datatype, so we continue that practice here. If we were only interested in implementing this FFT on a PC or other general purpose processor, we would probably have used **double** for the structure.

The calculation of the twiddle factors is accomplished by the function `init_W()`. Recall the twiddle factors are $W_N^n = \exp\left(-j\frac{2\pi n}{N}\right)$. By using the very helpful Euler's formula from complex analysis,

$$e^{jx} = \cos x + j \sin x,$$

our function `init_W()` can use the trigonometric equivalent of the complex exponential to make it easy to separate the real and imaginary parts of the twiddle factors. This works very well with the structure we defined above for complex numbers. Function `init_W()` is shown below; it runs only once and stores all the twiddle factors that will be needed for the specified length FFT.

Listing 8.4: A function for calculating the complex twiddle factors.

```
void init_W(int N, COMPLEX *W)
{
    int n;
    float a = 2.0*PI/N;

    for(n = 0 ; n < N ; n++) {
        W[n].real = (float) cos(-n*a);
        W[n].imag = (float) sin(-n*a);
    }
}
```

In the listing above, N is the length of the FFT, PI was defined earlier in the program, and W is a global array of complex numbers. It should be clear to you that function `init_W()` creates all the complex numbers needed for W_N^n.

The actual N-point butterfly for the FFT is performed by the code shown below, excerpted from the `fft_c()` function.

Listing 8.5: The C code for performing the FFT butterfly operation.

```
// perform fft butterfly
Window = 1;
for(len = n/2 ; len > 0 ; len /= 2) {
    Wptr = W;
    for (j = 0 ; j < len ; j++) {
        u = *Wptr;
        for (i = j ; i < n ; i = i + 2*len) {
            temp.real = x[i].real + x[i+len].real;
            temp.imag = x[i].imag + x[i+len].imag;
            tm.real = x[i].real - x[i+len].real;
            tm.imag = x[i].imag - x[i+len].imag;
            x[i+len].real = tm.real*u.real - tm.imag*u.imag;
            x[i+len].imag = tm.real*u.imag + tm.imag*u.real;
            x[i] = temp;
        }
        Wptr = Wptr + Window;
    }
    Window = 2*Window;
}
```

The input data is in array x, which is made up of complex datatype elements as defined by the structure discussed earlier, and the twiddle factors are accessed via pointer u. The variable len is used to successively split the data sets in half (see line 3 of the listing). The remaining lines simply perform the additions and multiplications required by the butterfly operations. You should work your way through this code with a small number of data elements (such as $N = 8$), while looking back frequently at the appropriate butterfly figure (such as Figure 8.5).

Finally, since the data coming out of the butterfly is in bit-reversed addressing order, we need to reorder the data back to "normal" order by "unscrambling" the elements of array x, which by now contains the FFT result, not the input data. This is accomplished by the code shown below.

Listing 8.6: A routine for "unscrambling" the order from bit-reversed addressing to normal ordering.

```
1  // rearrange data by bit reversed addressing
   // this step must occur after the fft butterfly
3  j = 0;
   for (i = 1; i < (n-1); i++) {
5      k = n/2;
       while(k <= j) {
7          j -= k;
           k /= 2;
9      }
       j += k;
11     if (i < j) {
           temp = x[j];
13         x[j] = x[i];
           x[i] = temp;
15     }
   }
```

Now that you understand the code...

Go ahead and copy all of the project files into a separate directory. Note that this is a very simple program, without any real-time requirements, so the project is quite small. When ready, open the project in an appropriate C programming environment[3] that targets your host PC's CPU, and compile (or build) the entire project. Once the build is complete, run the program on your host PC; the output can be seen on the StdIO window provided by your programming environment.[4]

To keep things as simple as possible, the input data is hard-coded into the program file as $x = \{0, 1, 2, 3, 4, 5, 6, 7, 0, 0, 0, 0, 0, 0, 0, 0\}$. This means you will be calculating a 16-point FFT. Based on our underlying knowledge of the Fourier transform, we can easily predict a few things about the result of an FFT on this data: (1) since the average value of the input data is non-zero, the frequency domain DC (or zero Hertz) value will also be non-zero; (2) since we have 16 input values we should have 16 output values (although the output will consist of 16 complex numbers); and (3) since the input data is real, the output data will be symmetrical about the $F_s/2$ point. While you are free to change the input data or modify

---

[3]Any of the various programming environments for C or C++ can be used, such as Microsoft Visual C/C++, GCC, lcc, MinGW, etc.

[4]We use the host PC for this example primarily because getting output via StdIO to show the FFT result is easy on a PC but not on a DSK.

the code to accept input data as an argument passed to the function, we wrote it this way so you could easily verify the correctness of the algorithm. It's also closer to how you might implement this in real-time, where the input would come from a predefined memory buffer. All you need to do now is compare the output of the C code running on the DSK to the result of the following MATLAB commands.

Listing 8.7: MATLAB commands used to confirm the correctness of your FFT.

```
x=[0 1 2 3 4 5 6 7 0 0 0 0 0 0 0 0];
2 X=transpose(fft(x))
```

We used the transpose operator in line 2 only so that the output would line up better as a column.[5] The MATLAB command window results should be similar to

```
X =

   28.0000
   -9.1371 -20.1094i
   -4.0000 + 9.6569i
    2.3801 - 5.9864i
   -4.0000 + 4.0000i
    3.2768 - 2.6727i
   -4.0000 + 1.6569i
    3.4802 - 0.7956i
   -4.0000
    3.4802 + 0.7956i
   -4.0000 - 1.6569i
    3.2768 + 2.6727i
   -4.0000 - 4.0000i
    2.3801 + 5.9864i
   -4.0000 - 9.6569i
   -9.1371 +20.1094i
```

These numbers should be essentially identical to the output of the FFT when run via C code on your host PC. Not only is our algorithm functioning correctly but our predictions about the FFT result are also verified: the DC value is non-zero (28.0000), there are 16 output values, and there is symmetry on either side of the $F_s/2$ value (the $F_s/2$ value is where $X[8] = -4.0000$). Feel free to try other input data sets and compare with the FFT from MATLAB. Once you are comfortable with the algorithm and the code, you can start thinking about how you would implement this on a DSK to run in real time.

There is much more to using the FFT and interpreting its results than we have room to discuss here. We will revisit this topic in the context of spectral analysis in Chapter 9.

8.5   Follow-On Challenges

Consider extending what you have learned.

1. Modify the non-real-time FFT code given in this chapter to run on a DSK inside a ProcessBuffer function. Extend it to create and test a frame-based implementation of an overlap-add filter that uses real-time fast convolution.

---

[5]Note that if we used the prime character (') at the end of line 2 as a shortcut for the transpose operation, we would have gotten the conjugate (or Hermitian) transpose. A shortcut for the nonconjugate transpose is the "dot prime" (. ') character pair.

2. Modify the non-real-time FFT code given in this chapter to run on a DSK inside a `ProcessBuffer` function (if you haven't already as part of the previous challenge). Extend it to create and test a frame-based implementation of an overlap-save filter that uses real-time fast convolution.

3. Determine a specific filtering situation where overlap-add or overlap-save is faster than one of the filtering techniques discussed earlier in this text.

4. Implement a Hilbert transform filter using the fast convolution approach.

8.6 Problems

1. Given an input data length of 4096 values, compare the approximate number of complex mathematical operations needed to evaluate a DFT versus a radix-2 FFT.

2. If you are using a radix-2 FFT and a sample frequency of $F_s = 48$ kHz, what is the minimum input data length needed to achieve a frequency resolution of approximately 50 Hz? Assume no smoothing window is being used on the data, and that the data length must be a power of two.

3. If fast convolution is used on a real input signal (i.e., having no imaginary values), why does the result of the inverse FFT typically contain non-zero imaginary values?

4. Suppose you were going to use fast convolution with the FFT to filter 50 samples of $x[n]$ with a 19th-order FIR lowpass filter $h[n]$. Assume the 50 samples of $x[n]$ are already stored, so you do not need to use real-time techniques such as overlap-add or overlap-save. Would you need to zero-pad either $x[n]$, $h[n]$, or both to avoid circular convolution effects? If so, specify the *minimum* number of zeros you would have to add to each if necessary.

5. The figure below is the plot of the magnitude spectrum from the output of a 20-point FFT, where the sample frequency was $F_s = 8$ kHz. Based on the magnitude spectrum, what specific things can you infer about the input signal provided to the FFT?

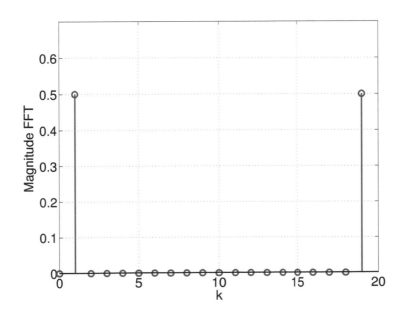

Chapter 9

Spectral Analysis and Windowing

9.1 Theory

$\mathbf{A}$S discussed in Chapter 8, the fast Fourier transform (FFT) allows us to transform a discrete-time signal from the sample (i.e., time) domain to the frequency domain. It is useful and often necessary to view the frequency content of a signal, and test equipment manufacturers market spectrum analyzers costing many thousands of dollars to perform this task. Nearly any engineer or technician working, for example, with communications or audio systems such as satellite up/down links, cellular telephone networks, radio/television stations, home theaters, or any high-end sound system *must* be able to analyze the frequency domain representation of signals. Rather than use a dedicated spectrum analyzer, we will explore how we can apply some basic DSP algorithms to achieve the same purpose.

Spectral analysis and estimation is a very broad topic in signal processing, and we will only scratch the surface of it here. If you wish to learn more about it, there are many fine texts available that cover the topic at different levels of detail (see, for example, [1,2,27,73–75]). Note that spectral estimation can be divided into nonparametric methods and parametric methods. By using the FFT we are using a nonparametric method, which is not optimal for certain special types of signals, but it is very easy to use and can be efficiently calculated. For this reason, FFT-based spectral analysis is by far the most common technique in use today. Digital oscilloscopes and spectrum analyzers typically implement a form of FFT-based spectral analysis. Parametric methods (such as those using ARMA, MUSIC, or ESPIRIT models) may be more sophisticated, but a discussion of them is well beyond the scope of this text.

9.1.1 Power Spectrum of a Signal

Our goal in this chapter is to obtain the distribution of power versus frequency for a given signal; this is called the *power spectrum*. Recall that the output values of an FFT are complex numbers; we will concentrate here only on the magnitude of the power spectrum, and not concern ourselves with the phase. While the phase response may be important for some applications, we don't pursue it here in order to keep the discussion to a reasonable length.

If a discrete-time signal $x[n]$ is provided as input to the FFT, the output is $X[k]$, i.e., $\text{FFT}\{x[n]\} = X[k]$. Recall that just as each increment of n in the time domain equates to a difference of $T_s = 1/F_s$ seconds in the signal, each increment of k in the frequency domain equates to a difference of $\Delta f = F_s/N$, where N is the length of the FFT. The value of Δf is called the *frequency resolution* of the spectrum. If $x[n]$ was originally a voltage versus time signal or a current versus time signal, then the resulting $X[k]$ would be voltage versus frequency or current versus frequency, respectively. Thus, to get the normalized power spectrum (i.e., normalized to an impedance of 1 Ω), we just use the relationship

$$|X[k]|^2 = (X[k]_{\mathrm{real}})^2 + (X[k]_{\mathrm{imaginary}})^2,$$

which will yield the squared magnitude in watts versus frequency.

For examples of how to interpret the result of the FFT-based power spectrum, let's recall a few things about the FFT. The FFT (just like the DFT) will output the same number of data points, in the form of complex numbers, as it is provided as input data points. If the input signal is real, the output magnitude will be symmetrical about the $F_s/2$ point. If N is even, $F_s/2$ is where $k = N/2$. If N is odd, $F_s/2$ is halfway between the two k values on either side of $N/2$, since k is an integer. From $k = 0$ up to $k = \lfloor N/2 \rfloor$, we interpret that value of k as corresponding to $f = k\Delta f = kF_s/N$, where $\lfloor \cdot \rfloor$ is the floor operator. Beyond the $k = \lfloor N/2 \rfloor$ point, the k values correspond to negative frequencies, and we interpret them as $f = -[(N - k)\Delta f] = -[(N - k)F_s/N]$. Now let's proceed to the examples.

Assume a signal $x(t)$ is sampled at $F_s = 48$ kHz for 2 seconds; we would obtain 96,000 data points such that $x[n]$ exists for $0 \le n \le 95999$. If we take a fairly large FFT of $x[n]$, for example, FFT$\{x[n]\}$ of just the first $N = 65536$ data points,[1] then $X[k]$ would be created for $0 \le k \le 65535$. In this case, $\Delta f \approx 0.732$ Hz. If the squared magnitude of this FFT showed a significant spike at $k = 100$ (and also at $k = N - 100 = 65436$ for the negative frequency component), it would mean the signal had significant power at $f \approx 732$ Hz. If instead we took a more reasonably sized FFT, for example, $N = 4096$, then $\Delta f \approx 11.7$ Hz. If the squared magnitude of *this* FFT showed a significant spike at $k = 100$ (and also at $k = N - 100 = 3996$ for the negative frequency component), it would mean the signal had significant power at $f \approx 1170$ Hz, not 732 Hz as before. Thus, changing only the length of the FFT changes the frequency resolution Δf, which changes how we need to interpret the FFT results.

For real-time spectral analysis, we need to keep the FFT size reasonably small for two reasons.

1. A large FFT may take too long to calculate to meet the real-time schedule.

2. A large FFT may take too long to present results (even if it can be calculated in real time), may exceed the desired response time, and may not respond well to signals containing quickly changing frequency content.

As seen above, large FFTs result in far greater frequency resolution (that is, where Δf is very small) than we are likely to need: a resolution of less than 7/10 of one hertz as in the first example above is probably overkill. On the other hand, if we choose a value for N that is *too* small, then while the FFT can be calculated quickly, the frequency resolution Δf is too coarse to be useful. As with most engineering trade-offs, the choice of the "best" FFT size is not clear cut.

In general, for real-time spectral analysis you would write a frame-based program (because the FFT needs more than one sample at a time) that continuously calculates the FFT of each new frame of data and provides the power spectrum output for presentation on the PC display. However, it's not quite that simple.

---

[1]This assumes a nonadaptive radix-2 FFT, which requires N to be a power of 2.

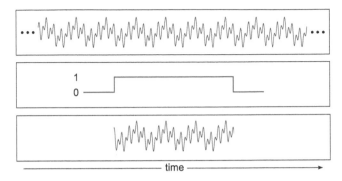

Figure 9.1: The time domain effect of applying a rectangular window. Top: a signal that lasts for an infinite time. Middle: a finite duration rectangular window. Bottom: The result of multiplying the infinite signal with the rectangular window is a finite duration signal.

It turns out that to get a more accurate estimate of a signal's power spectrum, it is sometimes better to add a few more steps to the computation. The Welch periodogram for example, a very popular method of calculating the power spectrum with the FFT, uses a smoothing window on each frame of data (as discussed below), averages the power spectrum of multiple frames of data, and overlaps the data by some percentage (often 50%) from one frame to the next. To discuss these finer points further would be beyond the scope of this text; see [27] for a very clear discussion.

9.1.2 The Need for Windowing

In many situations, we need to apply a smoothing window to each frame of data to get the best results from the FFT. If we don't apply a smoothing window to our data, then we have in effect applied a *rectangular* window, which has a constant value of 1 for its entire length.

Why is this true? As far as the FFT "knows," all data lasts an infinite amount of time, repeating for infinity with a period equal to the time duration of the given data. When we present only a finite length of data (as we must) to be transformed, this is the same as presenting an infinite length of data that has been multiplied with a finite length window having a constant value equal to 1. A visual example of this is shown in Figure 9.1. Why do we care? Recall that multiplication in the time domain is equivalent to convolution in the frequency domain. So the spectrum of the signal is effectively convolved with the spectrum of the window, and there's *always* a window of some sort—even if it's an unintentional rectangular window. What does the spectrum of a rectangular window look like?

A rectangular window is just like a single rectangular pulse (sometimes called a "rect function") that has a value of 1 for some finite region of time and a value of 0 everywhere else. You may recall from your signals and systems course that if we take the Fourier transform of a rectangular pulse, the resulting frequency spectrum is in the shape of a "sinc function," which is defined as $\operatorname{sinc}(x) = \sin(\pi x)/(\pi x)$. Another helpful recollection from Fourier theory is the reciprocal spreading property, which tells us in this case that as the rectangular pulse gets wider, the width of the sinc lobes get narrower. A "wider" rectangular pulse in this sense is equivalent to a rectangular window with a larger value of N (i.e., a "longer" window with more data points). This "rect $\leftrightarrow$ sinc" relationship can be observed in Figure 9.2.

Figure 9.3 depicts taking the FFT of a signal with no smoothing window applied to it first; you have in effect used a rectangular window. Because the result is as if the true

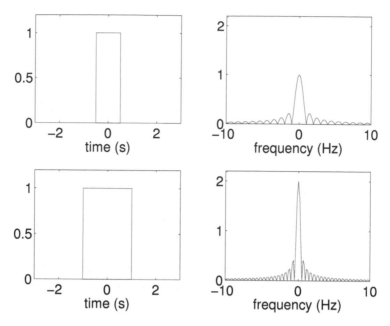

Figure 9.2: The "rect ↔ sinc" Fourier transform pair. The left two plots are rectangular pulses in the time domain. The right two plots are the corresponding magnitude spectra of the Fourier transform; the phase plots are not shown. Note that a wider pulse in the time domain results in narrower lobes of the sinc in the frequency domain.

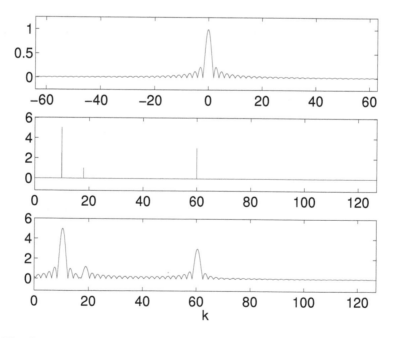

Figure 9.3: The frequency domain effect of applying a rectangular window. Top: the magnitude spectrum of a rectangular window is a sinc pulse. Middle: the theoretical spectrum (only positive frequencies shown) of some arbitrary infinite time duration signal that has three frequency components at $k = 10$, $k = 18$, and $k = 60$. Bottom: The result of convolving the window spectrum with the signal spectrum.

spectrum of the signal is convolved with the spectrum of the window, the observable signal spectrum is unavoidably "blurred."

This has two consequences of particular importance to spectral analysis that can be seen in the figure. First, the minimum width of a frequency component is limited by the width of the main lobe of the window's spectrum. Second, the ability to detect a weaker signal near a stronger signal is limited by the "height" of the sidelobes (called the sidelobe level).

The first effect is obvious in the bottom plot of Figure 9.3, where the frequency component "spikes" have been smeared to become wider lobes. If two frequency components are closer than half the main lobe width of the window, they will "blend into" each other and you will not be able to reliably distinguish them as separate components. The second effect can also be seen in the bottom plot of Figure 9.3, where the frequency component at $k = 18$ is almost obscured by the sidelobes from the component at $k = 10$. If the component at $k = 18$ had been slightly weaker in amplitude it would have been "covered up" by the nearby sidelobes. In general, the ratio of a weak component to a nearby strong component must be greater than the normalized sidelobe level of the window, or the weaker component will be obscured. Remember that we *always* have a window applied to our data; if we didn't explicitly apply a smoothing window to our data then we have in effect used a rectangular window. From the discussion above, it should be obvious that we need to know two critical characteristics about any windows we may use: the main lobe width and the sidelobe level.

9.1.3 Window Characteristics

Many smoothing windows have been developed over the years, most taking the name of the person who first proposed them. In addition to the rectangular window, there is the Bartlett (a triangular window), the Hamming, the von Hann (also called the Hanning or the Hann), the Blackman (also called the Blackman-Harris), the Kaiser, and the Dolph (also called the Chebyshev or the Dolph-Chebyshev). The time domain "shape" of some of these windows are shown in Figure 9.4.

The shape of the spectrum of each of these windows is somewhat similar to the sinc shape of the rectangular window's spectrum, in that there is a main lobe and some sidelobes. But the width of the main lobe and the sidelobe level differ from window to window; these are the two main criteria you use to select a window for a given spectral analysis application. Tracking down all the window characteristics in various DSP books is tedious, so we've collected the most important aspects of commonly used windows for you in Table 9.1.

In keeping with the practice of other DSP texts, the table shows the full main lobe width in normalized radian frequency (where π equates to $F_s/2$), with N being the length of the window, and the sidelobe level is shown in decibels. We don't show all the defining equations for the windows (which can be found in most theoretical DSP texts [2, 27]) because we'll discuss how you can easily create the windows you need using MATLAB®.

For spectral analysis, only the "Main Lobe Width" and "Sidelobe Level" columns in Table 9.1 are important. The other columns are useful if you ever design FIR filters using the window method; we included the extra columns here to collect all the window information in one place. What we most desire in a window is: (1) a narrow main lobe width so that we can resolve closely spaced frequency components and (2) a low sidelobe level so that we can resolve a weak signal near a strong signal. Unfortunately, these are two conflicting requirements. Take a moment to notice in Table 9.1 that, in general, the main lobe width (for a given data length N) tends to get wider as the sidelobe level gets lower. This can also be seen in Figure 9.5. Furthermore, the main lobe width will get narrower as the window length (which must be equal to the data length) gets longer—but the sidelobe level is independent of window length. As with most engineering decisions, the "best" choice of a window will be a tradeoff of these characteristics based on your specific needs.

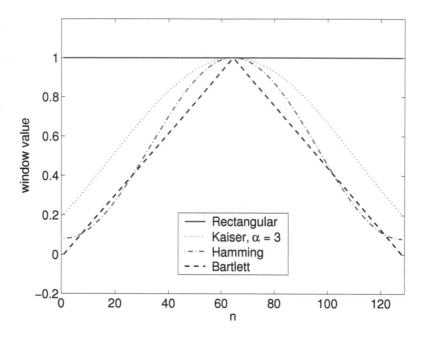

Figure 9.4: A few windows in the time domain. Note that all the windows smooth the data toward zero at the beginning and end of the data set, except for the rectangular window. The Bartlett window is sometimes called the triangular window.

Table 9.1: A summary of the characteristics of the most commonly used window functions.

Window[a] (length N)	Main Lobe Width	Sidelobe Level (dB)	Transition Bandwidth	Passband Ripple (dB)	Stopband Attenuation (dB)
rectangular	$4\pi/N$	-13.5	$1.8\pi/N$	0.75	21
Bartlett	$8\pi/N$	-27	$6.1\pi/N$	0.45	25
von Hann	$8\pi/N$	-32	$6.2\pi/N$	0.055	44
Hamming	$8\pi/N$	-43	$6.6\pi/N$	0.019	53
Blackman	$12\pi/N$	-57	$11\pi/N$	0.0017	74
Kaiser, $\alpha = 4$	$6.8\pi/N$	-30	$5.2\pi/N$	0.049	45
Kaiser, $\alpha = 8$	$10.8\pi/N$	-58	$10.2\pi/N$	0.00077	81
Kaiser, $\alpha = 12$	$16\pi/N$	-90	$15.4\pi/N$	0.000011	118
Dolph, $\alpha = -40$	$7.4\pi/N$	-40	NA	NA	NA
Dolph, $\alpha = -60$	$10.1\pi/N$	-60	NA	NA	NA
Dolph, $\alpha = -80$	$13.2\pi/N$	-80	NA	NA	NA

[a]Other window names: rectangular = boxcar, Bartlett = triangular, von Hann = Hann = Hanning, and Dolph = Chebyshev = Dolph-Chebyshev. In some books, the parameter α is called β instead. NA: not applicable, as the Dolph window is not often used for FIR filter design. Note: The "Main Lobe Width" column lists the full main lobe width, not the half main lobe width, to be consistent with the literature. The three rightmost columns are used for the window method of FIR filter design.

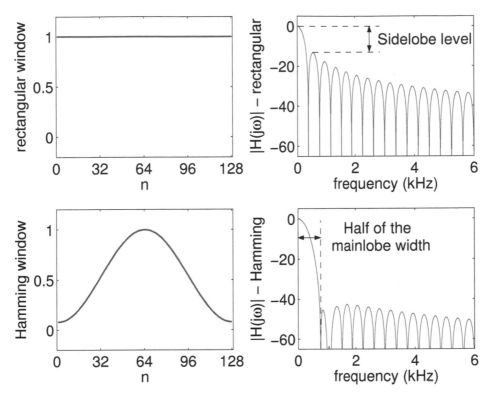

Figure 9.5: Two windows compared in the time and frequency domains. Note that a narrow main lobe also results in a high sidelobe level.

The main lobe width of the rectangular window is the "best" that we can do, since half the main lobe width is $2\pi/N = F_s/N$, which is the best resolution that we can ever get from an N-point FFT. But the sidelobe level of the rectangular window is the "worst" that we can do. Windows other than the rectangular window are very often recommended for spectral analysis. There is another reason that we may want to avoid the rectangular window: a phenomenon called "bias" in which the center peaks of two closely spaced frequency components appear to be farther away from each other than they really are (see [1] for a nice example). Applying one of the common smoothing windows instead of a rectangular window eliminates the bias problem.

To bring these windowing ideas into focus, let's try a couple of simple examples. Suppose we want to perform spectral analysis on a signal, sampled at 48 kHz, for which we expect there to be a frequency component at 14.0 kHz and another frequency component of nearly equal strength at 14.1 kHz. Thus, the frequency separation of the two components of interest is 100 Hz. Assume that, for some other reason, our data frame length is going to be fairly short at $N = 512$, so our window length must also be $N = 512$. We want to use a smoothing window to eliminate bias but don't want to smear these two components together with too wide a main lobe width. The sidelobe level is less important for this example because the magnitudes of the two signals are nearly equal. Can we use a Hamming window? From Table 9.1, half of the main lobe width of a Hamming window is $4\pi/N = 2F_s/N = 96000/512 = 187.5$ Hz, which is wider than the frequency separation of the two components of interest, so the answer is "No," we can't use a Hamming window—it will smear the two frequencies together—unless something changes. The only narrower window is the rectangular, but then we'll have a bias problem. The best alternative would be to increase the frame length to 1024 points, which would decrease the half main lobe width for the Hamming window to 93.75 Hz, less than the separation of the components of interest. In this case, the Hamming window would work.

Now suppose the second example is the same as before but that the "weak to strong" amplitude ratio between the two components of interest is 1:100 (or 0.01:1) instead of being nearly equal. The frame size is still 1024 so the Hamming window won't smear the two components into each other. But what about the sidelobes? When amplitudes will be very different, we need to check the sidelobe level. In decibels, a 0.01:1 amplitude ratio is $20 \log(0.01) = -40$ dB. From Table 9.1, we see that this eliminates the rectangular, Bartlett, and von Hann windows but that the Hamming window will work, although we're cutting it a bit close. The Blackman window would be better in terms of the sidelobe level, but the main lobe width would be too wide.

Given these examples, perhaps you can appreciate the thought process that goes into choosing an appropriate smoothing window. If resolving closely spaced frequencies of similar magnitude is more important, we will tend to choose a window with a narrow main lobe width. If resolving frequency components of very different magnitudes is more important, we will tend to choose a window with a low sidelobe level. In off-line applications, it is common to examine a signal with at least two windows, one with a narrow main lobe, the other with a low sidelobe level. However, we don't have that luxury if we are performing real-time spectral analysis, so in that situation we have to make an educated compromise when selecting the window. If we don't really know what frequencies and amplitudes may be lurking in the signal, at least we should know what could be hidden from us because of the window we choose!

9.2   winDSK Demonstration

The winDSK8 application has the ability to perform real-time spectral analysis, using a frame size of 512 samples. Plug an input signal into the DSK, start up winDSK8, and click the Oscilloscope button (called "Oscope/Analyzer" on the winDSK8 main interface). Two screens similar to Figure 9.6 appear; be sure the Spectrum Analyzer function is selected.

Note that the magnitudes of only the positive frequencies are displayed by the Spectrum Analyzer function. The frequency range for the x-axis is automatically adjusted to be 0 Hz to $F_s/2$ Hz, so to read the frequency scale we must know what sample frequency is being used. Under the Display category, you can also select a logarithmic y-axis (most common for displaying spectra) and choose to average the spectrum of a specified number of frames. Under the Windowing category you can choose which window type to apply; the available choices span the windows most commonly used for spectral analysis.

A logarithmic display of the spectrum of a 3 kHz sinusoidal signal sampled at 48 kHz is shown in the figure. The small spike close to DC is a 60 Hz power line artifact. You can experiment with a variety of input signals to the DSK and observe the associated spectral analyzer display.

Figure 9.6(b) shows the Scope display, which is the most common option for spectral analysis. Another useful display for observing how spectral components change over time is the waterfall spectral display, shown in Figure 9.7. This option, first mentioned in Chapter 6, adds a moving time-axis to the display. It is often called a *spectrogram*.[2] In winDSK8, the most recent data is shown at the top of the waterfall display.[3] Figure 9.7 is a waterfall spectral display of a theremin simulator with a sawtooth generator. This is a

---

[2]This is similar to MATLAB's `spectrogram` function (or the related `specgramdemo`).

[3]As mentioned in Chapter 6, this is similar to the type of readout provided by a typical sonar system on U.S. nuclear submarines.

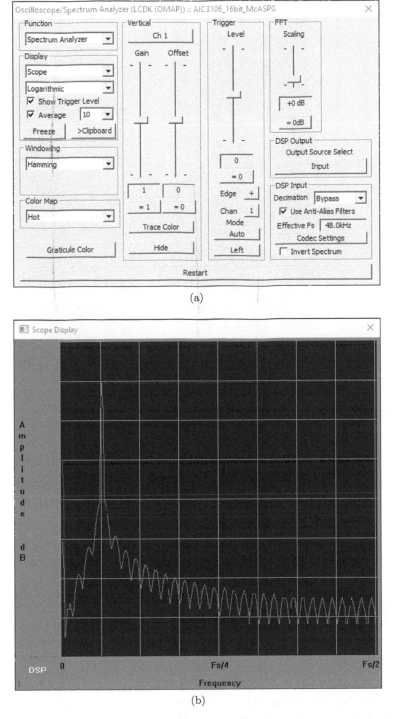

Figure 9.6: Spectrum analyzer windows (a) control and (b) display for winDSK8. Note that you can select options such as averaging, window type, log or linear y-axis, etc. from the control window. The signal displayed is a 3 kHz sinusoid, sampled at 48 kHz.

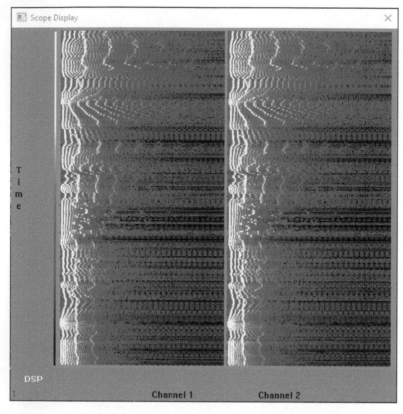

Figure 9.7: Spectrum analyzer waterfall display for winDSK8, showing spectral components of a theremin simulator. This type of display is also called a spectrogram.

fascinating electronic musical instrument; if you haven't heard of it, do a quick web search on "theremin" and be amazed.[4]

9.3   MATLAB Implementation

Spectral analysis of stored signals using MATLAB is very easy and flexible, but real-time spectral analysis with MATLAB is more difficult. Let's discuss topics related to non-real-time analysis first.

If you want to see how to generate, analyze, or use various types of data windows, explore MATLAB functions such as window, wintool, wvtool, sptool, and fdatool. Functions which create only a single type of window include rectwin, bartlett, hamming, hann, blackman, kaiser, and chebwin (the last of which creates a Dolph-Chebychev window). Use MATLAB's help command with any of these functions to get more detail.

For non-real-time spectral analysis in MATLAB, we'll assume you already have a discrete-time signal $x[n]$ stored on your computer in the MATLAB workspace as x. If you use the command pwelch(x) you'll quickly obtain a plot showing the power spectrum of signal $x[n]$ using the Welch periodogram method (a Hamming window is used by default). For example, Figure 9.8 shows the output obtained from the pwelch command when x contains 512 samples of a 7 kHz sinusoid sampled at 48 kHz. Type help pwelch to get information

---

[4]If you're a fan of some of the "classic" old-time science fiction movies, you will immediately recognize the sound of a theremin musical instrument, invented by Léon Theremin in 1928.

on this command and all of its many options. You may also want to explore functions such as `periodogram`, `pburg`, and `pmusic` for other methods of spectral analysis.

Obviously, what we have shown so far in MATLAB is not real-time. If you have the Data Acquisition Toolbox for MATLAB (available from The MathWorks), you can bring a signal in via your sound card and calculate the spectrum in real time. For those of you who do have the Data Acquisition Toolbox, we've included with the software for the book (in the Chapter 9 `matlab` directory) a MATLAB program called `specAn.m` which is a very simple real-time spectrum analyzer. It uses the sound card input of the PC to obtain the signal, with a default sample frequency of 8 kHz, and displays a real-time spectrum in a figure window very similar in appearance to Figure 9.8.

To use the program, copy `specAn.m` to some directory on your hard disk, and make that directory visible to MATLAB. Connect a signal source such as a CD player or a microphone to the input of your PC's sound card. In the MATLAB workspace, enter the command `specAn`, and press "Enter" on your keyboard to start the real-time process. To end the real-time process, click either mouse button anywhere on the figure window. If you want to use some other sample frequency F_s, specify that as an input argument (e.g., `specAn(44100)` for $F_s = 44.1$ kHz), keeping in mind that both MATLAB and your sound card will impose certain practical limits on F_s. If you don't have the Data Acquisition Toolbox, there is a MATLAB function called `audiorecorder` (see Chapter 2) that can bring samples into the MATLAB workspace via the sound card. However, we have found this function to be so much less capable than the functions in the Data Acquisition Toolbox (especially for a real time demonstration), that we haven't included a program using it. If possible, get access to the Data Acquisition Toolbox.

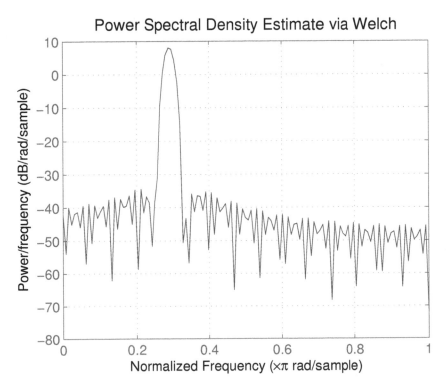

Figure 9.8: Spectrum plot from the `pwelch` command in MATLAB. The signal is a 7 kHz sinusoid, and the sample frequency is $F_s = 48$ kHz.

9.4 DSK Implementation in C

To achieve higher performance real-time spectrum analysis, we need to transition to a frame-based C program running on the DSK. However, we ideally want to view a live plot of the spectrum on the monitor of the host PC, which introduces an additional programming challenge. We have a general idea of how to program an FFT from Chapter 8, but how does the spectrum information get passed from the DSK back to the PC, and plotted on the monitor?

We could use some of the built-in capabilities of Code Composer Studio to do this, such as inserting a probe point at the appropriate place in the DSK program and using the rudimentary plot window available in Code Composer Studio. However, this approach will only work in DEBUG mode, and it halts the DSK's CPU for each plot update on the PC. While this technique might be useful in many situations (particularly for debugging purposes), it is not real-time operation.

Because this problem is more a problem of how to pass information back from the DSK to the PC and plot it than it is a problem of how to do spectral analysis on the DSK, we need to put off this discussion for now. In Appendix E you'll find a discussion of how to pass information back from the DSK and plot it on the PC monitor. This is explained in the appendix with a very basic real-time oscilloscope application first, followed by a short discussion and example of how to make the transition to real-time spectral analysis.

9.5 Conclusion

This concludes our coverage of what we call the *enduring fundamentals* of DSP, presented in the context of real-time operation. The next section of the book presents a series of projects that we hope you will find as fun and exciting as our students have. Don't stop now, for the fun is just beginning...

9.6 Follow-On Challenges

Consider extending what you have learned.

1. Use the winDSK8 spectrum analyzer to view a sinusoidal test signal. Increase the amplitude of this input signal until you exceed the limits of the ADC and clipping occurs. Does the spectrum change as you expect when the signal is clipped?

2. Use the winDSK8 spectrum analyzer to view a square wave test signal. Does the spectrum match what you expect from Fourier theory (i.e., do you see just odd harmonics that decrease in amplitude as they increase in frequency)?

3. Using the winDSK8 spectrum analyzer, select different windows and different numbers of frames for averaging. How does the spectral result change?

4. Explore all the options available for the `pwelch` function in MATLAB. Do the same for `periodogram`, `spectrogram`, `pburg`, and `pmusic`. Use various known input signals both with and without random noise added, and compare these different methods of spectral estimation.

5. Add features to the real-time spectrum analyzer example shown in Appendix E, such as those that are available in winDSK8.

9.7 Problems

1. For basic spectral analysis using the FFT (or DFT), proper window choice is crucial to success. Suppose some continuous-time signal data before sampling is known to be $x(t) = 2.1\cos(2\pi 50t) + 0.007\cos(2\pi 75t)$ V, and is sampled at a frequency of $F_s = 500$ Hz. A frame of $N = 256$ data points ($0 \le n \le 255$) is used for the FFT, with no zero padding. Assume an ideal ADC, and ignore any quantization effects. Choose, from the windows listed in Table 9.1, a window that should allow you to detect the two sinusoids in this signal using the FFT and *quantitatively* justify why the window you selected should work.

2. You wish to observe the magnitude spectrum of a signal consisting of a single sinusoid with an amplitude of 1.5 V and a frequency of 250 Hz, plus a DC offset voltage of 1.5 V. No other frequencies are present. You use exactly five cycles of the sinusoid (plus the DC offset) as input to an FFT. One cycle lasts 4 ms (since $T_0 = 1/F_0 = 1/250$), so five cycles last 20 ms. At a sample frequency of $F_s = 1$ kHz, this means you send 20 samples (data points) of the input signal to the FFT. Sketch an xy plot of the output of the magnitude of the FFT that results (you can ignore the phase of the FFT output). Be sure to show the output in the order in which the data comes from the FFT, with no shifting or centering of any kind. The vertical axis should be the magnitude, in linear units (not decibels), and scaled for the number of data points as appropriate. Label the units of both axes. Note that this sketch should be of the magnitude spectrum, not the power spectrum.

3. With respect to the previous question, how would the FFT magnitude plot be different if the only changes were that the sinusoidal frequency was increased to 600 Hz, and you send exactly 12 cycles to the FFT (yes, this means you are again providing 20 data points to the FFT). Sketch a plot of this new magnitude spectrum.

4. Assume you sample a continuous-time signal $x(t)$ at $F_s = 500$ Hz for a total time duration of 100 ms to obtain $x[n]$. Further, assume that $x(t)$ was sinusoidal. You then perform an FFT on $x[n]$ to obtain the magnitude spectrum as shown below.

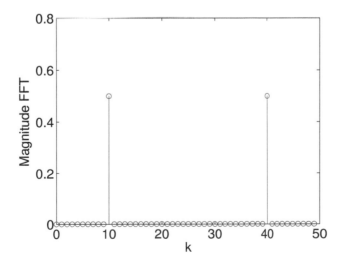

All the FFT magnitude values are shown; assume there was no zero padding, no windowing, no shifting or centering of the FFT output, and no aliasing occurred in the sampling process. Answer the following questions.

(a) How many samples of $x(t)$ did you obtain?

(b) What is the real-world frequency resolution (Δf) of the FFT?

(c) What was the real-world frequency of $x(t)$?

(d) Exactly how many periods of $x(t)$ were sampled?

Section II:
Projects

Chapter 10

Project 1: Guitar Special Effects

10.1 Introduction to Projects

SINCE this is the first chapter in the Projects section, let's explain how this part of the book differs from the previous section. All the the previous chapters cover topics we have called the "enduring fundamentals" of DSP. The topics were relatively broad, and the examples shown were meant only to illustrate that particular topic.

In the Projects section, we change our focus somewhat; we will now provide in each chapter at least one fully functional version of an interesting DSP application we have found to be popular with students over the years. In particular, the two general areas students seem to be drawn to when first learning DSP are audio (such as the special effects of this chapter and the graphics equalizer of the next chapter) and communications (such as the various receiver and transmitter projects of later chapters). While we provide fully functional code to get you started, we intentionally leave it to you to implement and improve the applications further. That's why they're called *projects*!

We remind the reader that most of the code shown for the projects in this and the following chapters is intentionally *not* fully optimized, because maximally efficient code is often very hard to understand—and our goal is for you to *understand* the code! You may want to explore ways in which you can improve the efficiency of these projects on your own. This first project chapter involves concepts that are fairly easy to understand; later project chapters progress to increasingly more involved examples.

10.2 Theory

10.2.1 Background

Special effects for electric guitars (and microphones) are a fun application of DSP. You can create all sorts of interesting sound variations quite easily with fairly simple DSP algorithms. Some of the more familiar effects include echo, chorus, flanger, phasing, reverb, tremelo, frequency translation, subharmonic generation, ring modulation, fuzz, compression/expansion, equalization, noise gating, and others. Whether you know them by these common names or not, you probably know what each of these effects "sounds" like if you've listened to even a moderate amount of popular music over the past 40 years or so. We will discuss a representative group of these effects in this chapter.

Special effects for electric guitars started to become more popular in the 1960s, not long after electric guitars themselves became widely available. Of course, in the early days, these special effects were typically created with hardwired analog circuit designs, and thus a single "effects box" (as they were called) could only produce a single type of effect. As a result, an electric guitar player who needed multiple effects used to be surrounded by a gaggle of effects boxes and pedals on the floor, each requiring its own foot switch, power, and signal cable. Later, some analog effects boxes were redesigned to include multiple related effects such as echo and reverb, or chorus and flanger, but the "rat's nest" of cables was still a problem. Another serious problem was the noise (particularly hum) which was added to the analog guitar signal, due in large part to using so many cables and connections between the guitar and the amplifier.

When DSP was first being taught in engineering colleges, algorithms were quickly derived that would produce the special effects being used by so many musicians. Unfortunately, the cost of the required hardware remained prohibitive for many years. But in the 1990s, this all changed and digital implementation of guitar special effects quickly replaced analog designs. A single DSP-based effects box is able to produce many variations of special effects, with improved signal-to-noise ratio and a single cable. As more people became familiar with DSP, new effects never produced with analog boxes were invented; this continues to this day.

10.2.2   How the Effects Work

A brief introduction to a few of these types of special effects was first given in Chapter 3 in the context of FIR filters. In this chapter, we'll discuss these and other special effects in a more general way.

The simplest special effect is an echo. A block diagram of how this can be implemented with a simple delay is shown in Figure 10.1. Notice the similarity of Figure 10.1 to Figure 3.9. The two diagrams in Figure 10.1 are equivalent, where the bottom diagram uses a more common representation for delay and gain. To set the amount of delay time, the value R specifies the number of sample periods of delay. For example, if the sample frequency is $F_s = 48$ kHz, then one sample period is $t_s = 1/F_s$ or 20.83 μs. Recall that in most DSP implementations, each sample period of delay requires a memory location; a 1-second delay in this case would thus require $R = 48000$ and need a memory array 48,000 locations in length. This has some practical ramifications that will be discussed later. Note that

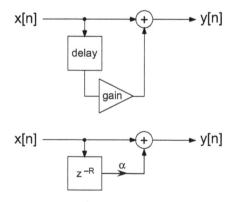

Figure 10.1: Block diagrams of a simple echo (or delay) effect using an FIR filter. The delayed version of the sound (delayed by R sample times), with amplification specified by gain value α, is added back to the non-delayed sound.

Figure 10.1 shows what is essentially an FIR filter, since only feedforward signal paths are used. This filter will result in a single echo, which may or may not be what you want. The filters in Figure 10.1 are of a type that is sometimes called "comb filters" for reasons that will become apparent.

To achieve multiple echos, we need to use a feedback signal path (sometimes called "regeneration" by musicians), which means we are now talking about an IIR filter. A block diagram of two simple ways this can be implemented is shown in Figure 10.2. To be consistent with most musical special effects references, the sign of the feedback coefficient (α) is the opposite of what was used in Chapter 4, but the transfer function equations presented later in this chapter will take this sign change into account. In IIR implementations, the "echoes" repeat forever, but the volume of the delayed sound decreases each sample time because of the stability condition of $|\alpha| < 1.0$. The repeated sound will thus "fade away" and be inaudible after some finite number of sample times. The filters in Figure 10.2, just like the one in Figure 10.1, are also called "comb filters." Both FIR and IIR comb filters are very common building blocks for the special effects used by musicians.

In addition to comb filters, another common filter used for special effects is the "allpass filter," which uses a combination of feedforward and feedback (with complementary gain values). Generic block diagrams of an allpass filter are shown in Figure 10.3. The version of the filter shown at the top of Figure 10.3 is the most basic implementation; the version

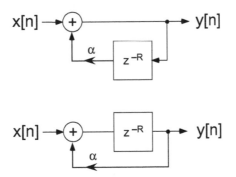

Figure 10.2: Block diagrams of a multiple echo effect using IIR filters. Ensure $|\alpha| < 1.0$ for stability.

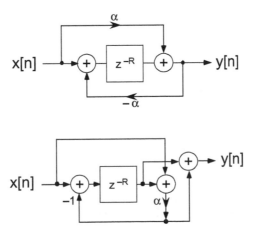

Figure 10.3: Block diagrams for allpass filters. Ensure $|\alpha| < 1.0$ for stability.

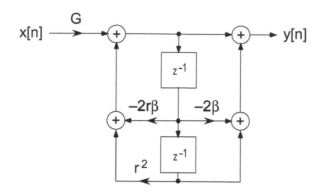

Figure 10.4: Block diagram for a second-order IIR notch filter, shown implemented as Direct Form II. The center notch frequency determines the value of β and the width of the notch is determined by r. See text for more detail.

shown at the bottom of the figure implements an identical filter (see [4]) but only requires a single multiplication operation.

The final type of filter we'll discuss is the "notch filter." While it is easy to create an FIR notch filter, an IIR implementation allows far more flexibility and is more commonly used. A block diagram for a versatile second-order IIR notch filter is shown in Figure 10.4.

FIR Comb Filters

Since comb filters, both FIR and IIR, are used so often in creating special effects, we will examine them in more detail. We begin with the FIR version shown earlier in Figure 10.1. The transfer function of the filter in Figure 10.1 is

$$H(z) = 1 + \alpha z^{-R}$$

and from this equation the frequency response can be calculated. For example, using the `freqz` command in MATLAB®, where $R = 10$ and $\alpha = 1$, yields the frequency response seen in Figure 10.5.

The magnitude of the frequency response (plotted here on a logarithmic (dB) scale) shows multiple evenly spaced passbands and stopbands of the filter. The magnitude of the frequency response resembles the teeth of a comb, which is where the name originated. Being a symmetric FIR filter, the phase response is linear in each of the passbands.[1] For our purposes, this means the delay time for all frequencies in the passband will be equal (i.e., constant group delay). The stopbands arise from the fact that the delay or phase shift of certain frequencies approaches 180 degrees, so when this is added back to the original signal these frequencies tend to cancel each other out. These stopbands, or nulls, occur at the frequencies along the unit circle of the z-plane where the zeros of the transfer function occur. To see this on a z-plane plot in MATLAB where α is represented by `alpha`, we can use the command `zplane([1 zeros(1, R-1) alpha], 1)`. Whether you prefer to think of it as due to phase cancellation or as due to zeros, the result is that frequencies in the stopbands are attenuated, so this filter provides both a delay *and* an associated change in the "tone" of the sound. The number of passbands and stopbands is directly related to the value of R, which can be easily seen in Figure 10.6.

---

[1]If you change the value of α to something other than 1.0, then the filter is no longer truly symmetric and the phase will thus no longer be truly linear.

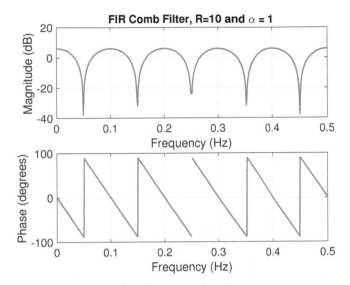

Figure 10.5: FIR comb filter response, with a normalized sample frequency of $F_s = 1$ Hz.

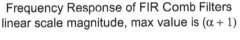

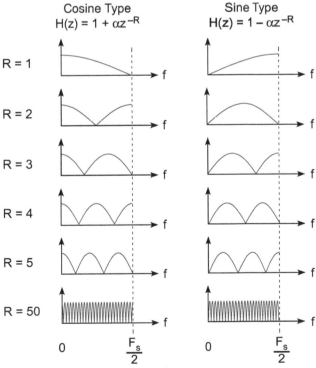

Figure 10.6: Effect of changing delay value R for an FIR comb filter. The linear scale magnitude of the frequency response is shown for two types of FIR comb filters.

We can infer many things from Figure 10.6. First, the number of stopbands is equal to $R/2$; for example, when $R = 5$, we have two and "one half" stopbands in the magnitude response of the filter. For "cosine type" comb filters, the stopbands are located at $0.5(F_s/R), 1.5(F_s/R), 2.5(F_s/R), \ldots$, and so on, however, many fit between 0 and $F_s/2$. For "sine type" comb filters, the stopbands are located at $0, (F_s/R), 2(F_s/R), 3(F_s/R), \ldots$, and so on, however many fit between 0 and $F_s/2$. Second, α affects the maximum value of the magnitude; for example, for the common setting of $\alpha = 1.0$, the maximum magnitude is 2.0 (on a logarithmic scale this would be +6 dB). When using real-world DSP hardware, we have to be careful in setting *alpha* not to exceed the dynamic range of the DAC; an overall scale factor of less than one may be needed. Third, if we *subtract* the delayed sample from the non-delayed sample instead of *adding* it, we get a different response, as seen on the right-hand side of Figure 10.6. Fourth, as we use longer delay times such as is shown for $R = 50$, the width of the passbands and stopbands is so small that the frequency response is essentially flat, which is similar to an allpass filter. An allpass filter passes all frequencies equally well (so the "tone" of the sound is unaffected), but due to its phase response a pure delay is provided. The difference in this respect between Figure 10.1 and Figure 10.3 is that Figure 10.3 provides an allpass response at *all* values of R, which will be very useful for some types of special effects.

IIR Comb Filters

The transfer function of the filter at the top of Figure 10.2 is

$$H(z) = \frac{1}{1 - \alpha z^{-R}} \qquad |\alpha| < 1,$$

which you should recognize as being IIR in nature. Again using the **freqz** command in MATLAB, where $R = 10$ but $\alpha = 0.8$ (for stability), the frequency response can be seen in Figure 10.7. The magnitude of the frequency response shows multiple evenly spaced passbands and stopbands of the filter, similar to the teeth of a comb. As an IIR filter, the disadvantages are that the phase response cannot be truly linear in each of the passbands

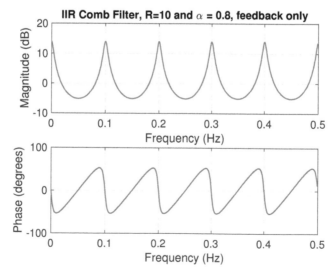

Figure 10.7: Response for the IIR comb filter shown at the top of Figure 10.2. The sample frequency has been normalized to $F_s = 1$ Hz.

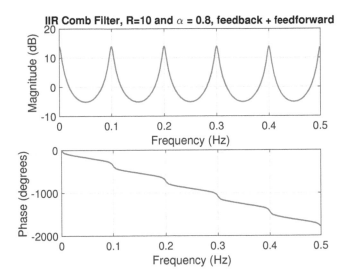

Figure 10.8: Response for the IIR comb filter shown at the bottom of Figure 10.2. The sample frequency has been normalized to $F_s = 1$ Hz.

and the filter can be unstable (if $\alpha \geq 1.0$ through design error or coefficient quantization). However, an advantage of the IIR version is that the passbands can be much sharper than is possible with the FIR version for similar memory size and/or computational requirements.

How is the the filter at the bottom of Figure 10.2 different from the filter at the top of Figure 10.2? The transfer function of the filter at the bottom of Figure 10.2 is

$$H(z) = \frac{z^{-R}}{1 - \alpha z^{-R}} \qquad |\alpha| < 1$$

which results in the frequency response shown in Figure 10.8. Note that, while the magnitude of the frequency response shows essentially identical passbands and stopbands as seen in Figure 10.7, the phase response of this filter is much closer to linear. This "almost linear" phase response provides a more uniform delay across the frequency range. For this reason, when an IIR comb filter is needed for certain audio special effects (particularly reverb), the version shown at the bottom of Figure 10.2 is often used. However, in this version the present time input $x[n]$ is delayed and not passed through directly to the output (i.e., there is no $x[n]$ term in the filter's difference equation, only an $x[n-R]$ term). Thus, there is no "present time" output from this filter, which for some other types of effects would be undesirable (e.g., if you plucked a note on your guitar, nothing would be heard until after the delay time has passed). Both versions shown in Figure 10.2 have their uses.

Allpass Filters

The transfer function of both of the filters shown in Figure 10.3 is

$$H(z) = \frac{\alpha + z^{-R}}{1 + \alpha z^{-R}} \qquad |\alpha| < 1$$

and from this the frequency response can be easily shown. The `freqz` command in MATLAB (using $R = 10$ and $\alpha = 0.8$) provides the frequency response shown in Figure 10.9.

Note that the magnitude of the frequency response shows a "flat" gain of 1 (i.e., 0 dB) for all frequencies from DC to $F_s/2$, from which the "allpass" name is derived. However,

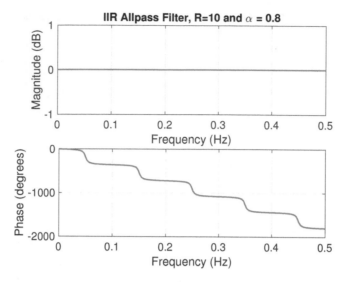

Figure 10.9: Response for the IIR allpass filters shown in Figure 10.3. The sample frequency has been normalized to $F_s = 1$ Hz.

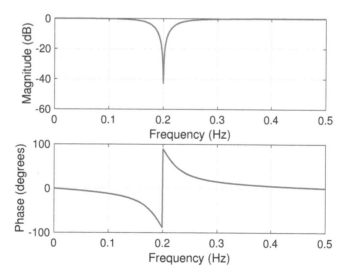

Figure 10.10: Response for the IIR notch filter of Figure 10.4. The sample frequency has been normalized to $F_s = 1$ Hz.

from the phase response we can see that this filter provides delay (note that the delay will be a different value in the narrow regions where the stopbands would exist for a comb filter using the same value of R). Thus, this filter is useful for situations such as reverb effects where you need to delay the sound without unduly "coloring" the tone of the sound.

Notch Filters

A notch filter is similar to a comb filter, but rather than having multiple evenly spaced stopbands, it has only a single stopband. An example frequency response of a notch filter is shown in Figure 10.10. Ideally, both the "sharpness" of the stopband and the location of the stopband on the frequency axis would be adjustable. An efficient and versatile design

Table 10.1: Typical methods for creating various special effects with basic filters. Delay times listed are only suggestions.

Effect	Filter	Type	Delay (ms)	Type of delay
single echo	comb	FIR	> 100	constant
multiple echos	comb	IIR	> 100	constant
doubling	comb	FIR or IIR	50–100	constant
chorus	comb	FIR	20–30	slowly varying
flanger	comb	FIR	1–10	slowly varying
flanger (metallic)	comb	IIR	1–10	slowly varying
phasing	allpass or notch	IIR	< 20	slowly varying
reverb	comb and allpass	FIR and IIR	multiple	constant

that achieves this is defined by the notch filter shown in Figure 10.4, which has the transfer function of

$$H(z) = G \frac{1 - 2\beta z^{-1} + z^{-2}}{1 + 2r\beta z^{-1} - r^2 z^{-2}} \qquad 0 \le r < 1, \ -1 \le \beta \le 1$$

where the notch center frequency is determined by β, the width of the notch is determined by r, and the term G is a scale factor used to adjust the overall filter gain. For a unity DC gain, set $G = \sum_i a_i / \sum_i b_i = (1 + 2r\beta - r^2)/(1 - 2\beta + 1)$. To set a particular notch center frequency f_c in the allowed range of 0 to $F_s/2$, simply set $\beta = \cos(2\pi f_c/F_s)$. Regarding the notch width, the closer r approaches 1.0, the narrower will be the notch (but if $r > 1.0$, the filter will be unstable). Experiment with different values for f_c and r.

Putting It All Together

Now that we have the building blocks (comb filters, allpass filters, notch filters) used for many of the most common special effects, let's put it all together. While up until now we have assumed a constant delay value of R (or a constant notch frequency determined by β), we will see that for many of the special effects we will need to vary the delay or notch frequency slowly over time. Table 10.1 lists the ways in which certain special effects can be created using the basic filters discussed above. In many cases, a very different sounding effect can be created with an identical filter form by simply changing the delay time or notch frequency (or by changing the range over which it varies). Some effects typically need just a single filter stage, while others (such as reverb) often need multiple filters to achieve the desired sound.

For example, a block diagram of the flanging effect is shown in Figure 10.11, where only a single comb filter is used. As before, α is the gain or scale factor, but instead of showing a constant R for delay, we now use $\beta[n]$, which represents a periodically varying delay. A method to vary the delay sinusoidally is described by

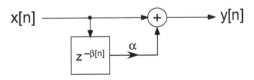

Figure 10.11: A block diagram of the flanging effect using a single comb filter.

$$\beta[n] = \frac{R}{2}\left[1 - \cos\left(2\pi\frac{f_0}{F_s}n\right)\right].$$

In the equation above, R is the maximum number of sample delays, f_0 is a relatively low frequency (often less than 1 Hz), and F_s is the sample frequency. This equation results in a slowly changing sinusoidally varying delay that ranges from 0 to R samples. Note that, as an alternative to sinusoidally varying the delay, musicians sometimes choose to use a triangle, sawtooth, or even an exponential function for $\beta[n]$ in order to obtain a somewhat different sound.

A block diagram of the chorus effect is shown in Figure 10.12. To generate a chorus effect that makes one musician sound similar to four musicians playing the same notes, three separate chorus signals (identical to flanging except having longer delay times) are summed with the original signal. For the best sound, each of the β's and α's should be independent.

The phasing effect can be achieved in various ways. One method uses the output of an allpass filter with a slowly varying delay that is added back to the original signal; due to the phase shift, some frequencies will tend to cancel (creating notches). This effect is very similar to the comb filter used in the flanger. Another method, which is easier to fine-tune to get exactly the sound you desire, uses the output of a notch filter with a slowly varying notch frequency that is added back to the original signal. Because it is easy to independently control the notch frequency and the notch width, this second method has many advocates.

Two block diagrams that can implement the phasing effect are shown in Figure 10.13. To generate a rich phasing sound, more than one separately phased signal can be summed with the original signal. For the best sound, it is recommended that the notch frequencies *not* be evenly spaced or harmonically related; experiment with all the parameters to obtain the sound you want.

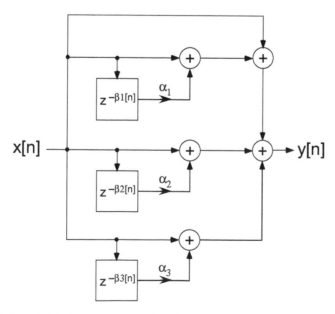

Figure 10.12: A block diagram of the chorus effect using three comb filters.

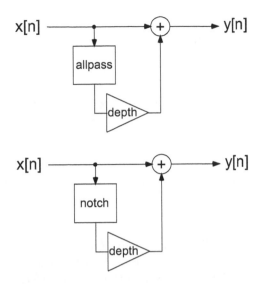

Figure 10.13: Block diagrams of the phasing effect using an allpass filter or a notch filter.

Reverb is an effect that we hear every day and in most cases take for granted. One proposed design [76] for a realistic-sounding reverb effect is shown in Figure 10.14. Modern music studios add some amount of reverb to almost every recording to compensate for consumers listening to the playback in relatively small rooms; without any added reverb the recording would have a "dead" sound to it. Reverb is caused by a multitude of sound

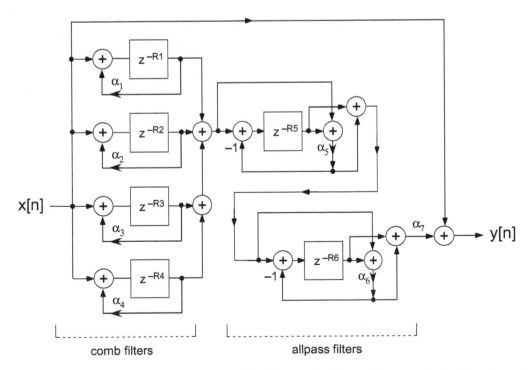

Figure 10.14: A proposed block diagram for the reverb effect using a combination of comb and allpass filters [76].

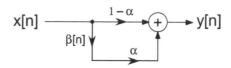

Figure 10.15: Block diagrams of the tremelo effect. The bottom block diagram, while less simple than the top, allows control of the amount or "depth" of the tremelo effect compared to the original signal.

reflections coming from the walls of the room or concert hall in which it is played; in a small room the delay times are too short to notice. In a larger room, we hear these reflections arrive at many different times, so for a realistic effect, we need to use multiple delay times. While the block diagram of Figure 10.14 may seem complex, it is actually much simpler than some of the modern studio-quality reverb algorithms. Discussion of these studio-quality algorithms would be beyond the scope of this chapter.

We now see that echo, chorus, flanger, phasing, and reverb are all created with some combination of delays that affect the phase of the signal, which is easy to do in DSP. Other effects such as tremelo, fuzz, compression/expansion, and noise gating are created by altering the amplitude (rather than the phase) of the signal.

In general, an intentional variation in the amplitude of a signal is called "amplitude modulation," or AM. This is used in radio communications systems, but also in special effects. The two most common special effects that use AM are tremelo and ring modulation.

Tremelo[2] (also spelled "tremolo") is simply a repetitive up/down variation in the volume of the signal.[3] Listen to the original version of the classic song "Crimson and Clover" by Tommy James and the Shondells for a great example of tremelo. Block diagrams that show how simple it is to implement tremelo are shown in Figure 10.15. The rate of the variation in volume is controlled by the time-changing nature of β, and the amount or "depth" of the tremelo effect compared to the original signal is controlled by α, where $0 \leq \alpha \leq 1$. Tremelo usually varies the volume at a constant sinusoidal rate, at a frequency below 20 Hz (some claim 7 Hz to be "ideal"), which can be expressed as

$$\beta[n] = \frac{1}{2}\left[1 - \cos\left(2\pi\frac{f_0}{F_s}n\right)\right].$$

In this equation, f_0 is the frequency of variation and F_s is the sample frequency. A communications engineer would view tremelo as form of amplitude modulation called "double sideband large carrier" (DSB-LC) because the "carrier" frequency (in tremelo this is just the original signal) will always show up in the output.

Ring modulation is a special effect whereby the guitar signal is multiplied by some other signal, usually an internally generated constant frequency sinusoidal signal such as $\beta[n] = \cos(2\pi(f_0/F_s)n)$. A block diagram that shows how simple it is to implement ring modulation is shown in Figure 10.16. Pure multiplication of any two frequencies f_1 and f_2 results in the sum $(f_1 + f_2)$ and the difference $(f_1 - f_2)$ frequencies. In communications

---

[2]This is not to be confused with the "tremelo technique" in classical guitar and flamenco guitar, which is a particular right-hand effect for the bass and treble strings.

[3]Some electric guitar and amplifier manufacturers confuse "tremelo" with "vibrato," but the correct definition of vibrato is an up/down variation in *pitch* not volume.

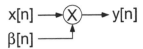

Figure 10.16: Block diagrams of the ring modulation effect. Signal $\beta[n]$ is usually an internally generated sinusoid, such as $\beta[n] = \cos(2\pi(f_0/F_s)n)$.

theory this technique is a form of amplitude modulation called "double sideband suppressed carrier" (DSB-SC). The "suppressed carrier" modifier refers to the fact that the "carrier" (in Figure 10.16 this would be $\beta[n]$) does not show up in the output (nor does the original guitar signal $x[n]$, for that matter). In fact, a ring modulator can create tremelo by setting $\beta[n] = [1 + \alpha\cos(2\pi(f_0/F_s)n)]$, where, as before, α controls depth for $0 \leq \alpha \leq 1$. In ring modulation, the frequency of $\beta[n]$ is usually higher than it is for tremelo; selecting a frequency somewhere in the 500 Hz to 1 kHz range is fairly common. Be aware that aliasing will occur if the ring modulator's sum frequencies exceed $F_s/2$ (a result which you may or may not want, depending upon the sound you seek).

Fuzz is an intentionally introduced distortion in the signal, typically caused by "clipping" or limiting the amplitude variations of the signal (see Figure 10.17 for a simple example). This effect was first discovered accidentally when the dynamic range of a tube-based amplifier stage was exceeded, which caused clipping, which in turn resulted in higher-frequency harmonics (harmonic distortion) being added to the original signal. Heated debates continue today about the "tube" sound of fuzz versus the "solid-state" or "transistor" sound of fuzz. Keep in mind that Figure 10.17 is a very simplistic example of clipping. The signal can be clipped so that the positive portion is limited to a different magnitude than the negative portion, or the clipping can be gradual rather than "flat." These variations (and others) will all produce a different sound of fuzz effect. Furthermore, the clipping is often followed by a frequency selective filter (lowpass or bandpass are the most common) to adjust the "harshness" or "color" of the fuzz sound. More sophisticated fuzz effects also have the option to engage a frequency selective filter before the clipping stage, in order to clip just a certain band of frequencies, then add this back to the unmodified or fully clipped signal. The possibilities are endless; experiment for the sound you like!

This has been a very brief discussion of the theory underlying the special effects used for electric guitars or microphones. Note that when combining multiple effects, the order of the effects in the signal chain will result in different sounds at the output. There are many articles and even entire books written on the subject of special effects, at both an engineering level and at the hobbyist level. See [4] for an excellent introduction, and [76–78] for other treatments. A web search on the Internet will also yield a plethora of information;

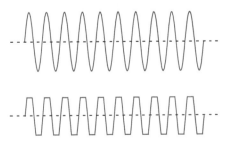

Figure 10.17: Clipping a signal produces the fuzz effect. Top: original signal. Bottom: symmetrically clipped signal. Asymmetrical clipping can be used for a somewhat different fuzz sound.

at the time of this writing one of the best sources was http://www.harmony-central.com/Effects/, particularly the "Effects Explained" link. A more theoretical treatment can be found at the site http://www.sfu.ca/sonic-studio/handbook/index.html. Both of these websites have many audio files that demonstrate the various effects.

10.3   winDSK Demonstration

See Section 3.2 for a discussion of the Audio Effects that can be produced by winDSK8. At the click of a mouse, you can create effects such as echo, chorus, flanger, tremelo, frequency translation, subharmonic generation, and ring modulation (by selecting the DSB-SC option for tremelo). Equalization is available in the Graphic Equalizer application provided with winDSK8, and the section also describes how the notch filter application can be operated as an FIR filter. You can use these functions of winDSK8 to quickly compare with your own special effects so you'll know if you're getting the kind of sound associated with a particular effect. Section 4.2 described how the notch filter application was actually implemented as an IIR second-order section, and described more variations on using the notch filter. The winDSK8 Notch Filter application provides the equivalent of what was shown earlier in this chapter in Figure 10.4, which was discussed in more detail in Section 10.2.2.

10.4   MATLAB Implementation

The next step in the path to real-time DSP is to explore these filters in MATLAB to be sure we understand them. At first, we are free to take advantage of the "vectorized" optimizations available in MATLAB along with various built-in functions and toolbox commands. As we've mentioned in previous chapters, this is handy when you want to quickly check aspects of a DSP algorithm such as the output signal, output spectrum, pole-zero plot, and so on. But before moving on to a C program running on real-time DSP hardware, we must "de-vectorize" the MATLAB code and stop using built-in functions and toolbox commands so that our m-file is as close as possible to a C implementation, while making sure the program still works as expected. Then, and *only* then, will we be ready to move on to the next step of creating a real-time program in C. This is the pattern that has consistently resulted in student success time after time, and this is the pattern we'll continue to follow for the projects.

In this section, we'll examine a subset of the filters described earlier in the chapter. None of these filters running under MATLAB operate in real time; in a later section we'll show example C code for real-time operation. In this section, we'll show two versions of an FIR comb filter, three versions of an IIR comb filter, two versions of an IIR notch filter, and one version of a flanger. Given this foundation, the reader should be able to create in MATLAB any of the special effects filters described in this chapter.

10.4.1   FIR Comb Filter

The program listed below, fir_comb1.m, takes advantage of the built-in function called filter.

Listing 10.1: A MATLAB FIR comb filter example.

```
% Method using the filter command

R=round(R);  % ensure R is an integer before proceeding
A=1; % the "A" vector is a scalar equal to 1 for FIR filters
```

```
  B=zeros(1,R+1);   % correct length of vector b
6 B(1)=1;  B(R+1)=alpha;
  % B vector is now ready to use filter command
8 y=filter(B,A,x);
```

This program can be found in the `matlab` directory of Chapter 10, along with all the other MATLAB code for this chapter; only the key parts of the programs are shown in this section. The program below implements the filter shown at the bottom of Figure 10.1, with the response shown in Figure 10.5. The input variables are x (input vector), R (number of sample time delays desired), and *alpha* (feedforward coefficient α). Obviously, this is an FIR filter.

The program `fir_comb1.m` processes all the samples in the entire x input vector, but of course not in real time. The program was easy to write, but it's not suitable for getting us to a C implementation in real time. Note that lines 5 and 6 ensure the B coefficient vector has the proper length and values.

The next program, `fir_comb2.m`, is an identical filter that while also not capable of real-time operation is much closer to C code and will help us transition to C later. This program has the same input variables as before.

Listing 10.2: A MATLAB FIR comb filter example closer to C.

```
  % Method using a more "C-like" technique
2
  R=round(R);   % ensure R is an integer before proceeding
4 N1=length(x);  % number of samples in input array
  y=zeros(size(x));  % preallocate output array
6 % create array and index for "circular buffer"
  buffer=zeros(1,R+1);
8 oldest=0;
  % "for loop" simulates real-time samples arriving one by one
10 for i=1:N1
      buffer(oldest+1)=x(i);  % read input into circular buffer
12    oldest=oldest + 1;  % increment buffer index
      oldest=mod(oldest,R+1);  % wrap index around
14    y(i)=x(i) + alpha*buffer(oldest+1);
  end
```

Instead of processing one sample at a time as we demonstrated for IIR filters in Chapter 4, this program uses a "for loop" to simulate samples arriving one by one, thus processing all the samples in the entire x input vector. This "for loop" would not be used in the real-time C program, but the code inside the "for loop" would be used in an interrupt service routine (ISR) for sample-by-sample processing. The use of the modulus operator in line 13 causes the index value `oldest` to "wraparound," creating a circular buffer as was discussed in Chapter 3 (see Figure 3.17). The use of "oldest + 1" in lines 11 and 14 is due to MATLAB's rule of the array index values starting at 1 instead of zero. Incrementing the index value in line 12 causes the index to point at the *oldest* sample in the buffer. If you aren't sure about how this works, draw a short circular buffer on a piece of paper and run through the whole circle a few times, placing samples in the buffer one by one. Now are you convinced?

You may want to use the handy program `demo_fir_comb2.m` to read in a WAV audio file, run the comb filter, and play the result. Experiment with different values, especially the delay value, referring to Table 10.1.

10.4.2   IIR Comb Filter

The program listed below, `iir_comb1.m`, again takes advantage of the built-in function called `filter`. It implements the IIR comb filter shown at the bottom of Figure 10.2, with the response shown in Figure 10.8. The input variables are the same as before (x is the input vector, R is the number of sample time delays desired), and *alpha* is now the feed**back** coefficient.

Listing 10.3: A MATLAB IIR comb filter example.

```
1  % Method using the filter command

3  R=round(R);   % ensure R is an integer before proceeding
   A=zeros(1,R+1);   % correct length of vector A
5  A(1)=1; A(R+1)=-alpha;
   % A vector is now ready to use filter command
7  B=zeros(1,R+1);   % correct length of vector B
   B(R+1)=1;   % use "B=1;" for other IIR version
9  % B vector is now ready to use filter command
   y=filter(B,A,x);
```

Lines 4 and 5 ensure the A coefficient vector has the proper length and values (take note of the sign needed for `alpha`). Lines 7 and 8 set up the B vector properly. If you would rather implement the IIR comb filter shown at the top of Figure 10.2, comment out line 7 and change line 8 to read "B=1;" as noted in the comment for line 9.

The next program, `iir_comb2.m`, is an identical filter that is much closer to C code and has the same input variables as before. It implements the filter in "Direct Form I" (see Figure 4.14).

Listing 10.4: A MATLAB IIR comb filter example closer to C, in Direct Form I.

```
1  % Method using a more "C-like" technique

3  R=round(R);   % ensure R is an integer before proceeding
   N1=length(x); % number of samples in input array
5  y=zeros(size(x));   % preallocate output array
   % create array and index for "circular buffer"
7  bufferx=zeros(1,R+1); % to hold the delayed x values
   buffery=zeros(1,R+1); % to hold the delayed y values
9  oldest=0; newest=0;
   % "for loop" simulates real-time samples arriving one by one
11 for i=1:N1
       bufferx(oldest+1)=x(i); % read input into circular buffer
13     newest=oldest; % save value of index before incrementing
       oldest=oldest + 1; % increment buffer index
15     oldest=mod(oldest,R+1); % wrap index around
       y(i)=bufferx(oldest+1) + alpha*buffery(oldest+1);
17     buffery(newest+1)=y(i);
   end
```

We again use a "for loop" to simulate samples arriving one by one, thus processing all the samples in the entire x input vector. Since this filter is derived from the block diagram (not the transfer function), we don't want a negative sign this time on the value of `alpha` for feedback (see line 16). The code shown implements the IIR comb filter shown at the bottom of Figure 10.2. To implement the IIR comb filter shown at the top of Figure 10.2, just make a change in line 16 such that the index used for `bufferx` is `newest` rather than `oldest`.

While a Direct Form I filter implementation is easy derive from the difference equation or transfer function, its key disadvantage is the need for two buffers (circular buffers as before): one to hold the delayed x values and one to hold the delayed y values. We can eliminate this inefficiency easily by using a Direct Form II implementation similar to Figure 4.16. This is shown below in `iir_comb3.m`.

Listing 10.5: A MATLAB IIR comb filter example closer to C, in Direct Form II.

```
% Method using a more "C-like" technique
2
R=round(R);  % ensure R is an integer before proceeding
4 N1=length(x); % number of samples in input array
y=zeros(size(x));  % preallocate output array
6 % create array and index for "circular buffer"
buffer=zeros(1,R+1); % to hold the delayed values
8 oldest=0; newest=0;
% "for loop" simulates real-time samples arriving one by one
10 for i=1:N1
       newest=oldest; % save value of index before incrementing
12     oldest=oldest + 1; % increment buffer index
       oldest=mod(oldest,R+1); % wrap index around
14     buffer(newest+1)=x(i) + alpha*buffer(oldest+1);
       y(i)=buffer(oldest+1);
16 end
```

While this implements exactly the same filter as before, only one circular buffer is needed. You may want to use the program `demo_iir_comb3.m` to read in a WAV audio file (perhaps from the `test_signals` directory), run the comb filter, and play the result. Experiment with different values, especially the delay value, referring to Table 10.1. Once again, the code shown in the listing implements the IIR comb filter shown at the bottom of Figure 10.2. To implement the IIR comb filter shown at the top of Figure 10.2, just make a change in line 15 such that the index used for `buffer` is `newest` rather than `oldest`.

Notice that all the filter programs above that use circular buffers and "for loops" run *much* faster than those using the built-in MATLAB `filter` command. The `filter` command is very general and is therefore not optimized to our specific use of it.

10.4.3 Notch Filter

We provide a notch filter program `notch1.m` that uses the built-in MATLAB `filter` command, but we don't bother to show its code here. A notch filter program `notch2.m` that implements a Direct Form II version in a very "C-like" manner is shown below. Its input variables are x (the input vector), $Beta$ (to set the notch frequency), and $alpha$ (to set the width of the notch).

Listing 10.6: A MATLAB IIR notch filter example, in Direct Form II.

```
% Method using a more "C-like" technique
2
N1=length(x); % number of samples in input array
4 y=zeros(size(x));  % preallocate output array
% create array and index for "circular buffer"
6 % This second order filter only needs a buffer 3 elements long
```

```
   buf=zeros(1,3); % to hold the delayed values
 8 oldest=0; nextoldest=0; newest=0;
   x=x*(1+alpha)/2; % scale input values for unity gain
10 % Set coefficients so calculation isn't done inside "for" loop
   % If sweeping Beta over time, do this inside "for" loop
12 B0=1; B1=-2*Beta; B2=1;
   A0=1; A1=Beta*(1+alpha); A2=-alpha;
14 % "for loop" simulates real-time samples arriving one by one
   for i=1:N1
16     newest=oldest; % save value of index before incrementing
       oldest=oldest + 1; % increment buffer index
18     oldest=mod(oldest,3); % wrap index around
       nextoldest=oldest + 1; % increment buffer index again
20     nextoldest=mod(nextoldest,3); % wrap index around
       buf(newest+1)=x(i)+A1*buf(nextoldest+1)+A2*buf(oldest+1);
22     y(i)=B0*buf(newest+1)+B1*buf(nextoldest+1)+B2*buf(oldest+1);
   end
```

This program uses similar techniques to the previous examples, but you should verify by comparing the code above to Figure 10.4 that the program really does result in the proper filter being implemented. Note that because this type of notch filter is always second order, we only need a circular buffer three elements long, and we access the current (**newest**) value, the **nextoldest** value which has been delayed by one sample time, and the **oldest** value which has been delayed by two sample times.

10.4.4   Flanger

Below is the MATLAB code for a flanger; it implements the filter shown in Figure 10.11. The input variables are x (input vector), t (maximum delay in seconds), $alpha$ (feedforward coefficient), $f0$ (variation frequency delay time), and Fs (sample frequency). This program is similar in many ways to Listing 10.2, except that the delay time is varied sinusoidally.

Listing 10.7: A MATLAB flanger example.

```
 1 % Method using a more "C-like" technique

 3 Ts=1/Fs;   % time between samples
   R=round(t/Ts); % determine integer number of samples needed
 5
   N1=length(x); % number of samples in input array
 7 Bn=zeros(1,N1); % preallocate array for B[n]
   arg=0:N1-1; arg=2*pi*(f0/Fs)*arg;
 9 Bn=(R/2)*(1-cos(arg)); % sinusoidally varying delays from 0-R
   Bn=round(Bn); % make the delays integer values
11
   y=zeros(size(x));   % preallocate output array
13 % create array and index for "circular buffer"
   buffer=zeros(1,R+1);
15 oldest=0;
   % "for loop" simulates real-time samples arriving one by one
17 for i=1:N1
       offset=R-Bn(i); % adjustment for varying delay
19     buffer(oldest+1)=x(i); % input sample into circular buffer
```

```
        oldest=oldest + 1; % increment buffer index
21      oldest=mod(oldest,R+1); % wrap index around
        offset=oldest+offset; % if delay=R this equates to fir_comb2
23      offset=mod(offset,R+1);
        y(i)=x(i) + alpha*buffer(offset+1);
25  end
```

Notice that lines 7 to 10 create $\beta[n]$, an array of sinusoidally varying integers ranging from 0 to R to be used as delay values. There are many ways to use $\beta[n]$ to make the index for the circular buffer to point to the value with the correct amount of delay. In the program above, we use a simple technique that clearly shows how this filter operation differs from the comb filter of Listing 10.2. Line 18 determines by how many locations the circular buffer index will need to be adjusted (compared to the comb filter of Listing 10.2) to account for the variable delay. For example, if $\beta[n] = R$ for a particular n, then the offset calculated in line 18 will be $R - R = 0$, and the index value calculated in line 22 will be the same as that used in Listing 10.2, which results in a delay of R. At the other extreme, if $\beta[n] = 0$, then the offset calculated in line 18 will be $R - 0 = R$, and the index value calculated in line 22 will be such that it will "wraparound" the circular buffer back to the current sample, which results in a delay of 0. Thus, the filter uses a sinusoidally varying delay, as needed for the flanger.

In Listing 10.7 above, the length of the array for $\beta[n]$ is the same as the length of the input vector, to keep things simple. When we transition to real-time C code, this would be impractical, as we can't predict how many input samples we'll be processing and probably wouldn't want to use an array that long anyway. So how do we overcome this? We just implement $\beta[n]$ as a separate circular buffer (with its own index variable) filled with sinusoidally varying values between 0 and R. How long should this buffer be? You don't need to store values in $\beta[n]$ that exceed one period of the sinusoid. A bit of thought should convince you that one period of the sinusoid must have a length of $Fs/f0$ elements. For example, if the sample frequency is 48 kHz and the frequency of the delay variation is 0.5 Hz (remember $f0$ is typically a very low frequency), then the array for $\beta[n]$ would need to be 96,000 elements long. There are techniques to cut this size to a half or a fourth of $Fs/f0$, but we leave that up to your imagination.

10.4.5   Tremelo

The concept of implementing $\beta[n]$ as a circular buffer is demonstrated below in the program tremelo.m, which implements the tremelo effect from the bottom of Figure 10.15.

Listing 10.8: A MATLAB tremelo example.

```
1  % Method using a "C-like" technique

3  N1=length(x); % number of samples in input array
   N2=Fs/f0;  % length for one period of a sinusoid
5  Bn=zeros(1,N2); % preallocate array for B[n]
   arg=0:N2-1; arg=2*pi*(f0/Fs)*arg;
7  Bn=(0.5)*(1-cos(arg)); % sinusoidally varying numbers from 0-1
   scale=1-alpha; % to scale the non-modulated component
9
   y=zeros(size(x));  % preallocate output array
11 % create index for "circular buffer" of Bn
   Bindex=0;
13 % "for loop" simulates real-time samples arriving one by one
```

```
    for  i=1:N1
15      y(i)=scale*x(i) + Bn(Bindex+1)*alpha*x(i);
        Bindex=Bindex + 1; % increment Bn index
17      Bindex=mod(Bindex,N2); % wrap index around
    end
```

The input variables are x (input vector), *alpha* (the gain of the amplitude modulated part of the signal), $f0$ (frequency of the modulation), and Fs (the sample frequency). This example also shows how simple multiplication allows you to adjust the amplitude of the signal. The fuzz effect, which clips amplitude, would be even easier to implement than tremelo.

The MATLAB code shown above (from the `matlab` directory of Chapter 10) provides the basic building blocks for you to create any of the special effects filters described under the Theory section of this chapter. We now turn our attention to the transition from MATLAB to real-time C code that will run on a DSK.

10.5   DSK Implementation in C

In this section, we get you started with making the transition from MATLAB code that is not real time to C code that will run in real time on the DSK. Once you see how to convert to C for a few types of filters, you will be able to create all the effects discussed in this chapter. We stay with sample-by-sample processing to keep the code simple, but there is no reason why you can't implement these same ideas using frame-based code.

10.5.1   Real-Time Comb Filters

We provide three versions of C code that implement comb filters in real time. All three versions are written in such a way that you can easily change between an FIR or an IIR filter by choosing which lines of code to uncomment. If you choose FIR, the C code closely follows the MATLAB example of Listing 10.2; if you choose IIR, the C code closely follows the MATLAB example of Listing 10.5 (i.e., Direct Form II so only one circular buffer is required).

The files necessary to run this application are in the `ccs\Echo` directory of Chapter 10. The primary files of interest are `ISRs_A.c`, `ISRs_B.c`, and `ISRs_C.c`. **Important:** you must have only *one* of these ISR files loaded as part of your project at any given time. The ISR files contain the necessary variable declarations and perform the actual filtering operation.

One aspect that needs to be discussed is how some of the variables are declared. Just as with the "C-like" MATLAB examples, an array implemented as a circular buffer will provide the delays needed for the filter.

Listing 10.9: Excerpt of variable declarations for the `ISRs_A.c` comb filter.

```
  Uint32 oldest = 0; // index for buffer value
2 #define BUFFER_LENGTH 96000 // buffer length in samples
  #pragma DATA_SECTION (buffer,"CE0"); // buffer in external SDRAM
4 volatile float buffer[2][BUFFER_LENGTH]; // for left and right
  volatile float gain = 0.75; // set gain value for echoed sample
```

The index value for the array is declared in line 1. The length of the buffer is defined in line 2, and the gain is defined in line 5, which is equivalent to R and α, respectively, in previous examples. Assuming a 48 kHz sample frequency, the value 96000 for R will provide a delay of 2 seconds. Lines 3 and 4 allocate memory needed for the buffer. Since we must have room for both left and right channel samples, the array actually requires $2 \times 96000 = 192000$ elements. Note that line 3 is critical, and its omission is a common error. The linker, which takes the outputs of the C compiler, will try to fit everything in the internal RAM for speed purposes, but an array of 192000 floats will not fit in the internal memory. Without line 3, the linker will generate an error message and the array will not be created. Unfortunately, this error message, which shows up in the bottom Code Composer Studio window, is often missed because it usually scrolls up and out of sight. But when you load and run the program without line 3 the filter output will be zero (silent). Line 3 directs the compiler to place the array that will be called `buffer` in the memory region we call `CE0`, which is external SDRAM. Thus, the buffer will have enough room to be created, the linker will not complain, and the program will run correctly. Another common error is not using the **volatile** keyword in lines 4 and 5 (see Appendix H for more about these issues).

The part of `ISRs_A.c` that performs the actual filtering operation is in the ISR function called `Codec_ISR()`. To allow for the use of a stereo codec, the program implements independent Left and Right channel filters. However, for clarity, only the Left channel will be discussed following the code listing.

Listing 10.10: Real-time comb filter from `ISRs_A.c`.

```
1  xLeft=CodecDataIn.Channel[LEFT];  // current LEFT input to float
   xRight=CodecDataIn.Channel[RIGHT];// current RIGHT input to float
3
   buffer[LEFT][oldest]=xLeft;
5  buffer[RIGHT][oldest]=xRight;
   newest=oldest; // save index value before incrementing
7  oldest=(++oldest)%BUFFER_LENGTH; // modulo for circular buffer

9  // use either FIR or IIR lines below

11 // for FIR comb filter effect, uncomment next two lines
   yLeft=xLeft + (gain * buffer[LEFT][oldest]);
13 yRight=xRight + (gain * buffer[RIGHT][oldest]);

15 // for IIR comb filter effect, uncomment four lines below
   //buffer[LEFT][newest]=xLeft + (gain * buffer[LEFT][oldest]);
17 //buffer[RIGHT][newest]=xRight + (gain * buffer[RIGHT][oldest]);
   //yLeft=buffer[LEFT][oldest];  // or use newest
19 //yRight=buffer[RIGHT][oldest];  // or use newest

21 CodecDataOut.Channel[LEFT]=yLeft;   // setup the LEFT value
   CodecDataOut.Channel[RIGHT]=yRight; // setup the RIGHT value
```

The real-time steps involved in comb filtering

An explanation of Listing 10.10 follows.

1. (Line 1): The ISR first converts the current sample (obtained from the codec as a 16-bit integer) to a floating point value and assigns it as current input element, equivalent to `x[0]`.

2. (Line 4): The current (i.e., the newest) sample is written into the circular buffer, overwriting the oldest sample.

3. (Line 6): The index value pointing to the newest value is saved before the next line of code causes the index to be incremented. This is used only for the IIR implementation. In fact, when running the FIR version it's likely that you'll get a compiler warning about the variable "newest" being set but not used. You can safely ignore this warning.

4. (Line 7): This is the line that causes the buffer to be "circular" in that the modulus operator (the % character in C and C++) causes the index to "wraparound" in the same way that mod() did in several of the earlier MATLAB examples. This line also includes the prefix ++, which increments the index value oldest *before* the modulus is applied. Thus, this line of code ensures the value of the index points to what is now the oldest sample in the circular buffer.

5. (Line 12): This line performs the FIR filter operation. Comment these lines out if you want the IIR comb filter.

6. (Lines 16 and 18): These lines together perform the IIR filter operation in a Direct Form II manner. Comment these lines out if you want the FIR comb filter. As shown, the code implements the IIR comb filter shown at the bottom of Figure 10.2. To implement the IIR comb filter shown at the top of Figure 10.2, simply change the index variable oldest in Line 18 to newest.

7. (Line 21): This line of code transfers the result of the filtering operation, $y[0]$, to the CodecDataOut.Channel[LEFT] variable for transfer to the DAC side of the codec via the remaining code of the ISR.

Now that you understand the code...

Go ahead and copy all of the files into a separate directory. Open the project in CCS and "Rebuild All." Once the build is complete, "Load Program" into the DSK and click on "Run." Your comb filter is now running on the DSK. Use a guitar or even a microphone as input and listen to the output. You should hear an echo (if FIR) or echoes (if IIR) spaced 2 seconds apart, due to the buffer length of each channel being 96000 long (assuming a sample frequency of 48 kHz). Feel free to change the definition of BUFFER_LENGTH to some other value to use a different value of R. After making the change, save the ISR file, rebuild the project, reload the program, and run it. In a similar fashion, you can experiment with changing the value of the gain variable to use a different value of α.

A small improvement to ISRs_A

While the modulus operator used on Line 7 above makes it easy to implement a circular buffer, it is not the recommended method for real-time processing. Modulus is the remainder after division, so using modulus in a line of code forces a division operation, which is costly in terms of CPU cycles since the DSP has no hardware support for division. A *far* more efficient way to implement a circular buffer is used in ISRs_B.c, where Line 7 is replaced with the two lines shown below.

Listing 10.11: Efficient circular buffer in the ISRs_B.c comb filter.

```
if (++oldest >= BUFFER_LENGTH) // implement circular buffer
       oldest = 0;
```

This is the only change between ISRs_A and ISRs_B. Even more efficient code could be realized by adopting the common practice of sizing your circular buffers to be a power of two (i.e., 2^n) in length, since the index wraparound can then be accomplished very quickly by "AND-ing" it with $2^n - 1$. But we leave it to you to implement that change if desired.

To switch from using ISRs_A to ISRs_B, right click ISRs_A.c in the left project window and select "Remove from Project." At the top of the Code Composer Studio window, click "Project," "Add Files to Project" and select ISRs_B.c. Then click "Rebuild All." Once the build is complete, "Load Program" (or "Reload Program") into the DSK and click on "Run." Your improved comb filter is now running on the DSK.

Incorporating interactive control

Code Composer Studio supports a general extension language (GEL) that allows you to rapidly create sliders, menu boxes, and other interfaces to be used with your program. However, in CCS version 4.2, it appears that the GEL control updates can now be made only while the program is fully halted, greatly limiting the usefulness of GEL controls (such as sliders) for CCS projects. We therefore no longer cover GEL controls in any detail.

Support software to facilitate the creation of real-time interactive controls is provided with the software for the book. If you are motivated to include such interactive controls in your real-time program, and are willing to invest just a bit of time and effort, you can make use of the functions called Windows Control Applications that accompany this book. They allow you to run a fully optimized RELEASE version of your compiled program and avoid any processor halts while still controlling your program. Similar techniques were used to create the winDSK8 application. See Appendix E for more information.

10.5.2 Other Real-Time Special Effects

The demonstrations above of how to convert MATLAB examples of comb filters to real-time C code that will run on the DSK should allow you to create any of the other special effects described in this chapter. A notch filter, tremelo, fuzz, and so on can all be converted to C and run in real time. For creating sinusoidally varying delay times for effects such as a flanger or chorus, consider creating the sinusoidal values for $\beta[n]$ in the StartUp.c module. You *don't* want to put something like that inside an ISR which executes over and over again at the rate of the sample clock!

When you start to concatenate multiple special effects, you may exceed the limits of the real-time schedule because you're trying to do too much in one sample time. This situation calls for converting your code to frame-based processing, using EDMA to transfer data without CPU overhead, and other techniques to extract higher performance from the DSP.

10.6 Follow-On Challenges

Consider extending what you have learned.

1. Add a time-varying (such as sinusoidal) delay time to the real-time comb filter, and choose an appropriate range of delay times to create the flanger effect.

2. Create three different comb filters similar to the flanger, but with longer delay times, and use them to create a chorus effect.

3. What do you expect to happen if you set $\alpha = 1.0$? Try it and find out. How would you modify the code to avoid this problem?

4. Implement a notch filter and use it for a phasing (i.e., phaser) effect.

5. Implement a tremelo effect.

6. Implement a ring modulator effect.

7. Implement a fuzz effect. Experiment with different ways of clipping the signal. Experiment with following and/or preceding the clipping operation with frequency selective filters.

8. Try combining more than one effect, such as a flanger followed by reverb.

9. Convert the real-time comb filter to frame-based operation.

Chapter 11

Project 2: Graphic Equalizer

11.1 Theory

THE parallel implementation of a 5-band FIR-based equalizer was first discussed in Chapter 3. A block diagram of such an equalizer and the generalized extension of this parallel implementation are shown in Figure 11.1. While this extension to M bands may not seem like a major change, increasing the computational complexity of the DSP algorithm by adding additional parallel filters will eventually result in being unable to meet the real-time schedule. At this stage in the equalizer's development, we must either settle for the current level of system performance or rethink our approach to implementing the algorithm. This is very similar to the approach taken in Chapter 3 where we progressed

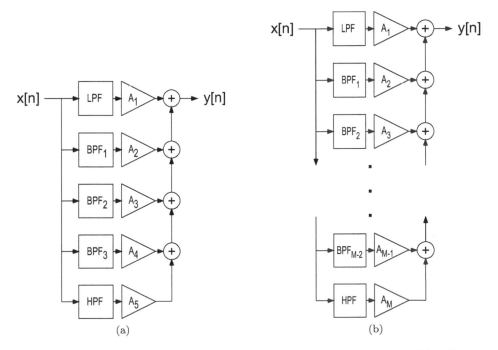

Figure 11.1: (a) Block diagram representing the winDSK8 5-band Graphic Equalizer application. (b) Generalized block diagram of an M-band graphic equalizer.

Figure 11.2: Photograph of a commercially available graphic equalizer, the EQ351 from Applied Research and Technology, Inc. This is a 31-band, 1/3 octave, ISO spaced, monaural graphic equalizer. See http://artproaudio.com/eqs/product/eq351/.

from an easily understood brute force implementation of the filter's dot-product, to a much more efficient, but more complicated to understand, implementation using a circular buffer.

One of the first results of "rethinking" our approach to implementing the equalizer is achieved when we realize that the gains associated with each of the parallel filters are not changed very often. If we assume that this is the case, why can't we calculate an equivalent filter, and implement this single filter instead of summing the outputs of M parallel filters?

Consider a 31-band audio equalizer similar to the commercially available model shown in Figure 11.2. If we are confident that the gain controls of the individual filters are only occasionally adjusted, then we can reduce the computational complexity of our DSP implementation by a factor of nearly 31, by *first* calculating an equivalent filter. A reduction factor of 31 is achieved by implementing a single filter instead of 31 filters, but this ignores the addition of the outputs of the 31 filters. For large order filters, these extra additions become negligible. This equivalent filter technique will allow us to implement an almost unlimited number of parallel filters.

The 31-band monaural audio equalizer shown in Figure 11.2 has center frequencies of 20, 25, 31.5, 40, 50, 63, 80, 100, 125, 160, 200, 250, 315, 400, 500, 630, 800, 1000, 1250, 1600, 2000, 2500, 3150, 4000, 5000, 6300, 8000, 10000, 12500, 16000, and 20000 Hz, which constitute frequency bands spaced 1/3 octave apart. An equivalent stereo equalizer would have identical but independent frequency bands for both the left and right channels.

11.2   winDSK Demonstration

Start the winDSK8 application, and the main user interface window will appear. Ensure the correct selections have been made in the "DSP Board" and "Host Interface" configuration panels of winDSK8 for each parameter before proceeding.

11.2.1   Graphic Equalizer Application

Clicking on the winDSK8 Graphic Equalizer button will run that program in the attached DSK, and a window similar to Figure 11.3 will appear. The Graphic Equalizer application implements a five-band audio equalizer, similar to the block diagram shown in Figure 11.1(a). If you're using a stereo codec on your DSK (and you have selected that codec from the winDSK8 main window), independently adjustable equalizers are active on both the left and the right channels.

The equalizer uses five FIR filters (a lowpass (LP) filter, 3 bandpass (BP) filters, and a highpass (HP) filter) operating in parallel. The gain sliders (A_1 to A_5) in the dialog box operate on memory locations used to control the gains of each filter and the overall system gain. The 5 FIR filters are designed as high-order ($N = 128$) filters; the resulting steep roll-off of these filters can be seen in Figure 11.4.

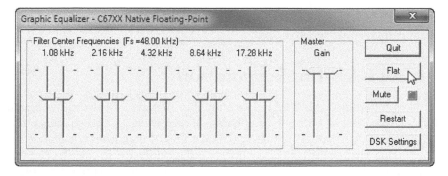

Figure 11.3: winDSK8 running the Graphic Equalizer application.

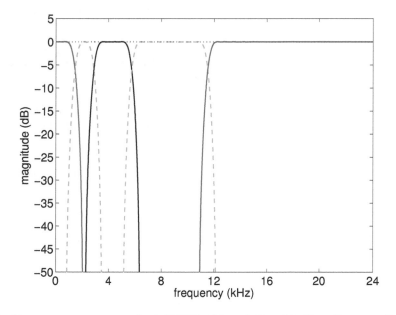

Figure 11.4: Frequency response of winDSK8's 5-band Graphic Equalizer application. The dotted straight line at 0 dB represents the sum of all five bands.

11.2.2 Effect of the Graphic Equalizer

There are a number of ways you can experience the effect of the graphic equalizer filtering. For example, you could connect the output of a CD player to the signal input of the DSK, and connect the DSK signal output to a powered speaker. Play some familiar music while you adjust the graphic equalizer slider controls and listen to the result. A more objective experiment would be to play the track of additive white Gaussian noise (AWGN) included with the software for the book (in directory `test_signals` play the file `awgn.wav`), which theoretically contains all frequencies. If the DSK signal output is then connected to a spectrum analyzer, you could observe which band of frequencies is affected, and how much it is affected, as you adjust the slider controls. If you don't have a spectrum analyzer available, a second DSK running winDSK8 can be used in its place (select the "Oscilloscope" button from the main screen, select "Spectrum Analyzer" from the next screen, and select "Log10" to display the result in decibels). Alternatively, you can use your computer's sound card to gather a portion of the DSK's output. This can be accomplished using the Windows sound recorder, the MATLAB® data acquisition (DAQ) toolbox, or the audio recorder that was recently introduced into MATLAB (version 6.1 or later). This recorded data can be analyzed and displayed using MATLAB.

11.3   MATLAB Implementation

As we stated in Chapter 3, MATLAB has a number of ways of performing filtering operations. In this chapter, we will only emphasize the creation of an equivalent filter based on the scaled sum of the parallel filters that make up the equalizer. As shown in the listing below, creating this equivalent filter is very straightforward as long as the equalizer is constructed using filters of equal order. "Zero padding" will be required to sum filters of differing length.

Listing 11.1: Calculating an equivalent impulse response.

```
% Simulation inputs
load('equalizer.mat')
A = [1.0 1.0 1.0 1.0 1.0]; % graphic equalizer scale factors

% Calculated terms
equivalentFilter = A(1)*filt1.tf.num + A(2)*filt2.tf.num + ...
    A(3)*filt3.tf.num + A(4)*filt4.tf.num + A(5)*filt5.tf.num;
```

A few items need to be discussed concerning this code listing.

1. The stored filter coefficients need to be loaded into the MATLAB workspace (line 2).

2. The filter scale factors, A_1, A_2, ..., A_5 are specified (line 3). In this example, all of the scale factors are set equal to 1. This results in a flat response.

3. The scale factors are multiplied by each of the filters' impulse response and then summed together (lines 6–7). The five filters used in this example were previously designed using the MATLAB function sptool. This function is capable of exporting structure-based variables to the MATLAB workspace. The variable filt1.tf.num contains the numerator coefficients num associated with the transfer function tf of filt1.

The first five subplots of Figure 11.5 show the impulse responses of each of the five FIR filters that make up the equalizer. The final subplot is the sum of all five impulse responses. The frequency response associated with these filters was shown in Figure 11.4.

With all of the filter gains set to 1.0, as they are in this example, the system should have a flat frequency response. Thus, it should come as no surprise that equivalent impulse response of the sum of all the equalizer filter impulse responses is a single delta function. That is, the frequency response and the impulse response are a Fourier transform pair, and the Fourier transform of a single delta function is a flat magnitude spectrum (equal power at all frequencies).

To change the frequency response of the equalizer, all we need to do is adjust the individual filter gains. The single line modification to the previous code listing is shown below.

Listing 11.2: Calculating a new equivalent impulse response.

```
A = [0.1 0.5 1.0 0.25 0.1]; % new graphic equalizer scale factors
```

The individual impulse responses and their sum are shown in Figure 11.6. The resulting equalizer's frequency response is shown in Figure 11.7. Finally, Figure 11.8 shows the equivalent filter's impulse and frequency response magnitude together.

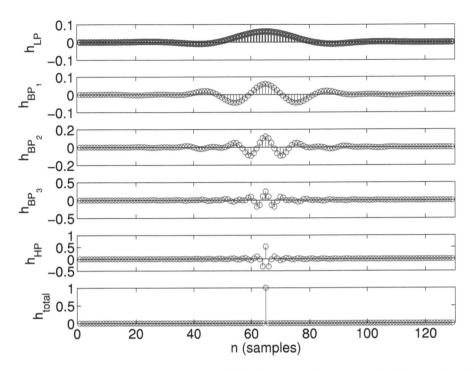

Figure 11.5: Impulse response of the five FIR filters and the sum (at bottom) of these impulse responses for unity gain at all bands.

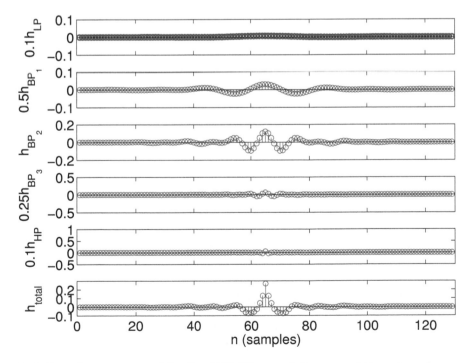

Figure 11.6: Impulse response of the five FIR filters and the sum of these impulse responses with unequal gain in the bands.

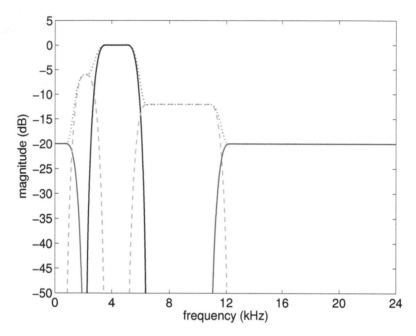

Figure 11.7: Frequency response of the five FIR filters and the equivalent filter.

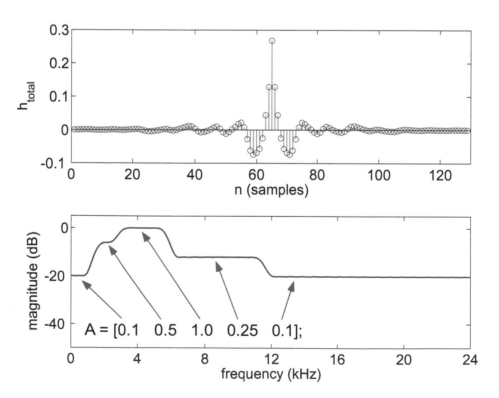

Figure 11.8: Impulse and frequency response of the equivalent filter.

11.4 DSK Implementation in C

11.4.1 Applying Gain to Filter Bands

When you understand the MATLAB code, the conceptual translation into C is fairly straightforward. The equalizer is actually implementing a single equivalent FIR filter, and any of the techniques discussed in Chapter 3 could be used. The new portion of this project is applying the gains to each filter band's coefficients and calculating the equivalent filter. This is accomplished in the `main.c` file, which is shown in Listing 11.3.

Listing 11.3: Graphic equalizer project main.c code.

```c
#include "DSP_Config.h"
#include "coeff.h"          // coefficients used by FIR filter
#include "coeff_lp.h"       // coefficients for equalizer
#include "coeff_bp1.h"
#include "coeff_bp2.h"
#include "coeff_bp3.h"
#include "coeff_hp.h"

volatile float new_gain_lp=1, new_gain_bp1=1, new_gain_bp2=1;
volatile float new_gain_bp3=1, new_gain_hp=1;
volatile float old_gain_lp=0, old_gain_bp1=0, old_gain_bp2=0;
volatile float old_gain_bp3=0, old_gain_hp=0;

void UpdateCoefficients()
{
  Int32 i;

  old_gain_lp  = new_gain_lp; // save new gain values
  old_gain_bp1 = new_gain_bp1;
  old_gain_bp2 = new_gain_bp2;
  old_gain_bp3 = new_gain_bp3;
  old_gain_hp  = new_gain_hp;

  for(i = 0; i <= N; i++) { // calculate new coefficients
    B[i] = (B_LP[i]  * old_gain_lp)  + (B_BP1[i] * old_gain_bp1)
      + (B_BP2[i] * old_gain_bp2) + (B_BP3[i] * old_gain_bp3)
      + (B_HP[i]  * old_gain_hp);
  }
}


int main()
{
    UpdateCoefficients(); // update FIR filter coefficients

    // initialize DSP board
    DSP_Init();
```

```
                // main stalls here, the interrupts control the operation
41          while (1) {
                    // check if any gains have changed
43              if ((new_gain_lp != old_gain_lp)
                        || (new_gain_bp1 != old_gain_bp1)
45                      || (new_gain_bp2 != old_gain_bp2)
                        || (new_gain_bp3 != old_gain_bp3)
47                      || (new_gain_hp != old_gain_hp)) {
                    UpdateCoefficients();
49              }
            }
51  }
```

An explanation of Listing 11.3 follows.

1. (Lines 2–7): Include the header files associated with the filter coefficients.

2. (Lines 9–12): Declare the filter gains. There are **old_gain** values, which are the gains that are in use, and there are **new_gain** values, which are the gains that have been updated.

3. (Line 14): Beginning of the **UpdateCoefficients** function.

4. (Lines 18–22): Copy the **new_gain** values to the **old_gain** values.

5. (Lines 24–28): Calculate the new equivalent filter coefficients, **B[i]**.

6. (Line 33): Call the **UpdateCoefficients** function to update filter coefficients.

7. (Line 39): Stalled, waiting for interrupts.

8. (Lines 41–47): If any of the equalizer gains have changed, call the **UpdateCoefficients** function.

11.4.2   GEL File Slider Control

Code Composer Studio supports a general extension language (GEL) that allows for sliders, menu boxes, and other interfaces to be rapidly created. The GEL file system uses the DEBUG portion of the CCS/DSK communication link to update variable values. Earlier versions of CCS temporarily halted the processor while the update took place, resulting in a momentary loss of the output signal. While this loss of signal is undesirable, the relative ease with which GEL file interfaces could be made to a CCS project made them a potentially useful tool. However, beginning with CCS version 4.2, it appears that the GEL control updates can be made only while the program is fully halted, greatly limiting the usefulness of GEL controls (such as sliders) for CCS projects. We therefore no longer cover GEL controls in any detail. Using GEL-based sliders used to be fairly easy, but the fact that the program must now be halted each time you adjust a slider keeps this from being useful for a real-time program. To get around this problem, Windows-based sliders (as part of a Windows Control Application) need to be created in such a way that the DSP can run without stopping. Support software to facilitate this is provided with the software for the book. See Appendix E for more information.

11.5 Follow-On Challenges

Consider extending what you have learned.

1. Design and implement your own monaural graphic equalizer. Select the frequency bands you desire and create an equivalent filter that will run in real time, using Windows-based sliders to control the gain of each frequency band.

2. Design and implement your own stereo graphic equalizer in a fashion similar to the monaural version.

Chapter 12

Project 3: Second-Order Sections

12.1 Theory

THE concept of using a second-order section (SOS) as a building block for IIR filters was first introduced in Section 4.3.3. Some advantages of using second-order sections for IIR filters were mentioned, such as the reduction of quantization effects on the filter coefficients. Note that, in practice, second-order sections are seldom used for FIR filters as they provide little to no advantage. For this project, we explore the use of second-order sections further. A block diagram showing how second-order sections can be used as building blocks for higher order filters was provided in Figure 4.18; for convenience, that figure is reproduced here as Figure 12.1. Odd-order filters can be implemented using SOS techniques by adding a first order section at the beginning or end of the cascaded sections.

In Section 4.3.3, an m-file called `ellipticExample` was introduced that implemented a fourth-order elliptic IIR filter. This m-file compared, among other things, the direct form implementation to the SOS implementation, when the filter coefficients were quantized to 16 bits of precision. For convenience, figures of both types of implementations are reproduced here as Figures 12.2 and 12.3. It was shown in Section 4.3.3 that, due to quantization effects, the direct form version was unstable, whereas the SOS version was stable. This is one of the primary reasons for the widely used practice of turning to SOS implementations for IIR filters: given the same order and specifications, an SOS version is far less affected by small variations in the coefficient values than any of the direct form versions. These

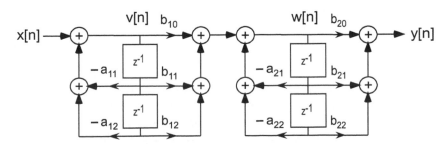

Figure 12.1: Block diagram associated with the second-order section (SOS) implementation of a fourth-order IIR filter, showing two SOS stages. Each SOS is a DF-II form.

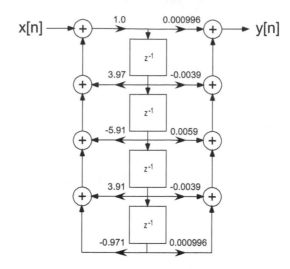

Figure 12.2: Block diagram of a direct form II (DF-II) fourth-order elliptic filter.

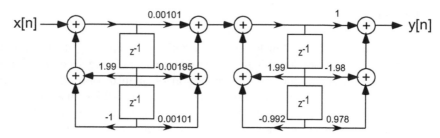

Figure 12.3: Block diagram of a second-order section (SOS) implementation of the same fourth-order elliptic filter as the filter shown in Figure 12.2.

coefficient variations occur when a filter is designed to the designer's satisfaction using high-precision numeric representation such as that found in MATLAB's FDATool,[1] but is then implemented on hardware that imposes lower precision (usually due to the CPU register size) on the coefficient values.

In a direct form implementation, the total "depth" of the sample delays is equal to the order of the polynomials in the numerator and denominator of the transfer function, as shown in Figure 12.2. Any perturbation in coefficient values is compounded at each additional level of delay. Because an SOS building block, by definition, is only two sample delays "deep," the amount of perturbation in coefficient values is kept small. In general, an SOS implementation is more robust.

The advantage of using SOS can be shown even when coefficient quantization is not an issue. Filter design algorithms can sometimes be challenged to find a stable direct form solution when the filter specifications are very stringent, yet have no problem finding a stable SOS solution. This is often a result of numerical problems due to roundoff errors that occur when the algorithm tries to form a single transfer function (i.e., just one numerator and one denominator polynomial), which implies a direct form solution. A pertinent example can be found in Section 3.6.2 of the biomedical signal processing text by Rangayyan [79]. The problem presented was an electrocardiogram (ECG) signal which had a significant low frequency artifact called a "wandering baseline," most likely due to patient movement during

---

[1]MATLAB typically defaults to using 64-bit double-precision floating point values for all calculations.

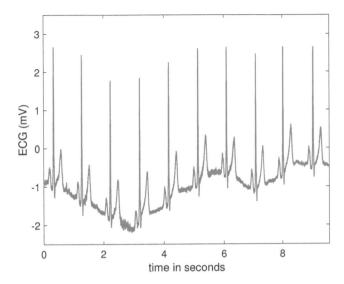

Figure 12.4: Electrocardiogram (ECG) with baseline drift; some higher frequency noise (power-line artifact) is also visible. Adapted from [79].

signal acquisition; see Figure 12.4. But the ECG has important diagnostic information at fairly low frequencies, and thus the solution for removing the baseline drift called for a sharp-cutoff HPF with a very low cutoff frequency. The suggested filter was an 8th-order Butterworth HPF, with a cutoff frequency of 2 Hz. Since the signal was acquired with $F_s = 1$ kHz, the ratio of f_c/F_s was only 0.002. That, combined with the order of the filter, posed a challenge for a stable design.

A Butterworth HPF having the desired specifications can be designed in MATLAB by using the **butter** command from the Signal Processing Toolbox, as shown below.

```
Fs=1000; Fc=2; N=8;
% convert Fc to Wc in pi units as required by "butter"
Wc=(Fc/Fs)*2;  % mult by pi is inherent in the definition
[b,a]=butter(N,Wc,'high'); % design the filter
```

This results in coefficients b_i and a_i ($i = 0, 1, 2, \ldots 8$) that define a single 8th-order polynomial for the numerator and a single 8th-order polynomial for the denominator of the transfer function. These can be used for any direct form implementation. A variation on the call to **butter** is shown next.

```
% now design the same filter again but using SOS
[z,p,k] = butter(N,Wc,'high');  % obtain poles, zeros, and gain
[sos,g] = zp2sos(z,p,k);        % Convert to SOS form
```

This results in a 4×6 matrix *sos*, where each of the four rows contains the coefficients for one of the four second-order sections needed for this filter, and g is the gain factor. Note that it's often a good idea to distribute gain across multiple SOS for high ordered filters.

Zoomed-in z-plane plots of the two resulting filter implementations are shown in Figure 12.5. Note that even with no coefficient quantization imposed on the filter, the direct form implementation places poles outside the unit circle, resulting in an unstable filter. The SOS implementation is stable, although the poles are so close to the unit circle that any potential coefficient quantization that a hardware target might impose could still be an issue. But the main point we want to make here is to show how a second-order section

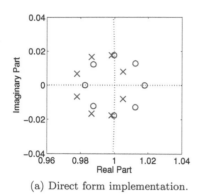

(a) Direct form implementation.

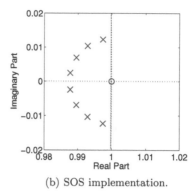

(b) SOS implementation.

Figure 12.5: Zoomed-in comparison of z-plane plots for an 8th-order Butterworth HPF. The almost vertical line in the center of each plot is the unit circle.

implementation is less prone to instability than a direct form implementation is, for the exact same filter specifications.

For further exploration by interested readers, we've included the MATLAB m-files `butterHPF_ex.m` and `ecg_noise_baseline_demo2.m`, and the data file `ecg_lfn_Fs1k.txt` of the wandering baseline ECG in the MATLAB directory for Chapter 12. It should be mentioned that even the stable version of the 8th-order Butterworth HPF has a phase response that would distort the waveshape of an EGC too much for clinical purposes if applied in the traditional manner. The filter's magnitude response can be applied in the frequency domain to the DFT of the ECG, or the `filtfilt` command can be used in the time domain, for excellent results; see Figure 12.6. Both methods are demonstrated in the `ecg_noise_baseline_demo2.m` program. However, either of these two methods implies frame-based processing if real-time operation is required.

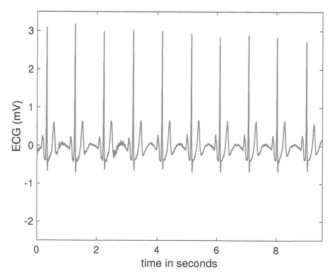

Figure 12.6: Electrocardiogram (ECG) of Figure 12.4, with baseline drift removed by frequency domain filtering using the SOS version of the 8th-order Butterworth HPF. The higher frequency noise was removed by an FIR LPF.

12.2 winDSK Demonstration: Notch Filter Application

The winDSK8 demonstration described in Section 4.2, which led the reader through using a second-order IIR notch filter, is performed using code that implements the filter as a single second-order section of the Direct Form II type. This same second-order IIR notch filter was revisited in Section 10.3. A block diagram of this notch filter was provided in Figure 10.4 on page 184, with more detail, including the transfer function, given on page 188. Readers may want to reacquaint themselves with the winDSK8 Notch Filter if needed.

12.3 MATLAB Implementation

As a convenient starting point, we have implemented a MATLAB simulation of a second-order low pass digital IIR filter. The simulation is coded in `SOSfilter.m`. This script file will plot both the frequency response of the filter (Figure 12.7) and the impulse response (IR) of the filter (Figure 12.8). In Figure 12.8, a comparison between the impulse response calculated using MATLAB's `impz` command is made to our algorithm's results when processing an input file that consists of only an impulse. This type of comparison is routinely performed to gain confidence in an algorithm. Calculating one of the mathematical norms of the two resulting signals would provide even higher levels of confidence in the algorithm, if you wish. The key parts of `SOSfilter.m` are shown in the listing below. The purpose of each part of the program should be evident from the comments in the listing.

Listing 12.1: A MATLAB simulation of a real time second-order low pass digital IIR filter.

```matlab
1  inputx = [1 0 0 0 0 0 0 0 0]; % impulse
   index = length(inputx); % length of x
3  yStorage = zeros(1, index);

5  x = [0 0 0];    %  input storage
   y = [0 0 0];    % output storage
7
   G = 0.248341078962541; % filter's gain
9  B = [1.0 2.0 1.0]; % numerator coefficients
   A = [1.0 -0.184213803077536 0.177578118927698]; % denominator
     [+]coefficients
11
   for n = 1:index % ISR simulation
13     % read in the current input value
       x(1) = inputx(n);
15
       % calculate the current output value
17     y(1) = -A(2)*y(2) - A(3)*y(3) + G*(B(1)*x(1) + B(2)*x(2) +
         [+]B(3)*x(3));
19     % prepare for next input value by updating stored values
       x(3) = x(2); x(2) = x(1);
21     y(3) = y(2); y(2) = y(1);

23     % update the storage array (save the filter's output values)
       % note: this is not part of the ISR; only needed for plotting
25     yStorage(n) = y(1);
   end
```

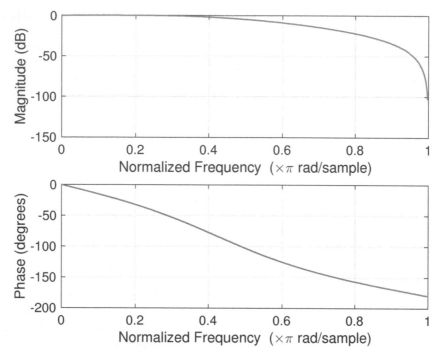

Figure 12.7: Frequency response of an IIR LPF implemented using SOS.

The next MATLAB file, SOSfilterRevA.m, modifies the SOSfilter.m program by turning the DF-I filtering operation into a function call. The function that is called by SOSfilterRevA.m is named sosFiltFunDFI.m, as shown below.

```
% perform the filtering operation
[x, y] = sosFiltFunDFI(x, y, B, A, G);
```

Everything else associated with this filter simulation remains the same as it was for the SOSfilter.m program. For consistency, the script file SOSfilterRevA.m generates the same two output plots as SOSfilter.m.

The next file, SOSfilterRevB.m, modifies the SOSfilterRevA.m program by turning the DF-I filtering operation into a DF-II filtering operation. The DF-II filter function called by SOSfilterRevB.m is named sosFiltFunDFII.m, as shown below.

```
% perform the filtering operation
[w, y] = sosFiltFunDFII(w, x, B, A, G);
```

Note that, unlike a DF-I function call, a DF-II function call uses w, where w is the current state of the filter. But DF-II is slightly more efficient than DF-I, as any DSP theory text will tell you. Everything else associated with this filter simulation remains the same. For consistency, this script file SOSfilterRevB.m also generates the same two output plots as SOSfilter.m.

12.4   DSK Implementation in C

The MATLAB programs just discussed simulate how an ISR would operate, but the execution was not in real time. Now let's look at an actual C-language ISR to run on your DSP board in real time. The next file, sosIIRmono_ISR.c, implements the DF-II IIR filter

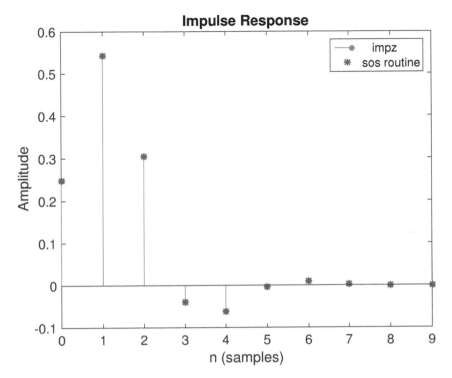

Figure 12.8: Impulse response of an IIR LPF implemented using SOS. Note the result of MATLAB's `impz` command is compared to processing an impulse through the filter.

as an interrupt service routine (ISR) written in C that runs in real-time using CCS. This will require one of the floating-point DSP boards and a working knowledge of real-time IIR filters that we developed in Chapter 4. This ISR does not use a filter function. Don't forget to add the `StartUp.c` file to your project!

12.4.1 Example SOS Code

The declarations associated with the SOS code implemented in C are shown in the listing that follows. Observe the similarities with the values defined in the MATLAB code of Listing 12.1.

Listing 12.2: Declarations associated with the SOS code.

```
float G = 0.248341078962541;      // filter's gain
float B[3] = {1.0, 2.0, 1.0}; // numerator coefficients
float A[3] = {1.0, -0.184213803077536, 0.177578118927698};  //
    [+]denominator coefficients
float w[3] = {0.0, 0.0, 0.0}; // filter's state
float x = 0.0;    // input value (buffered)
float y = 0.0;    // output values (buffered)
```

The purpose of each of the declarations should be evident from the comments in the listing above. Because this program implements the second-order section as a DF-II, the state of the filter (called w) is needed just as it was for the MATLAB simulation discussed earlier.

The algorithm execution associated with the SOS ISR provided in `sosIIRmono_ISR.c` is shown in the next listing.

Listing 12.3: Example SOS code from `sosIIRmono_ISR.c`.

```
x = CodecDataIn.Channel[LEFT]; // current input value; only LEFT
    [+]channel filtered

w[0] = x - A[1]*w[1] - A[2]*w[2];  // update state of the SOS
y = G*(B[0]*w[0] + B[1]*w[1] + B[2]*w[2]); // calculate new y

w[2] = w[1];  // setup for the next input
w[1] = w[0];  // setup for the next input

CodecDataOut.Channel[LEFT]  = y;      // setup the LEFT  value
CodecDataOut.Channel[RIGHT] = y;      // the LEFT output value
    [+]is written to the RIGHT channel
/* end of my DF-II IIR filter routine */

WriteCodecData(CodecDataOut.UINT); // send output data to
    [+]port
```

The purpose of each part of the program should be evident from the comments in the listing. If some part is unclear, a comparison of the C Listing 12.3 above with the very similar algorithm used in the MATLAB simulations provided earlier should clarify how the C program works.

The final file, `sosIIRmonoFun_ISR.c`, implements the DF-II IIR filter as an interrupt service routine (ISR) written in C that runs in real-time, but using a filter function called `IIR_SOS_DF2`. The function `IIR_SOS_DF2` simply provides the same code execution as seen in lines 3–7 of Listing 12.3. Other than this small change, the program is essentially the same as that shown in Listing 12.3, so there is little need to show another listing here. Open the file `sosIIRmonoFun_ISR.c` to see the specifics; note the function `IIR_SOS_DF2` is defined in the area where the global variables are declared. Again, don't forget to add the `StartUp.c` file to your project!

12.5   Points to Ponder

Now that (we hope) you're more comfortable with second-order sections, here are a couple of questions you may want to consider.

1. The second-order sections shown in this chapter were all DF-II. Would there be any advantage to using direct form II transpose (DF-IIt) for creating the second-order sections? See Figure 4.17 for an example of DF-IIt.

2. How does an SOS design compare to a parallel design? See Figure 4.19 for an example of a parallel filter implementation.

12.6   Follow-On Challenges

Consider extending what you have learned. This Project helped you with the implementation of a single SOS. Expand on what you have learned by accomplishing one or all of the following tasks.

1. Implement a higher-order, but even-ordered, filter using a cascade of multiple SOS using multiple function calls.

2. Write a new function that will implement the cascade of multiple SOS for you.

3. Write a new function that will implement an odd ordered filter using cascaded SOS and one additional filter stage.

4. How would you filter a stereo signal (signals from both the left and right channels)? Implement such a design.

Chapter 13

Project 4: Peak Program Meter

13.1 Theory

THE basic block diagram of the generic DSP system, shown in Figure 13.1, was first introduced in Chapter 2. We also emphasized in Chapter 2 that the analog signal that is digitized by the analog-to-digital converter (ADC) should not exceed the maximum voltage range of the converter. To avoid unintended distortion, be careful to ensure that the ADC is not driven beyond the maximum input voltage range, in either the positive or negative direction.

Even if the input analog signal remains within the proper range of the ADC, it is still possible to distort the signal by exceeding the output range of the digital to analog converter (DAC). As an example, the possible range of values for a 16-bit converter using two's complement representation is $+32767$ to -32768. Any operation within the DSP algorithm that results in an output value being written to the DAC that falls outside this range will also distort the signal. The only way the signal can exceed the output range for the DAC is if the DSP algorithm has a gain that exceeds 1.0, which implies that the algorithm results in an amplification of the signal. While gain greater than one is not strictly prohibited, saturating the DAC should be avoided, unless for some reason you actually *want* a distorted output.

Historically, volume unit (VU) meters were used in audio systems to monitor the signal's level. VU meters, however, have display accuracy problems that are largely due to the fact that the meter takes an average measurement that is severely restricted by the ballistics of the mechanical metering system. This can result in short, but very loud, transients being missed or improperly displayed.

More recently, audio equipment manufacturers developed the peak program meter (PPM) to overcome the VU meter's lackluster performance at displaying peak signal levels. The PPM improves on the VU meter's performance problems by integrating the signal for 5 ms. This integration process will then only detect peaks that are long enough to be heard by a typical human listener.

Figure 13.1: A generic DSP system.

13.2   winDSK Demonstration: commDSK

Start the winDSK8 application, and the main user interface window will appear. Ensure the correct selections have been made in the "DSP Board" and "Host Interface" configuration panels of winDSK8 for each parameter before proceeding. Clicking on winDSK8's commDSK button will run that program in the attached DSK, and a window similar to Figure 13.2 will appear.

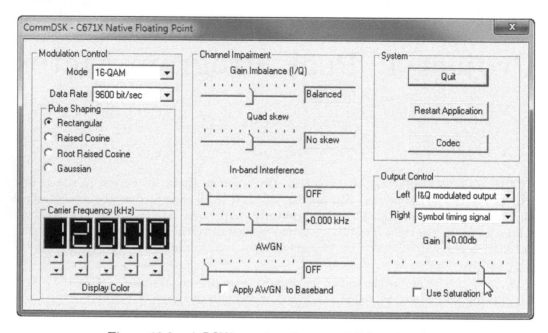

Figure 13.2: winDSK8 running the commDSK application.

In Figure 13.2, the "Output Control," "Left" box has been changed from "Symbol timing signal" to "I&Q modulated output."

The commDSK program is discussed in more detail in Chapter 18. Operation of a PPM can be seen by increasing the system gain. Increasing the system gain is accomplished by clicking on the gain slider located just below the box labeled "Gain," and then moving the slider to the right. This will result in positive gain numbers appearing in the "Gain" box. Additionally, as the "Gain" is increased, the two user LEDs on the OMAP-L138 Experimenter Kit, or three of the four user LEDs on an LCDK or C6713 DSK will function as a PPM.[1]

13.3   MATLAB Implementation

MATLAB® does not have an equivalent function for turning on an LED, except through an indirect use of the Data Acquisition Toolbox. We therefore omit a MATLAB discussion for this chapter.

---

[1]**Note:** While the LCDK and the C6713 DSK have four LEDs included on the board, the OMAP-L138 Experimenter Kit has only two LEDs that are easily accessible to your programs. To allow a similar four-level functionality with the OMAP-L138 Experimenter Kit, you could send signals to four digital output pins on the LCD connector J15 using the WriteDigitalOutputs function. See OMAPL138_Support_DSP.c in the common_code directory of the book's software. Specifically, bits 0–3 are sent to pins 6–9, respectively, of connector J15. Ground is available on that connector at pins 1, 5, and 10.

13.4 DSK Implementation in C

Like the VU meter and PPM, the primary function of this program is to detect and provide an LED indication/warning whenever an output value is approaching the range limit of the DAC. Since these conditions are checked every $T_s = 1/F_s$, a dwell time is also required to maintain the "ON" status of each of the LEDs. Without this dwell time, the LED would cycle on/off too rapidly to be visible. The output values above which an LED turns on were chosen to be ± 28000, ± 32000, and ± 32767. These turn-on levels are shown in Figure 13.3, where the sinusoidal signal is at maximum amplitude for the DAC.

13.4.1 Example PPM Code

The files necessary to run this application are in the **ccs\PPM** directory of Chapter 13. The primary files of interest are **main.c**, **PPM_ISRs.c**, **PPM_ISRs1.c**, **PPM_ISRs2.c**, and **PPM_ISRs3.c**. **Important:** you must have only *one* of the ISR files loaded as part of your project at any given time. The ISR files contain the necessary variable declarations and perform the actual filtering operation. The actual update to the LEDs is performed in **main.c**.

We will discuss **PPM_ISRs.c** first. The declarations associated with the PPM code are shown in the listing that follows.

Listing 13.1: Declarations associated with the PPM.

```
1 #define RESET 4800   // turns the LED off after 4800 samples

3 #define LED1_BIT 1
  #define LED2_BIT 2
5 #define LED3_BIT 4

7 volatile Uint8 LedMask = 0; // used by main() to update the LEDs
```

An explanation of Listing 13.1 follows.

1. (Line 1): Sets the minimum time that an LED will remain "ON." This time equals $(\text{RESET})(T_s)$, which in this case is $4800/48000 = 0.1$ seconds.

2. (Lines 2–5): Define constants that represent the "ON" state for each of the 3 LEDs.

3. (Line 7): Defines a variable, **LedMask**, which is used to control the LEDs.

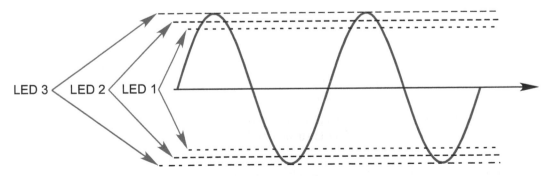

Figure 13.3: LED turn-on levels for the PPM.

A portion of the receive ISR in PPM_ISRs.c is shown in the listing below.

Listing 13.2: Example PPM code from PPM_ISRs.c.

```
1  // LED 1 logic
   if ((abs(outputLeft) > 28000)||(abs(outputRight) > 28000)) {
3      LedMask |= LED1_BIT;   // LED1 on
       LED_1_counter = RESET;
5  }
   else {
7      if (LED_1_counter > 0)
           LED_1_counter -= 1;
9      else
           LedMask &= ~LED1_BIT;   // LED1 off
11 }

13 // LED 2 logic
   if ((abs(outputLeft) > 32000)||(abs(outputRight) > 32000)) {
15     LedMask |= LED2_BIT;   // LED2 on
       LED_2_counter = RESET;
17 }
   else {
19     if (LED_2_counter > 0)
           LED_2_counter -= 1;
21     else
           LedMask &= ~LED2_BIT;   // LED2 off
23 }

25 // LED 3 logic
   if ((abs(outputLeft) > 32767)||(abs(outputRight) > 32767)) {
27     LedMask |= LED3_BIT;   // LED3 on
       LED_3_counter = RESET;
29 }
   else {
31     if (LED_3_counter > 0)
           LED_3_counter -= 1;
33     else
           LedMask &= ~LED3_BIT;   // LED3 off
35 }
```

Explanation of the PPM code

An explanation of Listing 13.2 follows.

1. (Lines 2–5): If either or both of the left or right channel levels is greater than 28,000 in magnitude, then LED 1 is turned on. A counter is also set to 4800. This counter keeps the light on for 0.1 seconds.

2. (Lines 6–11): This block of code decrements LED 1's counter and whenever the counter reaches zero, the LED is turned "OFF."

3. (Lines 14–17): If either or both of the left or right channel levels is greater than 32,000 in magnitude, then LED 2 is turned on. A counter is also set to 4800. This counter keeps the light on for 0.1 seconds.

4. (Lines 18–23): This block of code decrements LED 2's counter and whenever the counter reaches zero, the LED is turned "OFF."

5. (Lines 26–29): If either or both of the left or right channel levels is greater than 32,767 in magnitude, then LED 3 is turned on. A counter is also set to 4800. This counter keeps the light on for 0.1 seconds.

6. (Lines 30–35): This block of code decrements LED 3's counter and whenever the counter reaches zero, the LED is turned "OFF."

13.4.2   DSK LED Control

The LEDs are controlled using the `WriteLEDs` function. On the OMAP-L138 Experimenter Kit, signals to the LEDs are sent via an I^2C interface, which is too slow to use inside an ISR. The variable `LedMask` is used to pass the desired LED state to `main.c`, and the code in `main.c` updates the LEDs only when the state changes. To be consistent, the same approach is used for the LCDK and the C6713 DSK.

13.4.3   Another PPM Code Version

As noted above, four different versions of the PPM ISR code are provided with the software that accompanies the book. We have already discussed the pertinent parts of `PPM_ISRs.c`. We will now discuss `PPM_ISRs3.c`; explore the variations present in `PPM_ISRs1.c` and `PPM_ISRs2.c` on your own.

This implementation uses the same declarations as those shown earlier for `PPM_ISRs.c`. A portion of the ISR in `PPM_ISRs3.c` is shown in Listing 13.3.

Listing 13.3: Another approach to creating the PPM, excerpted from `PPM_ISRs3.c`.

```
1  maxOutput = _fabsf(outputLeft);
   if(maxOutput < _fabsf(outputRight))
3      maxOutput = _fabsf(outputRight);

5  if (maxOutput > 32767) {
       LED_3_counter = RESET;
7      LED_2_counter = RESET * 2;
       LED_1_counter = RESET * 3;
9  }
   else if (maxOutput > 32000) {
11     if(LED_2_counter < RESET)
           LED_2_counter = RESET;
13     if(LED_1_counter < RESET * 2)
           LED_1_counter = RESET * 2;
15 }
   else if (maxOutput > 28000) {
17     if(LED_1_counter < RESET)
           LED_1_counter = RESET;
19 }

21 workingLedMask = 0; // all LEDs off
   if (LED_3_counter) {
23     LED_3_counter--;
       workingLedMask |= LED3_BIT;  // LED3 on
```

```
25  }

27  if (LED_2_counter) {
        LED_2_counter--;
29      workingLedMask |= LED2_BIT;   // LED2 on
    }

31

    if (LED_1_counter) {
33      LED_1_counter--;
        workingLedMask |= LED1_BIT;   // LED1 on
35  }

37  LedMask = workingLedMask;    // update LED mask for main()
```

An explanation of Listing 13.3 follows.

1. (Lines 1–3): Determines maxOutput (the maximum of the absolute value of both the left and right output channels).

2. (Lines 5–9): If maxOutput is greater than 32,767 in magnitude, then LEDs 1, 2, and 3 are turned on. Counters for LED 1, 2, and 3 are set at 14400, 9600, and 4800. These counter values keep LEDs 1, 2, and 3 "ON" for 0.3, 0.2, and 0.1 seconds, respectively.

3. (Lines 10–15): If maxOutput is greater than 32,000 in magnitude, then LEDs 1 and 2 are turned on. Counters for LED 1 and 2 are set at 9600 and 4800. These counter values keep LEDs 1 and 2 "ON" for 0.2 and 0.1 seconds, respectively.

4. (Lines 16–19): If maxOutput is greater than 28,000 in magnitude, then LED 1 is turned on. The counter for LED 1 is set at 4800. This counter value keeps the LED "ON" for 0.1 seconds.

5. (Lines 21–35): Updates the LedMask based on the status of the LED counters.

6. (Line 37): Transfers the desired LED state to LedMask, which is used in main.c to update the status of the system's LEDs.

13.5   Follow-On Challenges

Consider extending what you have learned. Remember, to fully test the PPM as part of a larger program, some part of the DSP algorithm (other than the PPM part) should have a gain greater than 1. This can be accomplished easily by adding a multiplicative scale factor somewhere in the algorithm between the input and output.

1. Design and implement your own peak program meter.

2. If you have an LCDK or C6713 DSK, implement a peak program meter that utilizes all four LEDs.

3. If you have an OMAP-L138 Experimenter Kit, implement a peak program meter that utilizes the four digital output pins of the LCD connector J15.

Chapter 14

Project 5: Adaptive Filters

14.1 Theory

DIGITAL filters running in real-time can be very effective at removing undesirable noise or interference that is corrupting a signal. Some basic examples of FIR and IIR digital filters were first given in Chapters 3 and 4, and various implementations of digital filters were used in later chapters as well. Up until now, however, all the filters have been what are called "fixed coefficient" filters. That is, the response of the filters, once determined by the choice of coefficients, was fixed.[1] The coefficients did not change over time. This is by far the most common type of digital filter.

While this technique can work quite well when the undesirable parts of the input are unchanging, there are situations where this is not true. For example, the frequency components of an interfering signal might change over time, making a filter with a fixed passband and stopband ineffective. If the noise or interference is changing over time, an effective strategy would be to implement a filter that also changed over time, adapting as needed. Not surprisingly, this is called an adaptive filter. Adaptive filters are a subset of the topic of optimization theory.

This particular application of adaptive filters, called adaptive noise cancellation, is the easiest to understand [79–83]. In the basic block diagram shown in Figure 14.1, two inputs (on the left of the figure) are provided to the adaptive filter system. The upper input contains "signal plus noise" while the lower input contains "correlated noise." That is, the lower input is correlated with the additive noise present in the upper input, but *not* correlated with the desired signal. The adaptive filter (the box labeled with the transfer function $H_k(z)$ in the figure) uses the error signal to adjust its transfer function in real-time so as to optimally cancel out the noise at the output, leaving the desired signal with greatly reduced noise. The theory is straightforward, and will only be discussed briefly here.

14.1.1 A Problem Solved by Adaptive Filters

An example scenario in which adaptive noise cancellation is useful would be the noisy environment of a firefighter at the scene of an emergency, where the background noise from sirens, vehicles, various equipment, and other sources can be very loud. In this example, the "signal plus noise" represents the combined signals from the firefighter's helmet-mounted

---

[1]In Chapter 10, some filter responses did vary over time by varying the length of delay to achieve effects such as flanging and chorus. But this technique does not adapt to the input, and therefore would not be considered an adaptive filter technique.

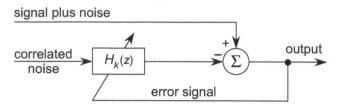

Figure 14.1: A basic block diagram of an adaptive filter used for noise cancellation.

monaural microphone (where the "signal" is his/her voice, and the "noise" is from a chain-saw running in the background being used to clear debris). The "correlated noise" signal represents just the chainsaw's signal, as detected by a second monaural microphone located on the firefighter's waist belt or lower torso, but nowhere near his/her mouth. The adaptive filter's purpose is to enhance the voice signal so that the firefighter may communicate effectively, for example, when using a radio communications link.

Since the chainsaw signal (the "noise") travels a slightly different path on its way to the two inputs shown in Figure 14.1, it is correlated but not equal in those two inputs. Thus, subtraction alone is not sufficient to mitigate the noise; the FIR filter must adapt to model the effects of the path difference between the two microphones and better cancel out the noise. As the firefighter moves, or the chainsaw user moves (or starts and stops the chainsaw cutting), the difference also changes. The frequency content and amplitude of the noise source (i.e., the chainsaw) changes in time as it cuts into debris or is just idling. Other noise sources may also contribute to the problem. The filter coefficients must continue to adapt and change as needed on the next update to best cancel out the noise, so that the firefighter's voice can be clearly understood at the radio receiver.

Another example scenario in which adaptive noise cancellation is particularly useful is the challenge of noninvasively detecting a fetal electrocardiogram (ECG) via skin electrodes when the maternal ECG will tend to overwhelm and significantly interfere with the desired signal [79,84]. In this example, the "signal plus noise" represents the combined ECG signals obtained from an abdominal-lead (where the "signal" is the ECG of the fetus, and the "noise" is the ECG of the expectant mother). The "correlated noise" signal represents just the mother's ECG, obtained from four chest leads. Not only is the maternal ECG much higher in amplitude than the fetal ECG, but the two contain nearly identical frequency components, making traditional fixed-coefficient filters useless. The adaptive filter's purpose is to effectively isolate the fetal ECG signal by suppressing the maternal ECG. The design described by Widrow et al. to solve this problem used all four chest-lead signals as a multi-channel "correlated noise" input, and one channel of "signal plus noise" from the abdominal-lead signal [84].

Adaptive noise cancellation, as shown in Figure 14.1, is one of many applications of adaptive filters. We make the common trade-off of accepting a higher filter order for guar-anteed filter stability,[2] and thus constrain the filter represented by $H_k(z)$ to be an FIR filter. Hence, the filter coefficients also completely define the impulse response $h_k[n]$, which is simply the inverse z-transform of $H_k(z)$. These coefficients change over time (they are typically updated every sample time) in order to adapt the filter to changes in the noise, and thus the subscript represents the impulse response and transfer function at some sample time k. Note that, since the filter coefficients change to adapt to the noise, we cannot

---

[2]In addition to the stability of the filter itself in Figure 14.1, the designer must also be concerned with the stability of the update algorithm that adjusts the filter coefficients. That is, will the update algorithm eventually converge on a solution after some number of updates, or will it "hunt" forever? If the latter situation is the case, the update algorithm is not stable for the given situation.

guarantee linear phase response of the FIR filter unless we impose the additional constraints of symmetry or anti-symmetry on the coefficients. Adding these additional constraints is not normally done.

While it's implied by the diagonal arrow passing through the filter box in Figure 14.1, we don't explicitly show a separate box for the particular update algorithm that changes the filter coefficients in response to changes in the noise. There are many approaches to such an update algorithm, each with its own advantages and disadvantages. Two of the most well-known classes of algorithms for adaptive filters are the least mean square (LMS) and the recursive least squares (RLS) methods. While RLS converges more quickly than LMS, and can thus better track rapidly changing noise, its much greater computational complexity often makes LMS the more attractive choice [79–83]. The LMS algorithm is also more straightforward to explain and demonstrate, so we concentrate here on the LMS adaptive filter.

14.1.2 The LMS Adpative Filter

Let the "signal plus noise" be $x[n] = v[n] + m[n]$, where $v[n]$ is the uncorrupted desired signal of interest and $m[n]$ is the noise that is unavoidably added to the desired signal. Let $r[n]$ be the "correlated noise," referred to by some texts as the reference input. Then the error signal, which is also the output of the adaptive filter in Figure 14.1, is $e[n] = x[n] - y[n]$, where $y[n]$ is the output of the FIR filter represented by $H_k(z)$.

If the FIR filter has adapted to fairly closely model the effects of the path difference between $m[n]$ and $r[n]$ in the firefighter scenario given above, then $y[n]$ is nearly the same as $m[n]$ and

$$e[n] = x[n] - y[n] \approx x[n] - \hat{m}[n] = \hat{v}[n] \qquad (14.1)$$

where the hat accent denotes an approximation to the actual value. Thus, when the FIR filter has properly adapted, the output $e[n]$ is a close approximation to $v[n]$, the uncorrupted desired signal of interest.

The key question is how do we get the FIR filter to properly adapt? That is, how do we get the FIR filter coefficients to update to a *new* set of coefficients that better solves the problem? The specific method of adaptation is what defines the type of adaptive filter. As a general strategy, adaptive filters strive to minimize the mean square error (MSE) that can be derived from the error signal $e[n]$. In the LMS approach, calculation of the true MSE (a nontrivial calculation) is avoided. The LMS algorithm uses the simplifying assumption that $e^2[n]$, the square of the instantaneous error signal, can be used as a "close enough" substitute for the true MSE.

To optimize the filter coefficients, a gradient descent technique is applied, and the criterion being minimized is simply $e^2[n]$. Calculating the gradient of $e^2[n]$ is straightforward (see [79], for example), and the final result of using the gradient with a user-defined convergence factor μ yields the update rule

$$\mathbf{w}[n+1] = \mathbf{w}[n] + 2\mu e[n]\mathbf{r}[n] \qquad (14.2)$$

where $\mathbf{w}[n]$ represents the present set of FIR filter coefficients, $\mathbf{w}[n+1]$ represents the next (updated) set of FIR filter coefficients, $\mathbf{r}[n]$ represents the set of all the present and delayed values of $r[n]$ that "fill" the FIR filter, and the bold letters indicate a vector quantity. This equation is also known as the Widrow-Hoff LMS method. Note that $\mathbf{w}[n]$, $\mathbf{w}[n+1]$, and $\mathbf{r}[n]$ are all vectors of the same length, determined by the designer's selection of the FIR filter order (recall that the filter length is one greater than the filter order). Some authors choose to write Equation 14.2 such that the number 2 in the second term to the right of the equal sign is absorbed into the value of μ.

The value of the convergence factor μ is also set by the user, typically in the range of $0 < \mu < 1$. Larger values of μ will result in bigger "jumps" for each update, which may allow faster convergence but also carry the danger of overshooting the desired coefficients. It has been shown that the LMS update algorithm will converge and remain stable if $0 < \mu < 1/p$, where p represents the largest eigenvalue of the autocorrelation matrix of $\mathbf{r}[n]$ (see [84]).

Most implementations of adaptive filters update the coefficients each sample time, so the sample-by-sample processing discussed in earlier chapters applies here. Even under the best circumstances, an adaptive filter will take more than one update to find the best (i.e., optimum according to the MSE criterion) set of coefficients to solve the problem. When an adaptive filter is first activated, one can often detect that the filter's performance begins poorly but it then "figures out" the set of coefficients that works well and performance can be quite good. As long as the noise source or path difference effects don't change too quickly, an LMS adaptive filter can "keep up" with it. Otherwise, a more complicated adaptive filter approach such as RLS may be needed.

With this very brief introduction to the theory underlying adaptive filters, we are ready to implement our own examples of adaptive noise cancellation using the LMS approach.

14.2   winDSK8 Demonstration

The winDSK8 program does not provide an example of an adaptive filter.

14.3   MATLAB Implementation

As an example of adaptive noise cancellation using MATLAB, we first recorded, in *.wav format, an uncompressed monaural voice signal (TBW's voice) for a duration of 22.272 seconds, at 16 bits/sample and a sample frequency of $F_s = 48$ kHz. We then generated, using the chirp command from MATLAB's Communications System Toolbox, a chirp signal of the same time duration as the voice signal to be used as interfering noise.[3] Specifically, we generated a sinusoidal up-chirp signal that begins at 1 kHz and ends at 5 kHz, with a linear sweep. Thus the frequency of the interfering signal is constantly changing, and the adaptive filter must constantly change to adapt to the noise.

To allow use of the MATLAB code by those readers who do not have access to the Communications System Toolbox, we stored the chirp signal in the file chirpSignal.mat. We also provide an alternate version of the m-file that does use the Communications System Toolbox, to provide flexibility for the reader.

The chirp signal is added to the voice signal (but in reversed order). Note that simple subtraction of the chirp from the voice will not work; the adaptive filter is necessary. We implement an LMS adaptive filter similar to that described in the Theory section, set up in a similar fashion to a real-time interrupt service routine (ISR). An excerpt of the m-file that implements this MATLAB simulation of an LMS adaptive filter for noise cancellation is shown in Listing 14.1.

Listing 14.1: A MATLAB simulation of the LMS adaptive filter.

```
1 %% Declarations and adaptive filter preparation
  clear;
3 N = 20; % number of adaptive filter coefficents (order is N-1)
  mu = 0.01; % convergence factor

5
```

---

[3]A chirp signal is one in which the frequency changes (or sweeps) with time.

```
   % load the chirp signal and read in the recorded voice signal
 7 load('chirpSignal.mat'); % the chirp noise data array
   [voice, Fs] = audioread('voiceRecording.wav');
 9 voice = voice'; % convert the column to a row

11 M = length(voice); % number of samples to be simulated
   r(2:N) = noise(N-1:-1:1); % create noise array, flipped around
13 w = zeros(1, N); % initialize the adaptive filter coefficents

15 xStorage = voice + noise; % create the signal plus noise
   xStorage = xStorage/max(abs(xStorage)); % normalize xStorage
17 yStorage = zeros(1, M); % array for filtered noise
   eStorage = zeros(1, M); % array for the "cleaned up" signal
19
   %% Algorithm for the adaptive filtering
21 for j = N:M
       %%% ISR simulation starts here: input the two channels
23     r(1) = noise(j); % interference (correlated noise)
       x = xStorage(j); % voice + interference
25
       % adaptively filter the interference signal
27     y = 0;
       for i = 0:N-1
29         y = y + w(i+1)*r(N-i);
       end
31
       % error signal is the filtered voice output
33     e = x - y;

35     % Widrow-Hoff LMS algorithm: update the coefficients
       for i = 1:N
37         w(i) = w(i) + 2*mu*e*r(N-i+1);
       end
39
       % prepare the r array for the next input sample
41     for i = N:-1:2
           r(i) = r(i-1);
43     end
       %%% the ISR simulation ends here
45
       % storage for post simulation use
47     yStorage(j) = y;
       eStorage(j) = e;
49 end
```

An explanation of Listing 14.1 follows.

1. (Line 3): Declare the number of filter coefficients. This is one less than the filter order.

2. (Line 4): Convergence factor, μ. This value is always between zero and one. Once your algorithm is working properly, adjusting the variables declared in lines 3 and 4 are your primary means of tuning the performance of your system.

3. (Line 7): Loads the variable noise, which contains the chirp signal.

4. (Line 8): Loads the voice signal from the provided wavfile.

5. (Line 9): MATLAB reads wav files as a column into the workspace. Monaural signals will have a single column, while stereo signals will have two columns. This command converts the column into an array (a row).

6. (Line 11): Determines the number of terms to be simulated.

7. (Line 12): Preloads the **r** array with correlated noise (a reverse-order of the chirp) with its initial values.

8. (Line 13): Declares and initializes the FIR filter coefficient array with all zeros.

9. (Line 15): Creates the corrupted signal by adding the noise (chirp).

10. (Line 16): Normalizes the corrupted signal (to a magnitude of one).

11. (Lines 17–18): Creates the arrays to store the values of y and e at the end of each simulated ISR call. These values may be useful for later analysis or plotting.

12. (Line 21): Begins the execution of a loop that single steps the simulated ISR through each of the input values.

13. (Lines 23–24): Simulates the beginning of the ISR by reading in the Left and Right channel values from either the stereo microphone (on the LCDK only) or stereo line inputs (available on all three boards).

14. (Lines 27–30): Implements an FIR filter (i.e., **w** convolved with **r**).

15. (Line 33): Subtracts the estimated noise from the corrupted signal. This results in the current best estimate of the noise-free signal.

16. (Lines 36–38): Implements the Widrow-Hoff LMS algorithm. This updates the adaptive filters coefficients.

17. (Lines 41–43): Prepares the **r** array (memory of previous input values of correlated noise) for the next sample by shifting the previous values by one sample. This is a *brute force* implementation of a linear memory model. Resources may be conserved by implementing a circular memory model (refer to Chapter 3).

18. (Line 44): All of the code between lines 23 and 43 will execute every time the simulated ISR is "called." This block of code should be almost identical to the actual ISR that your real-time DSP hardware will implement.

19. (Lines 47–48): Stores the latest value of y and e in the arrays created in lines 17 and 18. Storage of real-time variables may allow for subsequent analysis and plotting for a better understanding of the performance of the simulated system.

When you run this m-file in MATLAB, two figures will be created to illustrate the operation of the adaptive filter. The second figure created, which shows the original and the recovered voice plotted on top of one another, is shown here as Figure 14.2. You can see from the figure (and hear, when the m-file is run) that the filter initially takes some number of samples to adapt well to the noise.

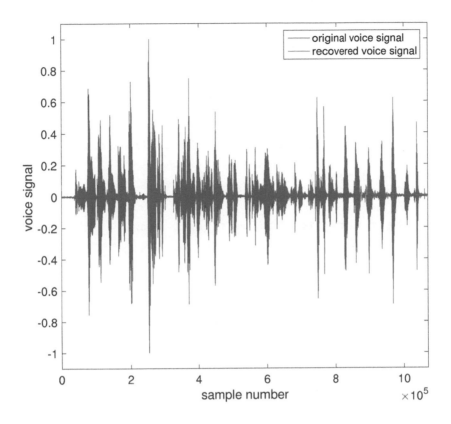

Figure 14.2: A comparison the the original, uncorrupted voice signal with the corrupted voice signal after the adaptive filter is used for noise cancellation.

14.4 DSK Implementation in C

To implement the adaptive noise canceling filter in real-time, the MATLAB program is converted to C. We hope the reader is getting used to this process by now. The most pertinent portions of the ISR are shown in Listing 14.2.

Listing 14.2: A portion of the adaptive filter project C code.

```
1 /* add your code starting here */

3 // read in the two channels of data
  r[0] = scaleFactor*CodecDataIn.Channel[ LEFT]; // noise
5 x    = scaleFactor*CodecDataIn.Channel[RIGHT]; // noisy voice
  // use watch window to reset the filter by changing "reset" to 1
7 if (reset == 1) {
        for(i=0; i<=N; i++) {
9               w[i] = 0;
        }
11       reset = 0;
  }

13
```

```
    // adaptively filter the interference signal
15  y = 0;
    for(i=0; i<=N; i++)        {
17          y += w[i] * r[N-i];
    }

19
    // error signal is the filtered voice output
21  e = x - y;

23  // Widrow-Hoff LMS algorithm: update the coefficients
    for(i=0; i<=N; i++)        {
25          w[i] += 2*mu*e*r[N-i];
    }

27
    // prepare the r array for the next input sample
29  for(i=N; i>0 ;i--)         {
            r[i] = r[i-1];
31  }

33  // scale the denoised signal for output
    CodecDataOut.Channel[ LEFT] = 32000*e;
35  CodecDataOut.Channel[RIGHT] = 32000*e;

37  /* end your code here */
```

Rather than provide a line-by-line explanation of this code, we think this is an excellent opportunity for the reader to practice comparing the MATLAB code of Listing 14.1 to the C code of Listing 14.2. The similarity of the MATLAB and C code should make this an easy exercise. Note that the method of using a watch window to "reset" the filter coefficients on the fly (see lines 6–12) does not have an exact counterpart in the MATLAB code. This reset method is mainly for convenience when testing the algorithm; it would not be used in production-level real-time code.

The code in Listing 14.2 is contained within the file ISRsAF.c in the ccs subdirectory of Chapter 14. By inspecting the code in this file, it should be clear that the input is provided to the stereo codec as interference (correlated noise) sent to the left channel, and the noisy voice is sent to the right channel. The filtered voice is output on both the left and right channels.

The ccs subdirectory of Chapter 14 also contains two audio wav files. The file chirp_noise.wav is a copy of the chirp signal used as the interfering noise in the MATLAB simulation, and the file AFtestSignal.wav is the voice signal with the interfering noise added to it, as used in the MATLAB simulation. The two files are provided mainly for an example, not necessarily for playback as inputs to the real-time adaptive filter. The real-time adaptive filter is intended for real-time inputs, not pre-recorded inputs.

14.5   Follow-On Challenges

Consider extending what you have learned.

1. Experiment with changing the convergence factor μ.

2. Experiment with changing the order of the FIR filter.

3. For a given implementation of your adaptive filter, use a noise source that changes faster and faster, until the filter can no longer "keep up" with it.

4. Implement a normalized LMS (i.e., NLMS) adaptive filter, and compare it to the plain LMS implementation. In the NLMS approach, Equation 14.2 is slightly modified to be

$$\mathbf{w}[n+1] = \mathbf{w}[n] + 2\mu e[n]\frac{\mathbf{r}[n]}{\|\mathbf{r}[n]\|^2}$$

where $\| \cdot \|$ represents the norm operation. A variation often used for the NLMS approach is

$$\mathbf{w}[n+1] = \mathbf{w}[n] + 2\mu e[n]\frac{\mathbf{r}[n]}{\alpha + \|\mathbf{r}[n]\|^2}$$

where α is some small value to avoid problems if $\|\mathbf{r}[n]\|^2 \approx 0$. As noted before, some authors prefer to absorb the 2 into μ for these equations.

Chapter 15

Project 6: AM Transmitters

15.1 Theory

ONE of the simplest modulation schemes is amplitude modulation, which is normally just abbreviated as AM. The commercial AM broadcast radio stations in the United States use a version of AM called double sideband large carrier (DSB-LC), sometimes also called double sideband with carrier (DSB-WC). See [64, 85] for some general theoretical background on amplitude modulated signals, and [86, 87] for more DSP-specific background on AM communications.

For several decades now, commercial AM radio broadcasts can be received on almost any consumer radio sold in the United States. Most U.S. commercial AM radio stations, which occupy the 550 to 1600 kHz band, are used primarily for public service, news, talk radio, and sports reporting, but only for limited music broadcasting. The majority of music programming has shifted to the more noise immune (and higher fidelity) stereo frequency modulation (FM) systems in the 88 to 108 MHz band. This is not to imply in any way that broadcast AM is no longer important! In fact, AM systems are still used all around the world. Additionally, AM provides an easily understood modulation scheme that can be thought of as the starting point for many of today's more complicated modulation schemes.

There are several ways in which AM (DSB-LC) can be generated. One method that is particularly easy to explain uses two steps:

1. offset the message signal $m(t)$ by adding a DC bias signal B, then

2. multiply the offset message signal $[B + m(t)]$ by some higher frequency sinusoidal carrier signal.

This process can be seen in Figure 15.1. To express this process mathmatically, the AM

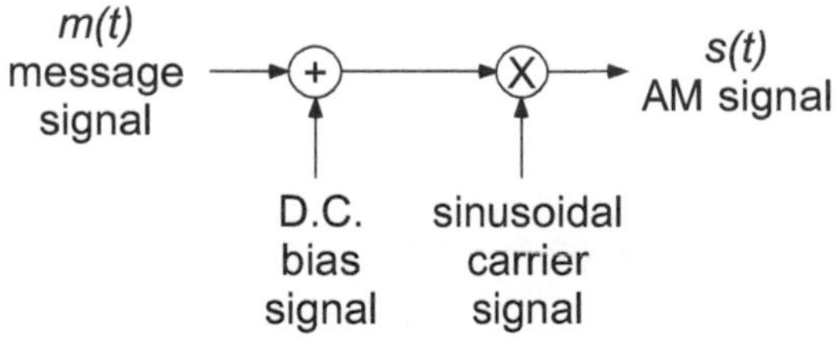

Figure 15.1: The block diagram for AM generation.

signal equation can be written as

$$s(t) = A_c[B + m(t)]\cos(2\pi f_c t), \tag{15.1}$$

where A_c is the carrier amplitude, f_c is the carrier frequency, and t represents time.

For distortion-free message recovery using envelope detection techniques (see Chapter 16), the term $B + m(t)$ must be kept greater than zero. This can be accomplished by adjusting either the bias signal value or the amplitude of the message. Figure 15.2 shows 100 ms of a voice signal. Figure 15.3 shows the result of adding the voice signal from Figure 15.2 and 5 mV of bias. In Figure 15.3 it is clear that the voice signal plus 5 mV does not always remain positive. Either the message amplitude needs to be reduced or the bias value needs to be increased. Otherwise, this will result in distortion if an envelope detector is to be used for message recovery. Figure 15.4 shows the result of adding the voice signal from Figure 15.2 and 20 mV of bias; it is clear that the voice signal plus bias now remains positive for the time period shown.

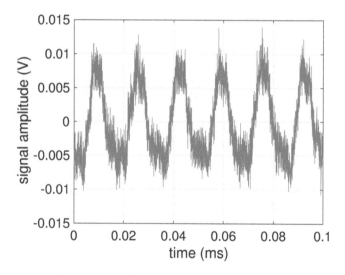

Figure 15.2: Plot of 100 ms of voice data.

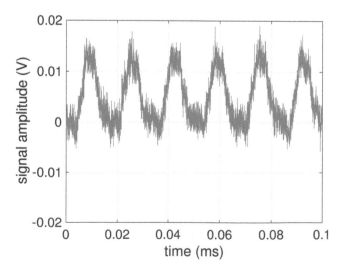

Figure 15.3: Plot of 100 ms of voice data with 5 mV of added bias.

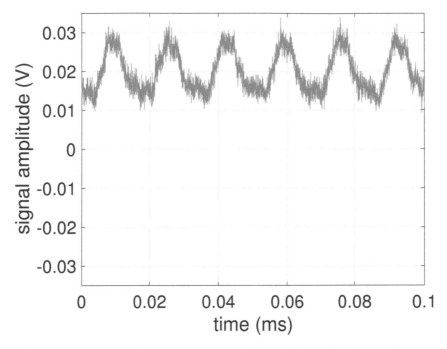

Figure 15.4: Plot of 100 ms of voice data with 20 mV of added bias.

The final step in the AM generation process is to multiply the properly biased message signal by a sinusoidal signal (called the *carrier*), as shown in Figure 15.5. The multiplication is a point-by-point operation, so the MATLAB® operator ".*" must be used.

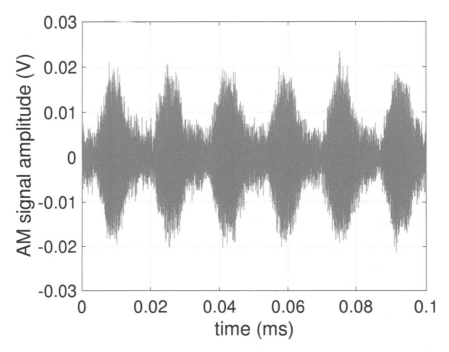

Figure 15.5: Voice signal modulating (DSB-LC) a 12 kHz carrier.

15.2   winDSK Demonstration

The winDSK8 program does not provide an equivalent function.

15.3   MATLAB Implementation

The output from a MATLAB simulation of the AM generation process is shown in Figure 15.6.

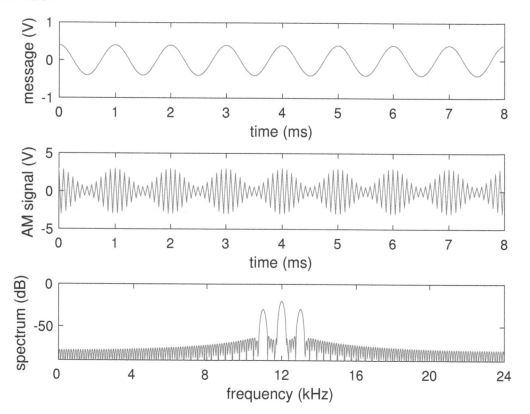

Figure 15.6: Sinusoidal signal modulating (DSB-LC) a 12 kHz carrier.

The simulation inputs, calculated terms, and simulation outputs are as follows.

- Simulation inputs

  - Simulation or sample frequency
  - Message frequency and amplitude
  - Bias level
  - Carrier frequency and amplitude
  - Simulation duration

- Calculated terms

  - Message value (we are calculating or simulating the message)
  - Carrier value

                        – AM signal value

       • Simulation outputs

                 – Plots of the message signal and the AM modulated signal

                 – Plot of the estimated power spectrum magnitude of the AM modulated signal

Figure 15.6 is divided into 3 subplots. Subplot 1 (top) plots the message signal (1000 Hz sinusoid with a 0.5 V amplitude) in the time domain. Subplot 2 (middle) plots the AM waveform in the time domain. Notice how the message waveform defines the AM signal's envelope. Also notice that the carrier appears to resemble a triangle wave. When a 12 kHz sinusoid is simulated using a 48 kHz sample frequency, only 4 samples per carrier cycle are present. For a unit amplitude cosine function, without any phase shift, the resulting carrier values are 1, 0, −1, and 0 per cycle. For a unit amplitude sine function, without any phase shift, the resulting carrier values are 0, 1, 0, and −1 per cycle. In either case, these values plot as a triangle wave. This is not a problem in a DSP system since the DAC incorporates a reconstruction (lowpass) filter. This filter will remove the high frequency components, only passing the fundamental frequency. This process turns the triangle wave back into a sinusoidal wave at 12 kHz.

Subplot 3 (bottom) plots the magnitude of the power spectral density (PSD) estimate of the AM signal. Additional details concerning spectral estimation can be found in Chapter 9. The m-file that created this plot is called **AM_SignalGeneratorAndPlotter.m**, and it can be found in the **matlab** directory for Chapter 15. The code listing is given below.

Listing 15.1: MATLAB example of AM (DSB-LC) generation.

```
1  %
   %   Generates an AM modulation figure that has 3 subplots:
3  %
   %   1 - message signal (time domain)
5  %   2 - AM signal (time domain)
   %   3 - PSD estimate of the AM signal
7  %

9  % Simulation inputs
   Fs = 48000;            % sample frequency
11 Fmsg = 1000;           % message frequency
   Amsg = 0.4;            % message amplitude
13 bias = 0.6;            % bias (offset)
   Fc = 12000;            % carrier frequency
15 Ac = 3;                % carrier amplitude
   duration = 0.008;      % duration of the signal in seconds
17 Nfft = 2048;           % number of points used for PSD frames

19 myFontSize = 12;    % font size for the plot labels

21 % Calculated terms
   NumberOfPoints = round(duration*Fs);
23 t = (0:(NumberOfPoints - 1))/Fs;        % establish time vector
   message = Amsg*cos(2*pi*Fmsg*t);        % create message signal
25 carrier = cos(2*pi*Fc*t);               % create carrier signal
   AM_msg = Ac*(bias + message).*carrier;  % create AM waveform

27
```

```
   % Simulation outputs
29 subplot(3,1,1)
   set(gca, 'FontSize', myFontSize)
31 plot(t*1000, message)
   xlabel('time (ms)')
33 ylabel('message (V)')
   axis([0 8 -1 1])
35
   subplot(3,1,2)
37 set(gca, 'FontSize', myFontSize)
   plot(t*1000,AM_msg)
39 xlabel('time (ms)')
   ylabel('AM signal (V)')
41
   subplot(3,1,3)
43 set(gca, 'FontSize', myFontSize)
   [Pam,frequency] = pwelch(AM_msg,length(message),0,Nfft,Fs,'psd');
45 plot(frequency/1000, 10*log10(Pam))
   xlabel('frequency (kHz)')
47 ylabel('spectrum (dB)')
   set(gca,'XTick', [0 4 8 12 16 20 24])
49 set(gca,'XTickLabel', [0 4 8 12 16 20 24]')
   axis([0 24 -50 0])
51
   print -deps2 AM_SignalPlot           % save eps file of figure
```

15.4   DSK Implementation in C

When you understand the MATLAB code, the concept translation into C is fairly straightforward. For the MATLAB simulation we listed the simulation inputs, calculated terms,
and the simulation outputs. While these concepts are similar for the DSK's code, the names
are modified. For the DSK, we will use the terms "declaration" and "algorithmic process."
We will need few modifications to the MATLAB thought process, however.

- The DSP must process the data from the ADC in real-time; therefore, we cannot
  wait for all of the message samples to be received prior to beginning the algorithmic
  process.

- Real-time DSP is inherently an interrupt driven process and the input samples should
  only be processed using interrupt service routines (ISRs). Given this observation,
  it is incumbent upon the DSP programmer to ensure that the time requirements
  associated with periodic sampling are met. Also, remember the input and output
  ISRs are asynchronous. Nothing will go in and out of your DSP hardware unless you
  program the DSP with an appropriate receive and transmit ISR.

- The digital portion of both an ADC and a DAC are inherently *integer* in nature.
  No matter what the ADC's input range is, the analog input voltage is mapped to
  an integer value. For a 16-bit converter using two's complement representation, the
  possible values range from $+32767$ to -32768. Since -32768 is the maximum negative
  value of the signal that can be received by the DSP, a bias level of no more than $+32768$

will be necessary to prevent envelope distortion at the receiver. You can always make the bias value larger than $+32768$ to explore the effects on AM signal generation.

Given these considerations, the program is broken into the following parts.

- Declaration

  - Bias level
  - Carrier frequency

- Algorithmic process

  - Read in a message sample from the ADC
  - Calculate the next carrier value
  - Calculate the AM signal value
  - Scale the AM signal value for the DAC
  - Write the AM signal value to the DAC

See the files associated with this project in the **ccs\AmTx** directory for Chapter 15. We provide two implementations of this project, a direct method (using the file **ISRs.c**) and a more efficient method (using the file **ISR_Table.c**). Select one (and only one) of these two files to include in your CCS project. If you're using **ISR_Table.c**, then modify **StartUp.c** so that the function call to FillSineTable() is not commented out.

If we directly implement the AM generation equation $s(t) = A_c[B + m(t)] \cos(2\pi f_c t)$ without considering the required scaling for the DAC, we will likely exceed the allowable range. We must assume that the full ADC range is possible for input data, so **CodecData. Channel[LEFT]** can range from -32768 to $+32767$. Thus **bias** must be at least $+32,768$ to prevent the combined term **bias+CodecData.Channel[LEFT]** from possibly becoming negative. Remember that this combined term must not be negative, or message distortion will occur at the output of the receiver when using an envelope detector. If **bias** is set to this minimum value of $+32768$, then the maximum value of **bias+CodecData.Channel[LEFT]** will be $32768 + 32767 = 65535$. The magnitude of the sine we will generate for the carrier is $|\sin(\cdot)| \leq 1$, so that means that a scale factor of 0.5 is needed to prevent the AM value from exceeding the allowable range of the DAC.[1] The only flexibility we lose by using this method is that we are no longer able to freely increase the "bias" value without also changing the 0.5 scale factor. The AM generation equation can therefore be implemented using the code statement shown in the listing below. Watch for line wraps due to margins in this and the following listings.

Listing 15.2: C code for scaled implementation of DSB-LC AM.

```
CodecDataOut.Channel[LEFT]=(float)0.5*(bias+CodecDataIn.Channel[
    [+]LEFT])*sinf(phase);
```

After profiling this code, it becomes obvious that the transmitter ISR is still the major user of DSP computational resources. This is due to the function **sinf**, which, although seemingly straightforward to calculate, is a call to a relatively "expensive" (in computational terms) routine prototyped in the header file **math.h**. As discussed in Chapter 5, numerous techniques exist to generate a sinusoid. The following code combines these concepts for AM signal generation. The only change to **StartUp.c** is to uncomment the line that makes

---

[1]Since division is more "expensive" computationally than multiplication, we multiply by 0.5 rather than divide by 2.

the function call to FillSineTable(); this version of the project will use the interrupt service routines contained in the file ISR_Table.c.

With the array SineTable filled, the line of code shown next extracts noninterpolated sine function values from the lookup table.

Listing 15.3: C code to extract the sine function values from the lookup table.

```
sine=SineTable[(Int32)(index/GetSampleFreq()*NumTableEntries)];
```

The code associated with the final calculations of the AM waveform generation and scaling follows.

Listing 15.4: C code for scaled implementation of DSB-LC AM with sine table lookup.

```
CodecDataOut.Channel[LEFT]=(float)0.5*(bias+CodecDataIn.Channel[
    [+]LEFT])*sine;
```

Code profiling using the new carrier generation algorithm reveals approximately an 80% reduction in computational resources used by the transmitter ISR.

15.5   Follow-On Challenges

Consider extending what you have learned.

1. Even though both output channels are used, the RIGHT channel data is just a copy of the LEFT channel data. Investigate how to use DSB-LC to transmit stereo information.

2. Since even momentary transmission with a modulation index greater than one results in distortion for a receiver using an envelope detector, how would you prevent this situation from occurring?

3. From a practical perspective, if the message signal that you are using to modulate the carrier has a baseband bandwidth that exceeds the carrier frequency, then aliasing will occur. Design and implement a system that digitally bandlimits (LP filters) the message signal *prior* to modulating the carrier signal.

4. What are the implications of setting the bias term to a value greater than +32768?

5. How would you implement a single sideband (SSB) AM transmitter?

6. Now that you understand AM transmitters, consider implementing a frequency modulation (FM) transmitter. In this case, instead of the input signal changing the carrier amplitude, the input signal changes the carrier frequency. Refer to any good communications textbook for a discussion about FM.

Chapter 16

Project 7: AM Receivers

16.1 Theory

AMPLITUDE modulation (AM) is a very popular modulation scheme. As we discussed in Chapter 15, AM signals are carried in the envelope of the carrier signal. An AM signal with carrier frequency $f_c = 550$ kHz, message frequency $f_{msg} = 5$ kHz, and modulation index $\mu = 0.8$, is shown in Figure 16.1. In this figure, the signal's envelope is clearly sinusoidal. Counting the envelope variations shows that the signal envelope experiences five periods in the displayed time duration of 1 millisecond. The message frequency can now be verified to be $f_{msg} = 5/0.001 = 5$ kHz. Since the carrier is displayed as solid shading in this figure, it is impossible to precisely determine its exact frequency without rescaling the plot. In fact, the carrier frequency is at $f = 550$ kHz, which means that this AM signal has $550,000/5,000 = 110$ Hz/period. That is, 110 cycles of the carrier occur for every cycle of the message. This represents the worst-case ratio for US-based commercial AM detection,

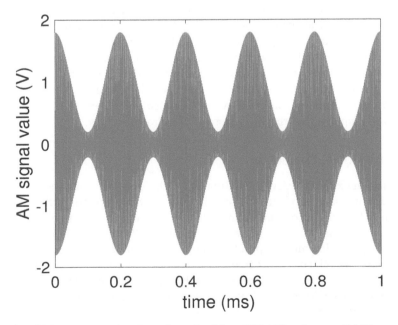

Figure 16.1: An AM signal in the time domain ($f_c = 550$ kHz, $f_{msg} = 5$ kHz, and $\mu = 0.8$).

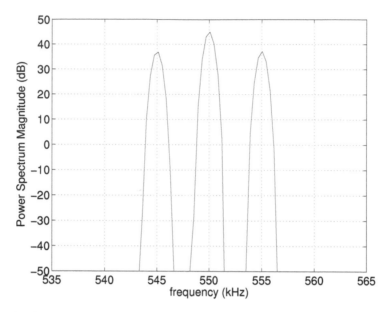

Figure 16.2: An AM signal shown in the frequency domain ($f_c = 550$ kHz, $f_{msg} = 5$ kHz, and $\mu = 0.8$). These are the only three frequency components in the signal.

since the minimum authorized carrier frequency is 550 kHz and the maximum allowed message frequency is 5 kHz. We are discussing messages that are sinusoidal in nature. We will use these sinusoidal tones as example messages to illustrate a number of different points. In actual radio systems, the messages will be much more complex and usually will occur at more than one frequency. It is also very common when discussing AM systems to treat the maximum message frequency as the message's bandwidth.

The AM signal shown in the time domain in Figure 16.1 is also shown in the frequency domain as Figure 16.2. Shown from left to right in this figure are the lower sideband (LSB), carrier frequency, and the upper sideband (USB). The LSB occurs at $f_c - f_{msg} = 545$ kHz, the carrier frequency is at $f_c = 550$ kHz, and the USB occurs at $f_c + f_{msg} = 555$ kHz. Theoretically, these spectral components should occur as delta functions (spectral lines with no width); however, this figure was created using the MATLAB `pwelch` function[1] using a Blackman-Harris windowing function. As discussed in Chapter 9, the spectrum of the windowing function in use is convolved with the *actual* spectrum. This is why the spectral components are displayed as "humps" instead of delta functions.

16.1.1   Envelope Detector

One of the most inexpensive AM demodulation techniques employs the envelope detector. Traditional circuit-based implementations of the envelope detector utilize a diode and an analog lowpass (LP) filter to demodulate the AM signal. The diode halfwave rectifies the incoming signal; that is, it passes either the positive half of the AM signal or the negative half of the AM signal, depending upon how the diode is connected in the circuit. The analog LP filter extracts the relatively low frequency message from the AM signal's envelope. The effect of halfwave rectification can be seen in Figure 16.3 (time domain) and Figure 16.4 (frequency domain), where an ideal diode is assumed to pass only the positive half of the AM signal. The nonlinear action of the diode has caused other frequency components to

---

[1]The MathWorks recommends using the `pwelch` function now instead of the older `psd` function.

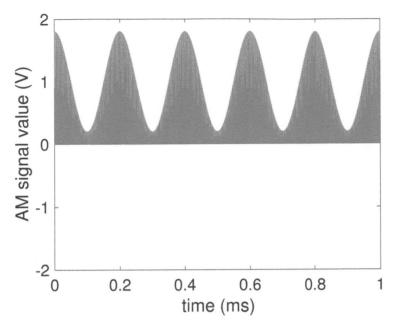

Figure 16.3: A halfwave rectified version of Figure 16.1 in the time domain.

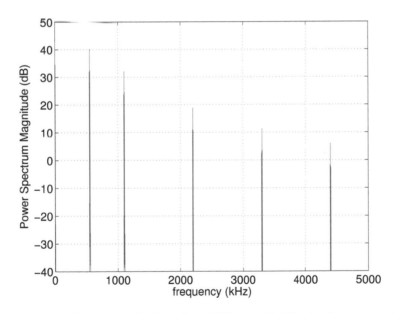

Figure 16.4: A halfwave rectified version of Figure 16.1 in the frequency domain.

appear in the signal, as is evident in Figure 16.4.

The scale of the plot makes it difficult to distinguish the individual lines of the LSB, the carrier, and the USB; each "spike" on the plot is actually multiple lines. But we can clearly see some components near DC (0 Hz), the fundamental frequency components (centered at $f_c = 550$ kHz), the second harmonic components (centered at $2f_c = 2 \cdot 550 = 1100$ kHz), and the other *even harmonic* components (centered at $nf_c = n \cdot 550$ kHz for $n = 4, 6, 8$). The even harmonics actually continue forever beyond the limits of the plot for $n = 10, 12, 14, \ldots$, but the amplitude of the harmonics approaches zero as their frequency increases. Figure 16.5

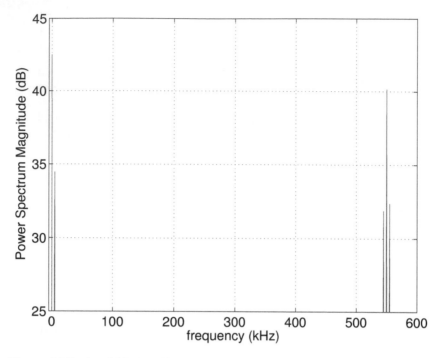

Figure 16.5: An AM signal's spectral content after halfwave rectification.

zooms in on the lower 600 kHz of Figure 16.4; look closely and observe five individual spectral components in Figure 16.5. These individual spectral components occur at the five frequencies that are listed below.

1. DC, at $f_{DC} = 0$ Hz

2. Message, at $f_{msg} = 5$ kHz

3. Lower sideband (LSB), at $f_c - f_{msg} = 545$ kHz

4. Carrier, at $f_c = 550$ kHz

5. Upper sideband (USB), at $f_c + f_{msg} = 555$ kHz

In the list of spectral components above, the second term is our message, and it can be extracted from the spectrum shown in Figure 16.4 by a LP filter. This filter needs to pass the f_{msg} term while providing significant attenuation at the LSB, f_c, and USB frequencies (and all the higher harmonics). These LP filter requirements lead to the design equation

$$BW \ll \frac{1}{\tau} \ll f_c - BW.$$

In this equation, BW is the message signal's bandwidth (in Hz), τ is the LP filter's time constant (in seconds), and f_c is the AM signal's carrier frequency (in Hz). In most radio frequency (RF) systems, $BW \ll f_c$, so the design equation is routinely approximated by

$$BW \ll \frac{1}{\tau} \ll f_c.$$

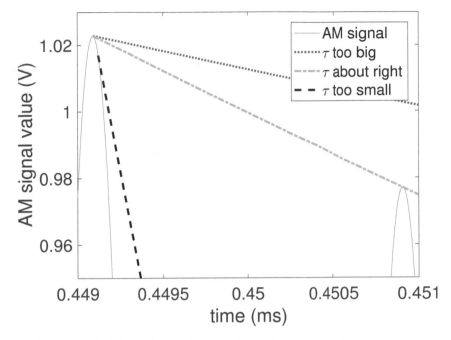

Figure 16.6: The effect of different LP filters on envelope recovery.

Continuing with our example of $f_{msg} = 5$ kHz and $f_c = 550$ kHz requires that

$$5 \text{ kHz} \ll \frac{1}{\tau} \ll 550 \text{ kHz}.$$

Setting $\frac{1}{\tau} \approx 120$ kHz easily satisfies the inequality and allows for direct AM detection/demodulation. Figure 16.6 shows the effect of this LP filter *in the time domain*. This figure shows an extremely magnified portion (showing just the top peaks) of Figure 16.3 with the discharge characteristics of three different LP filters superimposed onto the carrier waveform. The desired effect is for the LP filter to extract the message frequency by connecting the peaks of the halfwave rectified AM signal. Examples of filters that discharge too fast and too slow are also shown in the figure. Setting $\frac{1}{\tau} \approx 120$ kHz is seen to be "about right," as it almost perfectly "connects" the peaks during the filter's discharge process. As we will see below, this may not actually be the optimal choice. In all cases, the discharge rate of an analog filter is controlled by the time constant τ. For a simple first-order RC LP filter such as the one shown in Figure 4.1, the time constant is $\tau = RC$.

The previous figures demonstrate the worst-case scenario for using an envelope detector, in which the carrier is at the lowest frequency value allowed (by the FCC), and the message is at the highest frequency allowed. This is the worst case because the relative location of the peaks (in the time domain) drives our LP filter response in one direction, while the separation between the components we want to keep and the components we want to remove (in the frequency domain) drives our LP filter response in the opposite direction. In Figure 16.6, the $\frac{1}{\tau} \approx 120$ kHz filter's discharge characteristic appears to satisfy our needs. However, if we look at the filter response in the frequency domain, this choice does not look nearly as good. This can be seen in Figure 16.7 where the LP filter that seemed to meet our needs in the time domain provides less than 30 dB of attenuation at the carrier frequency of f_c. As previously stated, what is needed is a filter that passes f_{msg} and *significantly* attenuates f_c. From Figure 16.7 it is now clear that a higher performance filter (i.e., higher order) is required.

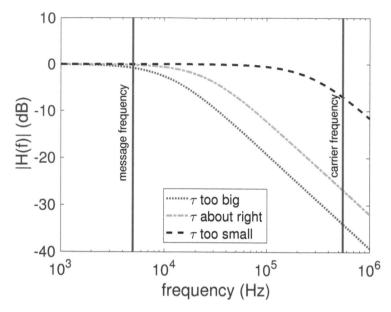

Figure 16.7: The effectiveness of the LP filters used for envelope recovery as viewed in the frequency domain.

Even after an acceptable envelope recovery (LP) filter is designed, there is one last unwanted spectral component at 0 Hz (DC) that needs to be removed. In an analog implementation, this can be accomplished with a single DC blocking capacitor.

Having made all of these observations, *actual* AM radios typically use a frequency selective, intermediate frequency (IF) stage prior to the envelope detector. This type of system is called a "superheterodyne receiver" or simply a "superhet." The IF-based system provides significant end-to-end gain without amplifier instability/oscillation, as well as providing for much better isolation of the desired frequency channel from any adjacent channels. Better channel isolation is accomplished by the use of a high performance IF filter which then allows the use of lower performance (i.e., less expensive) RF and audio frequency filters.

The discussion concerning the importance of the envelope detector's LP filter was necessary to demonstrate that while this technique works very well for commercial AM radio signal recovery, it may not work without severe distortion on our DSK-based AM system, which we limit to audio carrier frequencies to allow the use of the audio codec. This potential filtering problem can be inferred from Figure 16.8, where a 5 kHz message is AM modulated by a 12 kHz carrier. Because the carrier is no longer much higher in frequency than the message frequency (commercial AM carriers are more than 100 times higher than the message), it is difficult to see the message envelope in this audio waveform without the "message + DC" term also being shown in the plot. Despite the appearance of this time domain waveform, the message signal can still be extracted using a high performance LP filter. This can be confirmed by Figure 16.9, where it should be clear that if the LP filter passes the 5 kHz message and if the passband sharply drops off immediately *above* 5 kHz, then the "message + DC" term can be recovered without distortion from the other frequency components.

We must take great care in choosing frequencies for our audio carrier AM system. We set the carrier frequency to $f_c = 12$ kHz carrier (the center of the codec's alias-free frequency response limit when $F_s = 48$ kHz) to allow "room" for both lower and upper sidebands. But if we *increase* the message frequency too far (i.e., $f_{msg} \geq 6$ kHz), an envelope detector

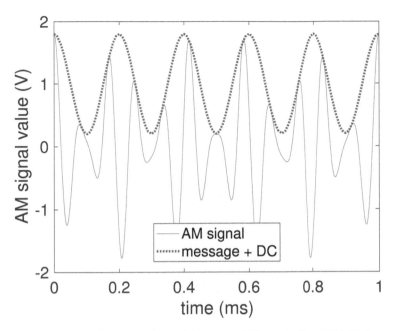

Figure 16.8: AM waveform ($f_{msg} = 5$ kHz and $f_c = 12$ kHz).

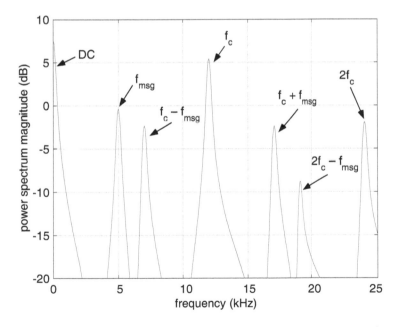

Figure 16.9: AM spectrum ($f_{msg} = 5$ kHz and $f_c = 12$ kHz).

will fail to recover the message properly. At $f_{msg} \geq 6$ kHz, the time domain waveform becomes almost incomprehensible and the spectral components associated with the output of the halfwave rectifier become inseparable using the traditional LP filter approach. These concepts can be seen in Figure 16.10 and Figure 16.11. While there are many known solutions to this problem, in the rest of this chapter the focus will be on the Hilbert-based AM receiver.

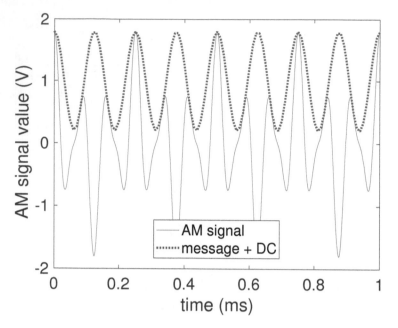

Figure 16.10: AM waveform ($f_{msg} = 8$ kHz and $f_c = 12$ kHz).

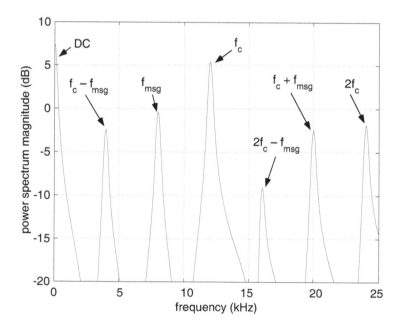

Figure 16.11: AM spectrum ($f_{msg} = 8$ kHz and $f_c = 12$ kHz).

16.1.2   The Hilbert-Based AM Receiver

The Hilbert-based AM receiver extracts the real envelope [86] from the received signal using the equation

$$r(t) = \sqrt{s^2(t) + \hat{s}^2(t)}\,.$$

In this equation, $r(t)$ is the real envelope of the AM signal. The envelope can be expressed as $r(t) = m(t) + \text{DC}$, where $m(t)$ is the message signal and "DC" represents the bias that was added at the AM transmitter to keep $m(t) + \text{DC} > 0$. Additionally, $s(t)$ is the received AM signal and $\hat{s}(t)$ is the Hilbert transform of $s(t)$. Once the real envelope is extracted, the DC term can be removed using an IIR-based DC blocking filter.

To create $\hat{s}(t)$, $s(t)$ must be passed through a system that implements the Hilbert transform. A continuous-time Hilbert transforming filter's impulse response is defined as

$$h(t) = \frac{1}{\pi t}$$

and the frequency response [87, 88] is defined as

$$H(j\omega) = \begin{cases} -j \text{ for } \omega > 0 \\ 0 \text{ for } \omega = 0 \\ +j \text{ for } \omega < 0 \end{cases}$$

The magnitude of the frequency response is one (except it is zero at exactly 0 Hz), and the filter introduces a $-90°$ phase shift for positive frequencies and a $+90°$ phase shift for negative frequencies. This phase shifting filter can either be closely approximated by an FIR digital filter or by using an "FFT/phase shift/IFFT" operation. In this chapter, we will use an FIR filter to approximate the Hilbert transform.

To design an FIR-based Hilbert transforming filter in MATLAB we will use the `firpm` command.[2] An example of how to use this command is shown below.

Listing 16.1: Using MATLAB to design a Hilbert transforming filter.

```
1  B = firpm(22, [0.1 0.9], [1 1], 'Hilbert');
```

In this listing, variable B will store the 23 filter coefficients, 22 is the filter order, 0.1 and 0.9 are the beginning and ending normalized frequencies over which we want the filter's magnitude response to remain constant, [1 1] represents the magnitudes at those two normalized frequencies, and 'Hilbert' tells MATLAB to design a Hilbert transforming filter. A stem plot of the resulting B coefficients is provided as Figure 16.12. Notice that, for Hilbert transforming filters such as this one, specified with a passband that is symmetric on the frequency scale and centered at $F_s/4$, we see that every other filter coefficient has a value of zero. This filter's coefficients are also antisymmetric about the center point (i.e., $h[n] = -h[N - n]$). These traits could be exploited to reduce the computational load of the DSP CPU.[3]

Specifying the Hilbert transforming filter's design parameters depends greatly on the characteristics of the signal that you are trying to transform. In Figure 16.13, three different filters of increasing order are shown. Each filter has the same bandpass (BP) filter specifications. For a given frequency range, the higher the filter order, the flatter the response becomes in the passband. Figure 16.14 shows that as the filter order increases, the filter's passband ripple decreases, but it will never completely disappear.

A sampled (i.e., discrete-time) system would replace $s(t)$ by $s[n]$ and $r(t)$ by $r[n]$ in the real envelope extraction equation. The block diagram associated with extracting the real envelope of the signal is shown in Figure 16.15. Note that to "line up" the unfiltered signal $s[n]$ with the filtered signal $\hat{s}[n]$, we need to delay the unfiltered signal by the group delay of the filter. The group delay associated with any linear phase FIR filter, such as the Hilbert

---

[2] The MathWorks recommends using the `firpm` function now instead of the older `remez` function.

[3] Any linear phase FIR filter will exhibit either symmetrical ($h[n] = h[N - n]$) coefficients or antisymmetrical ($h[n] = -h[N - n]$) coefficients.

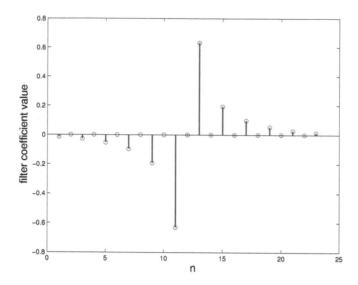

Figure 16.12: Stem plot of the coefficients associated with a 22nd-order FIR Hilbert transforming filter.

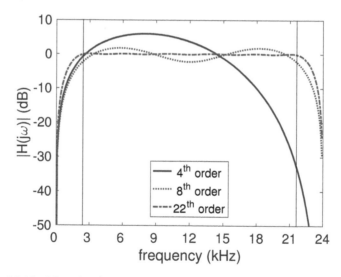

Figure 16.13: Magnitude responses of three Hilbert transforming filters.

transforming filter, is one-half of the filter order. For the 22nd-order filter in this example, the group delay will be 11 samples. Since the input values to this filter are already being stored for implementation using direct form I (DF-I) techniques, no additional input sample buffering is required for us to delay $s[n]$ as needed.

Finally, $r[n]$ must have its DC component removed. This is accomplished with a notch filter where the stopband frequency is set to 0 Hz. This filter places a zero on the unit circle at $z = 1$ to determine the location of the stopband, and a pole on the real axis very near this zero (e.g., $z = 0.95$) to make the slope of the stopband very sharp. The transfer function of this system is

$$H(z) = \left(\frac{1+r}{2}\right) \frac{1-z^{-1}}{1-rz^{-1}}.$$

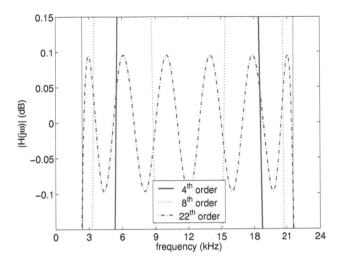

Figure 16.14: Zoomed magnitude response emphasizing the 22nd-order Hilbert transforming filter's passband ripple.

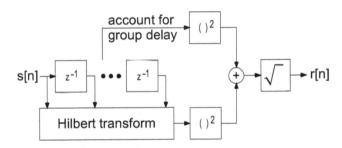

Figure 16.15: Method for real envelope recovery from an AM signal.

In this equation, r represents the location of the pole (we previously used the example where $r = 0.95$) and the $(1 + r)/2$ term normalizes the high frequency (passband) gain to 1.0 (0 dB). The difference equation associated with this system can be derived as follows.

$$H(z) = \frac{Y(z)}{X(z)} = \left(\frac{1+r}{2}\right)\frac{1 - z^{-1}}{1 - rz^{-1}}$$

$$Y(z)\left(1 - rz^{-1}\right) = X(z)\left(\frac{1+r}{2}\right)\left(1 - z^{-1}\right)$$

$$y[n] - ry[n-1] = \left(\frac{1+r}{2}\right)(x[n] - x[n-1])$$

$$y[n] = ry[n-1] + 0.5(1+r)(x[n] - x[n-1]).$$

We now have enough information to implement the AM demodulator shown in Figure 16.15.

16.2   winDSK Demonstration

The winDSK8 program does not provide an equivalent function.

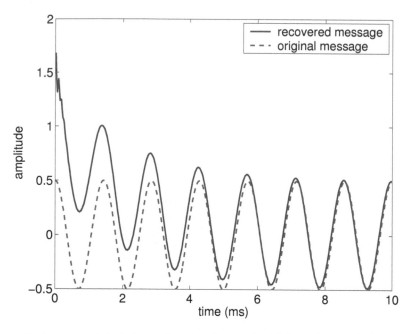

Figure 16.16: MATLAB simulation results of the Hilbert-based AM receiver.

16.3   MATLAB Implementation

The MATLAB listing provided below generates an AM signal, designs a Hilbert transforming filter, uses this filter to recover the real envelope of the signal, filters out the DC component, and displays both the original message and the recovered message. Figure 16.16 shows the output of this simulation. The initial decaying response of the recovered message is due to the startup transient associated with the DC blocking filter. Despite this transient, excellent agreement with the original message signal is achieved in fewer than 10 ms; thereafter, the demodulation would be nearly perfect. Additionally, the very small delay between the signals is due to the group delay of the DC blocking filter.

Failure to properly account for the group delay of the Hilbert transforming filter is a very common problem that will cause the receiver to fail. Being off by even a single sample delay while accounting for the group delay of the Hilbert transforming filter will prevent the proper operation of the system.

Listing 16.2: MATLAB simulation of a Hilbert-based AM receiver.

```
1 %  Hilbert-based AM receiver simulation
  %
3 % variable declarations
  Fs = 48000;              % sample frequency
5 Ac = 1.0;                % amplitude of the carrier
  fc = 12000;              % frequency of the carrier
7 Amsg = 0.5;              % amplitude of the message
  fmsg = 700;              % frequency of the message
9 HilbertOrder = 62;       % Hilbert transforming filter order
  r = 0.990;               % highpass filter pole magnitude
11 duration = 0.5;          % signal duration in seconds
  myFontSize = 16;         % font size for the plot labels
```

```
13
   % design the FIR Hilbert transforming filter
15 B = firpm(HilbertOrder, [0.05 0.95], [1 1], 'h');
   t = 0:1/Fs:duration;
17
   % generate the AM/DSB w/carrier signal
19 carrier = Ac*cos(2*pi*fc*t);
   msg = Amsg*cos(2*pi*fmsg*t);
21 AM = (1 + msg).*carrier;

23
   % recover the message
25 % note the HilbertOrder/2 delay to align the signals
   % use the MATLAB syntax of "..." to continue a line of code
27
   % apply Hilbert transform
29 AMhilbert = filter(B, 1, AM);

31 % get envelope, but account for filter delay
   OffsetOutput = sqrt((AM(1:2000)).^2 + ...
33   (AMhilbert((HilbertOrder/2+1):(2000 + HilbertOrder/2))).^2);

35 % remove DC component
   demodOutput = filter([1 -1]*(1 + r)/2, [1 -r], OffsetOutput);
37
   % create the desired figure
39 plot((0:(length(demodOutput)-1))/Fs*1000, demodOutput)
   set(gca, 'FontSize', myFontSize)
41 hold on
   plot((0:(length(demodOutput)-1))/Fs*1000, ...
43   msg(1:length(demodOutput)), 'r--')
   ylabel('amplitude')
45 xlabel('time (ms)')
   legend('recovered message', 'original message')
47 axis([0 10 -0.5 2.0])
   hold off
```

16.4 DSK Implementation in C

This version of the Hilbert-based AM receiver is very similar to the MATLAB simulation example. The intention of this first approach is understandability, which may come at the expense of efficiency.

The files necessary to run this application are in the `ccs\Proj_AmRx` directory of Chapter 16. The primary file of interest is the `AMreceiver_ISRs.c`, which contains the interrupt service routines. This file also contains the necessary variable declarations and performs the Hilbert-based AM demodulation.

If you are using a stereo codec (such as the on-board codec for the C6713 DSK or the OMAP-L138 boards), the program could implement independent Left and Right channel demodulators. For clarity, this example program will demodulate only one signal's message, but will output this message to both the Left and Right channels.

In Listing 16.3 shown below, array x (Line 1) contains the current and stored (i.e., past) received AM signal values. The Hilbert transforming filter's output value is y (Line 2). The present and most recent real envelope values ($r[n]$ and $r[n-1]$) are stored in **envelope** (Line 3) and the output of the DC blocking filter is stored in **output** (Line 4). Note that the **output** array has to be initialized as shown (Line 4), or it can get stuck with an initial value of NaN (not a number) and never recover. The DC blocking filter's only adjustable parameter is **r** (Line 5), which controls the location of the pole along the real axis. For proper operation, **r** should be slightly less than 1.0.

Listing 16.3: Variable declaration associated with a Hilbert-based AM receiver.

```
1 float x[N];              // received AM signal values
  float y;                 // Hilbert Transforming (HT) filter's output
3 float envelope[2];       // real envelope
  float output[2] = {0,0}; // output of the DC blocking filter
5 float r = 0.99;          // pole location for the DC blocking filter
  Int32 i;                 // integer index
```

The code shown below performs the actual AM demodulation operation. The six main steps involved in this operation will be discussed following the code listing.

Listing 16.4: Algorithm associated with Hilbert-based AM demodulation.

```
   /* algorithm begins here */
2  x[0] = CodecDataIn.Channel[LEFT];// current AM signal value
   y = 0;                   // initialize filter's output value
4
   for (i = 0; i < N; i++) {
6      y += x[i]*B[i];       // perform HT (dot-product)
   }
8
   envelope[0] = sqrtf(y*y + x[16]*x[16]); // real envelope
10
   /* implement the DC blocking filter */
12 output[0]=r*output[1]+(float)0.5*(r+1)*(envelope[0]-envelope[1]);
14 for (i = N-1; i > 0; i--) {
      x[i] = x[i-1];         // setup for the next input
16 }
18 envelope[1] = envelope[0]; // setup for the next input
   output[1]   = output[0];   // setup for the next input
20
   CodecDataOut.Channel[ LEFT] = output[0]; // setup the LEFT  value
22 CodecDataOut.Channel[RIGHT] = output[0]; // setup the RIGHT value
   /* algorithm ends here */
```

The six real-time steps involved in Hilbert-based AM demodulation

An explanation of Listing 16.4 follows.

   1. (Line 2): This code brings the current value of the AM signal into the DSP.

2. (Lines 3–7): This code initializes the filter's output and performs the Hilbert transform of the current and stored input values.

3. (Line 9): This code calculates the real envelope of the AM signal.

4. (Line 12): This code implements the DC blocking filter.

5. (Lines 14–19): These lines of code prepare the stored variables to receive the next input value.

6. (Lines 21–22): These lines of code output the message signal to both the Left and Right channels.

Now that you understand the code...

Go ahead and copy all of the files into a separate directory. Open the project in CCS and "Rebuild All." Once the build is complete, "Load Program" into the DSK and click on "Run." Your Hilbert-based AM receiver is now running on the DSK. AM modulated signals are available in the `test_signals` directory of the software for the book so you can test your AM receiver code. The file names begin with AM.

16.5 Follow-On Challenges

Consider extending what you have learned.

1. Implement the Hilbert transform-based AM receiver using an "FFT/phase shift/IFFT" technique to implement the Hilbert transform. This should reduce the DSP CPU computational load. See Chapter 8 for details concerning the FFT.

2. Design and implement different bandpass Hilbert transforming filters that are matched in bandwidth to the signal you are trying to recover. Experiment with different filter orders that will still recover the message signal.

3. Implement the Hilbert transform-based AM receiver taking advantage of the fact that every other coefficient for the Hilbert transforming filter is zero. This should reduce the DSP CPU computational load.

4. Implement the Hilbert transform-based AM receiver taking advantage of the fact that Hilbert transforming filters are antisymmetric filters. This should reduce the DSP CPU computational load.

5. Use circular buffering techniques to implement the Hilbert transform-based AM receiver. This should reduce the DSP CPU computational load.

6. Use frame-based techniques to implement the Hilbert-based AM receiver. This should reduce the DSP CPU computational load.

Chapter 17

Project 8: Phase-Locked Loop

17.1   Theory

THE phase-locked loop (PLL) is widely used in communications receiver systems. Since even the fundamental theory of phase-locked loops has been the topic of dozens of textbooks, we will only briefly discuss, then implement, a single PLL design: a discretized, second-order Costas loop [87, 88]. The simplified block diagram of such a system is shown in Figure 17.1. In this figure, $s[n]$ is the sampled input signal, $m[n]$ is an estimate of the message signal, T is the sample period, and ω_c is the carrier frequency.

The basic operation of the PLL is as follows. The incoming signal $s[n]$ is processed through a filter that implements a Hilbert transforming (HT) operation to create $\hat{s}[n]$. Recall from Chapter 16 that the frequency response magnitude of the HT operation is one (except it is zero at exactly 0 Hz), and it introduces a $-90°$ phase shift for positive frequencies and a $+90°$ phase shift for negative frequencies. A signal commonly called the "analytic signal" is formed from the sum of the input signal $s[n]$ and the HT-filtered version of the input signal $\hat{s}[n]$ that has been multiplied by the imaginary number j (where $j = \sqrt{-1}$). Recall that $jx = |x|\angle 90°$, so multiplication by j is equivalent to a $+90°$ phase shift for all frequencies. Note that you'll need to account for any group delay in the HT filtering operation to make sure the signals "line up" properly, as we did in Chapter 16. In

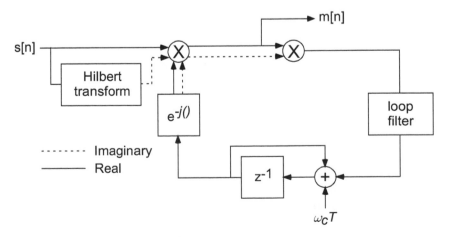

Figure 17.1: The simplified block diagram of a second order Costas loop.

equation form, the analytic signal is defined as $s[n] + j\hat{s}[n]$. This is why the block diagram uses solid and dashed lines to indicate the real and imaginary signals, respectively. All that remains, at this point, is to strip off the carrier signal.

The first multiplier in Figure 17.1 is actually an approximation of a phase detector. More specifically, the outputs of the complex exponential block $e^{-j(\cdot)}$ are sine and cosine waveforms that, ideally, are at the exact frequency and phase of the incoming signal's carrier. This complex oscillator, in an analog circuit, would be called a local oscillator (LO). The output of the multiplier, which can also be called a mixer, contains both the message signal and an approximation of the LO's phase error.

Various types of coherently detected amplitude modulated (AM) communication signals can be recovered by the real part of this mixer output, $m[n]$. Additional filtering may be required to recover a more accurate estimate of the transmitted message. Binary phase-shift keying (BPSK), the more general M-PSK, and quadrature amplitude modulation (QAM) can all be thought of as special cases of AM. More on this topic can be found in Chapters 18, 19, 20, and 21.

The multiplication of the real and imaginary outputs of the first mixer is the input to the loop filter. This filter is actually a lowpass filter which only allows an estimate of the LO's phase error to be fed back into the complex oscillator. The single input to the complex oscillator (LO) is the output of a 2-input phase accumulator. This accumulator combines the existing phase of the oscillator with the free-running oscillator's next phase increment, $\omega_c T$, and the estimate of the phase error out of the loop filter. The complex oscillator (LO) and the phase accumulator together are routinely referred to as a voltage-controlled oscillator (VCO).

If the LO's rest (or free-running) frequency, is *reasonably* close to the carrier frequency of the input signal, the PLL will almost immediately begin to remove any frequency and phase error between these signals, and "lock" the VCO frequency to the incoming carrier frequency. This is how the PLL got its name. The phase error feedback loop rapidly accomplishes this task without any operator interaction with the system.

17.2   winDSK Demonstration

The winDSK8 program does not provide an equivalent function.

17.3   MATLAB Implementation

17.3.1   PLL Simulation

The MATLAB® simulation of the PLL is shown in Listing 17.1.

Listing 17.1: Simulation of a PLL.

```
1 %   Simulation of a BPSK modulator and its coherent recovery
  %
3
  %   input terms
5 Fmsg = 12000;      % carrier frequency of the BPSK transmitter (Hz)
  VCOrestFrequencyError = 200*randn(1); % VCO's error (Hz)
7 VCOphaseError = 2*pi*rand(1);          % VCO's error (radians)
  Fs = 48000;                            % sample frequency (Hz)
9 N = 20000;                             % samples in the simulation
  samplesPerBit = 20;                    % sample per data bit
```

```
11 dataRate = Fs/samplesPerBit;          % data rate (bits/second)
   beta = 0.002;                         % loop filter parameter "beta"
13 alpha = 0.01;                         % loop filter parameter "alpha"
   noiseVariance = 0.0001;               % noise variance
15 Nfft = 1024;                          % number of samples in an FFT
   amplitude = 32000;                    % ADC scale factor
17 scaleFactor = 1/32768/32768;          % feedback loop scale factor

19 %  input term initializations
   phaseDetectorOutput = zeros(1, N+1);
21 vcoOutput = [exp(-j*VCOphaseError) zeros(1, N)];
   m = zeros(1, N+1);
23 q = zeros(1, N+1);
   loopFilterOutput = zeros(1, N+1);
25 phi = [VCOphaseError zeros(1, N)];
   Zi = 0;
27
   %  calculated terms
29 Fcarrier = Fmsg + VCOrestFrequencyError; % VCO's rest frequency
   T = 1/Fs;                             % sample period
31 B = [(alpha + beta) -alpha];          % loop filter numerator
   A = [1 -1];                           % loop filter denominator
33 Nbits = N/samplesPerBit;              % number of bits
   noise = sqrt(noiseVariance)*randn(1, N); % AWGN (noise) vector
35
   %  random data generation and expansion (for BPSK modulation)
37 data = 2*(randn(1, Nbits) > 0) - 1;
   expandedData = amplitude*reshape(ones(samplesPerBit,1)*data,1,N);
39
   %  BPSK signal and its HT (analytic signal) generation
41 BPSKsignal = cos(2*pi*(0:N-1)*Fmsg/Fs).*expandedData + noise;
   analyticSignal = hilbert(BPSKsignal);
43
   %  processing the data by the PLL
45 for i = 1:N
       phaseDetectorOutput(i+1) = analyticSignal(i)*vcoOutput(i);
47     m(i+1) = real(phaseDetectorOutput(i+1));
       q(i+1) = scaleFactor * real(phaseDetectorOutput(i+1)) ...
49             * imag(phaseDetectorOutput(i+1));
       [loopFilterOutput(i+1), Zf] = filter(B, A, q(i+1), Zi);
51     Zi = Zf;
       phi(i+1) = mod(phi(i) + loopFilterOutput(i+1) ...
53             + 2*pi*Fcarrier*T, 2*pi);
       vcoOutput(i+1) = exp(-j*phi(i+1));
55 end
   %  Plotting commands follow ...
```

An explanation of Listing 17.1 follows.

1. (Line 5): Define the system's carrier frequency as 12 kHz.

2. (Lines 6–7): Define errors in both the carrier's frequency and phase. These errors add realism to the simulation.

3. (Line 8): Defines the system's sample frequency as 48 kHz. This sample frequency matches the rate of the DSK's audio codec.

4. (Line 9): Defines the number of samples in the simulation.

5. (Lines 10–11): Together with the system's sample frequency, these lines of code specify the symbol rate. In this binary phase-shift keying (BPSK) simulation, the symbol rate is equal to the bit rate. It cannot be overemphasized that the requirement specified by Nyquist *must* be met! This requirement can be restated as "you must sample fast enough to prevent aliasing of your input signal." Given that we are implementing the BPSK signal as the multiplication of a 12 kHz carrier with an antipodal pulse train, it should be clear that some aliasing *will* occur since the bandwidth of a perfect antipodal pulse train is infinite.

6. (Lines 12–13): Specify the filter coefficients associated with the loop filter.

7. (Line 14): Like Lines 16–17, adding noise to the system adds realism to the simulation.

8. (Line 16): The full range of a 16-bit ADC and DAC is $+32767$ to -32768. This amplitude scale factor simulates an input signal near the full range of values allowed into the ADC without exceeding the range of the converter.

9. (Line 17): This term scales the phase error signal *prior* to this signal being fed back into the phase accumulator. As the PLL drives the system's phase error to near zero, we expect the phase error to be a very small number (a small portion of a radian).

10. (Lines 19–26): These lines of code establish the variables for sample-by-sample processing of the PLL simulation. Maintaining a vector instead of only the most recent value will allow for a number of performance plots to be generated.

11. (Lines 31–32): These are the coefficients associated with a single equivalent IIR filter implementation for the loop filter. This is done only for ease of simulation. In [87,88], the loop filter is implemented in parallel form, which can be seen in Figure 17.2.

12. (Lines 37–38): These lines of code create the BPSK baseband signal.

13. (Line 41): Mixes the BPSK baseband signal to the carrier frequency and adds noise to the signal.

14. (Line 42): Calculates the analytic signal of the input signal $s[n]$. Fortunately, MAT-LAB defines the analytic signal as $s[n] + j\hat{s}[n]$, which is the same definition we introduced earlier. At this point, we must recognize that the variable `analyticSignal` is a complex number.

15. (Line 46): Calculates the output of the first mixer.

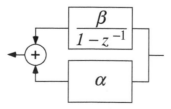

Figure 17.2: The block diagram of the parallel implementation of the loop filter.

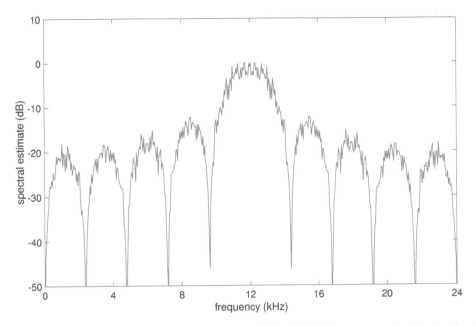

Figure 17.3: The normalized spectral estimate of the BPSK message signal mixed with a carrier frequency of 12 kHz.

16. (Line 47): Calculates the estimate of the message signal.

17. (Lines 48–49): Calculate and scale the output of the second mixer.

18. (Line 50): Performs the loop filtering operation.

19. (Line 51): Saves the filter state by copying the filter's final condition to the filter's initial condition variable.

20. (Lines 52–53): Calculate the next value contained in the phase accumulator. The `mod` command keeps the phase accumulator's output value between 0 and 2π.

21. (Line 54): Calculates the LO's output value. The complex exponential form can also be thought of as sine and cosine terms by using Euler's identity.[1]

Although not shown in the code listing, this simulation results in several plots that allow for a more detailed understanding of the PLL. Given the simulation's ability to randomly initialize the frequency and phase errors associated with the LO and the random nature of the noise that is added to the signal, the behavior of the simulation will be different *every* time the simulation is run. This random behavior can be controlled by either reinitializing the state of the MATLAB random number generator at the beginning of each simulation or by setting the variables in lines 16, 17, and 24 equal to zero. The state of the MATLAB random number generator can be reset using the MATLAB command `randn('state',0)`.

The normalized spectral estimate of the BPSK message signal mixed with a carrier frequency of 12 kHz is shown in Figure 17.3. The pole/zero plot of the loop filter is shown in Figure 17.4. In this figure, a pole is *on* the unit circle and, although it may not be evident from Figure 17.5, this results in infinite gain at 0 Hz (DC). An example of a well-behaved startup transient of the PLL is shown in Figure 17.6. While this type of behavior

---

[1]Specifically, $e^{-\phi} = \cos(-\phi) + j\sin(-\phi) = \cos(\phi) - j\sin(\phi)$, with the sign simplifications occurring because of the even and odd properties of the cosine and sine functions, respectively.

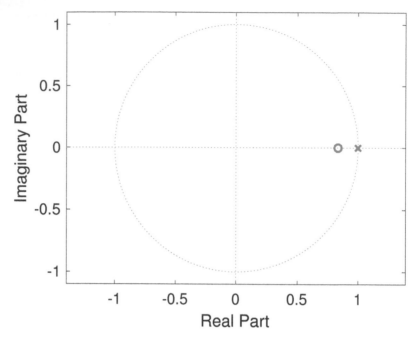

Figure 17.4: The pole/zero plot of the loop filter.

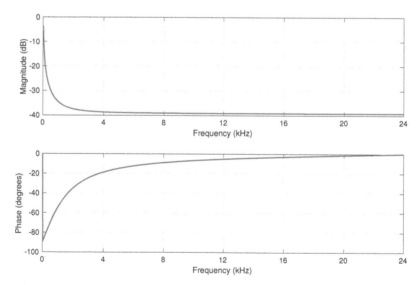

Figure 17.5: The frequency response of the loop filter.

is quite common, the second-order Costas loop is blind to 180-degree phase ambiguities, and the system's output may be as shown in Figure 17.7. In Figure 17.7, the "recovered message" is clearly 180 degrees out of phase from the "message" signal. This sign error will be disastrous (e.g., BPSK communication systems would result in 100% of the bits being received in error).[2] Assuming we are using a two's complement numeric representation,

---

[2]If this were an analog PLL performing coherent recovery of an analog voice signal, then this ±180° phase ambiguity would be of little or no concern because the human auditory system will not perceive a difference in the intended message. But for a digital signal, we cannot tolerate reversal of all the bits. The use of a known preamble code or using differentially encoded message data can solve this problem [64,85,89].

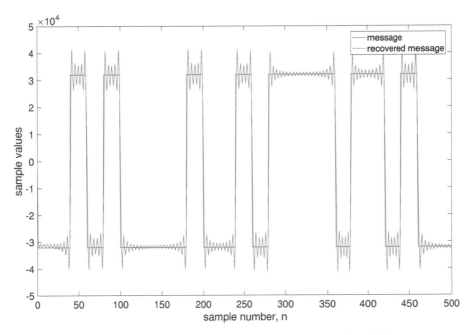

Figure 17.6: Well-behaved startup transient of the PLL.

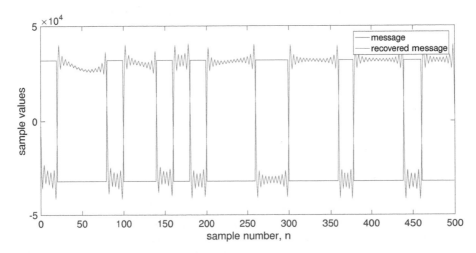

Figure 17.7: Well-behaved startup transient of the PLL with a 180-degree phase error.

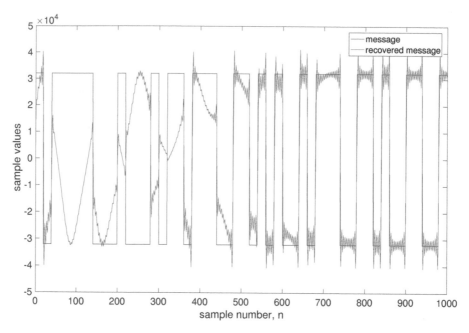

Figure 17.8: A more protracted startup transient of the PLL.

reversing the state of all the bits does *not* just constitute a change in sign! Finally, a very large frequency error was inserted into the LO to show a more protracted transient during PLL initialization. This is shown in Figure 17.8, where it took somewhere between 300 to 500 samples for the PLL to stabilize and track the incoming signal. In this simulation, there were 20 samples/symbol; this corresponds to 15 to 25 symbols that may not be properly recovered before the PLL stabilizes. Depending on the intended use of the communication system, this transient behavior of the PLL may be disastrous or of little concern.

17.3.2   A Few Updates to the MATLAB Implementation

As mentioned earlier, the simulation we presented was designed to be easily implemented in MATLAB. Since MATLAB is a very high-level language, a few of the specialized commands must be replaced by commands capable of being readily implemented in C/C++. Some issues to consider when transitioning the PLL code from MATLAB to C are given below.

1. The vector-based variables need to be replaced by sample-by-sample variables. This straightforward process will be explained in the next section.

2. There is no longer a need to intentionally offset the LO's frequency or phase and add noise to the incoming signal. While these terms were required to make the simulation more realistic, they are not required for real-time implementation.

3. While MATLAB can easily handle complex numbers, the C language does not have a native complex variable type. A common way to handle complex numbers is to declare real and imaginary variables associated with each of the complex terms. This is just a rectangular implementation of the MATLAB complex terms. Unlike MATLAB, when a rectangular version of the complex terms is used, it is incumbent on the system programmer to properly code the results associated with all of the complex mathematical operations. For example, if two complex numbers z_1 and z_2 are multiplied together the result would be $z_1 z_2 = (a+jb)(c+jd) = ac+jad+jbc-bd = (ac-bd)+j(ad+bc)$.

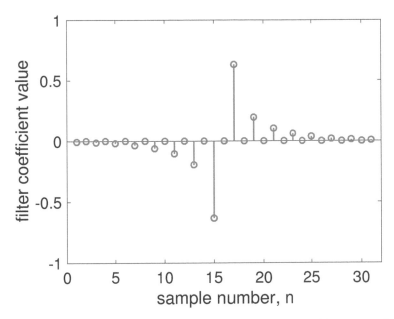

Figure 17.9: Filter coefficients associated with a 30th-order FIR Hilbert transforming filter.

4. The Hilbert transform of the incoming signal can be implemented in a number of ways. A sample-by-sample implementation would approximate the transform with a bandpass FIR filter. The FIR filter can be designed in MATLAB, for example, by using the command B = firpm(30, [0.1 0.9], [1.0 1.0], 'Hilbert'). In this command, 30 is the order of the filter, [0.1 0.9] is the normalized frequency range over which the specified amplitude response [1.0 1.0] applies, and 'Hilbert' tells MATLAB that a Hilbert transforming filter is to be designed. This is the identical syntax for the firpm command that we used in Chapter 16. A plot of the resulting filter coefficients is shown in Figure 17.9. Just as we saw with the Hilbert transforming filter we designed in Chapter 16, every other coefficient is zero, and the coefficients exhibit antisymmetry. We can take advantage of the large number of coefficients with a value of zero (and also the antisymmetry) to reduce the computational complexity of the filter. This filter has the frequency response shown in Figure 17.10. While this bandpass implementation of the Hilbert transforming filter may look flat in the passband, a closer inspection of the passband will reveal that some amount of passband ripple is unavoidable. This is clearly shown in Figure 17.11. Increasing the order of the filter or decreasing the normalized frequency range over which the specified amplitude response applies will decrease the passband ripple. The group delay of the Hilbert transforming filter is shown in Figure 17.12. This is an example of a symmetric FIR filter that has a constant group delay (due to its linear phase response). The group delay is equal to half the filter order.

5. Alternatively, an FFT/IFFT can be used to implement the Hilbert transform if a frame-based system is desired. This process can be implemented using the MATLAB code

```
transformedSignal = ifft(fft(signal).* ...
    [-j*ones(1,513) j*ones(1,511)]);
```

In this example, there are 1024 samples per frame.

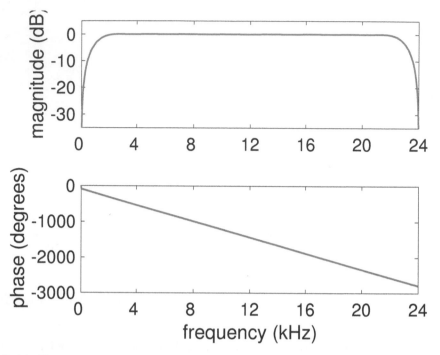

Figure 17.10: Frequency response associated with a 30th-order FIR Hilbert transforming filter.

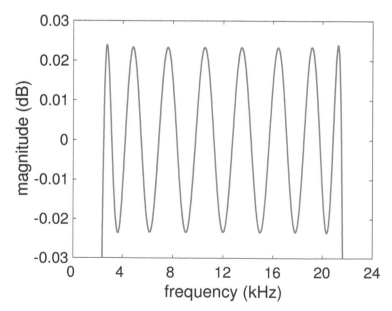

Figure 17.11: Close-up inspection of the passband of the frequency response associated with a 30th-order FIR Hilbert transforming filter. The passband ripple is now quite evident.

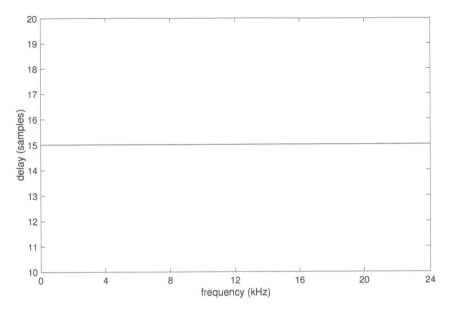

Figure 17.12: The group delay associated with a 30th-order FIR Hilbert transforming filter.

6. The loop filter can alternatively be implemented in its parallel form.

7. The modulus operation should be replaced by more basic C/C++ commands (e.g., an if statement followed by the subtraction of 2π whenever the accumulated phase is greater than 2π).

17.4 DSK Implementation in C

17.4.1 Components of the PLL

When you understand the MATLAB code, the translation of the concepts into C is fairly straightforward. The PLL has two major components: a Hilbert transforming FIR filter (any of the techniques discussed in Chapter 3 could be used to implement this filter), and the LO's control loop.

The files necessary to run this application are in the ccs\PLL directory of Chapter 17. The primary file of interest is the PLL_ISRs.c, which includes the interrupt service routines. This file includes the necessary variable declarations and performs the actual PLL algorithm.

If the DSK codec you're using is a stereo device (such as the on-board codec for the C6713 DSK or either of the OMAP-L138 boards), the program could implement independent Left and Right channel PLLs. For clarity, this example program will implement only one PLL, but will output a delayed version of the input signal and the recovered message signal. If both signals are displayed on a multichannel oscilloscope, the relationship between the modulated signal (input signal) and an estimate of the modulating signal (message) should be clear.

The declaration section of the code is shown in Listing 17.2.

Listing 17.2: Declaration portion of the PLL project code.

```
  float alpha =   0.01;          /* loop filter parameter */
2 float beta  = 0.002;           /* loop filter parameter */
  float Fmsg  = 12000;           /* vco rest frequency */
```

```
4  float  Fs = 48000;                    /* sample frequency */
   float  x[N+1] = {0,0,0,0,0,0,0,0,0,0,0,0,0,0,0,0,0,
6                   0,0,0,0,0,0,0,0,0,0,0,0,0,0,0,0}; /* input signal
                     [+]*/
   float  sReal;          /* real part of the analytic signal */
8  float  sImag;          /* imag part of the analytic signal */
   float  q = 0;          /* input to the loop filter */
10 float  sigma = 0;      /* part of the loop filter's output */
   float  loopFilterOutput = 0;
12 float  phi = 0;        /* phase accumulator value */
   float  pi = 3.14159265358979;
14 float  phaseDetectorOutputReal;
   float  phaseDetectorOutputImag;
16 float  vcoOutputReal = 1;
   float  vcoOutputImag = 0;
18 float  scaleFactor = 3.0517578125e-5;
```

An explanation of Listing 17.2 follows.

1. (Lines 1–2): Declare and initialize the loop filter coefficients. In this parallel implementation, beta should be much smaller than alpha.

2. (Lines 3–4): Declare the message (or carrier frequency) and the sample frequency, respectively.

3. (Lines 5–6): Declare and initialize the input signal's variable. An FIR filter, even if not initialized, will rapidly *flush* any unintended values from its storage variable. During this transient, it is *possible* that the output of the filter will be QNAN. This "not-a-number" state will be fed into the IIR-based loop filter. The filter cannot recover from this state. For this reason alone, **failure to properly initialize** variables is one of the most common causes of properly written algorithms that will not execute properly.

4. (Lines 7–8): Declare the real and imaginary parts of the analytic signal. These are two of the four inputs to the first mixer.

5. (Lines 9–11): Declare the intermediate variables needed by the loop filter and the loop filter's output.

6. (Line 12): Declares the VCO's current phase, which is the input argument to the LO.

7. (Lines 14–15): Declare the outputs of the first mixer.

8. (Lines 16–17): Declare the final two inputs to the first mixer.

9. (Line 18): Declares a scale factor that brings the product of the second mixer into a reasonable range for an error signal. Remember, the error signal (output of the loop filter) is needed to adjust the phase of the VCO. Assuming that the loop is reasonably close to locking, only small phase adjustments ($\ll$ 1 radian) should be added to the phase accumulator.

The algorithm section of the code is shown in Listing 17.3.

Listing 17.3: Algorithm portion of the PLL project code.

```c
// I added my PLL routine here
x[0] = CodecDataIn.Channel[LEFT]; // current LEFT input value
sImag = 0;                  // initialize the dot-product result

for (i = 0; i <= N; i+=2) { // indexing by 2, B[odd] = 0
    sImag += x[i]*B[i];       // perform the dot-product
}

sReal = x[15]*scaleFactor;  // grpdelay of filter is 15 samples

for (i = N; i > 0; i--) {
    x[i] = x[i-1];            // setup x[] for the next input
}

sImag *= scaleFactor;       // scale prior to loop filter

// execute the D-PLL (the loop)
vcoOutputReal = cosf(phi);
vcoOutputImag = sinf(phi);
phaseDetectorOutputReal=sReal*vcoOutputReal+sImag*vcoOutputImag;
phaseDetectorOutputImag=sImag*vcoOutputReal-sReal*vcoOutputImag;
q = phaseDetectorOutputReal * phaseDetectorOutputImag;
sigma += beta*q;
loopFilterOutput = sigma + alpha*q;
phi += 2*pi*Fmsg/Fs + loopFilterOutput;

while (phi > 2*pi) {
    phi -= 2*pi;     /* modulo 2pi operation */
}

// setup CODEC output values
CodecDataOut.Channel[LEFT]=32768*sReal; // input signal
CodecDataOut.Channel[RIGHT]=32768*phaseDetectorOutputReal; // msg
// end of my PLL routine
```

An explanation of Listing 17.3 follows.

1. (Line 2): Brings the input sample into the ISR.

2. (Lines 3–7 and 11–13): These lines of code take the Hilbert transform of the input signal using an FIR filter.

3. (Line 9): Accounts for the group delay of the FIR filter and scales the input signal *prior* to the loop filter.

4. (Line 15): Scales the output of the FIR filter. The outputs of lines 9 and 15 form the analytic signal and represent 2 of the 4 inputs into the first mixer.

5. (Lines 18–19): Calculate the outputs from the complex mixer. These calculations are the last 2 inputs into the first mixer.

6. (Lines 20–21): Calculate the outputs of the first mixer.

7. (Line 22): Calculates the output to the second mixer, which is the input to the loop filter.

8. (Lines 23–24): Calculate the intermediate results and the output of the loop filter.

9. (Line 25): Calculates the value of the phase accumulator, phi.

10. (Lines 27–29): Perform a modulus 2π operation on phi. The mod operator is available in the C implementation of CCS, but it is *only* defined for integer data types. Additionally, this subtraction of 2π technique is much faster than most operators requiring division. The while statement can be replaced by an if statement since the phase accumulator's value should only increase by ($\pi/2$ plus the loop filter's feedback signal) for each sample. A while statement is a more conservative solution to this problem.

17.4.2   System Testing

To test the operation of the PLL, test signals can be created in MATLAB, converted to wave files, and then played back through a computer's sound card. Note that some such signals are included in the test_signals directory of the software for the book. The filenames of these signals start with AM or with BPSK. MATLAB m-files that create these wave files are contained in the software for the book in the matlab directory for Chapter 17 and are named AMsignalGenerator.m and BPSKsignalGenerator.m. With a slight modification to these programs (that is, changing the sample rate to 44,100 Hz), the signals created by these m-files could also be recorded directly on to a CD-R of your choice, and then played back on any CD player. This effectively turns an inexpensive CD player into an inexpensive communications signal generator.

The response of the system to a 750 Hz sinusoidal message modulated (AM-DSB-SC) with a 12 kHz carrier, as viewed on a multichannel oscilloscope, is shown in Figure 17.13. A typical transient response of the system to a 750 Hz message modulated (AM-DSB-SC) with a 12 kHz carrier is shown in Figure 17.14. Finally, the response of the system to a 2400 bit per second (bps) BPSK signal with a 12 kHz carrier is shown in Figure 17.15. The BPSK signal was generated by a PC sound card and shows significant distortion due to the bandlimited response of the system.

17.5   Follow-On Challenges

Consider extending what you have learned.

1. Design and implement your own loop filter within the PLL.

2. Design and implement an algorithm that detects, then provides some indication to the user, when the PLL is *locked* and tracking the input signal.

3. There are three significant computational inefficiencies (bottlenecks) in the PLL ISR. Profile the ISR code and identify these bottlenecks.

4. Suggest possible improvements that minimize or remove these bottlenecks.

5. Implement at least one of your improvements and calculate the computational savings of your new code.

6. Implement a PLL using frame-based techniques.

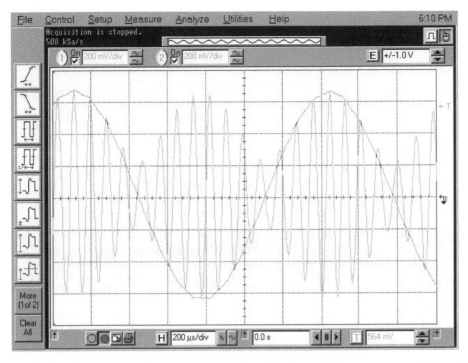

Figure 17.13: The response of the system to a 750 Hz sinusoidal message modulated (AM-DSB-SC) with a 12 kHz carrier, as viewed on a multichannel oscilloscope.

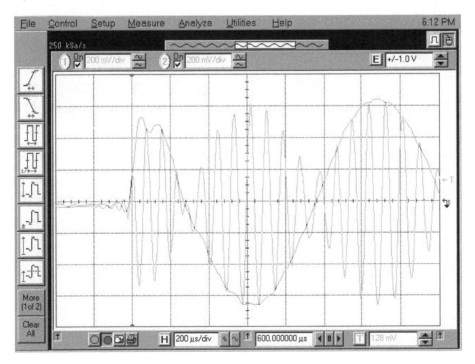

Figure 17.14: A typical transient response of the system to a 750 Hz sinusoidal message modulated (AM-DSB-SC) with a 12 kHz carrier.

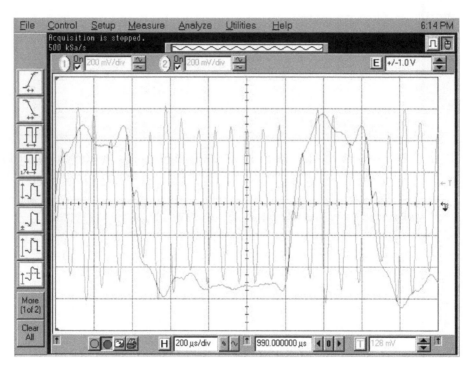

Figure 17.15: The response of the system to a 2400 bps message modulated (BPSK) with a 12 kHz carrier.

Chapter 18

Project 9: BPSK Digital Transmitters

18.1 Theory

IN Chapter 5, we introduced the basic concepts involved in periodic signal generation. Although we mentioned the idea, we intentionally deferred the discussion of aperiodic digital communications signals until now. Since digital communications signals can be generated using an unlimited number of different forms and specifications, we will only introduce one of these forms and a few of the techniques that can be used to produce this type of signal. Specifically, we will discuss

1. Random data and symbol generation.

2. Binary phase shift-keying (BPSK) using antipodal rectangularly shaped bits.

3. BPSK using impulse modulated (IM) raised-cosine shaped bits.

This is a good place to reiterate that this text gives only a brief review of the theory associated with the areas for which we use real-time DSP. For example, in this chapter we can't teach you the in-depth theory of digital communications; you'll need a good communications textbook for that, such as [64–66, 85].

18.1.1 Random Data and Symbol Generation

In an actual communication system, the data bits that eventually make up the transmitted symbols would come from an ADC or some other information source. Unfortunately, using real information sources can *greatly* increase the complexity of the system. Additionally, this tends to severely constrain the communication system design. While these constraints are necessary in the design of a real communication system, they tend to overly complicate matters for someone who is just getting started in communication system design and implementation.

To illustrate this point, let's imagine that we want to create a digital communications link capable of sending all of the data generated by the DSK's ADC for a very high fidelity (better than CD-quality) music signal. This implies stereo (2 channels of data), with 24 bits per sample, and a nominal sample rate (frequency) of 48,000 samples per second. This results in a data rate entering the DSK of $2 \times 24 \times 48,000 = 2,304,000$ bits per second (bps). Remembering that a T-1 data line, which represents the combined data signals from

24 telephone lines, only contains 1,544,000 bps, our desire to transmit such a signal may be a bit aggressive for our first digital communications project!

Instead, we will derive our data bits from a random number generator. A pseudonoise (PN or m-sequence) generator or an array of predeclared data could also be used. Speaking of bits, we need to briefly discuss bits versus symbols in digital communications, since they are often confused. Numeric values are represented in a computer or DSK as *bits*, but what we actually send over a communications link are *symbols*. If our communication system is using a set (called a constellation) of symbols that can take on four different values, then we have 2 bits per symbol. If our communication system is using a constellation of symbols that can take on 16 different values, then we have 4 bits per symbol. Remember that a digital communication system sends and receives symbols, not bits. With that being said, we are discussing BPSK in this chapter, where our symbols can take on only 2 different values. This means that for BPSK, we have 1 bit per symbol, so the bit rate and the symbol rate are identical.

A relatively straightforward starting point for the design of our digital communication system is to select a data rate such that there are an integer number of samples per symbol. That is, $F_s/R_d = k$, where F_s is the sample frequency, R_d is the data rate, and k is an integer. Using our nominal sample frequency of 48 kHz, and recognizing that we need at least 2 samples per symbol, we can choose from the data rates shown in Table 18.1. For the rest of this chapter, we will use $k = 20$, which implies a *great* number of things about our communication system. This includes, but is not limited to,

1. $F_s/20$ is the symbol rate, which is equal to 2400 symbols per second (sps).

2. The reciprocal of the symbol rate is the symbol period $= 1/2400 = 0.416666$ ms.

3. There are 20 samples associated with each and every symbol period.

While this may all seem very straightforward, a common mistake is to try to change one of these parameters (sample frequency, symbol rate, symbol period, or samples per symbol)

Table 18.1: Data rate (in symbols per second) using an integer number of samples per symbol, where the sample frequency is assumed to be $F_s = 48$ kHz. Note that for BPSK, "symbols per second" is identical to "bits per second."

F_s/k	k	Data Rate (sps)
$F_s/2$	2	24,000
$F_s/3$	3	16,000
$F_s/4$	4	12,000
$F_s/5$	5	9,600
$F_s/6$	6	8,000
$F_s/8$	8	6,000
$F_s/10$	10	4,800
$F_s/12$	12	4,000
$F_s/15$	15	3,200
$F_s/16$	16	3,000
$F_s/20$	20	2,400
$\vdots$	$\vdots$	$\vdots$
F_s/N	N	$48,000/N$

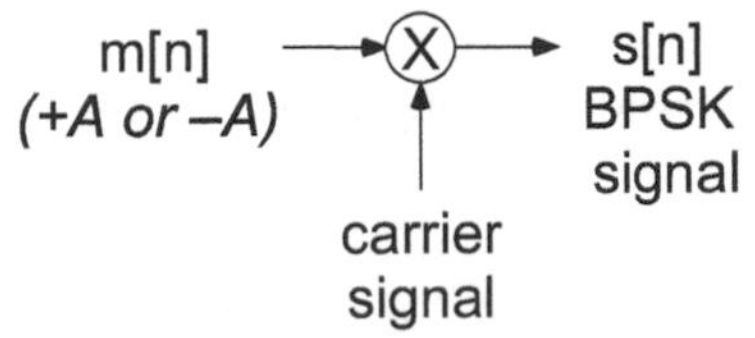

m[n] ──→ ⊗ ──→ s[n]
(+A or −A)   BPSK
                  signal
         │
      carrier
      signal

Figure 18.1: The block diagram associated with a rectangularly pulse shaped BPSK transmitter.

without realizing that they are *all* interrelated and therefore cannot be changed independently of one another.

In this project, our modulated message symbols will come out of the DSK's DAC as analog voltage levels. If we were actually going to transmit these symbols, this time-varying analog voltage level would then go to other stages such as a power amplifier and an antenna.

18.1.2 BPSK Using Antipodal Rectangularly Shaped Bits

This form of BPSK is infrequently used in actual communication systems, but it is by far the most understandable implementation. Specifically, the BPSK waveform is $s_{BPSK}[nT_s] = m[nT_s]cos[2\pi f_c nT_s]$, where n is a monotonically increasing integer, T_s is the sample period, m is the current bit's value, and f_c is the carrier frequency. Additionally, for antipodal signaling, m will be limited to the values $\pm A$, where A will routinely be an integer that is near the maximum value allowed by the DAC (e.g., $m = 30,000$ for 16-bits per sample). This form of BPSK is a special case of amplitude modulation (AM), in particular the type of AM known as double sideband-suppressed carrier (DSB-SC). A block diagram of this system is shown in Figure 18.1.

18.1.3 BPSK Using Impulse Modulated Raised-Cosine Shaped Bits

Due to its bandlimited nature, the raised-cosine filtered form of BPSK is commonly used in actual communication systems. The signal, however, is more complicated to understand and slightly more difficult to generate. In an impulse modulator, a scaled impulse is used to excite a pulse shaping filter once per symbol period. In our discussions, we will use a raised-cosine FIR filter as the pulse shaping filter. The output of this filter will then be multiplied by the carrier signal. A block diagram of this system is shown in Figure 18.2.

An example of how the impulse modulator functions is shown in Figure 18.3. In this figure, five positive-valued impulses form the input, $x[n]$, of the FIR filter. Each of the five output waveforms is shown individually on the $y[n]$ plot. The *actual* output of the filter would be the sum of the five sinc-shaped output waveforms.

Similarly, if antipodal impulse excitation of the FIR filter is provided, one possible result is shown in Figure 18.4. In both of these figures, notice how *all but one* of the sinc-shaped

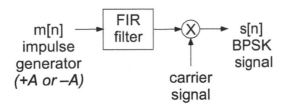

Figure 18.2: The block diagram associated with an impulse modulated BPSK transmitter.

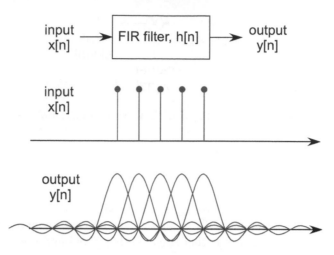

Figure 18.3: An example of how the impulse modulator functions (positive excitation impulses only).

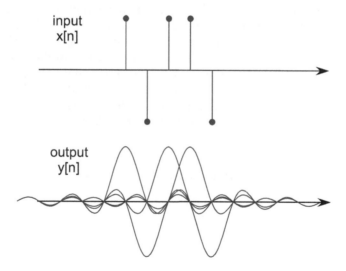

Figure 18.4: Another example of how the impulse modulator functions (antipodal excitation impulses).

waveforms have all of their zero crossings in common. This alignment of the zero crossings is by design, and is fundamental to minimizing intersymbol interference (ISI) within the system.

18.2   winDSK Demonstration

Start the winDSK8 application, and the main user interface window will appear. Ensure the correct selections have been made in the "DSP Board" and "Host Interface" configuration panels of winDSK8 for each parameter before proceeding. Clicking on winDSK8's commDSK button will run that program in the attached DSK, and a window similar to Figure 18.5 will appear.

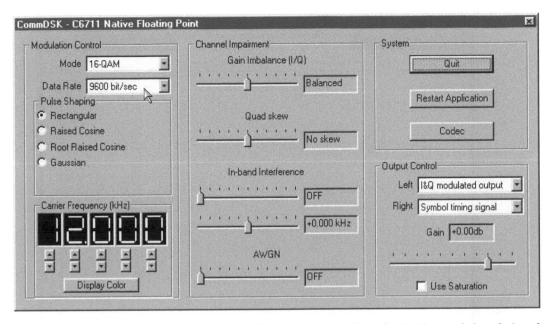

Figure 18.5: winDSK8 running the commDSK application. By default, the modulated signal appears on the Left output channel, and a timing signal appears on the Right output channel. These settings can be changed by the user if needed.

18.2.1 commDSK: Unfiltered BPSK

We need to change a few of the commDSK default settings for now. Change the "Mode" to "BPSK" and the "Data Rate" to "2400 bits/sec" (see Figure 18.6). An example waveform is shown in Figure 18.7. BPSK has only two possible symbols. In Figure 18.7, you can observe the transitions from one type of symbol to the other type of symbol by the sharp phase reversal in the waveform. With the horizontal scale being set to 500 μs per division,

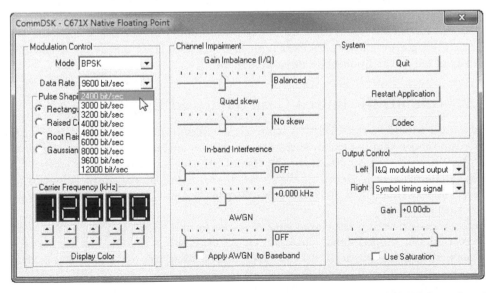

Figure 18.6: commDSK set to generate a rectangular pulse shaped, 2400 bps signal.

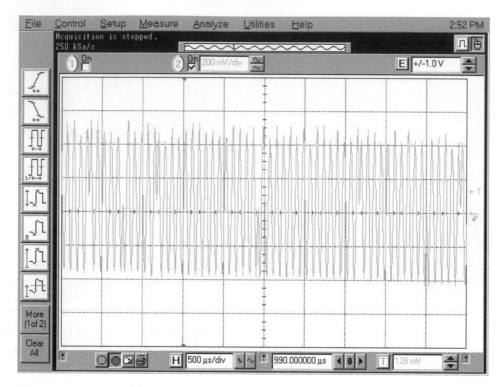

Figure 18.7: commDSK waveform of a rectangular pulse shaped, 2400 bps signal.

the first phase reversal appears to occur at about 350 μs from the left of the display window.

An averaged spectrum associated with this waveform is shown in Figure 18.8. The main lobe is centered at 12 kHz and the first spectral null above 12 kHz occurs at 14.4 kHz. This implies that the main lobe is 4.8 kHz wide (twice the symbol rate), with subsequent nulls occurring at 2.4 kHz spacing. The first side lobe has a relative magnitude that is approximately 13 dB down from the main lobe's peak. These are exactly the expected results associated with band-limited rectangularly-shaped BPSK. Ideally, a perfectly rectangular signal would have a spectrum that would extend to infinity on the frequency axis. But the DSK has a reconstruction lowpass filter built into its codec DAC that removes the majority of the signal energy at frequencies greater than 24 kHz.

18.2.2   commDSK: Raised-Cosine Filtered BPSK

Now we need to adjust commDSK to observe the effect of pulse shaping. We will apply a raised cosine pulse shaping effect, such that we will no longer have rectangular pulses. For the "Pulse Shaping" radio buttons on the commDSK user interface window, select "Raised Cosine." This change is shown in Figure 18.9. An example waveform is shown in Figure 18.10. In this mode, it is much easier to observe the transitions from one type of symbol to the other.

An averaged spectrum associated with this waveform is shown in Figure 18.11. Similar to the rectangular shaped signal, the main lobe is centered at 12 kHz, but the first spectral null above 12 kHz occurs at 13.8 kHz. This implies that the main lobe is 3.6 kHz wide $(2 \times (13.8 - 12) = 3.6)$. This agrees with the theoretical prediction of $BW = D(1 + \alpha) = 2400 \times (1 + 0.5) = 3600$ Hz, where BW is the signal bandwidth, D is the symbol rate, and α is the raised-cosine roll-off factor (the roll-off factor must remain between 0 and 1).

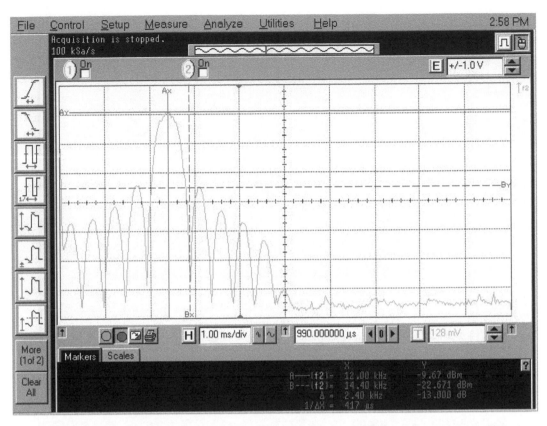

Figure 18.8: An averaged spectrum associated with a rectangular pulse shaped, 2400 bps signal generated by commDSK.

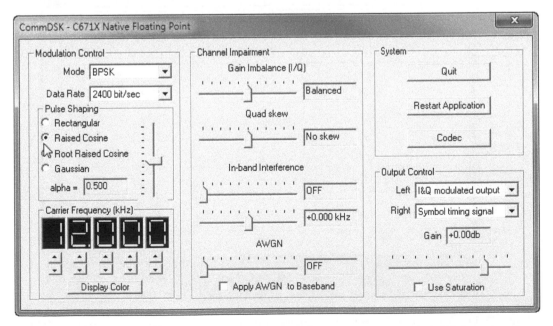

Figure 18.9: commDSK set to generate a raised-cosine pulse shaped, 2400 bps signal.

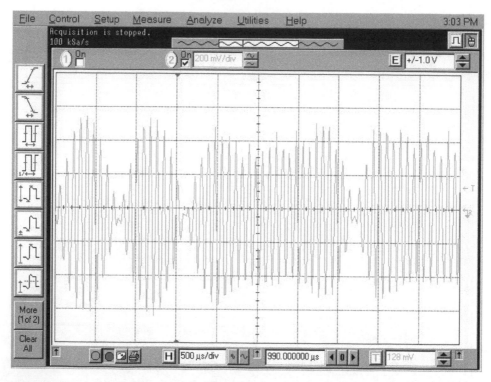

Figure 18.10: commDSK waveform of a raised-cosine pulse shaped, 2400 bps signal.

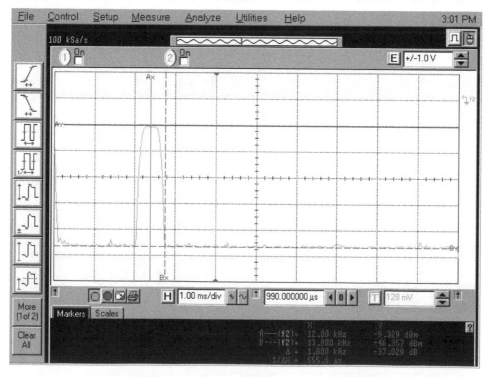

Figure 18.11: An averaged spectrum associated with a raised-cosine pulse shaped, 2400 bps signal generated by commDSK.

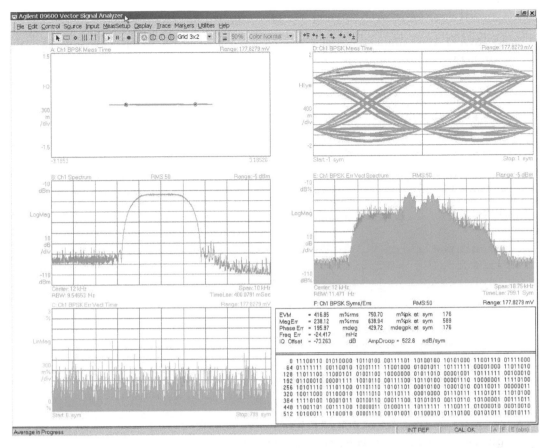

Figure 18.12: An example of a VSA display associated with a raised-cosine pulse shaped, 2400 bps, BPSK signal generated by commDSK.

In Figure 18.11, there are no sidelobes visible due to the apparent noise floor at approximately -46.357 dBm. With the peak of the main lobe at -9.329 dBm, the expected sidelobe level for raised cosine pulses with a roll-off factor of $\alpha = 0.5$ is lower than the observed noise floor. This noise floor is in fact a limitation of the 8-bit ADC associated with the digitizing oscilloscope that was used to produce this figure.

The commDSK program is capable of generating a number of different digital communications signals at a number of different data rates. These signals may also be distorted using the "Channel Impairment" section of commDSK. These impairments are very helpful if the signal is to be processed by a vector signal analyzer (VSA). An example of a VSA display is shown in Figure 18.12. In this figure, plot A is a trajectory/constellation diagram, plot B is the spectral estimate of the BPSK signal, plot C is the error vector magnitude (EVM), plot D is the eye-pattern, plot E is the EVM's spectral estimate, and plot F reports a number of statistics associated with the performance of the signal being analyzed. These plots can be used to infer a great deal about the communication system performance.

18.3 MATLAB Implementation

As discussed earlier, we will simulate generation of two types of BPSK signals: rectangular shaped BPSK signals and impulse modulated raised-cosine BPSK signals.

18.3.1   Rectangular Shaped BPSK Signal Generator

The first MATLAB® simulation is of a rectangular shaped BPSK signal generator; the code is shown in Listing 18.1.

Listing 18.1: Simulation of a rectangular shaped BPSK signal generator.

```
   %  input terms
 2 Fs = 48000;              % sample frequency of the simulation (Hz)
   dataRate = 2400;         % data rate
 4 time = 0.004;            % length of the signal in seconds
   amplitude = 30000;       % scale factor
 6 cosine = [1 0 -1 0];     % cos(n*pi/2) ... Fs/4
   counter = 1;             % used to get a new data bit
 8
   %  calculated terms
10 numberOfSamples = Fs*time;
   samplesPerSymbol = Fs/dataRate;
12
   %  ISR simulation
14 for index = 1:numberOfSamples
       % get a new data bit at the beginning of a symbol period
16     if (counter == 1)
           data = amplitude*(2*(rand > 0.5) - 1);
18     end
20     % create the modulated signal
       output = data*cosine(mod(index,4) + 1)
22
       % reset at the end of a symbol period
24     if (counter == samplesPerSymbol)
           counter = 0;
26     end
28     % increment the counter
       counter = counter + 1;
30 end
32
   %  Plotting commands follow ...
34 %
```

An explanation of Listing 18.1 follows.

1. (Line 2): Defines the system's sample frequency as 48 kHz. This sample frequency matches the rate of the DSK's audio codec.

2. (Line 3): Defines the data rate as 2400 bits per second (bps).

3. (Line 5): Scales the output signal near the full range of the 16-bit DAC.

4. (Line 6): Defines the output of the local oscillator (LO). This term is defined mathematically as $\cos(n\pi/2)$, for $n = 0, 1, 2$, or 3. This simplifies to $\cos(0\pi/2) = 1$,

$\cos(1\pi/2) = 0$, $\cos(2\pi/2) = -1$, or $\cos(3\pi/2) = 0$. Thus, the LO will *only* have an output value of $+1, 0, -1$, or 0. For this special case of signal generation, mixing with the LO requires very few computational resources.

5. (Line 7): The `counter` variable is used to determine the current position within a symbol.

6. (Lines 16–18): A new data bit is generated whenever `counter` is equal to 1.

7. (Line 21): Calculates the output value by multiplying (mixing) the data value with the LO's output. The `cosine` variable is accessed by the MATLAB `mod` command, which maintains the `index` value between 1 and 4.

8. (Lines 24–26): The `counter` variable is reset at the end of a symbol.

9. (Line 29): The `counter` variable is incremented at the end of the simulated ISR.

An example output plot from this simulation is shown in Figure 18.13.

18.3.2 Impulse Modulated Raised-Cosine BPSK Signal Generator

The second MATLAB simulation is of a impulse modulated raised-cosine BPSK signal generator; the code is shown in Listing 18.2. Note the local oscillator (LO) is at $F_s/4$ just like the previous simulation.

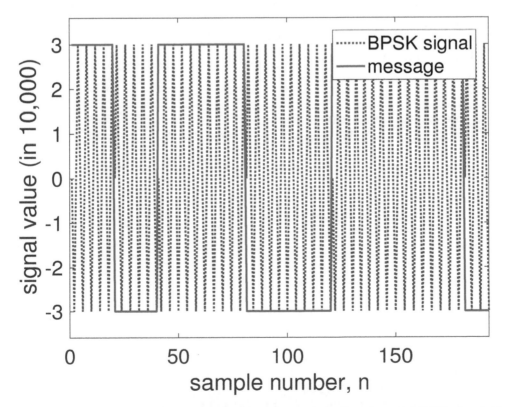

Figure 18.13: An example of the output from the rectangular shaped BPSK simulation. This signal has 2400 bps with a carrier frequency of 12 kHz.

Listing 18.2: Simulation of a impulse modulated raised-cosine BPSK signal generator.

```matlab
%   input terms
Fs = 48000;              % sample frequency of the simulation (Hz)
dataRate = 2400;        % data rate
alpha = 0.5;            % raised-cosine rolloff factor
symbols = 3;            % MATLAB "rcosfir" design parameter
time = 0.004;           % length of the signal in seconds
amplitude = 30000;      % scale factor
cosine = [1 0 -1 0];    % cos(n*pi/2) ... Fs/4
counter = 1;            % used to get a new data bit


%   calculated terms
numberOfSamples = Fs*time;
samplesPerSymbol = Fs/dataRate;

%   create filter
B = rcosfir(alpha, symbols, samplesPerSymbol, 1/Fs);
Zi = zeros(1, (length(B) - 1));


%   ISR simulation
for index = 1:numberOfSamples
    % get a new data bit at the beginning of a symbol period
    if (counter == 1)
        data = amplitude*(2*(rand > 0.5) - 1);
    else
        data = 0;
    end

    % create the modulated signal
    [impulseModulatedData, Zf] = filter(B, 1, data, Zi);
    Zi = Zf;
    output = impulseModulatedData*cosine(mod(index,4) + 1);

    % reset at the end of a symbol period
    if (counter == samplesPerSymbol)
        counter = 0;
    end

    % increment the counter
    counter = counter + 1;
end


%   output terms
%   Plotting commands follow
%   see the book software for the details
%
```

An explanation of Listing 18.2 follows.

1. (Line 2): Defines the system's sample frequency as 48 kHz. This sample frequency matches the rate of the DSK's audio codec.

2. (Line 3): Defines the data rate as 2400 bits per second (bps).

3. (Line 4): Defines the raised-cosine roll-off factor alpha.

4. (Line 5): Defines the length of the raised-cosine FIR filter. The filter length will be equal to 2*symbols + 1. This length is in "symbol periods."

5. (Line 7): Scales the output signal near the full range of the 16-bit DAC.

6. (Line 8): Defines the output of the local oscillator (LO). See the LO discussion related to Listing 18.1.

7. (Line 9): The counter variable is used to determine the current position within a symbol.

8. (Line 17): Designs the raised cosine filter using MATLAB's rcosfir function.[1]

9. (Lines 22–42): These lines of code simulate the real-time ISR.

10. (Lines 24–28): A new data bit is generated whenever counter is equal to 1.

11. (Lines 31–32): These lines of code implement the impulse modulator (IM). The IM is just an FIR filter with an input of one or more impulses followed by a large number of zeros. In this simulation, a single impulse with a value of 30,000 is followed by 19 sample values of zero (20 samples per symbol, remember?). The computational savings of this technique will become clear in the next section.

12. (Line 33): Calculates the output value by multiplying (mixing) the data value with the LO's output. The cosine variable is accessed by the MATLAB mod command which maintains the index value between 1 and 4.

13. (Lines 36–38): The counter variable is reset at the end of a symbol.

14. (Line 41): The counter variable is incremented at the end of the simulated ISR.

An example output plot (with a duration of 4 ms) from this simulation is shown in Figure 18.14. The large order of the FIR filter (120th-order) results in a large group delay (of 60 samples). This delay explains why the first "BPSK signal" peaks occur 60 samples after the first "message" impulse.

Even though the amplitude scale factor is set to 30,000, the system's simulation results in output values that approach $\pm 45,000$. These values are much greater than the DAC's maximum output values $(+32,767)$ and $(-32,768)$. This effect re-emphasizes the importance of first using a MATLAB simulation to determine an appropriate scale factor *prior* to implementing the algorithm in real-time hardware. The simulation time was increased to 2 seconds to allow a higher resolution estimate of the resulting normalized power spectral density; this is shown in Figure 18.15.

---

[1]When designing filters using MATLAB, be aware that as of this writing, the calling sequences of many filter design commands may still be in flux. The MathWorks seemed intent on moving to an object-oriented filter design process that is more cumbersome in many ways, but has recently backed off on that a little. Check the documentation for your version of MATLAB. You may want to read and run the code in filterDesignerComparison.m located in the MATLAB directory of Chapter 18.

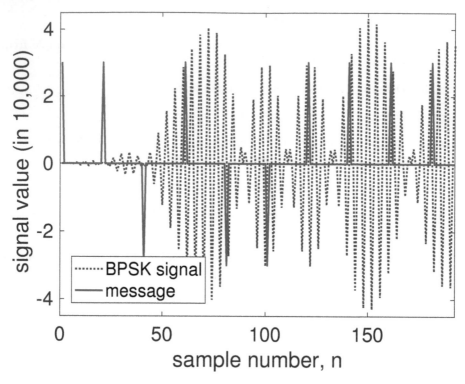

Figure 18.14: An example of the output from the impulse modulated BPSK simulation. This signal has 2400 bps, roll-off factor of $\alpha = 0.5$, and carrier frequency of 12 kHz.

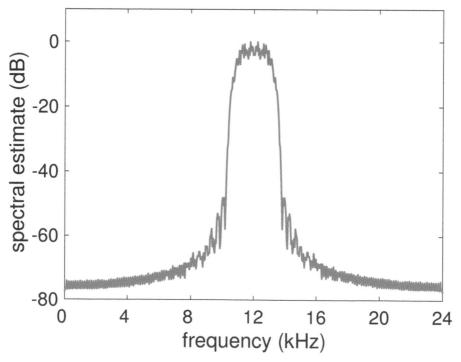

Figure 18.15: An example of the spectral estimate of an impulse modulated BPSK simulation. The signal has 2400 bps, roll-off factor of $\alpha = 0.5$, and carrier frequency of 12 kHz.

The benefits of a spectrally compact, raised-cosine pulse shaped signal cannot be over-emphasized. As calculated earlier, the null-to-null bandwidth of this raised-cosine signal, as compared to a rectangular signal, is 3600 Hz instead of 4800 Hz. To summarize:

1. The raised-cosine signal is more spectrally compact (smaller effective bandwidth).

2. The raised-cosine signal has a smaller null-to-null bandwidth (more spectrally efficient).

3. The raised-cosine signal is *fairly* easy to generate.

4. The digital communications receiver needed to recover the message from this raised-cosine signal will be more complex than if we used rectangular pulses.

18.4   DSK Implementation in C

When you understand the MATLAB code, the concept translation into C is fairly straightforward. The files necessary to run this application are in the **ccs\DigTx** directory of Chapter 18. The primary file of interest is the **rectangularBPSK_ISRs.c**, which contains the interrupt service routines. This file includes the necessary variable declarations and performs the BPSK generation algorithm.

Assuming the DSK's codec you're using is a stereo device, the program could implement independent Left and Right channel BPSK transmitters. For clarity, this example program will implement only one transmitter, but will output this signal to both channels.

18.4.1   A Rectangular Pulse Shaped BPSK Transmitter

The declaration section of the code is shown in Listing 18.3.

Listing 18.3: Declaration portion of the rectangular BPSK project code.

```
1  Int32 counter = 0; // counter within a symbol period
   Int32 symbol;         // current bit value ... 0 or 1
3  Int32 data[2] = {-20000, 20000}; // table lookup bit value
   Int32 x;                          // bit's scaled value
5  Int32 samplesPerSymbol = 20;      // number of samples per symbol
   Int32 cosine[4] = {1, 0, -1, 0}; // cos functions possible values
7  Int32 output;                     // BPSK modulator's output
```

An explanation of Listing 18.3 follows.

1. (Line 1): Declares and initializes the **counter** variable, which is used to indicate where the algorithm is relative to the beginning of the symbol (0) or the end of the symbol (19).

2. (Line 2): Declares the **symbol** variable, which is the current bit's value (0 or 1).

3. (Line 3): Declares and initializes the antipodal values associated with a 0 or a 1.

4. (Line 4): Declares the x variable, which is the current message's value.

5. (Line 5): Declares and initializes the **samplesPerSymbol** variable, which, as its name implies, is the number of samples in a symbol. For BPSK, a symbol and a bit are the same.

6. (Line 6): Declares and initializes the `cosine` variable that contains *all* of the possible LO's values for a 12 kHz cosine carrier.

7. (Line 7) Declares the BPSK modulator's output value.

The algorithm section of the code is shown in Listing 18.4.

Listing 18.4: Algorithm portion of the rectangular BPSK project code.

```
1  // I added my rectangular BPSK routine here
   if (counter == 0) {        // time for a new bit
3      symbol = rand() & 1;  // equivalent to rand() % 2
       x = data[symbol];      // table lookup of next data value
5  }

7  output = x*cosine[counter & 3]; // calculate the output value

9  if (counter == (samplesPerSymbol - 1)) { // end of the symbol
       counter = -1;
11 }

13 counter++;

15 CodecDataOut.Channel[LEFT]  = output; // setup the Left  value
   CodecDataOut.Channel[RIGHT] = output; // setup the Right value
17 // end of my rectangular BPSK routine
```

An explanation of Listing 18.4 follows.

1. (Lines 2–5): Once per symbol, create a random bit, and map that bit to an allowed level. This value remains constant over the next 20 samples.

2. (Line 7): Calculates the product of the current message value with the LO's value. This mixes the BPSK signal to 12 kHz.

3. (Lines 9–11): When `counter` = 19, the algorithm has reached the end of the symbol. At this point `counter` is reset to start the next symbol period.

4. (Line 13): Increments the `counter` variable in preparation for the next ISR call.

5. (Lines 15–16): Output the BPSK transmitter's current value to both the left and right channels.

18.4.2   A Raised-Cosine Pulse Shaped BPSK Transmitter

The declaration section of the code is shown in Listing 18.5. One item that isn't shown here is that the file `coeff.c` is also part of the CCS project. This file contains the coefficients of a 200th-order raised cosine FIR filter exported from MATLAB.

Listing 18.5: Declaration portion of the impulse modulation raised-cosine pulse shaped project code.

```
1  Int32 counter = 0;
   Int32 samplesPerSymbol = 20;
3  Int32 symbol;
   Int32 data[2] = {-15000, 15000};
```

```
5 Int32 cosine[4] = {1, 0, -1, 0};
  Int32 i;
7
  float x[10];
9 float y;
  float output;
```

An explanation of Listing 18.5 follows.

1. (Line 1): Declares and initializes the `counter` variable, which is used to indicate where the algorithm is relative to the beginning of the symbol (0) or the end of the symbol (19).

2. (Line 2): Declares and initializes the `samplesPerSymbol` variable, which, as its name implies, is the number of samples in a symbol. For BPSK, a symbol and a bit are the same.

3. (Line 3): Declares the `symbol` variable, which is the current bit's value (0 or 1).

4. (Line 4): Declares and initializes the antipodal values associated with a 0 or a 1.

5. (Line 5): Declares and initializes the `cosine` variable that contains *all* of the possible LO's values for a 12 kHz cosine carrier.

6. (Line 6): Declares the variable `i` that is used as the index in the dot-product.

7. (Line 8): Declares the `x` array that stores the current and past values of the message's value.

8. (Line 9): Declares the variable `y` that is the impulse modulator's current output value.

9. (Line 10) Declares the variable `output` that is the BPSK modulator's output value.

The algorithm section of the code is shown in Listing 18.6.

Listing 18.6: Algorithm portion of the impulse modulation raised-cosine pulse shaped project code.

```
// I added IM BPSK routine here
2
  if (counter == 0) {
4     symbol = rand() & 1; // faster version of rand() % 2
      x[0] = data[symbol]; // read the table
6 }

8
  // perform impulse modulation based on the FIR filter, B[N]
10 y = 0;

12 for (i = 0; i < 10; i++) {
      y += x[i]*B[counter + 20*i];   // perform the dot-product
14 }

16 if (counter == (samplesPerSymbol - 1)) {
      counter = -1;
18
```

```
      /* shift x[] in preparation for the next symbol */
20    for (i = 9; i > 0; i--) {
          x[i] = x[i-1];                // setup x[] for the next input
22    }
}
24
counter++;
26
output = y*cosine[counter & 3];
28
CodecDataOut.Channel[LEFT]  = output; // setup the LEFT  value
30 CodecDataOut.Channel[RIGHT] = output; // setup the RIGHT value
// end of IM BPSK routine
```

An explanation of Listing 18.6 follows.

1. (Lines 3–6): Once per symbol, create a random bit, and map that bit to an allowed level. This value remains constant over the next 20 samples.

2. (Lines 10–14 and 20–22): Perform the FIR filtering associated with the impulse modulator. The vector B contains the coefficients of the raised cosine filter designed with and exported from MATLAB, using the `rcosfir` function. Even though a 200th-order filter is being implemented, only 10 multiplies are required. This is because *all* of the other multiplies have a zero in the operation. These other multiplies are therefore *not* required since the outcome is already known! This is one of the most important advantages of an impulse modulator.

3. (Lines 16–17): When `counter` is equal to 19, the algorithm has reached the end of the symbol. At this point `counter` is reset to start the next symbol period.

4. (Line 25): Increments the variable `counter` in preparation for the next ISR.

5. (Line 27): Calculates the product of the current message value with the LO's value. This modulates the BPSK signal up to 12 kHz.

6. (Lines 29–30): Output the BPSK transmitter's current value to both the left and right channels.

18.4.3   Summary of Real-Time Code

Thus, we have created two real-time implementations of a BPSK transmitter. The second version, while more complicated, is closer to what is used in actual communication systems due to its superior spectral characteristics. The analog voltage output from the DSK's DAC represents message symbols at a data rate of 2,400 bps (remember that for BPSK, bits and symbols are equivalent). This data stream could be used with a second DSK that is configured as a digital receiver, a concept covered in Chapter 19.

18.5   Follow-On Challenges

Consider extending what you have learned.

1. In the MATLAB impulse modulator simulations we used a 120th-order FIR filter. In the real-time implementation we used a 200th-order FIR filter. What is the effect of using a smaller order filter on the system's performance?

2. Design a bandpass raised-cosine pulse shaping FIR filter/system that, when excited by a impulse, creates the modulated waveform directly (no separate mixer required).

3. Given your design in Challenge 2 above, what are the advantages and disadvantages of this approach?

4. How do the approaches discussed in this chapter compare to the analog filter approach? That is, compare to the method where you would generate a rectangular shaped BPSK signal and then filter the signal to the desired bandwidth using traditional analog filters.

Chapter 19

Project 10: BPSK Digital Receivers

19.1 Theory

IN Chapter 18, we introduced a few of the basic techniques that can be used to generate a binary phase shift-keying (BPSK) signal. Since there are an unlimited number of different forms and specifications associated with the generation of a BPSK signal, it should not be surprising that there are just as many variations of the receiver. In this chapter, we will introduce only one of these forms and a few of the techniques that can be used to recover the message contained within the BPSK signal.

Specifically, we will discuss a simplified BPSK receiver that must

1. Recover the carrier and remove its effects from the incoming signal. This will be accomplished using a phase-locked loop (PLL) (see Chapter 17). This process will recover a baseband version of the BPSK signal.

2. Process the recovered baseband signal through an FIR-based matched filter (MF). Assume our BPSK signal was generated at the transmitter using impulse modulated (IM) "root-raised-cosine" shaped pulses at 2,400 symbols per second. This is similar to, but an interesting and common variation of, the normal "raised cosine" shaped pulses we explored in Chapter 18. As is required for MF operation, the receiver will use an identical root raised-cosine filter to what was used in the transmitter. We selected a MF-based receiver because it results in the optimal signal to noise ratio (SNR) of the decision statistic in the presence of additive white Gaussian noise (AWGN) [65].

3. Finally, symbol timing must be recovered from the signal that comes from the receiver's MF. We will use a maximum likelihood (ML) based timing recovery loop to determine when to sample the matched filter's output. This sampling/decision process is equivalent to determining where, on average, the eye-pattern is the most "open." We will discuss eye-patterns in more detail later in the chapter. This sampling/decision process also converts a series of filtered sampled signal values back into a message bit (0 or a 1). Recall that for BPSK, bits and symbols are equivalent.

At this point in our discussion of a BPSK receiver, it cannot be emphasized enough that carrier recovery, matched filtering, and symbol timing recovery must *all* occur properly within the receiver in order for the individual message bits to be recovered correctly. The combination of these three required processes makes this a very challenging project. It may reduce your anxiety a bit when we tell you that this project actually consists of stringing together two concepts you've already seen and developing only one new concept. Specifically, the phase locked loop (PLL) was developed in Chapter 17 and the matched filter is just an FIR filter, which was developed in Chapter 3. The new portion of this project is the ML-based timing recovery system, which is where we will direct the majority of our discussion. Note that we will use the acronym NCO for "numerically controlled oscillator" to be consistent with the literature, but this is really just another name for a direct digital synthesizer (DDS) such as we discussed in Chapter 5.

The simplified block diagram of the end-to-end BPSK transmitter-channel-receiver is shown in Figure 19.1. In this figure, the receiver block diagram is contained within the dashed box. The timing recovery portion of the receiver is a simplified version derived from Figure 19.2. See [89] for more details.

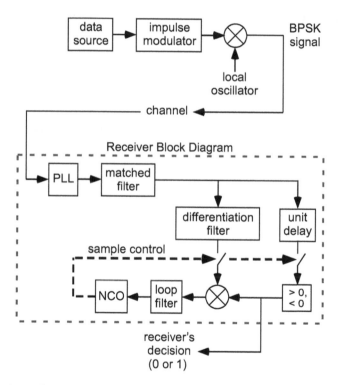

Figure 19.1: A simplified block diagram of a BPSK communications system (transmitter/channel/receiver). PLL: phase locked loop. NCO: numerically controlled oscillator.

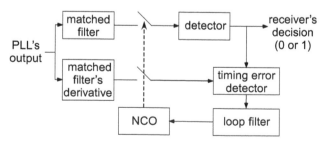

Figure 19.2: A maximum likelihood based timing recovery scheme. NCO: numerically controlled oscillator.

A few key simplifications of Figure 19.2 were made to arrive at Figure 19.1. Specifically,

1. Rather than implement two high-order FIR filters (both a matched filter and a "matched filter derivative" filter) as shown in Figure 19.2, we will implement only the matched filter, then *approximate* the derivative of the matched filter output.

2. The derivative operation will be implemented with a very simple second-order FIR filter that has a group delay of one sample. This unit delay must be accounted for to properly align the two signals.

3. The detector shown in Figure 19.2 will be implemented with a slicer. That is, positive signals will be mapped to $+1$ (message bit value of 1) and negative signals will be mapped to -1 (message bit value of 0). The detector block can be thought of as being the point where the receiver *decides* the value of the received message bit.

4. The timing error detector (TED) as shown in Figure 19.2 will be approximated by the multiplication operation.

19.1.1 The Output of the Matched Filter

After the PLL removes the effects of the transmitter's carrier, the signal is passed through a matched filter. As previously mentioned, this filter optimizes the signal-to-noise ratio of the decision statistic in the presence of AWGN. An example of the output of the matched filter is shown in Figure 19.3. In this figure, the time scale is 5.00 ms/div, and there are 10

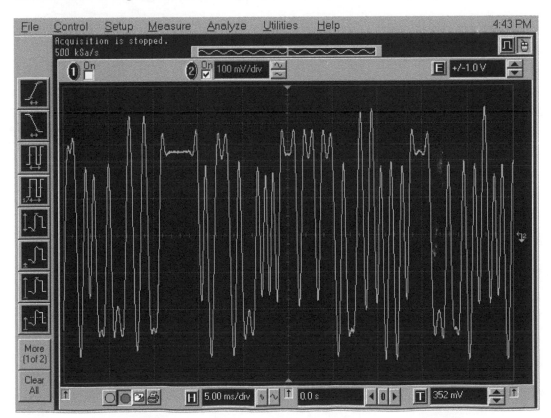

Figure 19.3: Output of the receiver's matched filter (120 bits).

horizontal divisions shown, so we see a 50 ms duration of data in the figure. At the given data rate of 2400 symbols/second (sps), this means the 50 ms "snapshot" is showing us 120 symbols of data. Since this is BPSK, 120 symbols is equivalent to 120 bits.

There was no noise intentionally added to the signal that resulted in Figure 19.3. How difficult is it for you to visually determine the values of all 120 symbols? Can you imagine trying to determine the message symbol values if a significant amount of noise had been added to the signal? Any real-world signal will unavoidably have noise added to it. Perhaps you can begin to appreciate how difficult a task the receiver must accomplish. The entire message symbol detection process is made possible by knowing when is the "best" time to sample the matched filter's output.

19.1.2   The Eye-Pattern

Before we commence our discussion of the timing recovery loop, we need to briefly review the concept of the eye-pattern. As previously mentioned, the BPSK receiver must remove the effects of the carrier (also called "down conversion"), filter the down-converted signal, and then sample the resulting signal at just the right time (timing recovery process) to convert (in this case) 20 samples (the number of samples in a transmitted symbol) back into a message symbol (+1 or −1). This process is equivalent to creating what is commonly called an eye-pattern and sampling this pattern at the point of maximum average eye opening. An example of an eye-pattern created using an oscilloscope and a recovered symbol timing signal to trigger the display is shown in Figure 19.4. In this figure, 100 ms of the

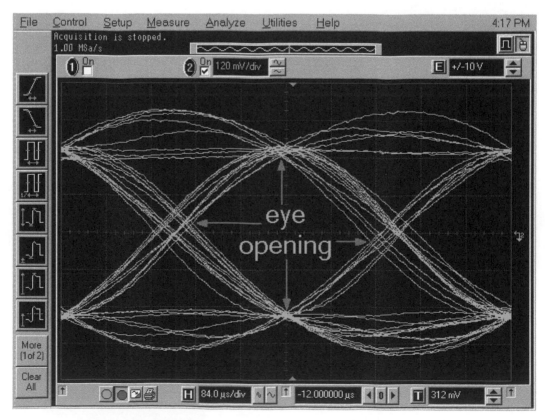

Figure 19.4: BPSK eye-pattern (100 ms of data from MF output).

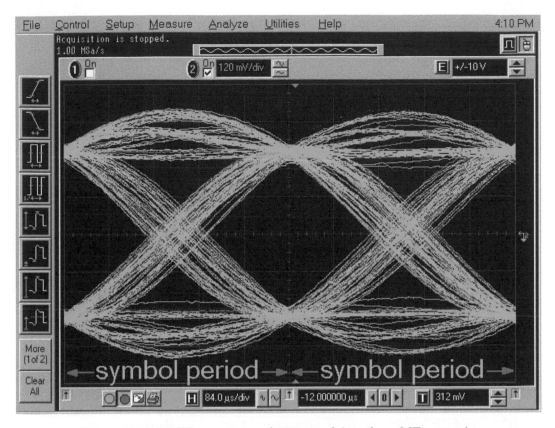

Figure 19.5: BPSK eye-pattern (1000 ms of data from MF output).

matched filter's output is displayed. The eye opening is labeled, but this opening is not symmetric. To achieve a symmetric eye opening, considerably more data (gathered over time) is required to be displayed. In Figure 19.5, a full second of matched filter output is displayed. The eye is now symmetric, and the symbol period is labeled on the horizontal axis. The symbol rate is 2400 symbols per second, which results in a symbol period of $1/2400 = 416.67$ μs. Considering that we wish to display three eye openings (i.e., two symbol periods), the time scale (the horizontal axis of the oscilloscope) needs to be set to $(1/2400) * 2/10 = 83.33$ μs/div, so the oscilloscope time-base was set to the nearest value of 84 μs/div.

At this point, it should be clear that eye-pattern displays of short periods of time allow for individual traces to be seen but that the characteristics of the eye opening can be misleading due to insufficient data. On the other hand, if a much longer time period is displayed, the individual traces on the eye-pattern will be obscured, but the average characteristics of the eye opening will be more clearly visible.

19.1.3   Maximum Likelihood Timing Recovery

As stated earlier, the approximation of the optimum ML timing recovery loop that we will implement is shown in the receiver block diagram portion of Figure 19.1. This diagram is a modified version of the optimal ML timing recovery loop discussed in Chapter 7 of the text by Mengali and D'Andrea [89]. The first step in this process is to multiply properly sampled outputs from the matched filter's decision ($+1$ or -1) by the derivative of the output of the matched filter (this multiplication takes the place of the timing error detector

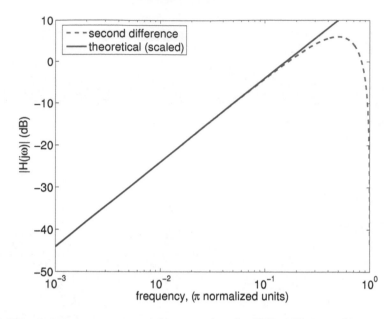

Figure 19.6: The frequency response of a second order FIR difference filter compared with a scaled version of the theoretical response.

in Figure 19.2). Therefore, we need to somehow implement the derivative operation. The derivative can be obtained using a number of different techniques, but we will approximate it with a simple difference operation using a second order FIR filter, $y[n] = x[n] - x[n-2]$, which has a group delay of one sample. As shown in Figure 19.6, this implementation is more than adequate since the difference operation very closely approximates the derivative operation for highly oversampled signals. As is almost always the case, the group delay associated with this filter must be accounted for prior to continuing with the algorithm.

An intuitive understanding of why this multiplication results in a signal that is proportional to the timing error can be seen in Figure 19.7. Recall that for this BPSK signal, a symbol value of -1 is equivalent to a bit value of 0, and a symbol value of $+1$ is equivalent to a bit value of 1. The eye-pattern traces labeled as "A_{01}" are associated with message bit transitions from 0 to 1 and the traces labeled as "A_{10}" are associated with message bit transitions from 1 to 0. For a random message of equiprobable bit values, the traces labeled "A_{01}" and "A_{10}," when taken together, should occur with a probability of 0.5.

The eye-pattern traces labeled as "B" represent extended strings of either ones or zeros (i.e., the bit value doesn't change). The eye-pattern traces labeled as "C" represent extended strings of either ones or zeros followed by a message bit change, or a message bit change followed by an extended string of either ones or zeros. For a random message of equiprobable bit values, the traces labeled "B" and "C," when taken together, should also occur with a probability of 0.5.

Only the "A" region traces result in a proper error signal being generated by the timing error detector (TED). In the "B" region, the slope (i.e., the derivative) of the traces is very close to zero, which results in almost no error signal being generated. In the "C" region, the traces result in an error signal of the "wrong" polarity. This wrong polarity signal can be viewed as either providing positive feedback or as a reinforcement of the system's error, which is not what we want. Fortunately, the effects of the "A" region are stronger than that of the combined "B" and "C" regions. Therefore, with the NCO set to free-run at the 2400 symbols per second rate, the system's error signal should only need to account for very

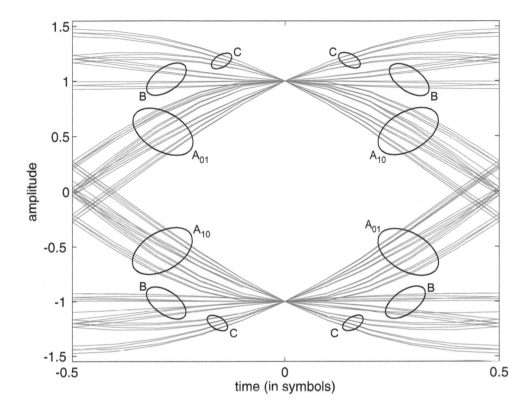

Figure 19.7: The timing recovery scheme for an ideal eye-pattern.

small differences between the transmitter's and the receiver's symbol clocks. This allows for proper operation of the timing recovery loop because, on average, the system tracks the maximum eye opening.

Finally, the sampling and decision at the output of the matched filter MF extracts the transmitted data symbols ($+1$ or -1). The slicer, which implements an even simpler decision, actually decides between $x > 0$ or $x < 0$. Based on the symbol recovered, the data bits (1 or 0) are obtained from the received BPSK signal.

Important: At this point in the book, we hope you've caught on to the need to go beyond the text and to read the *full* program listings associated with a given chapter of the software for the book. While many partial code listings and explanations have been given in previous chapters, the following discussion is intentionally not as detailed. This an attempt to help you further develop the ability to *teach yourself* how read and understand real-time DSP code; this is a necessary step toward creating your own original code. Try to go beyond what we've written.

19.2   winDSK Demonstration

The winDSK8 program does not provide an equivalent receiver function. The commDSK application of winDSK8 has transmitter functions only.

19.3   MATLAB Implementation

The MATLAB® simulation of the BPSK receiver is shown in Listings 19.1 and 19.2. Listing 19.1 details the variable declarations while Listing 19.2 details the simulated ISR portion of the MATLAB script file.

Listing 19.1: Declarations associated with the simulation of the BPSK receiver.

```
1  % generate the BPSK transmitter's signal
   [BPSKsignal, dataArray] = impModBPSK(0.1);
3
   % simulation inputs ... PLL
5  alphaPLL = 0.010;            % PLL's loop filter parameter "alpha"
   betaPLL  = 0.002;            % PLL's loop filter parameter "beta"
7  N  = 20;                     % samples per symbol
   Fs = 48000;                  % simulation sample frequency
9  phaseAccumPLL = randn(1);    % current phase accumulator's value
   VCOphaseError = 2*pi*rand(1); % selecting a random phase error
11 VCOrestFrequencyError = randn(1); % error in the VCO's rest freq
   Fcarrier = 12000;            % carrier freq of the transmitter
13 phi = VCOphaseError;         % initializing the VCO's phase

15 % simulation inputs ... ML timing recovery
   alphaML = 0.0040;   % ML loop filter parameter "alpha"
17 betaML  = 0.0002;   % ML loop filter parameter "beta"
   alpha   = 0.5;      % root raised-cosine rolloff factor
19 symbols = 3;        % MATLAB "rcosfir" design parameter

21 phaseAccumML = 2*pi*rand(1); % initializing the ML NCO
   symbolsPerSecond = 2401;     % symbol rate w/ offset from 2400
```

An explanation of Listing 19.1 follows.

1. (Line 2): Generation of the transmitter's signal.

2. (Lines 5–6): Loop filter parameters associated with the PLL.

3. (Lines 7–8): The sample frequency (samples per second) divided by the number of samples per symbol determines the number of symbols per second (symbol rate or baud).

4. (Lines 9–11, 13, 21, and 22): Add realism to the simulation by ensuring that errors exist in the PLL's initial frequency and phase and also in the ML timing recovery loop's initial phase and symbol rate.

5. (Line 12): Carrier rest frequency is set to match the transmitter's carrier frequency (12 kHz).

6. (Lines 16–17): Loop filter parameters associated with the ML timing recovery loop.

7. (Line 18): Root raised-cosine roll-off factor. This should match the roll-off factor of the transmitter.

8. (line 19): A MATLAB filter design parameter associated with the length (order) of the FIR filter that was designed using the `rcosfir` function.[1]

Listing 19.2: ISR simulation of the BPSK receiver.

```matlab
% commencing ISR simulation
for i = 1:length(BPSKsignal)
    %  processing the data by the PLL
    phaseDetectorOutput = analyticSignal(i)*vcoOutput;
    m = 6*real(phaseDetectorOutput);    % scale for a max value
    q = real(phaseDetectorOutput)*imag(phaseDetectorOutput);
    [loopFilterOutputPLL,Zi_pll]=filter(B_PLL, A_PLL, q, Zi_pll);
    loopFilterOutputPLLSummary = ...
        [loopFilterOutputPLLSummary loopFilterOutputPLL]; % plot
    phi = mod(phi + loopFilterOutputPLL + 2*pi*Fcarrier*T, 2*pi);
    vcoOutput = exp(-j*phi);

    %  processing the data by the ML-based receiver
    [MFoutput, Zi_MF] = filter(B_MF, 1, m, Zi_MF);
    [diffMFoutput,Zi_diff]=filter([1 0 -1], 1, MFoutput,Zi_diff);

    phaseAccumML = phaseAccumML + phaseIncML;
    if phaseAccumML >= 2*pi
        phaseAccumML = phaseAccumML - 2*pi;
        decision = sign(delayedMFoutput);
        [error, Zi_ML_loop] = filter(B_ML, A_ML, ...
            decision*diffMFoutput, Zi_ML_loop);
        phaseAccumML = phaseAccumML - error;
        errorSummary = [errorSummary error];           % plot
        decisionSummary = [decisionSummary decision]; % plot
    else
        errorSummary = [errorSummary 0];               % plot
    end

    delayedMFoutput = MFoutput; % accounts for group delay

    % state storage for plotting ... not part of the ISR
    delayedMFoutputSummary = ...
        [delayedMFoutputSummary delayedMFoutput];
    decisionSummaryHoldOn = [decisionSummaryHoldOn decision];
end

%  output terms
%  Plot commands follow ...
```

An explanation of Listing 19.2 follows.

1. (Lines 2–36): This "for" loop simulates the sample-by-sample processing of the received data.

---

[1]As mentioned in Chapter 18, the calling sequence of many filter design commands are in flux. You may want to read and run the code in `filterDesignerComparison.m` located in the MATLAB directory of Chapter 19.

2. (Lines 4–11): This block of code implements the PLL discussed in Chapter 17.

3. (Line 14): Performs the matched filtering of the data out of the PLL.

4. (Line 15): Performs the second difference of the output of the matched filter. This is a very good approximation of differentiation for this oversampled signal.

5. (Line 17): Updates the value of the phase accumulator associated with the ML timing recovery loop. For a free-running frequency of 2400 symbols per second, every time the ISR is called, the accumulator's value must increment by $2\pi/20 = \pi/10$ radians.

6. (Lines 18–28): Ensure that whenever the phase accumulator reaches 2π, the accumulator's value is reduced by 2π. For reasonable values of the ML timing loop error this is equivalent to a modulo 2π operation. On average, this block of code should only run once every 20 ISR calls. This effectively is a decimation by 20 operation which results in only these samples being passed to the ML timing recovery loop filter.

7. (Line 30): Accounts for the group delay of the second difference FIR filter.

Remember that the simulation randomly initializes the frequency and phase errors associated with the PLL and ML timing recovery loops; this (plus the random nature of any noise that may be added to the input signal) means that the behavior of the simulation will be different *every time* the program is run. This random behavior can be controlled by either reinitializing the state of the MATLAB random number generator at the beginning of each simulation or by setting the variables in lines 9, 10, 11, and 21 equal to zero. The state of the MATLAB random number generator can be reset using the MATLAB command `randn('state',0)`.

A simulation output example exhibiting excellent behavior of the PLL and ML timing recovery loops is shown in Figure 19.8. In this figure the first (top) subplot shows how the PLL's error damps toward zero error. The second subplot shows the ML timing error also settling toward an average value of zero. Remember that the phase angle between adjacent samples as measured by the ML timing recovery NCO is $\pi/10 \approx 0.314$ radians. In this example, the timing error never exceeds 0.1 radians. Keep in mind that the timing error is

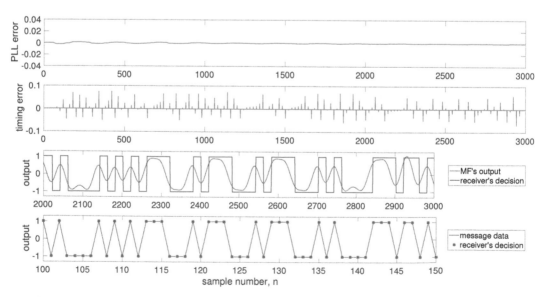

Figure 19.8: BPSK receiver exhibiting excellent PLL and ML timing recovery performance.

only defined when a sample is taken. So the subplot is showing an average of 19 zero error values for every non-zero value. The third subplot shows the output of the matched filter and the receiver's decision. This effectively turns the analog output of the MF back into a digital signal (data symbols). The fourth (bottom) subplot compares the transmitted and received symbols. In this simulation, the receiver processed about 15 symbols before the errors stopped occurring. Remember the symbol to bit mapping for this BPSK example is defined as $(+1 \rightarrow 1)$, $(-1 \rightarrow 0)$.

In Figure 19.9, everything in the first, second, and third subplots indicates that the algorithm is working quite well. The fourth subplot, however, clearly shows that the received symbols have been flipped (a transmitted -1 was interpreted as a $+1$, and a transmitted $+1$ was interpreted as a -1)! When we map the received symbols to bits, this will result in message bit flipping, and our bit error rate will be nearly 100%. This is unacceptable; a reasonable error rate is more on the order of one error for every million bits received! How did this catastrophe occur?

As we discussed in the PLL chapter, the Costas loop PLL is *blind* to 180-degree phase ambiguities. But there are ways to get around this problem. Sending a known preamble signal at the beginning of a transmission would allow you to identify the phase inversion so you could remove it. Another popular technique is to use differential encoding of the transmitted data (with the accompanying differential decoding after message recovery); this makes your data impervious to phase inversion at the cost of more complexity in the transmitter and receiver.

19.4 DSK Implementation in C

19.4.1 Components of the Digital Receiver

The real-time implementation of the BPSK receiver is shown in Listings 19.3 and 19.4. Listing 19.3 provides the declaration of most of the variables used, and Listing 19.4 implements

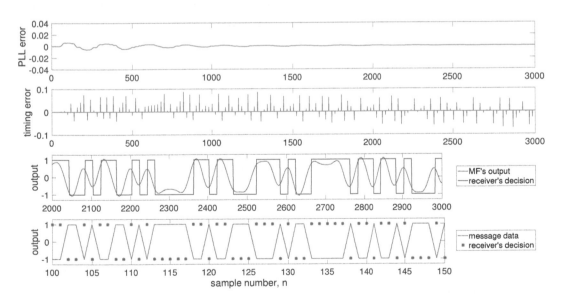

Figure 19.9: BPSK receiver exhibiting excellent PLL and ML timing recovery performance. However, the Costas loop locked up 180 degrees out of phase. This will result in message bit flipping, and a bit error rate of nearly 100%.

the algorithm. The files necessary to run this application are in the ccs\DigRx directory of Chapter 19. The primary file of interest is the BPSK_rcvr_ISRs.c, which contains the interrupt service routines. This file includes most of the necessary variable declarations and performs the BPSK receiver operation.

Listing 19.3: Declaration portion of the BPSK receiver project code.

```
1  float alpha_PLL = 0.01; // loop filter parameter float
   beta_PLL = 0.002; // loop filter parameter
3
   float alpha_ML = 0.1;    // loop filter parameter
5  float beta_ML = 0.02;    // loop filter parameter

7  float twoPi = 6.2831853072;    // 2pi
   float piBy2 = 1.57079632679;   // pi/2
9  float piBy10 = 0.314159265359; // pi/10
   float piBy100 = 0.0314159265359; // pi/100
11 float scaleFactor = 3.0517578125e-5;
   float gain = 3276.8;
13
   float x[N+1] = {0,0,0,0,0,0,0}; // input signal
15 float sReal = 0;  // real part of the analytical signal
   float sImag = 0;  // imag part of the analytical signal
17
   float phaseDetectorOutputReal[M+1] = {0,0,0,0,0,0,0,0,
19     0,0,0,0,0,0,0,0,0,0,0,0,0,0,0,0,0,0,0,0,0,
       0,0,0,0,0,0,0,0,0,0};  // real part of the analytical signal
21 float phaseDetectorOutputImag = 0;
   float vcoOutputReal = 1;
23 float vcoOutputImag = 0;
   float q_loop = 0;      // input to the loop filter
25 float sigma_loop = 0; // part of the PLL loop filter
   float PLL_loopFilterOutput = 0;
27 float phi = 0; // phase accumulator value

29 float *pLeft = phaseDetectorOutputReal;
   float *p = 0;
31 float matchedfilterout[3] = {0,0,0};

33 float diffoutput = 0;
   float sigma_ML = 0;   // part of the ML loop filter
35 float ML_loopFilterOutput = 0;
   float accumulator = 0;
37 float adjustment = 0;
   float data = 0;
39 volatile float ML_on_off = 1;

41 Int32 i = 0;
   Int32 sync = 0;
```

An explanation of Listing 19.3 follows.

1. (Lines 1–2): Declare the PLL's loop filter parameters.

2. (Lines 4–5): Declare the ML timing recovery loop's filter parameters.

3. (Lines 7–12): Declare various constants used in the algorithm.

4. (Lines 14–27): Declare variables needed to implement the PLL.

5. (Lines 29–31): Declare variables needed to implement the MF.

6. (Lines 33–38): Declare variables needed to implement the ML timing recovery loop.

7. (Line 39): Declares a flag to turn the ML timing recovery loop "ON" or "OFF." This can be used to demonstrate the effect of not having an error control process in the timing recovery loop.

8. (Line 41): Declares an integer index used in a loop.

9. (Line 42): Declares an integer synchronization signal that is used to send a timing pulse through the second codec channel. This timing pulse can be used to trigger an oscilloscope to create an eye-pattern.

Listing 19.4: Algorithm portion of the BPSK receiver project code.

```
// my algorithm starts here ...
// bring in input value
x[0] = CodecDataIn.Channel[LEFT];  // current LEFT input value

// execute Hilbert transform and group delay compensation
sImag = (x[0] - x[6])*B_hilbert[0] + (x[2] - x[4])*B_hilbert[2];
sReal = x[3]*scaleFactor; // scale and account the group delay

// setup x for the next input
for(i = N; i >0; i--) {
    x[i] = x[i-1];
}

sImag *= scaleFactor;

// execute the PLL
vcoOutputReal = cosf(phi);
vcoOutputImag = sinf(phi);
phaseDetectorOutputReal[0] = sReal*vcoOutputReal ...
    + sImag*vcoOutputImag;
phaseDetectorOutputImag = sImag*vcoOutputReal ...
    - sReal*vcoOutputImag;
q_loop = phaseDetectorOutputReal[0] * phaseDetectorOutputImag;
sigma_loop += beta_PLL*q_loop;
PLL_loopFilterOutput = sigma_loop + alpha_PLL*q_loop;
phi += piBy2 + PLL_loopFilterOutput;

while(phi > twoPi) {
    phi -= twoPi;  // modulo 2pi operation for accumulator
}

// execute the matched filter (MF)
```

```
     *pLeft  = phaseDetectorOutputReal[0];
34
     matchedfilterout[0] = 0;
36   p = pLeft;
     if(++pLeft > &phaseDetectorOutputReal[M])
38       pLeft = phaseDetectorOutputReal;
     for (i = 0; i <= M; i++) {   // do LEFT channel FIR
40         matchedfilterout[0] += *p— * B_MF[i];
           if(p < phaseDetectorOutputReal)
42               p = &phaseDetectorOutputReal[M];
     }
44
     // execute the differentiation filter
46   diffoutput = matchedfilterout[0] — matchedfilterout[2];

48   // execute the ML timing recovery loop
     sync = 0;
50   if(accumulator >= twoPi) {
         sync = 20000;
52       data = −1;
         if(matchedfilterout[0] >= 0) { // recover data
54           data = 1;
         }
56       adjustment = data*diffoutput;
         sigma_ML += beta_ML*adjustment;
58       // prevents timing adjustments of more than +/- 1 sample
         if (sigma_ML > piBy10) {
60           sigma_ML = piBy10;
         }
62       else if (sigma_ML < −piBy10) {
             sigma_ML = −piBy10;
64       }
         ML_loopFilterOutput = sigma_ML + alpha_ML*adjustment;
66
         // prevents timing adjustments of more than +/- 0.1 sample
68       if (ML_loopFilterOutput > piBy100) {
             ML_loopFilterOutput = piBy100;
70       }
         else if (ML_loopFilterOutput < −piBy100) {
72           ML_loopFilterOutput = −piBy100;
         }
74       if (ML_on_off == 1) {
             accumulator −= (twoPi + ML_loopFilterOutput);
76       }
         else {
78           accumulator −= twoPi;
         }
80   }

82   // increment the accumulator
     accumulator += piBy10;
```

```
84
   // setup matchedfilterout for the next input
86 matchedfilterout[2] = matchedfilterout[1];
   matchedfilterout[1] = matchedfilterout[0];
88
   CodecDataOut.Channel[LEFT] = sync; // O-scope trigger pulse
90 CodecDataOut.Channel[RIGHT] = gain*matchedfilterout[1];
   // ... my algorithm ends here
```

1. (Line 3): Brings the input value into the ISR.

2. (Line 6): Performs the Hilbert transform on the incoming signal. An inspection of the **B_hilbert** coefficients in the `hilbert.c` file included in this CCS project reveals an odd symmetry with the three odd-numbered terms all equal to zero. This greatly simplifies the dot-product required to implement this FIR filter. A zoomed-in comparison of the passband frequency response of the filter as designed in MATLAB and this filter with every other coefficient set equal to zero is shown in Figure 19.10. Notice that this filter is *very* close to "flat" in the frequency band of interest (12 kHz ± 2 kHz). This is not immediately obvious until you notice that the vertical axis units are milli-dB (mdB). The figure shows the very small but unavoidable passband ripple in both filters, but they are *very* close to being the same.

3. (Line 7): Applies a scale factor to the signal and accounts for the group delay of the Hilbert transforming FIR filter prior to the PLL.

4. (Lines 10–12): Update the buffered values of x for the next ISR call.

5. (Line 14): Applies a scale factor to the signal prior to the PLL.

6. (Lines 17–30): Implement the PLL.

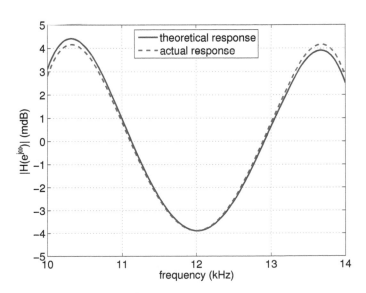

Figure 19.10: Comparison of the MATLAB designed Hilbert transform filter's passband frequency response and the same filter with every other coefficient set equal to zero. Note that the vertical axis scale is in milli-dB.

7. (Lines 33–43): Implement the FIR-based matched filter.

8. (Line 46): Implements the FIR-based second difference filter which is a very close approximation to differentiation.

9. (Line 49): Turns the codec's channel synchronization pulse off.

10. (Lines 50–80): Implement the ML timing recovery loop (the details follow).

11. (Line 50): When the total phase of the ML timing loop's NCO is $\geq 2\pi$, the sampling operation that supplies the next 2 inputs to the ML timing loop is activated.

12. (Line 51): Drives the codec's output synchronization pulse high.

13. (Lines 52–55): Implement the detector (slicer) to decide which symbol was received.

14. (Line 56): Performs the timing error detector operation (multiplication) of the properly aligned matched filter's output and its derivative.

15. (Lines 57–73): Implement the ML timing recovery loop's loop filter (the details follow).

16. (Lines 57–64): Implements the IIR portion of the filter. Note that a non-linear element (a limiter) prevents this filter's output from exceeding $\pm\pi/10$ radians (± 1 sample).

17. (Lines 65–73): Finishes the implementation of the loop filter and adds another limiter to prevent the total error from exceeding $\pm\pi/100$ (± 0.1 samples).

18. (Lines 74–79): Apply the ML timing recovery loop's error to the NCO if the ML loop is turned "ON," otherwise the loop free-runs at the nominal symbol rate (2400 sps).

19. (Line 83): Increments the ML timing loop NCO's phase by $\pi/10$ each time the ISR is called. This sets the NCO's free-running speed to the symbol rate (2400 sps).

20. (Lines 86–87): Update the buffered values of the matched filter's output in preparation for the next second difference operation.

21. (Lines 89–90): Output the synchronization signal to the codec's Left channel and the group-delayed matched filter output to the codec's Right channel.

19.4.2   System Testing

Creating an eye-pattern is an excellent way to determine how well your receiver is working. The DSK system should be set up as follows.

1. The software for the book contains wav-files (in the `test_signals` directory, where the file name starts with "BPSK RRC" for BPSK root raised cosine) that can be played through any wav-file playback device (CD player, PC sound card, etc....) to "stand in" for the BPSK transmitter. This signal should be connected as the input to the DSK's ADC. Alternatively, a second DSK could serve as the transmitter, running code similar to the C code for the impulse modulated BPSK transmitter in Chapter 18 (but using a *root* raised cosine filter, not a raised cosine filter). Or a second DSK could serve as the transmitter, running the `commDSK` application of winDSK8.

2. Use winDSK8 or an oscilloscope to verify that the input to the DSK is near, but does not reach, the maximum range of the DSK's codec (typically $-1 < x < +1$ volt).

3. Connect the signal source to the DSK's input.

4. Attach the two output channels (Left and Right) of the DSK's codec to two input channels of an oscilloscope in the following manner. Set the oscilloscope display to trigger off of the oscilloscope channel to which the Left output of the DSK (the sync pulse) is connected. Display both input channels of the oscilloscope on the screen.

5. Ensure that the BPSK input signal is playing, load the BPSK receiver's .out file into the DSK, and start the DSK (run).

With the oscilloscope's display persistence turned up, an image similar to Figure 19.11 should be visible.

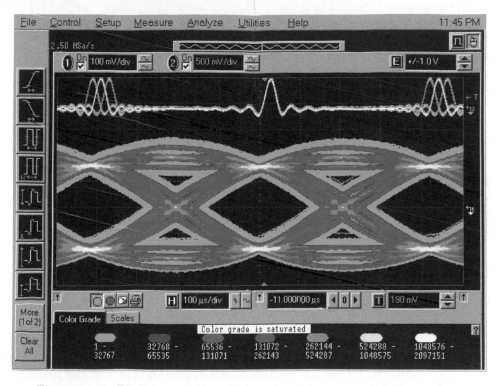

Figure 19.11: BPSK eye-pattern histogram with recovered timing pulses.

In this figure, a color-coded histogram (shown here in the text as shades of gray) has been produced that indicates where on the screen the MF output trace is most often located. Synchronization pulses are shown at the top of the display screen. The center synchronization pulse appears to be very stable, since it is being used to trigger the oscilloscope. The synchronization pulse immediately before and after this center pulse shows clear indications that the ML timing recovery loop occasionally tracked one sample to either side of the location of maximum eye opening. This very slight timing error results in a timing jitter that causes the eye opening to close slightly in both the vertical and horizontal directions. As the eye opening gets larger, the receiver is performing better.

Without the synchronization pulses displayed, a traditional eye-pattern should be displayed such as the one shown in Figure 19.12.

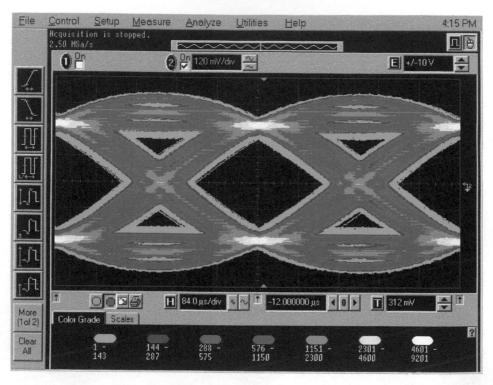

Figure 19.12: BPSK eye-pattern histogram.

19.5   Follow-On Challenges

Consider extending what you have learned.

1. Design and implement your own loop filter within the ML timing recovery loop.

2. Design and implement an algorithm that detects, then provides some indication to the user, when the ML timing recovery loop is *locked* and tracking the symbol rate.

3. Profile the ISR code and identify any bottlenecks.

4. Suggest possible improvements that minimize or remove these bottlenecks.

5. Implement at least one of your improvements and calculate the computational savings of your new code.

6. Implement the BPSK receiver using frame-based techniques.

Chapter 20

Project 11: MPSK and QAM Digital Transmitters

20.1 Theory

IN Chapter 18, we reviewed a few of the concepts involved in digital communications and developed an impulse modulated (IM), binary phase shift-keying (BPSK) transmitter. In this chapter, we will extend those concepts to increase the system's spectral efficiency (that is, squeeze more data into the same bandwidth). The system's spectral efficiency will be increased by adding a second dimension to the signal's constellation diagram, similar to a two-dimensional Cartesian coordinate system in x and y. This added dimensionality will result in each symbol representing multiple bits. Specifically, we will discuss

1. IM, quadrature phase shift-keying (QPSK) using root-raised-cosine (RRC) filtered symbols.

2. IM, 8-state phase shift-keying (8-PSK), 16-state phase shift-keying (16-PSK), and 32-state phase shift-keying (32-PSK).

3. IM, 16-state quadrature amplitude modulation (16-QAM).

This is a good place to reiterate that this text gives only a brief review of the theory associated with the areas for which we use real-time DSP. If you are not already familiar with digital communication techniques, a review of Chapter 18 or a more theoretical book on digital communications prior to proceeding would be in your best interest.

20.1.1 I- and Q-Based Transmitters

The block diagram of an impulse modulated, BPSK system as described in Chapter 18 is provided again in this chapter as Figure 20.1. This BPSK system transmits one bit at a time (i.e., one bit per symbol). To transmit two bits at a time (e.g., using QPSK), we will only *slightly* increase the transmitter's complexity. The block diagram of an impulse modulated QPSK system is shown in Figure 20.2.

There are three significant differences between the BPSK transmitter system shown in Figure 20.1 and the QPSK transmitter system shown in Figure 20.2.

1. The QPSK transmitter processes two bits at a time. This is accomplished by splitting the incoming data values into two parallel data streams using a serial-to-parallel

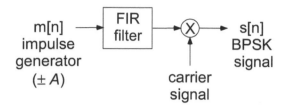

Figure 20.1: The block diagram associated with an impulse modulated BPSK transmitter.

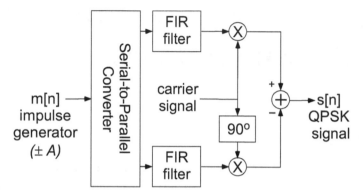

Figure 20.2: The block diagram associated with an impulse modulated QPSK transmitter.

converter. In Figure 20.2, it's most common to label the upper data stream as $x[n]$ and the lower data stream as $y[n]$, since they are related to the x and y coordinates of a two-dimensional signal constellation that will be discussed shortly. Note that while $x[n]$ and $y[n]$ come from a common data stream, for convenience we choose to interpret them such that there is an implied 90-degree (i.e., quadrature) phase difference between them in terms of how they are used to define a signal constellation.

2. The two parallel data streams, $x[n]$ and $y[n]$, are then filtered by identical FIR filters (for pulse shaping purposes) and modulated by a carrier signal. The upper mixer is called the "in-phase" or "I" mixer and the lower mixer is called the "quadrature" or "Q" mixer. The oscillator associated with the "Q" mixer is 90 degrees out of phase from the "I" mixer. If the system's carrier signal is assumed to be a cosine waveform, then the output of the 90-degree phase shifter will be a sine waveform at the same frequency. The two mixers and the 90-degree phase shifter taken together are routinely referred to as a complex mixer.

3. Finally, the two signal paths are recombined by subtracting the bottom signal from the top signal. A satisfying explanation for the necessity of the substraction operation requires a quick review of complex envelope notation [64]. Any physical bandpass waveform $s(t)$ can be expressed as the real part of the product of the signal's complex envelope, $g(t)$, and a complex exponential at the desired carrier frequency. To tie this back to Figure 20.2, $g(t)$ would come from the output of the serial-to-parallel converter, and the complex exponential would come from the two parts (regular and phase-shifted) of the carrier signal. See the short derivation below. While the derivation is written in terms of continuous time signals (e.g., $s(t)$) it applies equally well to

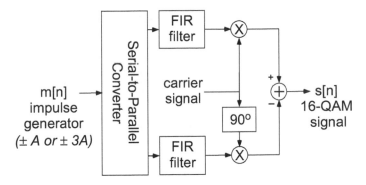

Figure 20.3: The block diagram associated with an impulse modulated 16-QAM transmitter.

discrete time signals such as $s[n]$.

$$s(t) = \text{Re}\left\{g(t)\,e^{j\omega_c t}\right\}$$

$$\text{where} \quad g(t) = x(t) + jy(t) \quad \text{and} \quad e^{j\omega_c t} = \cos(\omega_c t) + j\sin(\omega_c t)$$

$$s(t) = \text{Re}\left\{[x(t) + jy(t)][\cos(\omega_c t) + j\sin(\omega_c t)]\right\}$$

$$s(t) = \text{Re}\left\{x(t)\cos(\omega_c t) + jx(t)\sin(\omega_c t) + jy(t)\cos(\omega_c t) + j^2 y(t)\sin(\omega_c t)\right\}$$

$$s(t) = x(t)\cos(\omega_c t) - y(t)\sin(\omega_c t)$$

When properly implemented, this complex mixer translates the baseband I and Q signals to the frequency of the carrier signal, and since all of these signals are real valued (i.e., not complex), the resulting modulated signal is also real.

Once this slightly more complicated transmitter structure is understood, the modification required to implement other higher-order modulation schemes is straightforward. Specifically, only the excitation to the FIR filters must change. This can be seen in Figure 20.3 where four bits are transmitted at a time (16-QAM). In software, the serial-to-parallel conversion can be implemented by the program's logical structure and a table look up operation. The table lookup operation is routinely referred to as "symbol mapping," which is accomplished by a "symbol mapper."

20.1.2 A Few Constellation Diagrams

The constellation diagram associated with a QPSK signal is shown in Figure 20.4. Some comments need to be made concerning this figure. Specifically,

1. The horizontal axis is referred to as the I-axis.

2. The vertical axis is referred to as the Q-axis.

3. The four constellation points, represented by bold "plus" signs, form a circle.

4. The four constellation points can also be thought of in terms of their rectangular coordinates (+A and −A).

5. On subsequent diagrams, a significant amount of the constellation diagram's labeling will be omitted for clarity.

6. The observation that the constellation points can be identified in either polar form (magnitude and phase) or in rectangular form (I and Q values) can lead to a variety of different transmitter implementation methods. We will only implement a rectangular form of the transmitter.

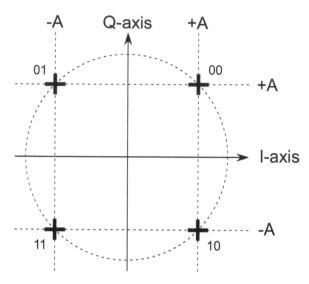

Figure 20.4: The constellation diagram associated with a QPSK signal.

7. The fact that the constellation points form a circle leads to this signal's characterization as "constant envelope." The constant envelope designation only truly exists for unfiltered signals. Since our implementation involves FIR filtering, the resulting signal will look very much like an AM (amplitude modulated) waveform.

8. The value of A is used to adjust the signal level exciting each of the impulse modulators (FIR filters).

9. This version of the QPSK constellation is not unique, but this is a commonly used diagram.

10. The four constellation points or states are each represented by two bits. Theoretically, any arrangement of the four constellation points on the I and Q plane is possible; however, some arrangements have more utility than others.

11. The two-bit binary value assigned to each constellation point is displayed near the constellation point.

12. The bit assignment shown is not unique, but this is a commonly used assignment.

13. For PSK systems, the bit assignments are almost always accomplished using a Gray code [90]. The use of a Gray code reduces the number of bit errors associated with the most common type of receiver error, called the "nearest neighbor" error. You should notice that when Gray code assignment is used, adjacent constellation points have only one bit difference (i.e., the Hamming distance [91] is equal to one). This results in a nearest-neighbor error contributing only a single bit error. A less thoughtful assignment of the bit values to each constellation point *could* result in every bit in the symbol being in error. This type of error would occur, for example, if we had just assigned values based on binary counting. Specifically, 00, 01, 10, and 11, which would place 00 and 11 next to each other (i.e., a Hamming distance equal to two).

14. The bandwidth of the transmitted signal $s[n]$ does not change (compared to BPSK) when the quadrature (Q) portion of the diagram is added. This doubling of the data

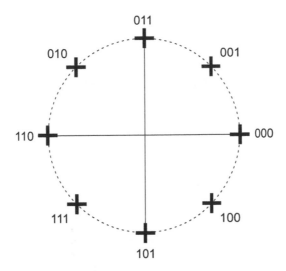

Figure 20.5: The constellation diagram associated with an 8-PSK signal.

rate, albeit with the same symbol rate and thus the same bandwidth, is one of the reasons that QPSK is so popular when compared to BPSK.

All of the other forms of phase shift-keying also place their constellation points on a circle. For example, the constellation diagram associated with an 8-PSK (three bits per symbol) signal is shown in Figure 20.5. This idea can easily be extended to 16-PSK (four bits per symbol), 32-PSK (5 bits per symbol), and so forth. As shown in Figure 20.6, as additional constellation points are added to the circle, the points become closer. While this fact in no way affects the transmitter, the receiver's task of being able to distinguish between points that are getting closer and closer together requires an increased signal-to-noise ratio for the same error performance. Yet again, a classic engineering tradeoff has been revealed: spectral efficiency versus signal quality (where the signal quality metric is signal-to-noise ratio, or more appropriately for digital communication systems, the energy per bit divided

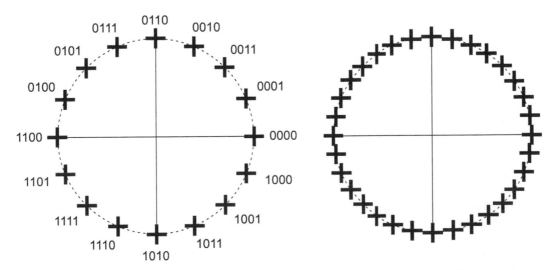

Figure 20.6: The constellation diagram associated with a 16-PSK and a 32-PSK signal.

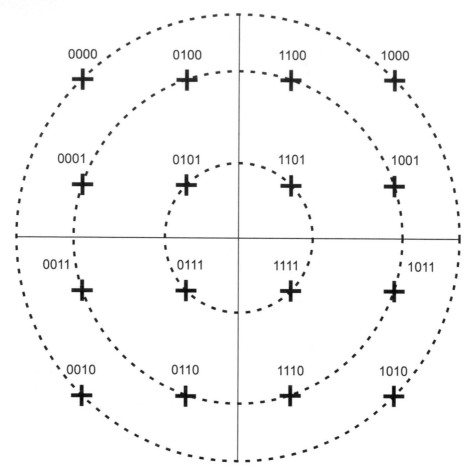

Figure 20.7: The constellation diagram associated with a 16-QAM signal.

by the noise power spectral density, E_b/N_0).

Alternatively, additional constellation points can be added to the I and Q plane using a combination of both amplitude *and* phase modulation. This modulation technique is called quadrature amplitude modulation (QAM or sometimes QUAM). The constellation diagram associated with a 16-QAM signal is shown in Figure 20.7. In the 16-QAM case, it should be clear that three distinct signal envelope levels will exist, since three circles of different radii are present. After filtering (with our pulse shaping FIR filters), these levels will not be at all distinct. Finally, it should be clear that Gray coding is not practical for QAM constellations; however, preferred coding assignments do exist.

20.2 winDSK Demonstration

Start the winDSK8 application, and the main user interface window will appear. Ensure the correct selections have been made in the "DSP Board" and "Host Interface" configuration panels of winDSK8 for each parameter before proceeding. Clicking on winDSK8's commDSK button will run that program in the attached DSK, and a window similar to Figure 20.8 will appear. In the "Modulation Control" section, select the "Mode" to QPSK and the "Data Rate" to 4800 bps.

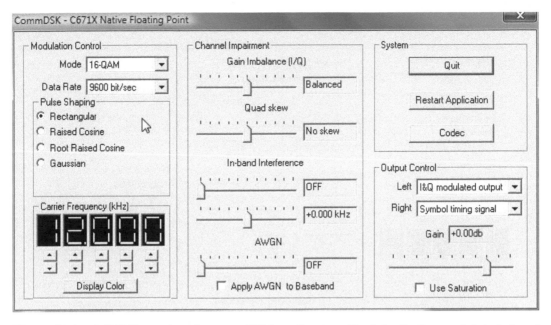

Figure 20.8: winDSK8 running the commDSK application. By default, the modulated signal appears on the Left output channel, and a timing signal appears on the Right output channel. These settings can be changed by the user if needed.

20.2.1   commDSK: Root-Raised-Cosine Filtered QPSK

Now adjust commDSK to observe the effect of pulse shaping. If you apply a root-raised-cosine pulse shaping effect, you will no longer have rectangular pulses. Select "Root Raised Cosine" from the "Pulse Shaping" radio buttons on the commDSK user interface window. This change is shown in Figure 20.9. An example waveform is shown in Figure 20.10. In this mode, it is much more difficult to detect the transition from one symbol to the next. An averaged spectrum associated with this waveform is shown in Figure 20.11. Similar to the rectangular shaped signal, the main lobe is centered at 12 kHz, but the first spectral null above 12 kHz occurs before 13.8 kHz. The higher frequency marker was left at 13.8 kHz as in Chapter 18. The markers are separated by 3.6 kHz ($2 \times (13.8 - 12) = 3.6$). The theoretical prediction for a *raised-cosine* pulse shaped system would be $BW = D(1 + \alpha) = 2400 \times (1 + 0.35) = 3264$ Hz, where BW is the signal's bandwidth, D is the symbol rate, and α is the raised-cosine roll-off factor that was used in this case (the roll-off factor must remain between 0 and 1). Remember that we are actually using a *root-raised-cosine* pulse shaping filter, but the bandwidths associated with these two systems are similar.

In Figure 20.11, no sidelobes are visible due to the apparent noise floor below -33 dBm. With the peak of the main lobe at -6.857 dBm, the expected sidelobe level for root-raised-cosine pulses with a roll-off factor of $\alpha = 0.35$ is lower than the observed noise floor. This noise floor is in fact a limitation of the 8-bit ADC associated with the digitizing oscilloscope that was used to produce this figure. The solid horizontal marker (Ay) is actually placed 40 dB below the dashed horizontal marker (By) to help illustrate this point.

The commDSK program is capable of generating a number of different digital communications signals at a number of different data rates. These signals may also be distorted using the "Channel Impairment" section of commDSK. These impairments are very helpful if the signal is to be processed by a vector signal analyzer (VSA). An example of a VSA display is shown in Figure 20.12.

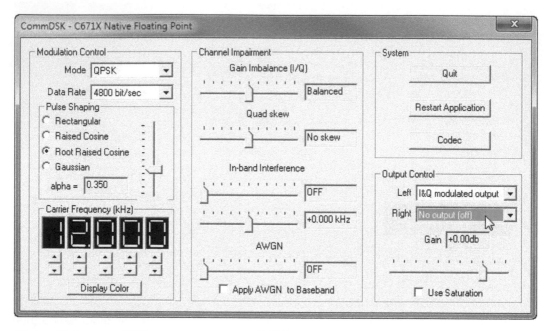

Figure 20.9: commDSK set to generate a QPSK, root-raised-cosine pulse shaped, 4800 bps signal.

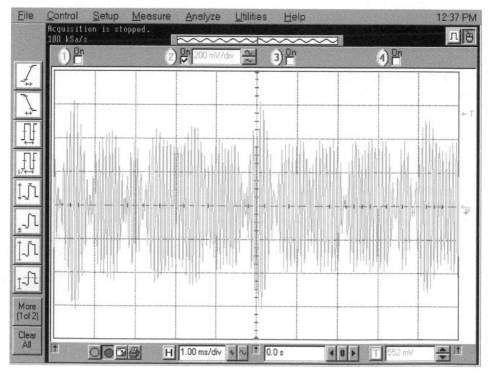

Figure 20.10: commDSK waveform of a QPSK, root-raised-cosine pulse shaped, 4800 bps signal.

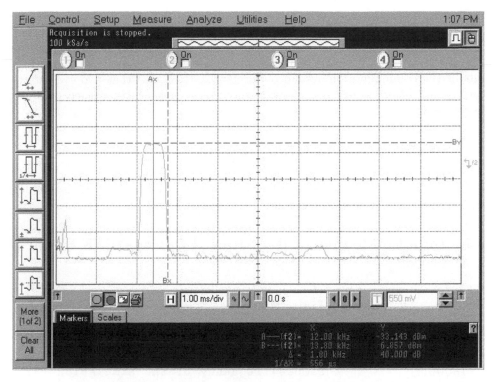

Figure 20.11: An averaged spectrum associated with a QPSK, root-raised-cosine pulse shaped, 4800 bps signal generated by commDSK.

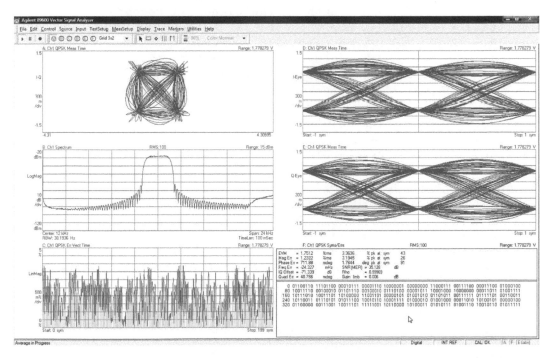

Figure 20.12: Example of a VSA display associated with a root-raised-cosine pulse shaped, 4800 bps, QPSK signal generated by commDSK.

In Figure 20.12, plot A is a trajectory/constellation diagram, plot B is the spectral estimate of the QPSK signal, plot C is the error vector magnitude (EVM), plot D is the I-eye-pattern, plot E is the Q-eye-pattern, and plot F reports a number of statistics associated with the performance of the signal being analyzed. These plots can be used to infer a great deal about the communication system performance. Recognize that two eye-patterns (I-eye-pattern and a Q-eye-pattern) are now required since we have added a second dimension to the constellation.

20.3   MATLAB Implementation

We will only simulate a single form of QPSK signal generation: the impulse modulated, root-raised-cosine QPSK signal generator.

20.3.1   Impulse Modulated Root-Raised-Cosine QPSK Signal Generator

The MATLAB® simulation is of an impulse modulated root-raised-cosine QPSK signal generator; the code is shown in Listing 20.1.

Listing 20.1: Simulation of an impulse modulated root-raised-cosine QPSK signal generator.

```
1  %  input terms
   Fs = 48000;            % sample frequency of the simulation (Hz)
3  dataRate = 4800;       % data rate
   alpha = 0.35;          % root-raised-cosine rolloff factor
5  order = 120;           % desired filter order
   time = 0.5;            % length of the signal in seconds
7  amplitude = 380000;    % amplitude scale factor
   cosine = [1 0 -1 0];   % cos(n*pi/2) ... Fs/4
9  sine =   [0 1 0 -1];   % sin(n*pi/2) ... Fs/4
   counter = 1;           % counter used to get new data bits
11
   %  calculated terms
13 numberOfSamples = Fs*time;
   symbolRate = dataRate/2; % for QPSK there are 2 bits/symbol
15 samplesPerSymbol = Fs/symbolRate;
17 %  design the pulse shaping filter
   B = firrcos(order, symbolRate/2, alpha, Fs, 'rolloff', 'sqrt');
19
   %  set the filter's initial conditions to zero
21 I_state = zeros(1, (length(B) - 1));
   Q_state = zeros(1, (length(B) - 1));
23
   %  ISR simulation
25 for index = 1:numberOfSamples
       % generate a new pair of data bits at the
27     % beginning of a symbol period
       if (counter == 1)
29         I_data = 2*(rand > 0.5) - 1; % generate a +1 or -1 (bit)
           Q_data = 2*(rand > 0.5) - 1; % generate a +1 or -1 (bit)
```

```
31    else
          I_data = 0;
33        Q_data = 0;
      end
35
      % create the modulated signal
37    [I_IM_data,I_state] = filter(B,1,amplitude*I_data,I_state);
      [Q_IM_data,Q_state] = filter(B,1,amplitude*Q_data,Q_state);
39    output = I_IM_data*cosine(mod(index,4) + 1) ...
              - Q_IM_data*sine(mod(index,4) + 1);
41
      % reset at the end of a symbol period
43    if (counter == samplesPerSymbol)
          counter = 0;
45    end
47    % increment the counter
      counter = counter + 1;
49 end
51 %   output terms
   %   Plotting commands follow ...
```

An explanation of Listing 20.1 follows.

1. (Line 2): Defines the system's sample frequency as 48 kHz. This sample frequency matches the rate of the DSK's audio codec.

2. (Line 3): Defines the data rate as 4,800 bits per second (bps). For QPSK this is 2,400 symbols per second, since two symbols are transmitted at a time.

3. (Line 4): Defines the root-raised-cosine roll-off factor alpha.

4. (Line 5): Defines the order of the root-raised-cosine FIR filter. In this case, the filter order is equivalent to six symbols.

5. (Line 7): Scales the output signal near the full range of the 16-bit DAC.

6. (Line 8): Defines the output of the in-phase (I) local oscillator (LO).

7. (Line 9): Defines the output of the quadrature (Q) local oscillator (LO).

8. (Line 10): The counter variable is used to determine the current position within a symbol.

9. (Line 18): Designs the root-raised-cosine filter using MATLAB's firrcos function. This function is part of MATLAB's signal processing toolbox.[1]

10. (Lines 25–49): These lines of code simulate the real-time ISR.

11. (Lines 28–34): New data bits are generated whenever counter is equal to 1.

---

[1] As mentioned in Chapter 18, the calling sequence of many filter design commands is in flux. You may want to read and run the code in filterDesignerComparison.m located in the MATLAB directory of Chapter 20.

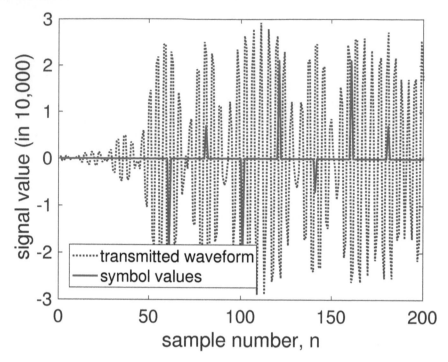

Figure 20.13: An example of the output from the impulse modulated, QPSK simulation. This signal has 4800 bps, a roll-off factor of $\alpha = 0.35$, and a carrier frequency of 12 kHz.

12. (Lines 37–38): These lines of code implement the impulse modulators (IMs). The IMs are just a pair of FIR filters with an input of one or more impulses followed by a large number of zeros. In this simulation, a single impulse with a value of 380,000 is followed by 19 sample values of zero (20 samples per symbol, remember?). The computational savings of this technique will become clear in the next section.

13. (Line 39–40): Calculates the output value by multiplying (i.e., mixing) the data value with the LO's output. The `cosine` and `sine` variables are accessed by the MATLAB `mod` command, which maintains the `index` value between 1 and 4.

14. (Lines 43–45): The `counter` variable is reset at the end of a symbol.

15. (Line 48): The `counter` variable is incremented at the end of the simulated ISR.

An example output plot (with a duration of about 4 ms) from this simulation is shown in Figure 20.13. The large order of the FIR filter (120th-order) results in a group delay of 60 samples. This group delay was compensated for by initializing the `dataArray` variable with 60 zeros. In this figure, the transmitted symbol values (i.e., the 2 bits) are displayed as a 4-level signal. This is intended to clearly show the four possible states of the system. Notice that when the polarity of the 4-level signal changes, the envelope of the QPSK signal collapses (i.e., drops dramatically). This phenomenon will cause significant implementation issues in an RF system if a nonlinear power amplifier is used. Slight variations of the QPSK scheme, such as staggered QPSK, offset QPSK, and $\frac{\pi}{4}$-Differential QPSK were invented to help minimize this effect.

The simulation time was increased to 2 seconds to allow a higher resolution estimate of the resulting normalized power spectral density; this is shown in Figure 20.14. The benefits

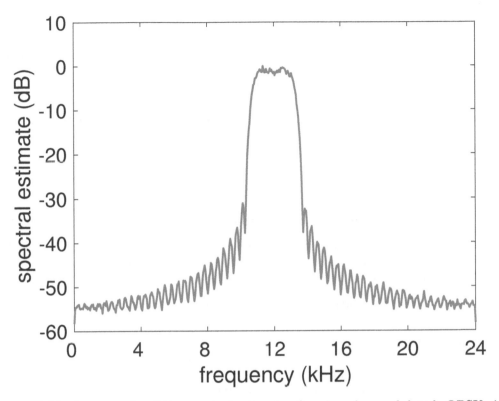

Figure 20.14: An example of the spectral estimate of an impulse modulated, QPSK simulation. This signal has 4800 bps, a roll-off factor of $\alpha = 0.35$, and a carrier frequency of 12 kHz.

of a spectrally compact, root-raised-cosine pulse shaped signal cannot be overemphasized. To summarize:

1. The root-raised-cosine signal is more spectrally compact (smaller effective bandwidth).

2. The root-raised-cosine signal has a smaller null-to-null bandwidth (more spectrally efficient).

3. The QPSK version of this root-raised-cosine signal is *fairly* easy to generate and of only slightly higher complexity than the BPSK system.

4. The migration from BPSK to QPSK doubles the data rate for a constant symbol rate system and, therefore, a constant bandwidth.

5. The digital communications receiver needed to recover the message from this root-raised-cosine signal will be more complex than if we had used rectangular pulses.

6. The matched filter associated with this root-raised-cosine signal's receiver would ideally experience no intersymbol interference (ISI). In practice, channel impairments, finite length filters, and other nonideal implementation effects will result in at least some ISI occurring.

20.4   DSK Implementation in C

When you understand the MATLAB code, the concept translation into C is fairly straight-forward. The files necessary to run this application are in the `ccs\Proj_QPSK_Tx` directory of Chapter 20. The primary files of interest are `impulseModulatedQPSK_ISRs.c` and `impulseModulatedQPSK_ISRs_revA.c`, which contain the interrupt service routines. These files include the necessary variable declarations and perform two different versions of the QPSK signal generation algorithm. Assuming the DSK's codec you're using is a stereo device, the program could implement independent Left and Right channel QPSK transmitters. For clarity, these example programs implement only one transmitter, but will output this signal to both channels.

20.4.1   A Root-Raised-Cosine Pulse Shaped QPSK Transmitter

The declaration section of the code is shown in Listing 20.2. One item that isn't shown here is the file `coeff.c` which is also part of the CCS project. This file contains the coefficients of a 120th-order root-raised-cosine FIR filter designed with and then exported from MATLAB.

Listing 20.2: Declaration portion of the impulse modulation root-raised-cosine pulse shaped QPSK project code.

```
Int32 counter = 0;
#define QPSK_SCALE 160000
const Int32 samplesPerSymbol = 20;
const Int32 cosine[4] = {1, 0, -1, 0};
const Int32 sine[4] = {0, 1, 0, -1};

const float QPSK_LUT[4][2] = {
// left (quadrature), right (in-phase)
{    1 * QPSK_SCALE,    1 * QPSK_SCALE}, /* QPSK_LUT[0]  */
{    1 * QPSK_SCALE,   -1 * QPSK_SCALE}, /* QPSK_LUT[1]  */
{   -1 * QPSK_SCALE,    1 * QPSK_SCALE}, /* QPSK_LUT[2]  */
{   -1 * QPSK_SCALE,   -1 * QPSK_SCALE}, /* QPSK_LUT[3]  */
};

float output_gain = 1.0;
float xI[6];
float xQ[6];
float yI;
float yQ;
float output;
```

An explanation of Listing 20.2 follows.

1. (Line 1): Declares and initializes the `counter` variable, which is used to indicate where the algorithm is relative to the beginning of the symbol (0) or the end of the symbol (19).

2. (Line 2): Defines and initializes the QPSK constellation scaling constant `QPSK_SCALE`. This constant is used in lines 7–13 to modify the excitation amplitude into the impulse modulation filters.

3. (Line 3): Declares and initializes the `samplesPerSymbol` variable, which, as its name implies, is the number of sample in a symbol. A symbol represents 2 bits in QPSK.

4. (Line 4): Declares and initializes the `cosine` variable that contains *all* of the possible LO's values for a 12 kHz cosine carrier.

5. (Line 5): Declares and initializes the `sine` variable that contains *all* of the possible LO's values for a 12 kHz sine carrier.

6. (Lines 7–13): Declares and initializes the QPSK constellation lookup table. In this table, the first column represents the Q-axis information and the second column represents the I-axis information.

7. (Line 15): Declares and initializes `output_gain` variable, which, as its name implies, is the output gain of the transmitter. Unlike `QPSK_SCALE`, this gain is adjustable while the program is running.

8. (Line 16): Declares the `xI` array that stores the current and past values of the message's in-phase bits.

9. (Line 17): Declares the `xQ` array that stores the current and past values of the message's quadrature bits.

10. (Line 18): Declares the variable `yI` that stores the current output of the in-phase impulse modulator.

11. (Line 19): Declares the variable `yQ` that stores the current output of the quadrature impulse modulator.

12. (Line 20): Declares the variable `output` that is the QPSK modulator's output value.

The algorithm section of the code is shown in Listing 20.3.

Listing 20.3: Algorithm portion of the impulse modulation root-raised-cosine pulse shaped project code.

```
   // I added my impulse modulated QPSK routine here
 2 if (counter == 0) {
       symbol = rand() & 3; /* generate 2 random bits */
 4     xI[0]  = QPSK_LUT[symbol][RIGHT];
       xQ[0]  = QPSK_LUT[symbol][ LEFT];
 6 }

 8 // perform impulse modulation based on the FIR filter, B[N]
   yI = 0;
10 yQ = 0;

12 for (i = 0; i < 6; i++) {
       yI += xI[i]*B[counter + 20*i]; // perform the "I" dot-product
14     yQ += xQ[i]*B[counter + 20*i]; // perform the "Q" dot-product
   }
16
   if (counter >= (samplesPerSymbol - 1)) {
18     counter = -1;

20     // shift xI[] and xQ[] in prep to receive the next input
       for (i = 5; i > 0; i--) {
22         xI[i] = xI[i-1];  // setup xI[] for the next input value
```

```
            xQ[i] = xQ[i-1];  // setup xQ[] for the next input value
24    }
   }

26
   counter++;

28
   output = output_gain*(yI*cosine[counter&3] - yQ*sine[counter&3]);

30
   CodecDataOut.Channel[LEFT]  = output; // setup the LEFT  value
32 CodecDataOut.Channel[RIGHT] = output; // setup the RIGHT value
   // end of my impulse modulated QPSK routine
```

An explanation of Listing 20.3 follows.

1. (Lines 2–6): Once per symbol period, we generate a random number that is bitwise ANDed with 3. This bit masking operation generates the variable **symbol** which is then used to access the QPSK lookup table. The appropriate row is selected by **symbol** and the new values for **xI** and **xQ** are assigned. In a practical communications system, the data bits would come from a data source instead of a random number generator.

2. (Lines 8–15 and 20–24): Performs both the I and Q FIR filtering associated with the impulse modulators. The vector **B** contains the coefficients of the root-raised-cosine filter designed with and exported from MATLAB, using the **firrcos** function. Even though a 120th-order filter is being implemented, only 6 multiplies are required. This is because *all* of the other multiplies have a zero in the operation. These other multiplies are therefore *not* required since the outcome is already known! This is one of the most important advantages of an impulse modulator.

3. (Lines 17–18): When **counter** is equal to 19, the algorithm has reached the end of the symbol. At this point, **counter** is reset to start the next symbol period.

4. (Line 27): Increments the variable **counter** in preparation for the next ISR.

5. (Line 29): Calculates and scales the current output value. This results in a QPSK signal centered at 12 kHz.

6. (Lines 31–32): Output the QPSK transmitter's current value to both the left and right channels.

20.4.2   A More Efficient RRC Pulse Shaped QPSK Transmitter

The declaration section of the code is shown in Listing 20.4. The code listing improves the computational efficiency of the complex mixer by recognizing that only one of the mixers will have a non-zero output value.

Listing 20.4: Declaration portion of the more efficient impulse modulation root-raised-cosine pulse shaped QPSK project code.

```
1 Int32 counter = 0;
  #define QPSK_SCALE 10000
3 const Int32 samplesPerSymbol = 20;

5 const float QPSK_LUT[4][2] = {
  // left (quadrature), right (in-phase)
7 {    1 * QPSK_SCALE,   1 * QPSK_SCALE}, /* QPSK_LUT[0]  */
```

```
    {     1 * QPSK_SCALE, -1 * QPSK_SCALE}, /* QPSK_LUT[1]  */
 9  {    -1 * QPSK_SCALE,  1 * QPSK_SCALE}, /* QPSK_LUT[2]  */
    {    -1 * QPSK_SCALE, -1 * QPSK_SCALE}, /* QPSK_LUT[3]  */
11 };

13 float output_gain = 1.0;
   float xI[6];
15 float xQ[6];
   float output;
```

An explanation of Listing 20.4 follows.

1. (Line 1): Declares and initializes the `counter` variable, which is used to indicate where the algorithm is relative to the beginning of the symbol (0) or the end of the symbol (19).

2. (Line 2): Defines and initializes the QPSK constellation scaling constant `QPSK_SCALE`. This constant is used in lines 7–13 to modify the excitation amplitude to the impulse modulation filters.

3. (Line 3): Declares and initializes the `samplesPerSymbol` variable, which, as its name implies, is the number of samples in a symbol. A symbol represents 2 bits in QPSK.

4. (Lines 5–11): Declares and initializes the QPSK constellation lookup table. In this table, the first column represents the Q-axis information and the second column represents the I-axis information.

5. (Line 13): Declares and initializes `output_gain` variable, which, as its name implies, is the output gain of the transmitter. Unlike `QPSK_SCALE`, this gain is adjustable while the program is running.

6. (Line 14): Declares the `xI` array that stores the current and past values of the message's in-phase bits.

7. (Line 15): Declares the `xQ` array that stores the current and past values of the message's quadrature bits.

8. (Line 16): Declares the variable `output` that is the QPSK modulator's output value.

9. (comparing to the previous listing): There is no need for the `cosine` and `sine` oscillators since their function (multiplication by −1, 0, or +1) is taken care of within the program's case statement. Additionally, `yI` and `yQ` are not needed since the system's output is assigned directly to the variable `output`.

The algorithm section of the code is shown in Listing 20.5.

Listing 20.5: Algorithm portion of the improved efficiency impulse modulation root-raised-cosine pulse shaped project code.

```
   // I added my impulse modulated, QPSK routine here
 2 if (counter == 0) {
       symbol = rand() & 3; /* generate 2 random bits */
 4     xI[0]  = QPSK_LUT[symbol][RIGHT];  // lookup the I symbol
       xQ[0]  = QPSK_LUT[symbol][ LEFT];  // lookup the Q symbol
 6 }
```

```
8  output = 0;
   switch(counter & 3) {
10 case   0: // perform the I IM-based on the FIR filter, B[N]
       for (i = 0; i < 6; i++) {
12         output += xI[i]*B[counter + 20*i]; // "I" dot-product
       }
14     break;
   case 1: // perform the Q IM-based on the FIR filter, B[N]
16     for (i = 0; i < 6; i++) {
           output -= xQ[i]*B[counter + 20*i]; // "Q" dot-product
18     }
       break;
20 case 2: // perform the -I IM-based on the FIR filter, B[N]
       for (i = 0; i < 6; i++) {
22         output -= xI[i]*B[counter + 20*i]; // "-I" dot-product
       }
24     break;
   default: // perform the -Q IM-based on the FIR filter, B[N]
26     for (i = 0; i < 6; i++) {
           output += xQ[i]*B[counter + 20*i]; // "-Q" dot-product
28     }
       break;
30 }
   if (counter == (samplesPerSymbol - 2)) {
32     /* shift xI[] in preparation to receive the next I input */
       for (i = 5; i > 0; i--) {
34         xI[i] = xI[i-1];  // setup xI[] for the next input value
       }
36 }
   else if (counter >= (samplesPerSymbol - 1)) {
38     counter = -1;  // reset in prep for the next set of bits
       /* shift xQ[] in preparation to receive the next Q input */
40     for (i = 5; i > 0; i--) {
           xQ[i] = xQ[i-1];  // setup xQ[] for the next input value
42     }
   }
44
   counter++;
46
   CodecDataOut.Channel[LEFT]  = output_gain*output; // LEFT output
48 CodecDataOut.Channel[RIGHT] = CodecDataOut.Channel[LEFT]; // copy
   // end of my impulse modulated, QPSK routine here
```

An explanation of Listing 20.5 follows.

1. (Lines 2–6): Once per symbol period, we generate a random number that is bitwise ANDed with 3. This bit masking operation generates the variable symbol which is then used to access the QPSK lookup table. The appropriate row is selected by symbol and the new values for xI and xQ are assigned.

2. (Line 8): Initialize the system's output prior to filtering.

3. (Line 9): Establishes a switch construct based upon a logical AND of the current

value of `counter` and number 3. This results in a modulo 4 switch operation to take advantage of the non-zero values of the cosine and sine oscillators.

4. (Lines 10–14): Performs only the I dot product since the Q dot product will be multiplied by zero.

5. (Lines 15–19): Performs only the Q dot product since the I dot product will be multiplied by zero. The extra negative sign accounts for the subtraction prior to the output.

6. (Lines 20–24): Performs only the negative of the I dot product since the Q dot product will be multiplied by zero.

7. (Lines 25–29): Performs only the negative of the Q dot product since the I dot product will be multiplied by zero. The extra negative sign accounts for the subtraction prior to the output.

8. (Lines 31–36): When `counter` is equal to 18, the algorithm can prepare for the next `xI` value.

9. (Lines 37–43): When `counter` is equal to 19, the algorithm can prepare for the next `xQ` value. The algorithm has also reached the end of the symbol and `counter` is reset to start the next symbol period.

10. (Line 45): Increments the variable `counter` in preparation for the next ISR.

11. (Line 47): Scales the output value and assigns the result to the left channel.

12. (Line 48): Copies the left channel output value to the right channel's output.

20.4.3 Summary of Real-Time Code

We have created two real-time implementations of a QPSK transmitter. The second version, though somewhat more complicated, requires about half of the computational resources than the more easily understood, first version. The waveforms from either transmitter could be used with a second DSK that is configured as a QPSK receiver, a concept that is discussed in Chapter 21.

20.5 Higher-Order Modulation Schemes

Assuming that we maintain a constant symbol rate of 2,400 symbols per second, we have increased from 1 bit/symbol using BPSK modulation, to 2 bits/symbol using QPSK modulation. The next two obvious steps are to proceed to 3 bits/symbol and then 4 bits/symbol. This can be accomplished in a straightforward manner using 8-PSK modulation and 16-QAM modulation, respectively. The constellations associated with these modulations schemes were previously shown as Figure 20.5 and Figure 20.7.

To implement an 8-PSK transmitter, you will need to generate 3 random data bits per symbol. This can be accomplished using, `symbol = rand() & 7;`. The final change to the code will require a lookup table that represents the 8-PSK constellation. To implement a 16-QAM transmitter you will need to generate 4 random data bits per symbol. This can be accomplished using, `symbol = rand() & 15;`. The final change to the code will require a lookup table that represents the 16-QAM constellation.

In both of these cases, the *symbol* rate will remain at 2,400 symbols per second, the same as for the BPSK and QPSK modulation examples previously discussed. However, for 8-PSK modulation the *data* rate would be 7,200 bits per second, and for 16-QAM modulation the *data* rate would be 9,600 bits per second (compared to 2,400 bps for BPSK and 4,800 bps for QPSK). Since it's the symbol rate, not the data rate, that determines the signal bandwidth, you can appreciate the advantage these higher-order modulation schemes offer.

20.6   Follow-On Challenges

Consider extending what you have learned.

1. In both the MATLAB impulse modulator simulation and in the real-time implementations we used a 120th-order root-raised-cosine FIR filter. What is the effect of using a lower-order filter on the system's performance?

2. Research and implement a different modulation scheme.

3. Implement a different data rate. Hint: you will want to consider maintaining an integer number of samples per symbol.

4. Explain whether the impulse modulators could be implemented using an IIR filter.

5. How would you design a raised-cosine or root-raised-cosine IIR filter?

6. How do the approaches discussed in this chapter compare to the analog filter approach? That is, compare to the method where you generate a rectangular shaped QPSK signal and then filter the signal to the desired bandwidth using traditional analog filters.

7. Should you desire to work with a much lower-order IIR filter, you will want to explore the MATLAB command `sosfilt`. Notice that this toolbox function does not allow you to retain the filter's final condition. Write a MATLAB function that allows the filter state to be retained.

Chapter 21

Project 12: QPSK Digital Receivers

21.1 Theory

IN Chapter 20, we introduced a few of the basic techniques that can be used to generate a QPSK signal. Since there are an unlimited number of different forms and specifications associated with the generation of a QPSK signal, it should not be surprising that there are just as many variations of the receiver. In this chapter, we will introduce only one of these forms and a few of the techniques that can be used to recover the message contained within a QPSK signal.

Specifically, we will discuss a QPSK receiver that will

1. Remove the majority of the frequency translating effects of the signal's carrier from the incoming QPSK signal. This will be accomplished using a complex mixer driven by a free-running oscillator set to the expected incoming signal's carrier frequency. At this stage in the receiver, the system will not be frequency-locked or phase-locked.

2. Process the near-baseband signal through IIR-based matched filters (MF). An IIR-based approach will be used to greatly reduce the computational resources required for this operation. Assume our QPSK signal was generated at the transmitter using impulse modulated (IM) "root-raised-cosine" shaped pulses at 2,400 symbols per second. This is similar to, but an interesting and common variation of, the normal "raised cosine" shaped pulses we explored in Chapter 18. As is required for MF operation, the receiver will use an identical pair of root raised-cosine filters to that which was used in the transmitter.[1] We selected a MF-based receiver because it results in the optimal signal to noise ratio (SNR) of the decision statistic in the presence of additive white Gaussian noise (AWGN) [65].

3. Provide amplitude adjustment by an automatic gain control (AGC). The AGC applies an adjustable, multiplicative scale factor to the output of the matched filters in an attempt to stabilize the magnitude of the recovered signal's constellation.

4. Control the phase rotation of the constellation using a de-rotation algorithm. The phase rotator attempts to stabilize the phase of the signal's constellation.

---

[1] As mentioned in Chapter 18, the calling sequence of many filter design commands is in flux. You may want to read and run the code in `filterDesignerComparison.m` located in the MATLAB® directory of Chapter 21.

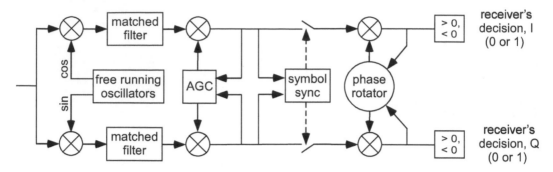

Figure 21.1: A simplified block diagram of a QPSK receiver. The signal from the transmitter/channel enters the system from the left.

5. Finally, symbol synchronization (or timing recovery) must be accomplished. We will use a maximum likelihood (ML) based timing recovery loop to determine when to sample the matched filter's outputs. This sampling/decision process is equivalent to determining where, on average, the eye-pattern is the most "open." This sampling/decision process also converts a series of filtered sampled signal values back into message bits (0 or a 1).

At this point in our discussion, it cannot be overemphasized that *all* five of the above actions must be completed properly and in the correct order for the individual message bits to be recovered effectively. The simplified block diagram of our QPSK receiver is shown in Figure 21.1.

Note that in general, the technical aspects of transmitters are "easier" than those of receivers, and so, due to page constraints, receivers are not covered in as much detail as are transmitters by the majority of textbooks. In particular, not very many texts on digital communications provide much detail at all regarding the theoretical intricacies of digital receivers, particularly for modulation schemes beyond BPSK. Two notable exceptions are [66, 92]; both can be used as excellent references concerning digital receivers.

If we were to plot the outputs of the two matched filters against each other, we would ideally see the traditional phase trajectory diagram without the highlighted constellation diagram sample points. We say *ideally* in that it is almost guaranteed, due to a lack of frequency-lock or phase-lock, that the diagram will be slowly rotating and of the wrong magnitude or scale. This can be seen in Figure 21.2. If we focus on just the first quadrant, as shown in Figure 21.3, it should be clear that adjusting the *actual* point of magnitude r_1 to the *desired* point of magnitude r_2 is just a scaling operation. This scaling will be performed using AGC, the block diagram for which is shown in Figure 21.4. In this block diagram, *calculate envelope* is accomplished by $\sqrt{I^2 + Q^2}$. The de-rotation algorithm is accomplished by rotating the *actual* constellation by an angle of θ. While a number of different algorithms exist for this angle determination, we are using a maximum likelihood phase error detector, the block diagram for which is shown in Figure 21.5. In this diagram, we used small *humps*, on three occasions, to make it clear that two lines may cross other lines, *but do not connect*, except at their ends.

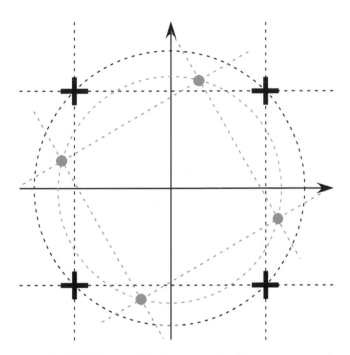

Figure 21.2: A QPSK constellation in need of de-rotation and scaling.

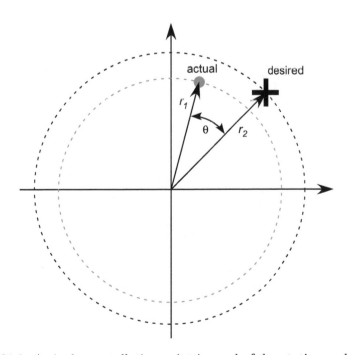

Figure 21.3: A single constellation point in need of de-rotation and scaling.

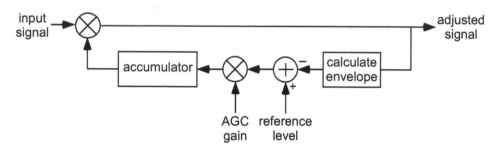

Figure 21.4: A basic block diagram associated with an AGC.

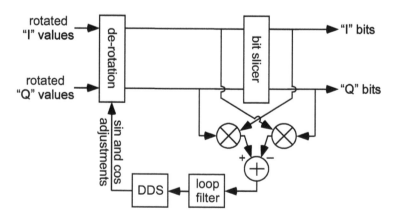

Figure 21.5: The block diagram of a maximum likelihood phase error detector. DDS is the acronym for direct digital synthesizer, as discussed in Chapter 5.

21.2 winDSK8 Demonstration

The winDSK8 program does not provide an equivalent receiver function. The commDSK application of winDSK8 has transmitter functions only.

21.3 MATLAB Implementation

We have chosen to develop the QPSK receiver in two parts. The first part will develop the receiver through the AGC, while the second part will complete the receiver system implementation. In both cases, a slightly modified QPSK transmitter from what we presented previously is required. This transmitter is based closely on the system developed in Chapter 20, but modified for this receiver example to allow for the constellation to be slightly rotated. This small amount of rotation will allow you to verify that your constellation de-rotation loop is functioning properly. Such rotation will not be necessary in your real-time system since there is no inherent synchronization between the transmitter and the receiver, and some rotation is inevitable. As a reminder, in MATLAB® simulations, common timing within the transmitter and receiver m-files provides for a very unrealistic degree of synchronization between the transmitting and receiving system, so we have to "force" some real-world effects into the m-file. This modified m-file also omits the plots that were needed in Chapter 20.

Listing 21.1: Modified sections of the QPSK signal generator.

```
% to rotate the constellation
rotation = pi/6;
cr = cos(rotation);
sr = sin(rotation);
output = (I_IM_data*cr-Q_IM_data*sr)*cosine(mod(index,4)+1) ...
       - (Q_IM_data*cr+I_IM_data*sr)*sine(mod(index,4)+1);
```

21.3.1 Through the AGC

The code for a MATLAB simulation of a QPSK receiver, through the AGC, is shown in Listing 21.2.

Listing 21.2: Simulation of a QPSK receiver (through the AGC only).

```
% save the original values from the transmitter simulation
temp = outputArray;

% apply an additional scale factor to test the AGC
outputArray = 0.1*outputArray;   % 0.1 ... attenuation

% initialize the matched filters
ZiI = zeros(1,120);
ZiQ = zeros(1,120);

% preallocate the storage arrays
scaledI = zeros(1,numberOfSamples);
scaledQ = zeros(1,numberOfSamples);
I_mixer_output = zeros(1,numberOfSamples);
Q_mixer_output = zeros(1,numberOfSamples);
```

```
16
   reference = 18000; % reference value (AGC's goal)
18 AGCgain = 1.0; % initial AGC gain
   alpha = 0.005/reference; % AGC loop gain
20
   % ISR simulation ... storage is for plotting purposes
22 for index = 1:numberOfSamples
       % multiplication by the free running oscillators
24     I_mixer_output(index) = ...
           outputArray(index)*cosine(mod(index,4)+1);
26     Q_mixer_output(index) = ...
           outputArray(index)*sine(mod(index,4)+1);
28
       % matched filters
30     [I(index), ZiI] = filter(B, 1, I_mixer_output(index), ZiI);
       [Q(index), ZiQ] = filter(B, 1, Q_mixer_output(index), ZiQ);
32
       % apply the AGC gain
34     scaledI(index) = AGCgain*I(index);
       scaledQ(index) = AGCgain*Q(index);
36
       % calculate the new AGC gain
38     magnitude = sqrt(scaledI(index)*scaledI(index) + ...
           scaledQ(index)*scaledQ(index));
40     error = reference - magnitude;
       scaledError = alpha*error;
42     AGCgain = AGCgain + scaledError;
   end
44
   %  output terms
46 %  Plotting commands follow ...

48 % restore the saved values ... this allows for repeated execution
   outputArray = temp;
```

Since a number of variables carry forward from the execution of the modified_QPSK_DIGTx_listing_01.m file, you *must* run this script file *before* you run any of the receiver files. An explanation of Listing 21.2 follows.

1. (Line 2): Saves the outputArray values from the QPSK transmitter m-file. This is necessary since the AGC will modify these values. This operation works as a pair with Line 49.

2. (Line 5): Scales the outputArray to 10 percent of its initial value. This will allow you to observe and test the AGC's operation.

3. (Lines 8–9): Initializes to zero the initial conditions associated with the two matched filters.

4. (Lines 12–15): Preallocates variables for storage. This allows for a number of output plots.

5. (Lines 17–19): Defines the AGC's control parameters. The reference variable is the target value that the AGC is trying to achieve. The AGCgain variable is the

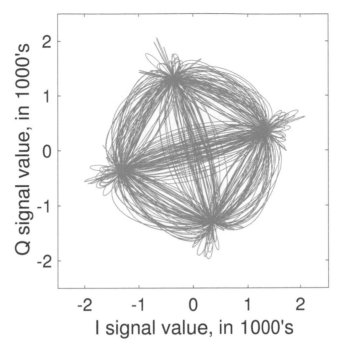

Figure 21.6: QPSK phase trajectory plot prior to AGC.

current gain of the AGC system. Finally, the variable `alpha` is the loop gain of the AGC's control loop. Setting this variable to a larger value results in a quick response, but a great deal of noise-like effects on the signal's magnitude. Setting the variable to a smaller value results in a much slower response, but a very consistent signal magnitude.

6. (Lines 24–27): Multiplies the incoming signal by the free-running oscillator values.

7. (Lines 30–31): Performs the matched filtering and maintains the state of the filter for the subsequent simulated ISR calls.

8. (Lines 34–35): Scales the signal by the current AGC gain.

9. (Lines 38–39): Calculates the magnitude of the signal. This occurs *after* the scaling by the current AGC's gain.

10. (Line 40): Calculates the error signal; the difference between the magnitude and the `reference` value declared on line 17.

11. (Line 41): Scales the `error` by the AGC's loop gain, `alpha`.

12. (Line 42): Implements the *accumulator* operation referred to in Figure 21.4.

13. (Line 49): Restores the values saved in line 2. This allows for repeated execution of the receiver code without needing to rerun the transmitter code.

An example output plot of the signal's constellation *prior* to the AGC is shown in Figure 21.6. Notice the constellation's small magnitude (relative to a 16-bit DAC's input range of +32767 to −32768) and its angular rotation. The de-rotation of the constellation will be addressed in subsequent sections of this chapter. An example output plot of the first

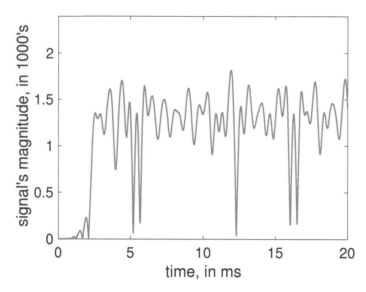

Figure 21.7: QPSK magnitude plot prior to AGC.

20 ms of the signal's magnitude *prior* to the AGC is shown in Figure 21.7. Notice again the constellation's small magnitude (relative to a 16-bit DAC's input range of +32767 to −32768). Also notice the initial transient lasts only a couple of milliseconds as the QPSK transmitter's filters *warm up* (i.e., fill with valid values). Also of interest is when the signal's magnitude nears zero. This is the motivation for such modulation schemes as offset QPSK and $\pi/4$ differential QPSK. An example output plot of the signal's constellation, *after* the AGC, is shown in Figure 21.8, and an example output plot of the first 500 ms of the signal's magnitude, also *after* the AGC, is shown in Figure 21.9. Notice in Figure 21.8 the constellation's magnitude after AGC, compared to a 16-bit DAC's input range of +32767 to −32768 (shown as a box around the constellation). Notice in Figure 21.9 that the AGC's transient only lasts a couple of hundred milliseconds.

21.3.2   A Complete QPSK Receiver

The MATLAB simulation of the complete QPSK receiver is shown in Listing 21.3.

Listing 21.3: Simulation of the complete QPSK receiver.

```
1 % save the original values from the transmitter simulation
  temp = outputArray;
3
  % apply an additional scale factor to test the AGC
5 outputArray = 0.4*outputArray;    % 0.4 ... attenuation

7 % initialize the matched filters
  ZiI = zeros(1,120);
9 ZiQ = zeros(1,120);

11 % preallocate the storage arrays
   Iscaled = zeros(1,numberOfSamples);
13 Qscaled = zeros(1,numberOfSamples);
   I_mixer_output = zeros(1,numberOfSamples);
```

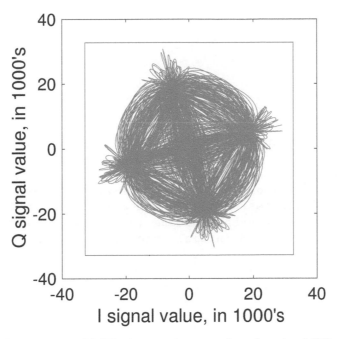

Figure 21.8: QPSK phase trajectory plot after the AGC.

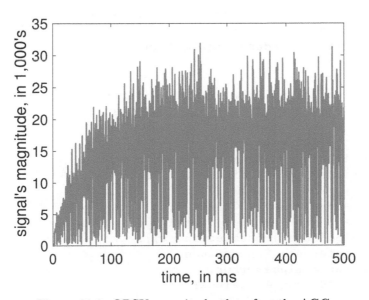

Figure 21.9: QPSK magnitude plot after the AGC.

```matlab
15  Q_mixer_output = zeros(1,numberOfSamples);
    IsampledPlot = [];
17  QsampledPlot = [];
    phaseAdjPlot = [];
19  phasePlot = [];
    thetaPlot = [];
21
    % AGC variables
23  reference = 18000; % reference value (AGC's goal)
    AGCgain = 1.0; % initial AGC gain
25  alpha = 0.001/reference; % AGC loop gain

27  % symbol timing recovery variables
    phase = pi/6;   % symbol timing recovery loop's phase
29  phaseInc = 2*pi/samplesPerSymbol; % phase increment for the NCO
    phaseGain = 0.2e-6; % symbol timing loop gain
31  Ziphase = zeros(1,13); % initial conditions for the MA filter

33  % constellation de-rotation variables
    thetaGain = 1.0e-7; % the gain that controls the de-rotation loop
35  st = 1;
    ct = 1;
37  phaseAdj = 0;
    theta = 0;
39
    % ISR simulation ... storage is for plotting purposes
41  for index = 1:numberOfSamples
        % multiplication by the free running oscillators
43      I_mixer_output(index) = ...
            outputArray(index)*cosine(mod(index,4)+1);
45      Q_mixer_output(index) = ...
            outputArray(index)*sine(mod(index,4)+1);
47
        % matched filters
49      [I_mf(index), ZiI]=filter(B, 1, I_mixer_output(index), ZiI);
        [Q_mf(index), ZiQ]=filter(B, 1, Q_mixer_output(index), ZiQ);
51
        % apply the AGC gain
53      Iscaled(index) = AGCgain*I_mf(index);
        Qscaled(index) = AGCgain*Q_mf(index);
55
        % calculate the new AGC gain
57      magnitude = sqrt(Iscaled(index)*Iscaled(index) + ...
            Qscaled(index)*Qscaled(index));
59      error = reference - magnitude;
        scaledError = alpha*error;
61      AGCgain = AGCgain + scaledError;

63      phase = phase + phaseInc;

65      % timing recovery loop
```

```matlab
       if(phase >= 2*pi)
67          phase = phase - 2*pi;

69         % derotation and sampling
           st = sin(theta);
71         ct = cos(theta);
           Isampled = Iscaled(index)*ct - Qscaled(index)*st;
73         Qsampled = Qscaled(index)*ct + Iscaled(index)*st;
           IsampledPlot = [IsampledPlot Isampled];
75         QsampledPlot = [QsampledPlot Qsampled];

77         % slicer ... bit decisions
           if(Isampled > 0)
79             di = 1;
           else
81             di = -1;
           end
83         if(Qsampled > 0)
               dq = 1;
85         else
               dq = -1;
87         end

89         % derotation adjustment ... calculate the new theta
           thetaAdj = (di*Qsampled - dq*Isampled)*thetaGain;
91         theta = theta - thetaAdj;
           if(theta > 2*pi)
93             theta = theta - 2*pi;
           end

95
           % timing adjustment
97         symTimingAdj = di*(Iscaled(index)-Iscaled(index-2)) + ...
               dq*(Qscaled(index)-Qscaled(index-2));
99         % 13th order MA filter
           [phaseAdj, Ziphase]=filter(phaseGain*ones(1,14)/14,1, ...
101            symTimingAdj, Ziphase);
           phase = phase - phaseAdj;
103    end

105    % derotation
       I(index) = Iscaled(index)*ct - Qscaled(index)*st;
107    Q(index) = Qscaled(index)*ct + Iscaled(index)*st;
       phaseAdjPlot = [phaseAdjPlot phaseAdj];
109    phasePlot = [phasePlot phase];
       thetaPlot = [thetaPlot theta];
111 end

113 % output terms
    % Plotting commands follow ...
115 % restore the saved values ... this allows for repeated execution
    outputArray = temp;
```

Since a number of variables carry forward from the execution of the `modified_QPSK_DIGTx_listing_01.m` file, you *must* run this script file *before* you run any of the receiver files. An explanation of Listing 21.3 follows.

1. (Line 2): Saves the `outputArray` values from the QPSK transmitter m-file. This is necessary since the AGC will modify these values. This operation works as a pair with Line 117.

2. (Line 5): Scales the `outputArray` to 40 percent of its initial value. This will allow you to observe and test the AGC's operation.

3. (Lines 8–9): Initializes to zero the initial conditions associated with the two matched filters.

4. (Lines 12–20): Preallocates variables for storage. This allows for a number of output plots.

5. (Lines 23–25): Defines the AGC's control parameters. The `reference` variable is the target value that the AGC is trying to achieve. The `AGCgain` variable is the current gain of the AGC system. Finally, the variable `alpha` is the loop gain of the AGC's control loop. Setting this variable to a larger value results in a quick response, but causes a great deal of noise-like effects on the signal's magnitude. Setting the variable to a smaller value results in a much slower response, but a very consistent signal magnitude.

6. (Line 28): Sets the symbol timing recovery loop to something *other* than zero.

7. (Line 29): Declares the phase increment associated with the free running oscillator's rate of 2400 symbols per second. This corresponds to one rotation per symbol, or 2π divided by the number of samples in a symbol. For QPSK at 4800 bps and a sample frequency of 48,000 Hz, this corresponds to $2\pi/20 = \pi/10$.

8. (Line 30): Defines the symbol timing loop's gain. This parameter is very sensitive to even small variations.

9. (Line 31): Initializes to zero the initial conditions associated with the symbol timing loop filter. This is a 13th-order (i.e., 14 coefficient) filter.

10. (Line 34): Defines the de-rotation loop's gain.

11. (Lines 35–38): Initializes `st`, sine of theta, `ct`, cosine of theta, `phaseAdj`, the adjustment to the de-rotation phase (theta), and `theta`, the de-rotation angle theta.

12. (Lines 41–103): This is the actual ISR simulation.

13. (Lines 43–46): Multiplies the incoming signal by the free running oscillator values.

14. (Lines 49–50): Performs the matched filtering and maintains the state of the filter for the subsequent simulated ISR calls.

15. (Lines 53–54): Scales the signal by the current value of the AGC gain.

16. (Lines 57–58): Calculates the magnitude of the signal. This occurs *after* the scaling by the AGC's current gain value.

17. (Line 59): Calculates the error signal, which is the difference between the magnitude and the `reference` value declared on line 17.

18. (Line 60): Scales the **error** by the AGC's loop gain, **alpha**.

19. (Line 61): Implements the *accumulator* operation referred to in Figure 21.4.

20. (Line 63): Increments the timing recovery loop's phase by the phase associated with one symbol period ($\pi/10$).

21. (Lines 66–103): These are the timing recovery and de-rotation loops. These algorithms should run at the symbol rate (2400 symbols/second).

22. (Lines 66-67): If the **phase** variable is greater than 2π, it's time to sample the constellation and to perform a modulus 2π operation.

23. (Lines 70–73): Calculates the sine of theta and the cosine of theta and then de-rotates the constellation sample values.

24. (Lines 78–87): Performs the bit decision process. This is referred to as *slicing*.

25. (Line 90–102): Implements the algorithm shown in Figure 21.5.

26. (Line 90): Implements the maximum likelihood phase estimation (high signal-to-noise ratio (SNR) case).

27. (Line 91): Applies the negative feedback to **theta**.

28. (Lines 92–94): Performs a modulus 2π operation on **theta**.

29. (Lines 97–98): Calculates the symbol timing adjustment. We are using a second difference to minimize the effects of higher frequency (i.e., closer to $F_s/2$) noise.

30. (Lines 100–101): Performs the loop filtering operation. Ideally, the maximum likelihood symbol timing recovery loop uses an accumulator as its filter. During the initial MATLAB simulations, this approach resulted in an unsatisfactory oscillation in the system's tracking. A moving average (MA) filter solved this problem.

31. (Line 102): Applies the phase adjustment to the **phase** variable.

32. (Lines 106–110): Calculates and stores intermediate results for subsequent plotting.

33. (Line 116): Restores the values saved in line 2. This allows for repeated execution of the receiver code without needing to rerun the transmitter code.

A number of MATLAB plots are provided at the completion of this QPSK receiver simulation m-file. Only the plot of the constellation diagram is shown in Figure 21.10. In this figure you can see the combined effects as the AGC, de-rotation, and symbol timing loops all converge on the expected four *crisp* constellation points. This is a 2-second simulation and the last 400 sample points are plotted in white. This is what causes the *white holes* at the four expected constellation points.

21.4 DSK Implementation in C

When you understand the MATLAB code for the QPSK receiver, the concept translation into C is fairly straightforward. The files necessary to run this application are provided in the ccs\Proj_QPSK_Rx directory of Chapter 21. The primary files of interest are ISRs_AGC.c and ISRs_Rx.c, which contain the interrupt service routines. These files include the necessary variable declarations and perform two different versions of the QPSK signal generation

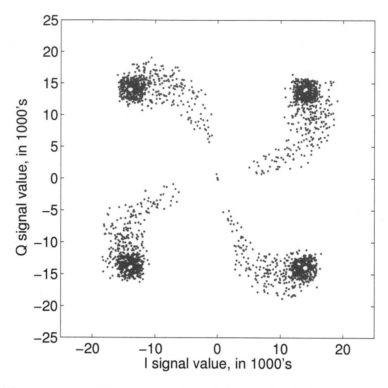

Figure 21.10: QPSK constellation plot from simulation start-up.

algorithm. Assuming the DSK's codec you're using is a stereo device, the program could implement independent Left and Right channel QPSK receivers. For clarity, these example programs implement only a single receiver, but will output this one signal to both L and R channels.

21.4.1   Through the AGC

The declaration section of the code is shown in Listing 21.4.

Listing 21.4: Declarations for the "through AGC" portion of the QPSK receiver code.

```
  Int32 i;
2 Int32 fourcount = 0;
  Int32 costable[4] = {1, 0, -1, 0};
4 Int32 sintable[4] = {0, 1, 0, -1};

6 float Output_Q[5] = {0, 0, 0, 0, 0};
  float Output_I[5] = {0, 0, 0, 0, 0};
8
  /* IIR-based matched filters using second order sections (SOS) */
10 float SOS_Gain = -0.005691614547251;

12 float Stage1_B[3] = {1.0,-0.669057621555000,-0.505837557192856};
  float Stage2_B[3] = {1.0,-1.636373970290336, 0.793253123708712};
14 float Stage3_B[3] = {1.0,-2.189192793892326, 1.206129332609970};
  float Stage4_B[3] = {1.0,-1.927309142277217, 0.981006820709641};
```

```
16
   float Stage1_A[3] = {1.0,-1.898291587416584, 0.901843187948439};
18 float Stage2_A[3] = {1.0,-1.898520943904540, 0.909540256532186};
   float Stage3_A[3] = {1.0,-1.906315962519294, 0.928697673452646};
20 float Stage4_A[3] = {1.0,-1.920806676700677, 0.957209542544347};

22 float Stage1_Q[3] = {0, 0, 0};
   float Stage2_Q[3] = {0, 0, 0};
24 float Stage3_Q[3] = {0, 0, 0};
   float Stage4_Q[3] = {0, 0, 0};
26
   float Stage1_I[3] = {0, 0, 0};
28 float Stage2_I[3] = {0, 0, 0};
   float Stage3_I[3] = {0, 0, 0};
30 float Stage4_I[3] = {0, 0, 0};

32 float I, Q;
   float magnitude;
34 float reference = 15000.0;      // reference value
   float error;    // error signal
36 float AGCgain = 1.0;    // initial system gain
   float scaledError;
38 float alpha = 1e-7; // approximately 0.002/reference
```

An explanation of Listing 21.4 follows.

1. (Line 1): Declares the i variable, which is used in a number of for loops.

2. (Line 2): Declares and initializes the fourcount variable, which is used as a counter that cycles through the pattern …0, 1, 2, 3, 0, 1, 2, 3, …

3. (Lines 3–4): Declares and initializes the costable and sintable variables, which are used as the free-running oscillators at a frequency of 12 kHz $(F_s/4)$.

4. (Lines 6–7): Declares and initializes the Output_Q and Output_I variables, which are used as the input and output of each of the four IIR-based second-order section (SOS) matched filter stages.

5. (Line 10): Declares and initializes the SOS_Gain variable, which is the overall gain of the matched filters.

6. (Lines 12–20): Declares and initializes the SOS filters coefficients.

7. (Lines 22–30): Declares and initializes the states of the SOS filters.

8. (Line 31): Declares and initializes the I and Q variable, which are the outputs of this system.

9. (Lines 33–38): Declares and initializes the variables involved in the AGC's control parameters. The magnitude variable is the magnitude of the received signal. The reference variable is the target value that the AGC is trying to achieve. The error variable is the error between the reference and the magnitude. The AGCgain variable is the current gain of the AGC system. The scaledError variable is an intermediate variable. Finally, the variable alpha is the loop gain of the AGC's control loop.

The algorithm section of the code is shown in Listing 21.5.

Listing 21.5: Algorithm portion of the "through AGC" portion of the QPSK receiver code.

```
      // multiplication by the free running oscillators
 2    Output_I[0] = ...
      SOS_Gain*CodecDataIn.Channel[LEFT]*sintable[fourcount];
 4    Output_Q[0] = ...
      SOS_Gain*CodecDataIn.Channel[LEFT]*costable[fourcount];

 6
      // 8th order, IIR-based matched filters
 8    Stage1_Q[0] = Stage1_A[0]*Output_Q[0] -
      Stage1_A[1]*Stage1_Q[1] -
10    Stage1_A[2]*Stage1_Q[2];
      Output_Q[1] = Stage1_B[0]*Stage1_Q[0] +
12            Stage1_B[1]*Stage1_Q[1] +
      Stage1_B[2]*Stage1_Q[2];

14
      Stage1_I[0] = Stage1_A[0]*Output_I[0] -
16            Stage1_A[1]*Stage1_I[1] -
      Stage1_A[2]*Stage1_I[2];
18    Output_I[1] = Stage1_B[0]*Stage1_I[0] +
              Stage1_B[1]*Stage1_I[1] +
20    Stage1_B[2]*Stage1_I[2];


22    Stage2_Q[0] = Stage2_A[0]*Output_Q[1] -
              Stage2_A[1]*Stage2_Q[1] -
24    Stage2_A[2]*Stage2_Q[2];
      Output_Q[2] = Stage2_B[0]*Stage2_Q[0] +
26            Stage2_B[1]*Stage2_Q[1] +
      Stage2_B[2]*Stage2_Q[2];
28    Stage2_I[0] = Stage2_A[0]*Output_I[1] -
              Stage2_A[1]*Stage2_I[1] -
30    Stage2_A[2]*Stage2_I[2];
      Output_I[2] = Stage2_B[0]*Stage2_I[0] +
32            Stage2_B[1]*Stage2_I[1] +
      Stage2_B[2]*Stage2_I[2];

34
      Stage3_Q[0] = Stage3_A[0]*Output_Q[2] -
36            Stage3_A[1]*Stage3_Q[1] -
      Stage3_A[2]*Stage3_Q[2];
38    Output_Q[3] = Stage3_B[0]*Stage3_Q[0] +
              Stage3_B[1]*Stage3_Q[1] +
40    Stage3_B[2]*Stage3_Q[2];
      Stage3_I[0] = Stage3_A[0]*Output_I[2] -
42            Stage3_A[1]*Stage3_I[1] -
      Stage3_A[2]*Stage3_I[2];
44    Output_I[3] = Stage3_B[0]*Stage3_I[0] +
              Stage3_B[1]*Stage3_I[1] +
46    Stage3_B[2]*Stage3_I[2];

48    Stage4_Q[0] = Stage4_A[0]*Output_Q[3] -
```

```
                        Stage4_A[1]*Stage4_Q[1] -
50          Stage4_A[2]*Stage4_Q[2];
            Output_Q[4] = Stage4_B[0]*Stage4_Q[0] +
52                      Stage4_B[1]*Stage4_Q[1] +
            Stage4_B[2]*Stage4_Q[2];
54          Stage4_I[0] = Stage4_A[0]*Output_I[3] -
                        Stage4_A[1]*Stage4_I[1] -
56          Stage4_A[2]*Stage4_I[2];
            Output_I[4] = Stage4_B[0]*Stage4_I[0] +
58                      Stage4_B[1]*Stage4_I[1] +
            Stage4_B[2]*Stage4_I[2];


60
            // update the filter's state
62          for (i=0; i<2; i++) {
            Stage1_Q[2-i] = Stage1_Q[(2-i)-1];
64                  Stage2_Q[2-i] = Stage2_Q[(2-i)-1];
                    Stage3_Q[2-i] = Stage3_Q[(2-i)-1];
66                  Stage4_Q[2-i] = Stage4_Q[(2-i)-1];

68                  Stage1_I[2-i] = Stage1_I[(2-i)-1];
                    Stage2_I[2-i] = Stage2_I[(2-i)-1];
70                  Stage3_I[2-i] = Stage3_I[(2-i)-1];
                    Stage4_I[2-i] = Stage4_I[(2-i)-1];
72          }


74          // apply the AGC gain
            I = AGCgain*Output_I[4];
76  Q = AGCgain*Output_Q[4];

78  // calculate the new AGC gain
    magnitude = sqrtf(I*I + Q*Q);
80  error = reference - magnitude;
    scaledError = alpha * error;
82  AGCgain = AGCgain + scaledError;

84  // increment the counter ... 0, 1, 2, 3, ... repeat
    fourcount++;
86  if (fourcount > 3) {
        fourcount = 0;
88  }

90          // output I and Q for a "versus" plot on an oscilloscope
            CodecDataOut.Channel[RIGHT] = I;
92          CodecDataOut.Channel[LEFT]  = Q;
```

An explanation of Listing 21.5 follows.

1. (Lines 2–5): Multiplies the incoming signal by the free running oscillator values.

2. (Lines 8–59): Performs the matched filtering operations.

3. (Lines 62–72): Updates the state of the filter for subsequent ISR calls.

4. (Lines 75–76): Scales the signal by the current value of the AGC gain.

5. (Line 79): Calculates the magnitude of the signal. This occurs *after* the scaling by the AGC's current gain value.

6. (Line 80): Calculates the error signal, which is the difference between the `magnitude` and the `reference` value.

7. (Line 81): Scales the `error` by the AGC's loop gain, `alpha`.

8. (Line 82): Implements the *accumulator* operation referred to in Figure 21.4.

9. (Lines 85–88): Increments the `fourcount` variable and performs a modulus four operation.

10. (Lines 91–92): Writes the `I` and `Q` variables to the output.

21.4.2   A Complete QPSK Receiver

The declaration section of the code is shown in Listing 21.6.

Listing 21.6: Declaration portion of the complete QPSK receiver project code.

```
   Int32 i, di, dq;
 2 Int32 fourcount = 0;
   Int32 costable[4] = {1, 0, -1, 0};
 4 Int32 sintable[4] = {0, 1, 0, -1};

 6 float Output_Q[5] = {0, 0, 0, 0, 0};
   float Output_I[5] = {0, 0, 0, 0, 0};

 8
   /* IIR-based matched filters using second order sections (SOS) */
10 float SOS_Gain = -0.005691614547251;

12 float Stage1_B[3] = {1.0,  -0.669057621555000,-0.505837557192856};
   float Stage2_B[3] = {1.0,  -1.636373970290336, 0.793253123708712};
14 float Stage3_B[3] = {1.0,  -2.189192793892326, 1.206129332609970};
   float Stage4_B[3] = {1.0,  -1.927309142277217, 0.981006820709641};

16
   float Stage1_A[3] = {1.0,  -1.898291587416584, 0.901843187948439};
18 float Stage2_A[3] = {1.0,  -1.898520943904540, 0.909540256532186};
   float Stage3_A[3] = {1.0,  -1.906315962519294, 0.928697673452646};
20 float Stage4_A[3] = {1.0,  -1.920806676700677, 0.957209542544347};

22 float Stage1_Q[3] = {0, 0, 0};
   float Stage2_Q[3] = {0, 0, 0};
24 float Stage3_Q[3] = {0, 0, 0};
   float Stage4_Q[3] = {0, 0, 0};

26
   float Stage1_I[3] = {0, 0, 0};
28 float Stage2_I[3] = {0, 0, 0};
   float Stage3_I[3] = {0, 0, 0};
30 float Stage4_I[3] = {0, 0, 0};
```

```
32  float I, Q;
    float Iscaled[3] = {0, 0, 0};
34  float Qscaled[3] = {0, 0, 0};
    float Isampled, Qsampled;
36  float magnitude;
    float reference = 15000.0;        // reference value
38  float error;      // error signal
    float AGCgain = 1.0;        // initial system gain
40  float scaledError;  // error signal scaled by the AGC loop gain
    float alpha = 1.0e-7;    // approximately 0.002/reference
42
    float phase = 0.5; // initial phase for the timing recovery loop
44  float phaseInc = 0.314159265358979; // phase increment (2pi/20)
    float phaseGain = 0.2e-6;    // gain for the symbol timing loop
46
    float thetaGain = 1.0e-7;    // gain for the de-rotation loop
48  float st = 1.0;        // sin(theta)
    float ct = 1.0;        // cos(theta)
50  float phaseAdj = 0;        // phase adjustment associated with theta
    float symTimingAdj[14] = {0,0,0,0,0,0,0,0,0,0,0,0,0,0};
52  float theta = 0;      // constellation de-rotation angle
    float thetaAdj;
```

1. (Line 1): Declares the i variable, which is used in a number of **for** loops. Declares the **di** and **dq** variables, which represent the output bits (digital I and digital Q).

2. (Line 2): Declares and initializes the **fourcount** variable, which is used as a counter that cycles through the pattern . . . 0, 1, 2, 3, 0, 1, 2, 3, . . .

3. (Lines 3–4): Declares and initializes the **costable** and **sintable** variables, which are used as the free running oscillators at a frequency of 12 kHz ($F_s/4$).

4. (Lines 6–7): Declares and initializes the **Output_Q** and **Output_I** variables, which are used as the input and output of each of the four IIR-based second-order section (SOS) matched filter stages.

5. (Line 10): Declares and initializes the **SOS_Gain** variable, which is the overall gain of the matched filters.

6. (Lines 12–20): Declares and initializes the SOS filters coefficients.

7. (Lines 22–30): Declares and initializes the states of the SOS filters.

8. (Line 32): Declares and initializes the **I** and **Q** variables, which are the outputs of this system.

9. (Lines 33–34): Declares and initializes the buffers need to calculate the derivative of **Iscaled** and **Qscaled**.

10. (Line 35): Declares the de-rotated I and Q sample points. The collection of these points forms the constellation diagram.

11. (Lines 36–41): Declares and initializes the variables involved in the AGC's control parameters. The **magnitude** variable is the magnitude of the received signal. The

reference variable is the target value that the AGC is trying to achieve. The error variable is the error between the reference and the magnitude. The AGCgain variable is the current gain of the AGC system. The scaledError variable is an intermediate variable. Finally, the variable alpha is the loop gain of the AGC's control loop.

12. (Line 43): Declares and initializes the phase variable, which is used to track symbol timing. When phase is $\geq 2\pi$, symbol sampling takes place. The symbol sampling should take place at "maximum eye opening."

13. (Line 44): Declares and initializes the phaseInc variable to $\pi/10$. This is the incremental phase associated with a symbol rate (baud) of 2400.

14. (Line 45): Declares and initializes the phaseGain variable. This variable sets the gain in the symbol timing tracking loop.

15. (Line 47): Declares and initializes the thetaGain variable. This variable sets the gain in the constellation de-rotation control loop.

16. (Lines 48–49): Declares and initializes the st and ct variables. These variables represent the sine and cosine of the angle theta.

17. (Line 50): Declares and initializes the phaseAdj variable. This variable represents the calculated phase adjustment within the symbol timing control loop.

18. (Line 51): Declares and initializes the symTimingAdj variable. This variable is calculated based on the bit decisions and an estimate of the signal's slope. These values are then buffered and used in a moving average (MA) filter to determine the symbol timing error, phaseAdj.

19. (Line 52): Declares and initializes the theta variable. This variable represents the constellation's rotation angle. This angle, once known, is removed by the de-rotation algorithm.

20. (Line 53): Declares and initializes the thetaAdj variable. This variable represents the phase adjustment within the constellation de-rotation control loop.

The algorithm section of the code is shown in Listing 21.7.

Listing 21.7: Algorithm portion of the complete QPSK receiver project code.

```
1   Output_I[0] =
    SOS_Gain*CodecDataIn.Channel[LEFT]*sintable[fourcount];
3   Output_Q[0] =
    SOS_Gain*CodecDataIn.Channel[LEFT]*costable[fourcount];
5
    // 8th order, IIR-based matched filters
7   Stage1_Q[0] = Stage1_A[0]*Output_Q[0] -
            Stage1_A[1]*Stage1_Q[1] -
9   Stage1_A[2]*Stage1_Q[2];
    Output_Q[1] = Stage1_B[0]*Stage1_Q[0] +
11          Stage1_B[1]*Stage1_Q[1] +
    Stage1_B[2]*Stage1_Q[2];
13
    Stage1_I[0] = Stage1_A[0]*Output_I[0] -
15          Stage1_A[1]*Stage1_I[1] -
```

```
            Stage1_A[2]*Stage1_I[2];
17          Output_I[1] = Stage1_B[0]*Stage1_I[0] +
                    Stage1_B[1]*Stage1_I[1] +
19          Stage1_B[2]*Stage1_I[2];


21          Stage2_Q[0] = Stage2_A[0]*Output_Q[1] -
                    Stage2_A[1]*Stage2_Q[1] -
23          Stage2_A[2]*Stage2_Q[2];
            Output_Q[2] = Stage2_B[0]*Stage2_Q[0] +
25                  Stage2_B[1]*Stage2_Q[1] +
            Stage2_B[2]*Stage2_Q[2];
27          Stage2_I[0] = Stage2_A[0]*Output_I[1] -
                    Stage2_A[1]*Stage2_I[1] -
29          Stage2_A[2]*Stage2_I[2];
            Output_I[2] = Stage2_B[0]*Stage2_I[0] +
31                  Stage2_B[1]*Stage2_I[1] +
            Stage2_B[2]*Stage2_I[2];

33
            Stage3_Q[0] = Stage3_A[0]*Output_Q[2] -
35                  Stage3_A[1]*Stage3_Q[1] -
            Stage3_A[2]*Stage3_Q[2];
37          Output_Q[3] = Stage3_B[0]*Stage3_Q[0] +
                    Stage3_B[1]*Stage3_Q[1] +
39          Stage3_B[2]*Stage3_Q[2];
            Stage3_I[0] = Stage3_A[0]*Output_I[2] -
41                  Stage3_A[1]*Stage3_I[1] -
            Stage3_A[2]*Stage3_I[2];
43          Output_I[3] = Stage3_B[0]*Stage3_I[0] +
                    Stage3_B[1]*Stage3_I[1] +
45          Stage3_B[2]*Stage3_I[2];


47          Stage4_Q[0] = Stage4_A[0]*Output_Q[3] -
                    Stage4_A[1]*Stage4_Q[1] -
49          Stage4_A[2]*Stage4_Q[2];
            Output_Q[4] = Stage4_B[0]*Stage4_Q[0] +
51                  Stage4_B[1]*Stage4_Q[1] +
            Stage4_B[2]*Stage4_Q[2];
53          Stage4_I[0] = Stage4_A[0]*Output_I[3] -
                    Stage4_A[1]*Stage4_I[1] -
55          Stage4_A[2]*Stage4_I[2];
            Output_I[4] = Stage4_B[0]*Stage4_I[0] +
57                  Stage4_B[1]*Stage4_I[1] +
            Stage4_B[2]*Stage4_I[2];

59
            // update the matched filter's state
61          for (i=0; i<2; i++) {
            Stage1_Q[2-i] = Stage1_Q[(2-i)-1];
63                  Stage2_Q[2-i] = Stage2_Q[(2-i)-1];
                    Stage3_Q[2-i] = Stage3_Q[(2-i)-1];
65                  Stage4_Q[2-i] = Stage4_Q[(2-i)-1];
```

```
67          Stage1_I[2-i] = Stage1_I[(2-i)-1];
            Stage2_I[2-i] = Stage2_I[(2-i)-1];
69          Stage3_I[2-i] = Stage3_I[(2-i)-1];
            Stage4_I[2-i] = Stage4_I[(2-i)-1];
71      }

73      // apply the AGC gain
        Iscaled[0] = AGCgain*Output_I[4];
75  Qscaled[0] = AGCgain*Output_Q[4];

77  // calculate the new AGC gain
    magnitude=sqrtf(Iscaled[0]*Iscaled[0]+Qscaled[0]*Qscaled[0]);
79  error = reference - magnitude;
    scaledError = alpha * error;
81  AGCgain = AGCgain + scaledError;

83  // increment the counter ... 0, 1, 2, 3, ... repeat
    fourcount++;
85  if (fourcount > 3) {fourcount = 0;}

87  phase = phase + phaseInc;
    // timing recovery and de-rotation control loops
89  if(phase > 6.283185307179586) {
        // GPIO control ... turn ON GPIO pin 6
91      WriteDigitalOutputs(1);
        phase -= 6.283185307179586;
93
        // de-rotation
95      st = sinf(theta);
        ct = cosf(theta);
97      Isampled = Iscaled[0]*ct - Qscaled[0]*st;
        Qsampled = Qscaled[0]*ct + Iscaled[0]*st;
99
        // slicer ... bit decisions
101     if(Isampled > 0) {di = 1;}
        else {di = -1;}
103
        if(Qsampled > 0) {dq = 1;}
105     else {dq = -1;}

107     // de-rotation control ... calculate the new theta
        thetaAdj = (di*Qsampled - dq*Isampled)*thetaGain;
109     theta = theta - thetaAdj;
        if(theta > 6.28318530717) {theta -= 6.28318530717;}
111
        // symbol timing adjustment
113     symTimingAdj[0] = di*(Iscaled[0] - Iscaled[2]) +
            dq*(Qscaled[0] - Qscaled[2]);
115
        // MA filter of symTimingAdj (loop filter)
117     phaseAdj = 0;
```

```
        for (i = 0; i < 14; i++) {phaseAdj += symTimingAdj[i];}
119     phaseAdj *= phaseGain/14;
        for (i = 13; i > 0; i--) {
121         symTimingAdj[i] = symTimingAdj[i-1];
        }
123         phase -= phaseAdj;

125     // GPIO control ... turn OFF GPIO pin 6
                WriteDigitalOutputs(0);
127     }

129 I = Iscaled[0]*ct - Qscaled[0]*st;
    Q = Qscaled[0]*ct + Iscaled[0]*st;
131
    // update memory
133 Iscaled[2] = Iscaled[1];
    Iscaled[1] = Iscaled[0];
135 Qscaled[2] = Qscaled[1];
    Qscaled[1] = Qscaled[0];
137
        CodecDataOut.Channel[RIGHT] = I;
139     CodecDataOut.Channel[LEFT]  = Q;
```

An explanation of Listing 21.7 follows.

1. (Lines 1–4): Multiplies the incoming signal by the free running oscillator values.

2. (Lines 6–58): Performs the matched filtering operations.

3. (Lines 61–71): Updates the state of the filter for subsequent ISR calls.

4. (Lines 74–75): Scales the signal by the current AGC gain.

5. (Line 78): Calculates the magnitude of the signal. This occurs *after* the scaling by the current AGC's gain.

6. (Line 79): Calculates the error signal; the difference between the magnitude and the **reference** value.

7. (Line 80): Scales the **error** by the AGC's loop gain, **alpha**.

8. (Line 81): Implements the *accumulator* operation referred to in Figure 21.4.

9. (Lines 84–85): Increments the **fourcount** variable and performs a modulus four operation.

10. (Line 87): Increments the **phase** variable by $\pi/10$. This is the phase associated with a symbol period.

11. (Lines 89–127): Implements the timing recovery and de-rotation control loops. The control loops *activate* if the phase exceeds 2π.

12. (Line 91): Turns "ON" GPIO pin number 6. This digital signal can be used to trigger an oscilloscope.

13. (Line 92): Performs a modulus 2π operation.

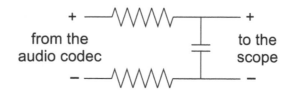

Figure 21.11: A lowpass filter for connecting to test and measurement equipment.

14. (Lines 95–98): Calculates the sine and cosine of `theta` and then de-rotates the I and Q samples.

15. (Lines 101–105): Performs the bit decision operation (slicer).

16. (Lines 108–110): Calculates the new value of `theta`.

17. (Lines 113–114): Calculates the adjustment to the symbol timing.

18. (Lines 117–123): Implements a MA loop filter and corrects the timing recovery loop's phase.

19. (Line 126): Turns "OFF" GPIO pin number 6. This digital pulse is *very narrow* but should occur at the symbol rate (2400 Hz). If you are using a digital oscilloscope, be sure that your oscilloscope's sample frequency captures *every* timing pulse.

20. (Lines 129–130): Calculates the output values I and Q. This code is required to ensure that an output occurs from each ISR call.

21. (Lines 133–136): Buffers the values so that the derivative can be calculated.

22. (Lines 138–139): Writes the I and Q variables to the output.

21.4.3   System Testing

Both the C6713 DSK and the OMAP-L138 boards utilize audio codecs for their conversions both to and from the analog world. Audio codecs in general are designed with the assumption that they are only concerned with signal processing within the human hearing range (typically, 20 Hz to 20 kHz). Despite this, it is common for the digital-to-analog converters (DACs) in audio codecs to output energy outside of this band. In the case of the OMAP-L138 Experimenter Kit, for example, there is significant energy above the audio band that extends to about 2.5 MHz, which can be problematic when using test and measurement equipment to evaluate your real-time project.[2] This out-of-band energy can be significantly suppressed using a simple circuit similar to that shown in Figure 21.11. Even after applying this type of RC filter, it is not uncommon for the test and measurement equipment (e.g., an oscilloscope) to display a phase trajectory, constellation, or eye pattern that shows a significant amount of what appears to be *noise*. These signal variations are probably not noise per se, but rather are caused by a number of non-noise phenomena such as ground loops and coupling capacitors.

   Using a traditional oscilloscope, set for "channel 1" versus "channel 2" to obtain a two-dimensional "plot" of the I and Q signals, a display similar to that shown in Figure 21.12 should be obtained from the QPSK receiver project running in real-time. If a "histogram" option is available for the oscilloscope, a display similar to that shown in Figure 21.13 can be obtained.

---

[2]There is much less out-of-band energy present in the LCDK. See Appendix I for more detail.

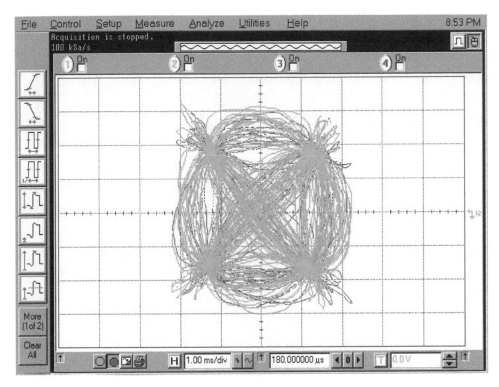

Figure 21.12: A stabilized QPSK phase trajectory.

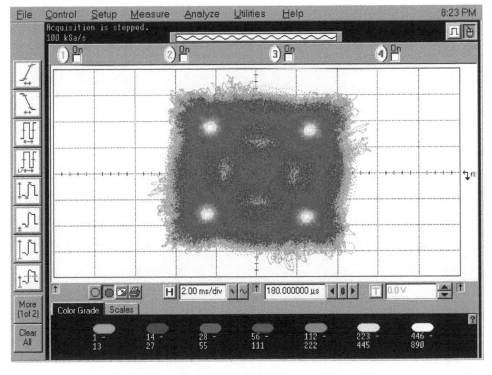

Figure 21.13: A stabilized QPSK phase trajectory histogram.

Note that Figures 21.12 and 21.13, taken from the receiver DSK, result from two DSKs in operation simultaneously; one DSK is acting as the real-time QPSK transmitter, and the other DSK is acting as the real-time QPSK receiver. The two DSKs are connected only via the codec output of the transmitter and the codec input of the receiver, so there is no synchronization between the DSKs. All synchronization is provided by the real-time code.

21.5   Follow-On Challenges

Consider extending what you have learned.

1. Design and implement your own loop filter within the ML timing recovery loop.

2. Design and implement an algorithm that detects, then provides some indication to the user, when the AGC loop has converged to a constant gain value.

3. Design and implement an algorithm that detects, then provides some indication to the user, when the de-rotation loop has converged to a constant theta value.

4. Design and implement an algorithm that detects, then provides some indication to the user, when the ML timing recovery loop is *locked* and tracking the symbol rate.

5. Profile the ISR code and identify any computational bottlenecks.

6. Suggest possible improvements that minimize or remove these bottlenecks.

7. Implement at least one of your improvements and calculate the computational savings of your new code.

8. Implement differential encoding and decoding to remove the phase ambiguity of the QPSK system.

9. Implement the QPSK receiver using frame-based techniques.

Section III:
Appendices

Appendix A

Code Composer Studio: An Overview

A.1 Introduction

CODE Composer Studio™ (CCS) is Texas Instruments' (TI) integrated development environment (IDE) for developing application programs on a wide variety of their DSPs. In CCS, the editing, code generation, and debugging tools are all integrated into one unified environment. You can select the target DSP, adjust the optimization parameters, and set the user preferences as you desire.

An application program is developed based on the concept of a project, where the information in the project file determines what source code files are used and how they will be processed. Learning to use Code Composer Studio is a necessary step in bridging the gap between DSP theory and real-time DSP if you plan to use TI processors. We recommend that you devote some time to getting to know CCS.

In the first edition of this book, we included in Appendix A a tutorial on how to use CCS for a typical project. That information is still provided (in updated form) for this edition, but to allow more versatility in the formatting of the tutorial information, **we have moved nearly all of it to the book website.** Look for links on the website associated with phrases such as "New material for Appendix A, the tutorial for Code Composer Studio (CCS)." These expanded tutorials are based on versions we have given as part of our Real-Time DSP Workshops at various IEEE and ASEE conferences, and have been "field tested" by many people.

Note: We *highly* recommend you visit the book website to read the latest information regarding CCS, since even small changes can cause you great frustration. For example, C6713 DSK users now need to specify a different compiler version to be used with CCS than those users with OMAP-L138 boards, due to a subtle change in output file format.

A.2 Starting Code Composer Studio

This book assumes that you have CCS properly installed on a computer running a relatively recent version of the Windows operating system. As stated in Chapter 1, this book also assumes your version of CCS is version 6.1 or later. If your version is earlier than 6.1, you can usually obtain an updated version via download from TI. If CCS is not yet installed, please install it now before continuing. This short overview and the tutorial on the book website are much more effective if you can follow along on your computer.

How do you know if CCS is installed? Before moving on to the tutorial on the website, find on your computer either an icon or an entry on the start menu for CCS and use that to start the program.[1] As the program is starting, you should see a CCS splash screen similar to Figure A.1. There may be a progress bar at the bottom of the splash screen to indicate how far the program initialization has proceeded. This initialization can take several seconds depending on your system.

When the initialization is complete, the splash screen should disappear and the main project window should appear in its place. This main project window should look similar to Figure A.2, which shows a typical project already loaded into the CCS environment. Note the hierarchal structure of the files associated with your project are shown on the left-most pane in Figure A.2, the C source code is shown in the largest pane, and so forth. If you have gotten this far, you are ready to turn to the tutorial on the book's website.

A.3   Conclusion

After completing the CCS tutorial from the book's website, you will be much more confident using this powerful development tool, and will probably avoid some of the problems and frustrations that can come with unfamiliarity with CCS. We also hope that, in the context of your new familiarity with CCS, the format of all our CCS projects included with this book will make sense to you.

---

[1]CCS may have more than one icon and/or more than one start menu entry if you have installed the program for more than one target DSP.

Figure A.1: The opening splash screen for Code Composer Studio version 6.1.

Figure A.2: The main project screen for Code Composer Studio version 6.1.

Appendix B

DSP/BIOS

B.1   Introduction

SOME readers are curious about DSP/BIOS, which is a real-time operating system specific to the Texas Instruments DSPs [93,94]. This appendix provides a short description of DSP/BIOS, and several projects intended to get you started in the DSP/BIOS environment.

B.1.1   DSP/BIOS Major Features

The major features of DSP/BIOS include:

- The scheduler and its associated thread classes provide a mechanism for arranging and controlling the software's execution. The scheduler is preemptive, meaning that it will periodically interrupt the currently executing thread, determine what the highest priority thread is that is ready to execute, and start that thread running. One of the DSP's hardware timers is used to implement this preemptive behavior. The available thread types will be discussed in more detail later in the chapter.

- Memory manager to control the operation of the memory/cache architecture and control allocation of memory resources.

- Instrumentation that provides deterministic, minimally-invasive analysis, profiling, and statistical functions.

- Communications resources, including queues, pipes and streams, and a device driver mechanism.

- Support libraries providing standardization of access and hardware abstraction across multiple DSPs. These include the board support library (BSL) providing board-level functional support and the chip support library (CSL) providing DSP device-level support.

B.1.2   DSP/BIOS Threads

DSP/BIOS provides several classes of threads that can be scheduled for execution:

- Hardware Interrupt (HWI): Executed in response to a hardware interrupt, so should be very short and fast. Typically, these threads simply transfer data, and schedule a software interrupt for any further processing. The DSP/BIOS interrupt dispatcher can be used to permit ordinary C functions to serve as interrupt service routines.

- Software Interrupt (SWI): Software interrupts are typically posted (scheduled) by a HWI, and handle more involved interrupt processing while allowing hardware interrupts to be processed without delay. The posting mechanism has a mailbox variable that can be used to condition posting of ISR (i.e., can countdown to posting, or use bits as flags). SWIs are preempted by HWIs and higher priority SWIs.

- Periodic Function (PRD): Periodic functions are a class of SWI that are scheduled at regular intervals. DSP/BIOS automatically implements a hardware timer HWI and SWI for PRD scheduling. PRDs are preempted by HWIs and higher priority SWIs.

- Tasks (TSK): Tasks are functions that run to completion once scheduled, and are intended for longer duration, more complex processing that must be done when required. TSKs are preempted by HWIs, SWIs, PRDs, and higher priority TSKs.

- Idle Functions (IDL): Idle functions execute when DSP/BIOS has no other pending threads. They are most useful for true background tasks, like system maintenance and self-test. If multiple IDLs are present, they are run to completion in round-robin order.

B.2   DSP/BIOS Sample Projects

Sample project documentation and the complete source code is available in the `threads` directory of Appendix B.

Appendix C

Numeric Representations

IN the digital domain, a given number may be stored and used in a number of different representations. A number may be exactly representable in one form, but not in others. How the number is represented will affect the accuracy of calculations, the memory and bus bandwidth requirements, and the speed of calculations that can be attained.

C.1 Endianness

Typically, computer memories are addressable in bytes. If a data element is larger than one byte, then a decision must be made as to how the individual bytes of the data element are to be stored in memory. Given a 32-bit (4 byte) data element with hexadecimal value 12345678h, the data can be ordered in memory in two distinctly different ways. Assuming the data is stored at address 00001000h, it could be represented in either of the orderings shown below.

Address	00001000h	00001001h	00001002h	00001003h
Big-endian	12h	34h	56h	78h
Little-endian	78h	56h	34h	12h

The choice of storage method determines what is commonly referred to as *endianness*, so named since it is based on which *end* of a number is stored in the first byte of the memory space that the number occupies. *Big-endian* organization places the most significant byte of the data at the first address, while *little-endian* places the least significant byte of the data at the first address. There is no advantage of one over the other, and both are used in practice. In fact, the TMS320C6x DSPs are capable of operating with either endianness based on the setting of a processor pin at reset. By default, the DSK is configured to operate in little-endian mode.

To verify the DSK's endianness, open Code Composer Studio, and use View→Memory to open two memory windows at address 00000000h. Set the properties on one memory window to `32-Bit Hex - TI Style` and the other to `8-Bit Hex - TI Style`. Then, in the 32-bit window, set the value at address 00000000h to 12345678h. After making the change, observe how the bytes of the value are stored in the 8-bit window in order to determine the endianness in use.

While endianness will likely not affect typical single-processor DSP code, you should be aware of it, particularly if transferring information between processors, working in a multiprocessor environment with shared memory, or manipulating individual bytes of multi-byte data elements directly.

C.2   Integer Representations

Integer representations use a number of bits to represent just the integer part of a number; that is, they cannot represent any fractional part of a number. Integer representations can be broadly divided into those that represent signed numbers and those that represent unsigned (nonnegative) numbers.

In general, an unsigned integer can represent any value in the range from 0 to $2^n - 1$, where n is the width of the unsigned integer in bits. For example, with an 8-bit unsigned integer value, the minimum value will be $00000000_2 = 0_{10}$. The maximum value will be $11111111_2 = 255_{10} = 2^8 - 1$.

Signed representations can represent both positive and negative values, using one of several conventions. The most commonly used is the 2's-complement representation. In this representation, the most significant bit determines the sign of the number, with a 1 signifying a negative number. The determination of a positive value is straightforward in that it can simply be interpreted as an unsigned number. However, if a number is negative, then it is easiest to determine its value by negating it and interpreting the resulting positive value as the magnitude of the negative value. To negate a 2's-complement number, simply complement the number (flip the value of each bit) and add 1. If the addition carries beyond the number of bits in the number, the carry is discarded.[1] The number that remains is interpreted as though it is unsigned, and a negative sign is added. This is illustrated for six different 8-bit 2's-complement numbers below, with only the first of the numbers being positive.

binary value	complement	add 1	decimal value
01100011	(not needed)	NA	99
11100011	00011100	00011101	−29
11111111	00000000	00000001	−1
11111110	00000001	00000010	−2
10000001	01111110	01111111	−127
10000000	01111111	10000000	−128

While the 2's-complement representation may seem strange, it has a great advantage over other representations in the design of computer arithmetic hardware. In general, 2's-complement integers can represent any value in the range from (-2^{n-1}) to $(+2^{n-1} - 1)$, where n is the width of the 2's-complement integer in bits. For example, with an 8-bit 2's-complement integer value, the minimum value will be $10000000_2 = -128_{10}$. The maximum value will be $01111111_2 = +127_{10}$.

Another relatively common method for representing signed binary integers is to use the sign-magnitude convention. In this case, the most significant bit again determines the sign with a 1 signifying a negative number, but the remaining bits are interpreted as an unsigned magnitude. This has an advantage in that the representation is symmetric about 0, as compared to the 2's-complement representation where it can represent one more negative value than positive value. For example, with an 8-bit sign-magnitude integer value, the lowest value will be $11111111_2 = -127_{10}$. The highest value will be $01111111_2 = +127_{10}$. The values 00000000_2 and 10000000_2 both represent 0.

Note that for an integer representation, every possible bit combination is in fact a valid value—this makes it impossible to represent or detect erroneous values in hardware without modifying the representation.

---

[1]An alternate method of negating a 2's-complement number: begin at the least significant bit, and move to the left, keeping digits unchanged up to and including the first "1" that is encountered. Then complement all the remaining bits.

C.3 Integer Division and Rounding

In general, if we were asked to round the result of a division, the common solution is to see if the fraction part is 0.5 or greater; if so, add 1 to the result, then simply truncate to the integer value. However, integer division hardware produces the integer quotient and a remainder, not a fractional value. So, to do rounding, one method would be to add one to the quotient if the remainder is greater than the divisor divided by two. However, this requires the following additional steps:

1. obtain the divisor divided by two

2. compare to the remainder

3. conditionally add one to the quotient

A more efficient approach is to recognize that if we add one half of the divisor to the dividend before division, the result will be rounded. This requires the following additional steps:

1. obtain the divisor divided by two (with any remainder truncated)

2. add to the dividend before the division

The truncated result will in fact be rounded, as shown below for an 8-bit unsigned integer.

Operation	Dividend	Divisor	Quotient
$47 \div 3$	00101111_2 (47)	00000011_2 (3)	00001111_2 (15)
$(47+(3\div2))\div3$	00110000_2 (48)	00000011_2 (3)	00010000_2 (16)

When programming computer hardware that does not have a hardware integer divider (i.e., the TMS320C6x family), great pains are taken in algorithm implementation to avoid division by anything other than a power of two. This allows the division operations to be accomplished using bit-wise shifts, since every right-shift is equivalent to division by two, as shown below for an 8-bit unsigned integer. (Conversely, a left shift is equivalent to a multiplication by two.) Even in machines having a hardware integer divider, it is much faster to perform division by powers of 2 as shifts.

Initial Value	Shift	Equivalent to	Result
00101111_2 (47_{10})	right 1	$\div2$	00010111_2 (23_{10})
00101111_2 (47_{10})	right 2	$\div4$	00001011_2 (11_{10})
00101111_2 (47_{10})	right 3	$\div8$	00000101_2 (5_{10})
00101111_2 (47_{10})	right 4	$\div16$	00000010_2 (2_{10})
00101111_2 (47_{10})	right 6	$\div64$	00000000_2 (0_{10})
00101111_2 (47_{10})	left 1	$\times2$	01011110_2 (94_{10})
00101111_2 (47_{10})	left 2	$\times4$	10111100_2 (188_{10})
00101111_2 (47_{10})	left 3	$\times8$	01111000_2 (120_{10})

Note that in the last result, overflow occurred and the result is erroneous. This highlights a significant limitation in the dynamic range available when using integer representations. Floating point representations help to mitigate this problem, although they are subject to similar issues as well.

C.4 Floating-Point Representations

In floating-point representations, numbers are stored as a mantissa and exponent value, similar to the scientific notation we commonly use. However, instead of being stored in the form $(mantissa_{10} \times 10^{exponent_{10}})$, a floating-point representation is stored in a binary format as $(mantissa_2 \times 2^{exponent_2})$. Commonly used floating-point representations include the IEEE single-precision and double-precision formats [95], as illustrated in Figure C.1.

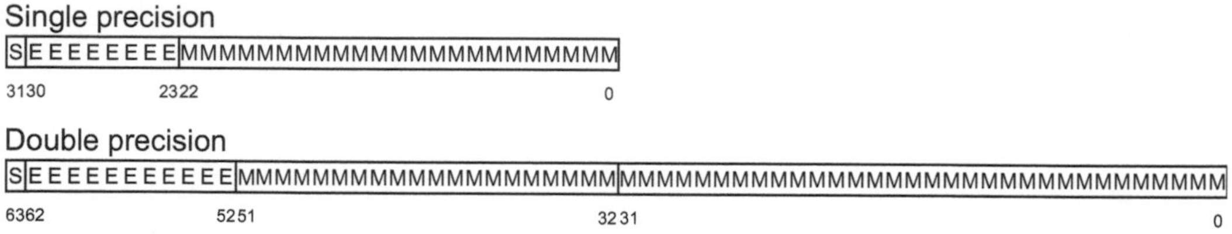

Single precision

S	E E E E E E E E	M M M M M M M M M M M M M M M M M M M M M M M

3130   2322   0

Double precision

S	E E E E E E E E E E E	M M M M M M M M M M M M M M M M M M M M	M M M M M M M M M M M M M M M M M M M M M M M M M M M M M M M M

6362   5251   3231   0

Figure C.1: Single- and double-precision IEEE 754 floating-point representations.

The following discussion focuses on the single-precision representation in detail; the double-precision representation is conceptually similar. In the single-precision representation, the S bit determines the sign of the number, where a 0 value indicates a positive number and a 1 value indicates a negative value. This can be expressed as -1^S. The 8-bit exponent portion of the number is biased by 127 (called "excess 127"), such that an exponent value of 00000000_2 is interpreted as a value of -127, a value of 11111111_2 (255_{10}) is interpreted as $+128$, and a value of 01111111_2 (127_{10}) is interpreted as an exponent of 0. This results in an potential exponent term multiplier of 2^{-127} to 2^{+128}, but as we shall see later, some exponent values are reserved for special cases. The 23-bit mantissa portion is interpreted as a binary value $1.MMM \cdots MMM$, where the radix point is a binary point, not a decimal point. The value of each mantissa bit therefore takes on the values shown below.

$$1 \; . \; \underset{2^{-1}}{M} \quad \underset{2^{-2}}{M} \quad \underset{2^{-3}}{M} \quad \cdots \quad \underset{2^{-21}}{M} \quad \underset{2^{-22}}{M} \quad \underset{2^{-23}}{M}$$

By assuming the leading bit to be a 1 (the normalized condition), the allowable range of the mantissa can be seen to be from a low of (1.0), where all M bits are 0, to a high of $(2.0 - 2^{-23})$, where all M bits are 1. Example floating-point values are shown in Table C.2.

As the last entry in Table C.2 shows, even though the floating point number has a seemingly benign value such as 0.1, it may well not be possible to represent it exactly in a given format. In fact, 0.1 can be exactly represented only by the *infinite* binary series

$$\sum_{i=1}^{\infty} \frac{1}{2^{4i}} + \frac{1}{2^{4i+1}},$$

and so any use of it in calculations is inexact. Although the difference may seem trivial, using the value in a repeated calculation leads to larger accumulated errors, and a form of quantization noise will be found in the results.

If a leading 1 in the mantissa is assumed, then it is not possible to exactly represent 0.0. To overcome this, a special case is designated to represent 0.0 exactly; if the exponent and the mantissa fields are both all 0's, then the value of the number is defined by the IEEE standard to be exactly 0.0.

Table C.1: Example floating-point values in the IEEE 754 format.

Hexadecimal	SEEE EEEE EMMM MMMM MMMM MMMM MMMM MMMM
	$= -1^S \times (1.\text{MMMMMMMMMMMMMMMMMMMMMMM}_2) \times 2^{\text{EEEEEEEE}_2 - 127}$
0x3F800000	0011 1111 1000 0000 0000 0000 0000 0000
	$= -1^0 \times (1.00000000000000000000000_2) \times 2^{127-127}$
	$= 1 \times (1) \times 2^0 = 1.0$
0xBF800000	1011 1111 1000 0000 0000 0000 0000 0000
	$= -1^1 \times (1.00000000000000000000000_2) \times 2^{127-127}$
	$= -1 \times (1) \times 2^0 = -1.0$
0xC2820000	1100 0010 1001 0011 0000 0000 0000 0000
	$= -1^1 \times (1.00100110000000000000000_2) \times 2^{133-127}$
	$= -1 \times (1 + 2^{-3} + 2^{-6} + 2^{-7}) \times 2^6 = -73.5$
0x7F00000	0111 1111 0000 0000 0000 0000 0000 0000
	$= -1^0 \times (1.00000000000000000000000_2) \times 2^{254-127}$
	$= 1 \times (1) \times 2^{127} = 1.7014118 \times 10^{38}$
0x3DCCCCCD	0011 1101 1100 1100 1100 1100 1100 1101
	$= -1^0 \times (1.10011001100110011001101_2) \times 2^{123-127}$
	$= 1 \times (1 + 2^{-1} + 2^{-4} + 2^{-5} + 2^{-8} + 2^{-9} + 2^{-12} + 2^{-13}$
	$\quad + 2^{-16} + 2^{-17} + 2^{-20} + 2^{-21} + 2^{-23}) \times 2^{-4}$
	$= 0.10000000149012 \approx 0.1$

Although the floating point representation permits the representation of a much wider range of values, there exists the potential for other inaccuracies in mathematical computation. One such effect that may occur happens when adding a small number to a much larger number. In order to add or subtract two floating point numbers, they must be converted to the same exponent value, then the mantissas can be added. After adding the mantissas, the resulting number is normalized by determining the most significant 1 bit, then adjusting the exponent so that bit becomes the assumed 1 bit in the representation. If two numbers are added together where one number is substantially larger than the other, the result may not be accurate. By way of illustration, assume that there are two operands with values as given below.

```
            SEEE EEEE EMMM MMMM MMMM MMMM MMMM MMMM
Operand1    0100 1011 1000 0000 0000 0000 0000 0000   (16,777,216.0)
Operand2    0011 1111 1000 0000 0000 0000 0000 0000   (1.0)
```

After converting both numbers to the same exponent by converting Operand2 to an exponent of 151 (10010111_2), the mantissa addition would take place as shown below (exponents not shown).

```
              1.MMM MMMM MMMM MMMM MMMM MMMM MMMM MMMM MMMM MMMM MMMM
Mantissa1     1.000 0000 0000 0000 0000 0000 ---- ---- ---- ---- ----
Mantissa2     0.000 0000 0000 0000 0000 0000 1000 0000 0000 0000 0000
Sum           1.000 0000 0000 0000 0000 0000 1000 0000 0000 0000 0000
Sum mantissa      000 0000 0000 0000 0000 0000
```

In order to store the resultant mantissa, it must be truncated to 23 bits. When this is done, it can be seen that the original Operand1 mantissa value has not changed, and therefore the addition operation had no effect. A more complete discussion of numerical accuracy in computing can be found in [96, 97].

In addition to storing normalized numbers, special representations are used in the IEEE floating-point standard to express non-normalized numbers as well as various invalid numbers and error conditions, such as NaN (not a number); see Table C.2. A complete discussion of these can be found in [95].

Table C.2: Representations of special numbers in the IEEE 754 floating-point standard. The X means "don't care" regarding the sign.

Number	Sign	Exponent	Fractional part of mantissa
0	X	all zeros	all zeros
∞	0	all ones	all zeros
$-\infty$	1	all ones	all zeros
NaN	X	all ones	any non-zero number

An additional figure for IEEE 754 that compares the formats is shown as Figure C.2. Note that while quad precision is also defined by the standard, this representation is not widely supported by hardware. However, quad precision is sometimes implemented in software for special needs.

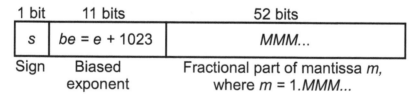

Single precision: 32 bits

1 bit	8 bits	23 bits
s	$be = e + 127$	$MMM...$
Sign	Biased exponent	Fractional part of mantissa m, where $m = 1.MMM...$

Double precision: 64 bits

1 bit	11 bits	52 bits
s	$be = e + 1023$	$MMM...$
Sign	Biased exponent	Fractional part of mantissa m, where $m = 1.MMM...$

Quad precision: 128 bits

1 bit	15 bits	112 bits
s	$be = e + 16383$	$MMM...$
Sign	Biased exponent	Fractional part of mantissa m, where $m = 1.MMM...$

Figure C.2: Comparison of IEEE 754 floating-point representations. In each case, the number represented is $(-1)^s \times (m \times 2^e)$, where s, m, and e are all base 2 numbers.

C.5   Fixed-Point Representations

Although floating-point data representation and manipulation are more intuitive to most engineers, the use of floating-point is not without penalty. First, the floating-point representations may be wider than necessary and therefore increase system cost and power consumption with no benefit. Also, integer hardware is significantly simpler than floating-point hardware, so it can be designed to operate faster and consume less power. These attributes are the reason that floating-point DSPs are usually not used in high-volume portable product applications, notably in most cellular telephones. In these commodity market environments, cost and low power consumption are dominating factors, and the additional programming complexity required to implement algorithms on fixed-point hardware can be amortized over a large number of units. Also, for a given width (i.e., 32 bits), the fixed-point number will have better resolution (and hence a lower noise floor) than a floating-point representation (assuming the proper scaling is performed). This is due to the fewer number of bits in the floating-point mantissa as compared to the fixed-point number.

Fixed-point representations are used to allow the implementation of fractional arithmetic using only integer arithmetic hardware. In fixed-point, a binary point is assumed to exist at a fixed location in a 2's-complement number, typically in a 16-bit value. The location of the binary point is indicated by the **Q-number** notation, such that a **Qn** number is assumed to have **n** bits to the right of the binary point. The most commonly used are the **Q15** and **Q12** formats, as illustrated below.

$$
\begin{array}{lll}
\texttt{Q15} & \texttt{S.XXX XXXX XXXX XXXX} & 1000000000000000_2 = -1.0000000 \\
 & & 0111111111111111_2 = +0.9999695 \\
\texttt{Q12} & \texttt{SXXX. XXXX XXXX XXXX} & 1000000000000000_2 = -8.0000000 \\
 & & 0111111111111111_2 = +7.9997559
\end{array}
$$

To determine the decimal value of a fixed-point number, first determine if it is positive or negative. The sign bit **S** is 1 for negative numbers and 0 for positive numbers. For a negative number, convert it to the corresponding positive value as was done for 2's-complement integers. Then determine the value based on the sum of the individual bits multiplied by their weight.

	binary value	complement	add 1	decimal value
Q15	0.110100000000000	not needed	NA	$\frac{1}{2} + \frac{1}{4} + \frac{1}{16} = 0.8125$
Q12	0110.100000000000	not needed	NA	$4 + 2 + \frac{1}{2} = 6.5$
Q15	1.110100000000000	0.001011111111111	0.001100000000000	$-(\frac{1}{8} + \frac{1}{16}) = -0.1875$
Q12	1110.100000000000	0001.011111111111	0001.100000000000	$-(1 + \frac{1}{2}) = -1.5$

It is important to note that fixed-point arithmetic is intended to be accomplished on standard 2's-complement integer arithmetic hardware, so it must yield correct results without modification. Using the **Q15** values of 0.375 ($\frac{3}{8}$) and -0.25 ($-\frac{1}{4}$), addition using integer logic is illustrated below.

$$
\begin{array}{rl}
0.375 = & 0.011000000000000 \\
+ \quad -0.250 = & \underline{1.110000000000000} \\
& 10.001000000000000 \qquad \textit{but carry out is lost} \\
& 0.001000000000000 \qquad\quad = 0.125 \; \checkmark
\end{array}
$$

Binary multiplication of two n-bit numbers results in a $2n$-bit result. The result of multiplying two Q15 numbers is a 32-bit number in Q30 representation with a redundant sign bit. To return the result to Q15 format, it is shifted right 15 bits and truncated to 16 bits. (Note that multiplying negative numbers requires a different algorithm, not illustrated here.)

$$
\begin{array}{rl}
0.375 = & \quad 0011\ 0000\ 0000\ 0000 \\
\times\ \ 0.750 = & \quad \underline{0110\ 0000\ 0000\ 0000} \\
& 0\ 0110\ 0000\ 0000\ 000 \\
& \underline{00\ 1100\ 0000\ 0000\ 00} \\
& 0001\ 0010\ 0000\ 0000\ 0000\ 0000\ 0000\ 0000 \\
\text{(shift right 15 bits)} \rightarrow & 0\ 0010\ 0100\ 0000\ 0000 \\
\text{(truncate to 16 bits)} \rightarrow & 0010\ 0100\ 0000\ 0000 = 0.28125\ \checkmark
\end{array}
$$

It is useful to note that the exponent in floating-point provides automatic scaling, whereas in fixed-point the scaling must be performed in the algorithm as required to prevent overflow. Q15 is commonly used in signal processing since multiplication of two Q15 numbers will never overflow beyond the range of the Q15 number, with the exception of the (-1×-1) case.

C.6   Summary of Numeric Representations

A summary of the numeric range, precision, and dynamic range of various number representations is provided in Table C.3. Signed integer calculations are based on the 2's-complement representation. Numeric range shows the most negative and most positive values that can be represented. Precision is defined as the smallest increment that the given representation can represent in normalized form. For floating-point representations, the precision figure is based on the smallest mantissa increment that can be used in an addition/subtraction with a value of 1.0 and still affect the resultant mantissa value. Dynamic range D for all representations can be calculated (in decibels) as $D = 20\log\left(\frac{\text{numeric range}}{\text{precision}}\right)$. Note that the floating-point representations can represent a much larger range of values than the precision represented by the mantissa (for example, a range in excess of 1600 dB for single-precision values), however, for any given value being represented there is a related range of values that can be added to the current value without the computation's effect being lost. In a sense, the exponent of the floating-point number could be thought of as determining where the current dynamic range of the floating-point number exists in the much larger value space of the numeric representation.

Table C.3: Summary of numeric representations.

Bits	Format	Numeric Range	Precision	Dynamic Range
8	Unsigned integer	$0 \rightarrow +255$	1	≈ 48 dB
8	Signed integer	$-128 \rightarrow +127$	1	≈ 48 dB
16	Unsigned integer	$0 \rightarrow +65,536$	1	≈ 96 dB
16	Signed integer	$-32,768 \rightarrow +32,767$	1	≈ 96 dB
16	Fixed-point (Q12)	$-8.0 \rightarrow \approx +7.999756$	≈ 0.000244	≈ 96 dB
16	Fixed-point (Q15)	$-1.0 \rightarrow \approx +0.9999695$	≈ 0.0000305	≈ 96 dB
32	Unsigned integer	$0 \rightarrow +4,294,967,296$	1	≈ 193 dB
32	Signed integer	$-2,147,483,648 \rightarrow +2,147,483,647$	1	≈ 193 dB
32	Single-precision	$\approx \pm 3.402823 \times 10^{38}$	$\approx 1.19 \times 10^{-7}$	≈ 138 dB
64	Double-precision	$\approx \pm 1.797693 \times 10^{308}$	$\approx 2.22 \times 10^{-16}$	≈ 314 dB

Appendix D

TMS320C6x Architecture

T HE first section of this appendix is intended to serve as a basic primer on computer architecture to the extent necessary to have a better understanding of the TMS320C6x architecture. It is assumed that the reader has a basic understanding of microprocessor operations. The second section then discusses the TMS320C6x architecture in some detail. Readers familiar with computer architecture may find it unnecessary to read the first section in order to understand the second section. For more detailed information on the TMS320C6x processors, the reader is referred to the technical documentation from Texas Instruments (for example [71, 98]).

D.1 Computer Architecture Basics

One definition of computer architecture is "... an abstract interface between the hardware and the lowest level software of a machine that encompasses all the information necessary to write a machine language program that will run correctly, including instructions, registers, memory size, and so on" [99]. When selecting and using a processor to perform a given task, the underlying construction of the processor will determine what it does well and what it does not, and ultimately, whether it meets the design requirements.

A basic microprocessor system is illustrated in Figure D.1. The central processing unit (CPU) contains registers (in this example, R0–R7) and the functional units (in this example just an arithmetic-logic unit (ALU)), all interconnected by signaling buses and sequenced by the timing and control unit. The memory system and input/output (I/O) subsystems are connected to the CPU by the system bus. The clock generator provides the timing for the logic operation and the reset circuit ensures the processor starts from a known state. A number of peripheral devices are commonly found in the I/O subsystem of a microprocessor system.

- Parallel I/O ports interface to external devices for control or sensing.

- Serial ports facilitate communications with local or distant devices using various serial protocols and hardware.

- Counter/timers are used to established precise timing intervals, generate rectangular waveforms, and to count external events.

Although the I/O and memory are shown in Figure D.1 as external to the CPU, in practice they may be integrated onto the actual processor device.

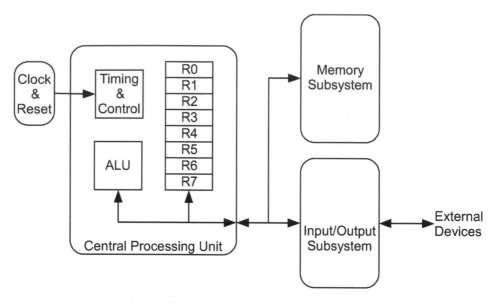

Figure D.1: Basic microprocessor system.

D.1.1 Instruction Set Architecture

One way to differentiate processors is in the make-up of their *instruction set architecture* (ISA), the set of commands that the processor can execute and the hardware required to execute them. On one end, the *complex instruction set computer* (CISC) supports instructions that can perform complicated tasks. For example, a single instruction may execute a complete FIR filter routine or search for a given value in an array. At the other extreme, *reduced instruction set computers* (RISC) have only a limited number of low-level instructions. So, more complex tasks must be accomplished as a series of simple instructions. In particular, a RISC instruction set usually only permits operations on data stored in the processor's registers, and has a very limited number of instructions that move data between memory and the registers. Since the CISC machine effectively executes complex tasks in hardware, it should have (and often does have) a performance advantage on a limited set of very specific task(s). However, complex instruction sets make it extremely difficult to optimize the performance of a processor in a general sense (and to develop efficient compilers for high-level languages), so nearly all general-purpose microprocessors are now RISC. (Although the ubiquitous Intel 80x86 architecture is programmed using a CISC instruction set, Pentium Pro and later implementations perform real-time translation of those instructions into RISC-like micro-operations that are then executed by the processor core.) The ARM family of processors, such as the ARM926EJ-S core in the OMAP-L138 multi-core system-on-chip, is RISC.

D.1.2 Register Architectures

Another broad classification of processor architectures is based on the possible locations of an instruction's source and destination operands. There are two common architectures classified in this way.

Register-memory: architectures allow one or more instruction operands to be located in memory. This architecture is commonly used in CISC machines.

Load-store: architectures require that all instruction operands be in registers. Only a

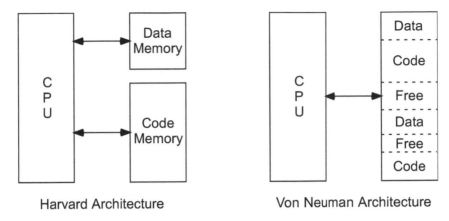

Figure D.2: Memory architectures.

very few instructions have access to memory, and these typically perform only simple transfers from memory to a register (load) or from a register to memory (store). The TMS320C6x DSPs use a load-store architecture.

D.1.3 Memory Architectures

The organization of processor memory space is a key element of the overall operation of the system. The information in memory consists of two distinct types:

1. instructions that the processor will execute exist in *code space*, and

2. information that the processor accesses as part of its program execution is stored in *data space*.

In the design of the processor, these two spaces can be placed into physically independent memories, or can exist in the same physical memories, as shown in Figure D.2. Architectures with separate code and data spaces are referred to as *Harvard* architectures. The primary advantage of the Harvard architecture is that there can be simultaneous operations in code and data memory, increasing memory bandwidth. Also, since the code and data spaces have different buses to the processor, their widths can be different in order to optimize each, and the code can be absolutely protected from inadvertent corruption by data operations. The primary disadvantage is that code and data can only be placed in their respective spaces, so any free memory in code space cannot be used for data, and vice versa. The Harvard architecture is commonly used in microcontrollers and special purpose processors, including the Texas Instruments TMS320C2x and TMS320C5x families of DSPs.

Processors where the code and data exist in the same memory space are referred to as *Von Neumann* (or *Princeton*) architectures. The primary advantage is that all of memory is available for code or data in any proportion, giving it much greater memory allocation flexibility. The disadvantages include the fact that code and data cannot be simultaneously accessed, and that the possibility exists for corruption between the code and data spaces. This architecture is used by nearly all general purpose microprocessors and numerous specialized processors as well, due primarily to its flexibility. The Texas Instruments TMS320C6x family of DSPs uses a Von Neumann architecture for external memory.

In addition to their main memories, modern processor systems often have *cache memories*. These are very fast local memories of a limited size that are often internal to the processor itself, and typically operate without any explicit control by the processor. The purpose of the cache memory is to retain a subset of all instructions in the hope that a significant percentage of the overall instruction stream will be present in the cache when needed and therefore the processor will not have to wait for it to be read from the slower main memory. If an object is in the cache when it is requested by the processor, it is said to be a *cache hit*. If it is not in the cache, it is said to be a *cache miss*. The underlying principle that makes this technique very effective is that programs typically display somewhat predictable behavior that can be exploited. (Note that if the instruction stream were truly random, then a cache would be of no use.) In particular, most caches are optimized to take advantage of the following properties.

Temporal locality: this is the property whereby code or data that is accessed has a high likelihood of being needed again in the near future. By keeping recently used code and data in the cache, the possibility of reuse is high.

Spatial locality: this is the property whereby code or data that is close to a memory location that was accessed is more likely to be needed than other memory locations that are more distant. To exploit spatial locality, most processor caches automatically fetch a larger block of data from the main memory when any location in the block is accessed.

Since cache memories have limited size, various algorithms are used to try to maintain only the information that is most likely to be needed in the cache. Caches can provide a substantial performance improvement; in fact, modern general-purpose processors rely heavily on multi-level cache hierarchies to achieve good performance. However, caches make it difficult to predict program execution time since it becomes probabilistic whether the needed instructions or data are in the cache, or must be fetched from slower main memory. This is a common theme in modern computer architecture, where many of the techniques used to speed up the execution of general-purpose processors also make it difficult or impossible to predict the program execution time.

D.1.4   Fetch-Execute Model

In its simplest form, a processor operates by reading an instruction from memory (referred to as a fetch), then it executes the instruction. In order to execute an instruction, the processor must first decode the instruction to determine what it is to do, read in any required operands, perform the required action, and then write the result to the proper location. While this sequential behavior results in a very simple design, performance suffers. For example, once the instruction is fetched, the bus to code memory will be idle until the instruction is completely executed. Similarly, the functional units that actually perform the operation (i.e., an adder or multiplier) are idle during the instruction fetch, the instruction decode, and while the results are being written out. Obviously, if all of the parts of the system could be kept busy simultaneously, performance would be improved.

D.1.5   Pipelining

In order to improve the utilization of the processor hardware, it is divided into stages, each of which handles a distinct portion of the total processing of an instruction. As an instruction is processed through one stage of the pipeline, it is passed to the next stage. Since the pipeline can only go as fast as the slowest stage, it is designed to be balanced where each stage has a similar delay. A representative pipeline with four stages is shown in Figure D.3 (note that modern processors may use deeper pipelines with more than 20 stages). The pipeline stages are abbreviated F, D, E, and W, as defined next.

Figure D.3: Pipeline stages.

F (fetch) is responsible for reading the next instruction from memory.

D (decode) decodes the instruction to determine what action and operands are required.

E (execute) loads operands (if any) and performs the required operation.

W (write-back) stores the results of the operation into the destination.

If we assume that each stage of the pipeline has a 10 ns delay, then if each instruction were required to complete before the next could be fetched it would take 40 ns for each instruction, and the processor could execute 25 million instructions per second (MIPS). With each stage of the pipeline able to operate independently on a different instruction, it will still take 40 ns for an instruction to be completely executed. This is an important observation: in general, pipelining does not improve the latency of a system. However, an instruction now finishes the journey through the pipeline every 10 ns, so the processor now operates at 100 MIPS, a 400% increase in throughput. In this case, the processor would have four instructions *in flight* (being executed) at once. This performance increase can only be achieved if the pipeline receives a steady stream of instructions and has unfettered access to the operands required as input and output of the instructions.

Consider the example instruction stream shown in Figure D.4. The operation of the four stage pipeline with instruction stream from Figure D.4 is shown in Figure D.5. Each column represents the state of the pipeline at a given processor clock, with time advancing left to right in the figure. This figure illustrates several common issues that limit pipeline performance.

- In the execution of `Instruction1`, the execute stage is shown as being delayed waiting for the required operands. This could be due to the delay in reading from memory after a cache miss, or waiting for a previous instruction's result to become available (in a longer pipeline). This delay is referred to as a *pipeline stall*, and causes all instructions at earlier stages to be delayed as well. Note that `Instruction2` cannot advance to the execute stage, and `Instruction3` cannot advance to the decode stage. Although not shown here, later pipeline stages could continue to operate and the instructions in them move forward, creating a *pipeline bubble* (empty pipeline stages).

- When `Instruction4` causes a jump or branch, execution now proceeds out of sequence. In this case, the address to fetch the next instruction from is not known until the completion of the write-back stage. The later instructions currently following this instruction must be discarded in a *pipeline flush*. Then the pipeline begins to refill as fetches occur in sequence again. Pipeline flushes are very costly in terms of time, especially in deeper pipelines. For this reason, modern high-performance processors use *branch prediction* to "guess" what the next instruction will be, and execute that instruction. If the guess is correct, then the pipeline remains full and maximum performance is obtained. If the guess is wrong, then those instructions must be discarded and the correct instructions executed. Fortunately, branch prediction algorithms typically have an accuracy in excess of 95 percent. Another technique used to minimize pipeline flushes is *predicated execution*, where an instruction's execution is predicated on a value in a specified register. Depending on the value in the predicate register, the instruction either executes normally, or it is passed through the pipeline as a

Address	Instruction	Action
00001000h	Instruction1	
00001004h	Instruction2	
00001008h	Instruction3	
0000100Ch	Instruction4	(jump to 00001040h)
00001010h	Instruction5	
00001014h	Instruction6	
00001018h	Instruction7	
⋮	⋮	
00001040h	InstructionX	
00001044h	InstructionY	
00001048h	InstructionZ	

Figure D.4: Example instruction sequence with an unconditional jump.

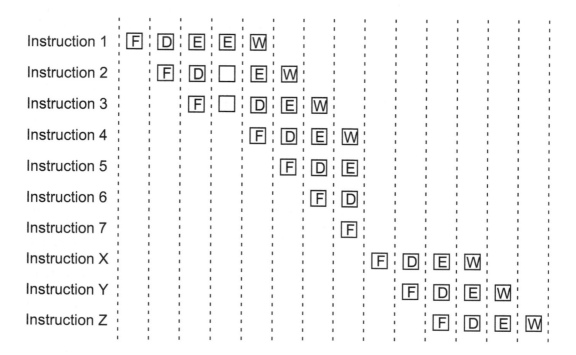

Figure D.5: Pipeline operation of instructions in Figure D.4.

no-operation (NOP) instruction. This permits conditional execution without flushing the pipeline. Yet another technique to mitigate the negative performance effects of branches is to use *delayed branch* instructions. In this case, the pipeline is **not** flushed when the fetch of the branch target is started. Instead, the instructions in the pipeline continue to move through it as normal. These instructions are said to be in the *delay slots* of the delayed branch instruction. From a programming perspective, a delayed branch instruction must be followed by some number of instructions that will be executed before the actual branch in program flow occurs. If there are no useful instructions that can be placed in the delay slots, NOPs must be inserted. This can mitigate the negative performance effects of branches, but adds to the complexity of programming the processor. The TMS320C6xxx branch instruction is implicitly a delayed branch instruction.

D.1.6 Single- versus Multiple-Issue

The processors described to this point have been *single-issue* processors, that is, they only execute one operation at a time. Even though pipelining introduces a form of parallelism, the actual execution of the instructions is still sequential. For example, if there were a series of three ADD instructions, the actual addition operations would occur in the Execute stage of the pipeline, and so would occur in sequence. In order to speed up execution further, a *multiple-issue* processor is designed to execute more than one operation in parallel. Multiple-issue processors require the evaluation of a number of considerations.

- Clearly, to do more than one operation requires that the processor have multiple instances of the required hardware. Examples of *functional units* would typically be ALUs, specialized adders and multipliers, and load-store units.

- If the processor is going to execute instructions in parallel, then it must be able to determine which can be safely executed at any given time. This issue will be discussed in more detail in Section D.1.7.

- It is likely that the functional units will have unequal delays, so even if instructions are executed in order it is possible (and likely) that the operations will be completed out of order. This makes the state of the processor at any instant (i.e., which instructions are executed and which are not) difficult to determine. So, there must be a mechanism in place to ensure that the operation results are stored in the proper order to preserve their interdependencies, and to permit the processor to precisely suspend and restore execution in order to service interrupts.

D.1.7 Scheduling

On a multiple-issue processor, *scheduling* is necessary to determine the order in which instructions can safely be executed. The scheduling must ensure that any dependencies between instructions are preserved as they are executed and their results stored. For example, in the example below, the first and third instructions can be executed in any order since they are independent, but the second instruction may *only* be executed when the result from the first instruction is available.

        ADD R1, R2, R3   adds R1 & R2 and places result in R3
        MUL R1, R3, R4   multiplies R1 & R3 and places result in R4
        ADD R1, R5, R6   adds R1 & R5 and places result in R6

Scheduling can either be completed in real-time on the processor hardware (dynamic scheduling) or can be done in advance by the code generation tools (static scheduling). This choice leads to fundamentally different architectures that are each well suited to specific environments.

Dynamic scheduling is primarily used with code that was not written to be intrinsically parallel. The processor attempts to discover parallelism in the code (*instruction level parallelism*, or ILP) by examining the interdependencies between instructions, managing functional unit assignments, and ensuring that results are stored in the proper order. This gives dynamic scheduling a great advantage in that it can exploit parallelism in code that was not written in a parallel fashion, permitting it to run unaltered serial code on a parallel architecture (dynamic scheduling is used in nearly all processors used in computer workstations). The primary disadvantage is that scheduling is a nontrivial process, so doing it in real-time requires a significant additional amount of hardware with the attendant cost and power consumption. Due to the hardware requirements, typical dynamic scheduling hardware is only able to look at a window of only several hundred instructions, limiting its ability to find parallelism. *Superscalar* processors use multiple functional units and dynamic scheduling, with the processor enforcing all dependencies between instructions. The exact execution order is not known until run-time, but execution is guaranteed to produce the same results as would serial execution of the code.

Static scheduling removes the burden of scheduling from the processor and instead requires code that explicitly specifies what instructions may be executed in parallel. In this case, the compiler is responsible for determining which instructions may be executed in parallel, and for ensuring that the result of an operation will in fact be ready before it is used in another instruction. The primary advantages of static scheduling are that the compiler can look for parallelism across the entire program and so hopefully determine a more efficient execution order, and that it eliminates the need for the dynamic scheduling hardware — a significant power and cost savings. The main disadvantage is that the code that is generated is very machine dependent and may be less adaptive to changing system dynamics. The statically scheduled *very-long instruction word* (VLIW) architecture used in the TMS320C6x fetches eight instructions in parallel (a *fetch packet*) to simultaneously pass to its eight functional units. If a functional unit is not used, then it is passed a no-operation (NOP) instruction. The high-level language compilers do all instruction scheduling and enforce dependencies. Writing assembly language for this architecture is a challenge, but is typically only done for very time critical code to maximize the functional unit utilization and reduce execution time.

For more detailed reading on VLIW processor design and their use in embedded systems, the reader is referred to the excellent book by Fisher, Faraboschi, and Young [100].

D.2   TMS320C671x Architecture

The TMS320C67xx DSP is an 8-way VLIW implementation of a RISC load-store architecture. The CPU core contains 32 general-purpose registers (A0-15, B0-15) and eight functional units split into two clusters, as shown in Figure D.6. Each functional unit has a primary specialization but most are capable of multiple operations. The primary functions of each are shown in the following table.

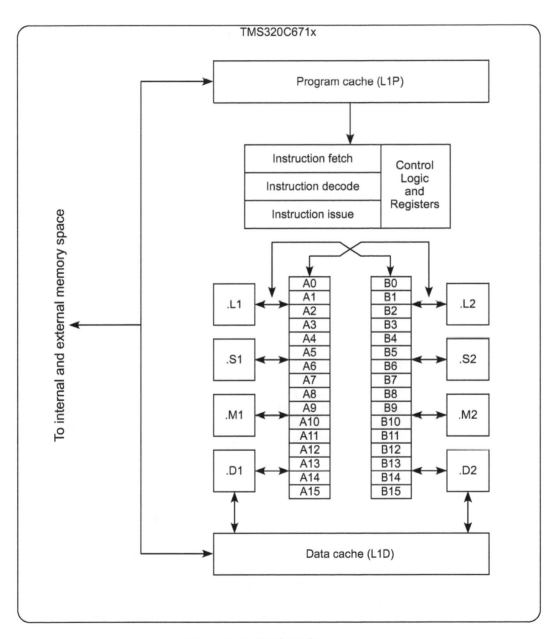

Figure D.6: TMS320C671x core.

Unit	Integer operations	Floating-point operations
.L	Logical	Arithmetic
	Arithmetic / compare	Integer/floating-point conversions
.S	Shifts and bit fields	Compare
	Logical	Reciprocal
	Arithmetic	Reciprocal square root
	Branches	Absolute value
	Constant generation	Single-/double-precision conversions
.M	Multiply	Multiply
.D	Load and store	Load and store
	Address calculation	
	Addition/subtraction	

The A and B register banks both have data buses for transferring data to and from the functional units associated with them, as well as for loading and storing operands. Two cross paths to permit the use of a single A-side register with a B-side functional unit, and vice versa. As one might imagine, determining the optimum combination of registers and functional units to use and efficiently scheduling the instruction stream can be a daunting task.

D.2.1   Memory System

The overall layout of the TMS320C671x processor's memory organization is shown in Figure D.7. The memory system is a Von Neumann architecture with a unified main memory space, but the cache memory is split into program and data paths. This is a very common design, since the program and data flows behave very differently (e.g., the program cache is never written to). The processor core must access memory through one of two caches, one for data operands (L1D) and one for instruction fetches (L1P). This notation is used to indicate that these are level 1 caches, that is, the caches closest to the processor core. These caches do not appear in the processor memory map, and are not directly accessible to the programmer. If the data is not available in the L1 cache or is being written to memory, then the request is passed to the L2 cache/SRAM controller. This controller manages a 64 KB block of memory that can be used either as a level 2 cache or as simply memory, in 16 KB blocks, by programming the associated control registers. For programs that need 64 KB or less of memory, the entire block can be left as memory. If a larger program is being run from off-chip memory, then the cache memory can significantly improve execution time. Or, a program may be made more efficient by using some portion of memory as L2 cache with the rest being used for on-chip memory to store frequently accessed data or code. In the TMS320C6713, there is an additional 192 KB block that can only be used as on-chip memory.

If a memory request cannot be filled by the L2 controller (the requested data is not in the L2 cache or memory), it is passed to the enhanced direct memory access (EDMA) controller, which then executes the transfer. The EDMA controller is an on-chip peripheral device that can be programmed to automatically transfer data under software control, however, those transfers requested by the L2 controller are transparent to the programmer. Since the processor may well be fetching instructions and transferring data at the same time, the EDMA controller is designed to handle simultaneous requests according to a priority

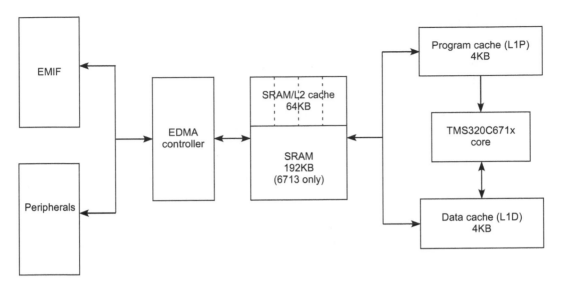

Figure D.7: TMS320C671x memory organization.

scheme. Based on the address of the memory request, the data transfer will be made to on-chip memory, one of the on-chip peripherals, or to an external memory device using the external memory interface (EMIF).

The EMIF is designed to provide a *glueless* interface to a number of different external memory devices, including various dynamic memories (e.g., SDRAM, SBSRAM, etc.) as well as static memory devices (e.g., ROM, SRAM, FIFOs, etc.). The term "glueless" refers to the fact that the processor and the memory device can be connected directly together without requiring any additional logic devices to create a compatible interface between the two (this implementation of interface logic is commonly referred to as *glue logic*). Eliminating the need for glue logic reduces both space and power requirements.

D.2.2 Pipeline and Scheduling

The TMS320C671x's VLIW architecture utilizes static scheduling. The hardware handles pipeline stalls typically caused by cache misses, but does not enforce any scheduling. Branch prediction is not used, but predicated execution instructions allow for conditional code without forcing pipeline flushes. The functional units require different amounts of time to complete their operations, for example, the ADD instruction result is available in the next clock cycle, but the MPY (multiply) instruction result is not available until after an additional 1 clock cycle delay. The branch instructions execute such that branch does not actually occur until 5 clock cycles after it is executed. The combination of all these constraints makes simply reading the assembly language difficult, and makes assembly language programming much more complex and tedious. Because of this, most programming is done in a high-level language such as C, and only very time-critical routines are hand-coded in assembly language.

Since the functional units are pipelined, they can also contain a number of instructions in the process of execution. For example, to perform a tight loop where a single execution packet is repeatedly executed, the branch unit would have multiple branch instructions in-flight, with a branch instruction completing at every clock cycle until the loop finished. In this way, implementation of the pipeline increases efficiency.

D.2.3   Peripherals

The TMS320C671x DSP incorporates a number of on-chip peripheral devices. Timers are typically used to provide precise periodic interrupts to the DSP, to generate rectangular waveforms for external devices (i.e., a clock for an ADC), and to count external events. Each timer consists of a counter register that is incremented by the DSP clock or an external signal, a period register that is used to determine when to reset the counter register, and a control register that is used to configure the timer. Basically, the timer operates by incrementing the counter register until it matches the period register; when they match the counter is reset to 0 and an interrupt is generated. This interrupt provides a very accurate time reference. One of the common uses of the timer interrupt is to permit the DSP/BIOS operating system to gain control of the DSP at prescribed intervals in order to perform preemptive multitasking.

The EDMA controller is used to offload data movement from the DSP. As mentioned above, the EDMA controller operates transparently in handling transfers required by the L2 cache controller. It can also be explicitly programmed to service interrupts by transferring data between the device and memory, or to move data from one region in memory to another. The EDMA controller is capable of sophisticated data movements, such as moving a two-dimensional region of a large array to a smaller array so that the extracted data is contiguous in memory.

Serial ports provide an interface mechanism to communicate with serial devices (i.e., many codecs) using a number of different formats. Once configured, they permit the DSP to simply write a value to the serial port in order to have it sent in the appropriate serial format (or to read a value that has been received). The serial ports can be serviced directly by the DSP, or the EDMA controller can be used to automatically transfer serial port data to and from memory. The EDMA controller is then programmed to interrupt the DSP when a complete frame of data has been transferred. This eliminates the need for the processor to perform basic data movements, freeing up processing power for more complex tasks.

D.2.4   Host Port Interface

The TMS320C6x DSPs all incorporate a Host Port Interface (HPI). The HPI makes it possible for an external (host) processor to access the entire memory space of the DSP. In addition to reading and writing memory locations, the host processor can also configure any of the DSP's peripherals. The DSP is also designed so that it can be forced to boot using the HPI port. In this mode, the DSP holds itself in reset until signaled by the host processor to begin execution. While the DSP is in reset, the host can load the desired program into the memory of the DSP, configure the peripherals, and then issue a *host port interrupt* to start the DSP running. While the DSP is running, the host processor can still read and write to the DSP memory space.

The Host Port Interface provides a very effective means for a central processor to control the operation of multiple DSPs. It is also used for high-speed communication between two DSPs, or a DSP and general-purpose processor. The winDSK8 software and the other software tools described in Appendix E all use the HPI.

D.3   TMS320C674x Architecture

The OMAP-L138 is a heterogeneous multi-core processor containing an ARM926EJ-S 32-bit RISC general-purpose microprocessor, a TMS320C6748 DSP, and a host of peripheral devices [101]. A comprehensive discussion of the OMAP-L138 architecture is beyond the scope of this text, but this section will highlight the enhanced capabilities of the C6748

DSP relative to the C6713 DSP. Note that since our programming is done in a high-level language, we are not directly exposed to these low-level enhancements, but the compiler is able to take advantage of them and produce more compact, faster code. Some particularly interesting enhancements of the C6748 are listed below.

- The C674x instruction set is a superset of the C67x+ floating-point instruction set and the C64x+ fixed-point instruction set. The C67x+ instructions are an extended version of the C671x instruction set. The C64x+ instructions are generally focused on supporting image and video processing operations.

- The C6748 doubles the register file size to two banks of 32 registers, reducing the need to repeatedly load and store memory variables during periods of heavy register usage. The L1D and L1P caches are also much larger (32 kB versus 4 kB).

- The functional units support many single instruction, multiple data (SIMD) operations. For example, a .M unit can do a single 32-bit by 32-bit multiply, two simultaneous 16-bit by 16-bit multiplies, or four simultaneous 8-bit by 8-bit multiplies. Multiplication of complex numbers is also directly supported.

- Many instructions can be expressed as compressed (16-bit) instructions if only certain registers can be specified. This increases the number of instructions that can be contained in a fetch packet, thereby improving performance and reducing code size.

For our purposes of presenting real-time DSP in this book, the differences between the C6748 and the C6713 have been kept relatively invisible. However, the reader should note that even if they had the same clock frequency, in many cases identical C code would run faster on a C6748 than on a C6713.

Appendix E

Related Tools for DSKs

E.1 Introduction

THIS appendix contains information on several tools that are available for use with the OMAP-L138 and TMS320C6713 DSKs. (Note that to use the tools with the TMS320C6713 DSK, the board must be equipped with the Educational DSP, LLC HPI daughtercard.) The Host Port Interface provides external access to the DSPs memory space, as described in Appendix D. This allows the tools to download and start programs, then read and write DSP memory locations to get data back from the DSK and to control the program.

E.2 Windows Control Applications

To control the DSK from a Windows application, programs must be created for both the host computer and the DSK. The sample host computer Windows application is written in Microsoft Visual C++. The interface between the host computer and the DSK can be serial RS-232 or USB. The details of this interface are hidden in a dynamic link library (DLL) file that is included with the host computer program. To transfer data to and from the DSK, the host computer must know the variable addresses where the data is stored on the DSK. To simplify this process, a predefined data structure is used, and the interface software has the ability to determine where the data structure is located in the DSK's memory space.

The host computer can perform a few basic operations:

- Reset the DSP.

- Load a program onto the DSP.

- Start the DSP program.

- Read and write DSP memory.

Control of a DSP program is implemented by writing to variables in the DSP memory space. Program status and output data are obtained by reading from variables in the DSP memory space. However, keeping track of the specific addresses of all the variables in the DSP program is tedious and error-prone, since variable locations can change each time a program is recompiled. To simplify the process of finding variable addresses, the DSP software establishes a special data structure (HostInterfaceData) so that the variables will be in a known location.

The host software first loads the program onto the DSK. Then, the location of the HostInterfaceData structure is determined by reading the symbol table embedded in the executable file. The host application can determine a variable's address by adding the desired variable's offset within the HostInterfaceData structure to the address of the HostInterfaceData symbol. This address is then used in the host read and write functions that access the DSP's memory.

E.2.1   Sample Windows Control Application

Detailed documentation and the complete source code for the sample Windows Control applications are available in the WIN_CONTROL_APPS directory of Appendix E. The basic Windows Control application implements a simple audio talk-through with a gain control. Further enhancements show how to create a simple oscilloscope and spectrum analyzer.

E.3   MATLAB Exports

Using the MATLAB® program SPTool is a convenient, graphical way to design digital filters.[1] To be able to use those designs in Code Composer Studio (CCS), we need to export them into a C language format. There are four MATLAB m-files discussed in this appendix and included with the software for the book that can be used to help automate this process (see the Appendix E MatlabExports directory). In all cases, two files are created, a C header file (filename.h) declaring the variables, and a C source file (filename.c) defining them. You can use any file name you wish by specifying it in the argument list for the m-file, as shown in the examples below. These files can then be included in your CCS project. In this appendix it is assumed that the reader is familiar with using MATLAB and SPTool. It is recommended that you add a MATLAB path to the directory where you have installed the m-files.

E.3.1   Exporting Direct-Form II Implementations

The filt structure created by MATLAB SPTool contains Direct-Form II numerator coefficients in filt.tf.num and denominator coefficients in filt.tf.den. If the filter is designed as a finite impulse response (FIR) filter, then only the numerator coefficients need to be exported using fir_dump2c.m for floating-point coefficients, or fir_dump2c_Qxx.m for fixed-point coefficients.

To use fir_dump2c.m, the following steps should be taken:

- Export the filter design from SPTool to the workspace. Ensure that you have specified an FIR filter design. (The remainder of this procedure assumes that filter design was exported with name filt1.)

- Execute a MATLAB cd command to change to the desired destination directory for the exported files.

- Run the m-file by typing

  ```
  fir_dump2c('coeff','B',filt1.tf.num,length(filt1.tf.num))
  ```

  at the MATLAB command line.

---

[1]If using another filter design method in MATLAB, such as FDATool, simply adapt the procedure for using the m-files as needed. The m-files will still eliminate the burden of converting from MATLAB variables into the format needed by the C language.

This creates two files, `coeff.c` and `coeff.h`, which declare a `float` array B of length
B_SIZE.

To use `fir_dump2c_Qxx.m`, the following steps should be taken:

- Export the filter design from SPTool to the workspace. Ensure that you have specified
  an FIR filter design. (The remainder of this procedure assumes that filter design was
  exported with name `filt1`.)

- Execute a MATLAB `cd` command to change to the desired destination directory for
  the exported files.

- Run the m-file by typing

  `fir_dump2c_Qxx('coeff','B',filt1.tf.num,length(filt1.tf.num),15)`

  at the MATLAB command line.

This creates two files, `coeff.c` and `coeff.h`, which declare a `short` array B of length
B_SIZE. The last parameter (`Qxx`) determines the location of the binary point. Fixed-point
number representations are discussed in Appendix C.

If the filter is designed as an infinite-impulse response (IIR) filter, then the numerator
and denominator coefficients can either be exported individually using the methods described for FIR filters above, or both can be exported simultaneously using `df2_dump2c.m`.

To use `df2_dump2c.m`, the following steps should be taken:

- Export the filter design from SPTool to the workspace. (The remainder of this procedure assumes that filter design was exported with name `filt1`.)

- Execute a MATLAB `cd` command to change to the desired destination directory for
  the exported files.

- Run the m-file by typing

  `df2_dump2c('HPF_coeff','HPF',filt1.tf)`

  at the MATLAB command line.

This creates two files, `HPF_coeff.c` and `HPF_coeff.h`, which declare the `float` arrays HPF_A
of length HPF_A_SIZE (denominator coefficients), and HPF_B of length HPF_B_SIZE (numerator coefficients). The array length is determined by the length of the `filt1` numerator
and denominator vectors.

E.3.2 Exporting Second-Order Section Implementations

An SPTool filter design can be converted from direct-form II to second-order sections by
using the MATLAB function `tf2sos` (you may want to type `help tf2sos` in MATLAB for
more details). Running `tf2sos` creates an $L \times 6$ matrix, where L is the number of second-
order sections needed to implement the filter, with each row of the matrix containing the
coefficients $(b_0, b_1, b_2, a_0, a_1, a_2)$ for a single second-order section. These second-order section
coefficients can be exported using `sos_dump2c.m`.

To use `sos_dump2c.m`, the following steps should be taken:

- Export the filter design from SPTool to the workspace. (The remainder of this procedure assumes that filter design was exported with name `filt1`.)

- Convert the filter design to second-order sections by typing

  `filt1.sos=tf2sos(filt1.tf.num,filt1.tf.den)`

  at the MATLAB command line.

- Execute a MATLAB `cd` command to change to the desired destination directory for the exported files.

- Run the m-file by typing

  `sos_dump2c('coeff','bqd_coeff',filt1.sos,size(filt1.sos,1))`

  at the MATLAB command line.

This creates two files, `coeff.c` and `coeff.h`, which declare the two-dimensional `float` array `bqd_coeff` of size `bqd_coeff_SIZE`-by-5. The a_0 coefficient is assumed to be 1 and is not used in the actual filter implementation, so it is ignored in the export.

E.4   MATLAB Real-Time Interface

The MATLAB real-time interface is a software tool that permits MATLAB to interface directly with a DSK. Data can be imported from the DSK inputs into MATLAB variables, and variables can be written to the DSK outputs. The data transfer capabilities are limited by the bandwidth of the host PC to DSK connection, and the speed of the host computer. At lower sample frequencies, real-time behavior can be maintained. At higher sample frequencies, only a portion of the total codec data stream will be able to be transferred.

An interface that allows the direct importation of real-time DSK data into MATLAB can be used for a number of purposes. The most basic approach is to simply use the DSK as a data acquisition board to obtain live data, and perform all signal processing in MATLAB. This also permits the use of the MATLAB visualization features with real-time DSK data. An interesting example of this approach was the development of real-time, acoustic beam-forming systems using multichannel analog input daughtercards on the DSK. Details of these projects are available in a number of references, including [40, 44, 50].

The MATLAB real-time interface driver software and example MATLAB scripts are available in the Appendix E `MatlabInterface` directory. Detailed descriptions of the interface functions are available in the `MatlabInterface\Matlab_API.pdf` document that can be found in the Appendix E subdirectory of the `docs` directory of the book's software.

Appendix F

Using the Code Generator with MATLAB

F.1 Introduction

THIS book is based on the premise that first perfecting a DSP algorithm in MATLAB and then migrating the resulting m-file to real-time C code is a valuable skill. One of the alternatives to developing this skill is to use an automated code-generation tool called the MATLAB Coder^{TM} to convert a MATLAB function "auto-magically" into C code. Using a code generator can potentially save time, but the user has much less control over the form of the software created, and will probably have less understanding of the generated software. If errors crop up, this can make debugging quite difficult. Ultimately, the decision of which approach to use is yours. The authors are strong advocates of the first approach, but we didn't want to completely ignore the MATLAB Coder option in case some of our readers are interested in that approach.

The MATLAB Coder generates standalone C and C++ code from MATLAB code. The generated source code is portable and readable. The MATLAB Coder supports a subset of core MATLAB language features, including program control constructs, functions, and matrix operations. It can also generate MEX functions that let you accelerate computationally intensive portions of MATLAB code and verify the behavior of the generated code. See http://www.mathworks.com/products/matlab-coder/ for more details.

The MATLAB Coder is a separate MathWorks product and as such, an additional expense. During its installation, you will be reminded that you must also install one of the supported C/C++ compilers. For MATLAB Release 2016a, the list of supported compilers can be found at http://www.mathworks.com/support/compilers/R2016a/index.html.

F.2 An FIR Filter Example

F.2.1 Before Using the MATLAB Coder

In Chapter 3, we developed a brute force approach to FIR filtering using MATLAB and the resulting code was shown in Listing 3.2. The code shown in Listing F.1 is a functionalized version of Listing 3.2. The FIR filtering function used in Listing F.1 is shown in Listing F.2. The m-script names include the letters "fun" which is a reference to the fact that these files are function-based.

Listing F.1: The `funFIR.m` code, a functionalized version of Listing 3.2.

```
 1  %  This m-file is used to convolve xLeft[n] and B[n] without
    %  using the MATLAB filter command.  This is one of the
 3  %  first steps toward being able to implement a real-time
    %  FIR filter in DSP hardware. This m-file uses a function to
 5  %  calculate the output value, yLeft[0].
    %
 7  %  In sample-by-sample filtering, you are only trying to
    %  accomplish 2 things,
 9  %
    %  1.  Calculate the current output value, yLeft[0], based on
11  %      just having received a new input sample, xLeft[0].
    %  2.  Setup for the arrival of the next input sample.
13  %
    %  This is a BRUTE FORCE approach!
15  %
    %  written by Dr. Thad B. Welch, PE {t.b.welch@ieee.org}
17  %  copyright 2001, 2015
    %  completed on 13 December 2001 revision 1.0
19  %  updated to a function-based script on 21 July 2015 rev 1.1

21  % Simulation inputs
    xLeft = single([1 2 3 0]);            % input vector xLeft
23  N = int16(3);                         % order of filter=length(B)-1
    B = single([0.25 0.25 0.25 0.25]);    % FIR filter coefficients B[n]
25  yLeft = single(0);                    % declare output variable y

27  % Calculated terms (functionalized)
    [xLeft, yLeft] = funFilter(xLeft, B, N);
29
    % Simulation outputs
31  xLeft                                 % notice xLeft(1) = xLeft(2)
    yLeft                                 % average of last 4 input values
```

Listing F.2: The `funFilter.m` code, which defines the function used in Listing F.1.

```
    function [xLeft, yLeft] = funFilter(xLeft, B, N)
 2
    % initializes the output value
 4  yLeft = single(0.0);

 6  % performs the dot product of B and x
    for i = 1:N+1
 8      yLeft = yLeft + B(i)*xLeft(i);
    end
10
    % shift the stored x samples to the right
12  for i = N:-1:1
        xLeft(i+1) = xLeft(i);
14  end
```

To allow for easy comparison between the real-time C code from Listings 3.3 and 3.4, and the C code that we are about to generate, a few code modifications were made. Specifically, the modifications are listed next.

1. The variable x was renamed xLeft, and the variable y was renamed yLeft.

2. All of the variable types were declared, xLeft as single, N as int16, B as single, and yLeft as single.

3. The FIR filter routine was made into a separate MATLAB function and given the name funFilter.m. Remember, there is already a MATLAB function named filter and you must avoid using existing function or variable names to represent more than one thing. If you are not sure if a variable or function name that you are considering using exists, use the MATLAB **which** command (for example, **which filter**).

If you run the funFIR.m script, you will get the same results as in Chapter 3, as shown below.

```
xLeft =
    1    1    2    3
yLeft =
    1.5000
```

F.2.2 Using the MATLAB Coder

Now the Coder tool can be used. From the MATLAB command line, type **coder** and then press the "Enter" key. A dialog box similar to the figure below will appear.

Notice the progress indicator near the top of this dialog box. We are currently in the first of six steps which is labeled, Select. Use the browse option (indicated by the ellipsis "...") to the right of the highlighted window) to find and enter funFilter.m which contains our FIR filter function. This will result in a dialog box similar to the next figure shown.

Since we have run this process a number of times, a yellow highlighted box has appeared to remind us that this project already exists. We will select the option to `Overwrite` the project. After clicking on `Overwrite`, the yellow highlighted information will disappear and we are ready for the next step. This is indicated by the flashing Next in the lower right corner. Clicking on Next will result in a dialog box similar to the next figure shown.

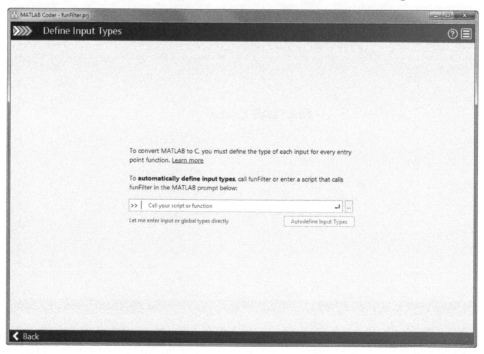

We have chosen to enter the name of the script `funFIR.m` so that the resulting code will be very similar to what we created in Chapter 3. Use the browse option (indicated by the ellipsis "..." to the right) to find and enter `funFIR.m`, which sets up our filtering example and calls our FIR filter function. Click on the Autodefine Input Types button. This will result in a dialog box similar to the next figure shown.

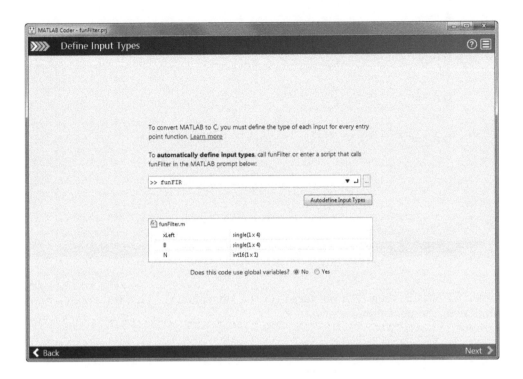

Click on Next. This will result in a pop-up box similar to the next figure shown.

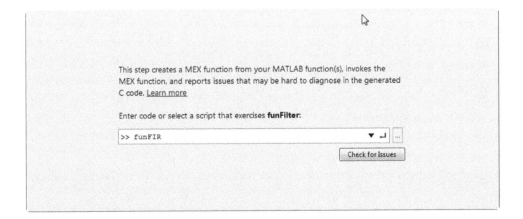

Click on Check for Issues. This will result in a dialog box similar to the next figure shown.

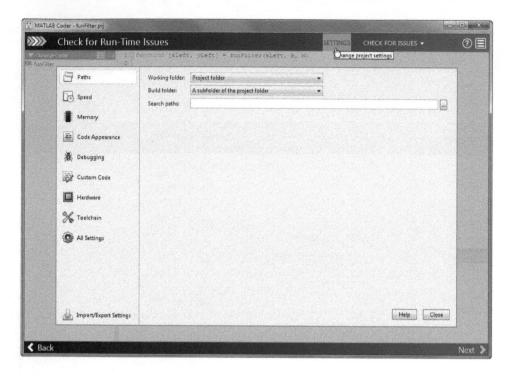

Click on **SETTINGS**, then click on Speed (in the left column). This will result in a dialog box similar to the next figure shown.

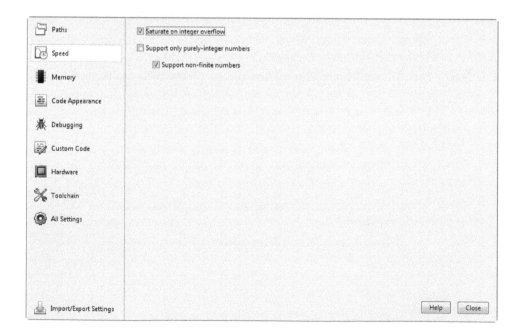

Uncheck the boxes for Saturate on integer overflow and Support non-finite numbers. Click on Close and click on the **CHECK FOR ISSUES** button. This will result in a pop-up box similar to the next figure shown.

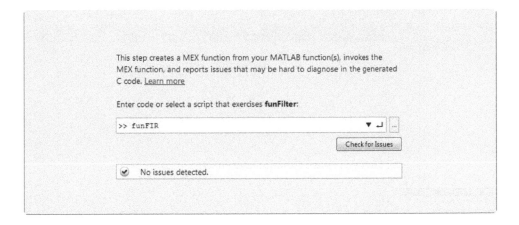

Click on Next in the lower right corner. This will result in a dialog box similar to the next figure shown.

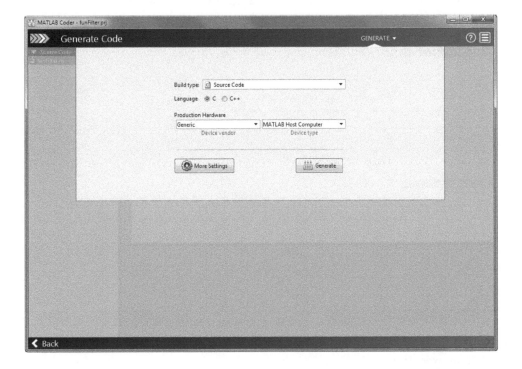

Under Production Hardware, pulldown the Device vendor menu and select Texas Instruments. Pulldown the Device type menu and select C6000. Click on the Generate button. This will result in something similar to the next figure shown.

Scrolling down in the listing, the important results are shown in the next figure shown.

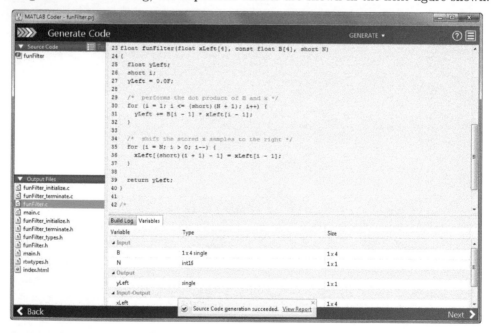

We are now ready to use the pertinent parts of the auto-generated code in a CCS project for real-time execution.

F.2.3   Transferring to a CCS Project

We will now copy and paste the appropriate section of the auto-generated code listing from the previous figure into our real-time project in CCS. Specifically, we will need to use the following parts.

- Paste lines 25 and 26 from the previous figure into the variable declarations section of the ISR in the CCS project.

- Paste lines 27–37 from the previous figure into the algorithm section of the ISR in the CCS project.

The real-time project is now almost ready to run, using the C code generated by the MATLAB Coder.

F.2.4 Observations

After following this procedure, there are a few things to notice.

1. The MATLAB Coder created a number of files (11 by our count).

2. We will use **none** of those 11 files!

3. We only need to extract the variable declarations and algorithm parts from the `funFilter.c` file.

4. Lines 25 and 26 in the auto-generated code only declared `yLeft` and `i`. The variables `xLeft` and `B` will **also need to be declared** before the project can be run in CCS.

Another minor observation you may notice, when comparing the real-time C code from Chapter 3 with the code generated by the MATLAB Coder, is that MATLAB appears to have trouble accepting the fact that in C code, a memory location with an index of zero is perfectly valid. This probably stems from the original FORTRAN legacy of MATLAB, which is why even today MATLAB only allows array index values to start at 1. When MATLAB was rewritten in C++ many years ago, this behavior was maintained to keep from "breaking" any existing MATLAB code. Indeed, one of the strengths of MATLAB is how well backward compatibility is maintained. The authors have m-files written over 25 years ago that still run without error on the latest version of MATLAB; very few software tools can claim that.

F.3 Conclusion

Is the MATLAB Coder for you? If you are willing to develop your MATLAB algorithm as a function, declare your variables in your MATLAB code as if you were using a declarative language (such as C), develop a script file that calls this function, and then reintegrate the resulting C code into your real-time code's ISR file, then this approach may work for you.

As mentioned at the start of this appendix, the authors are strong advocates of first perfecting your DSP algorithm in MATLAB, and then manually migrating the resulting m-file to real-time C code. In our opinion, this results in a better understanding of the real-time code.

Appendix G

Battery Power for the DSP Boards

G.1   Introduction

SOME users may desire to operate their DSP board on battery power. Possible reasons for this would certainly include portability, but also electrical isolation from the AC power system. The latter may be desirable, for example, to provide increased patient safety when the DSP board input is connected to a biomedical signal source such as an electrocardiogram (ECG) provided via surface electrodes and appropriate bioinstrumentation buffer circuitry. We have proven that it is quite feasible to use any of the DSP boards supported by this text with battery power.

All of the supported DSP boards are powered by an AC power supply that converts wall outlet power to approximately 5 volts DC. These boards connect to the AC power supply via a DC power plug, which is also called a barrel connector. The outer portion of the barrel is 5.5 mm in diameter (ground) and the inner post is 2.5 mm in diameter (+5 volts DC). The approximate quiescent currents for these boards are shown in Table G.1. When the DSP core is performing low-intensity calculations, these currents will rise slightly (10–20%). Higher-intensity calculations will draw higher amounts of current; this will very much be application dependent, so investigate your particular application.

G.2   Method

All of the DSP boards supported by this text operate with a modest amount of current, at +5 volts, as mentioned above. This allows any of the boards to be easily operated independent of AC power. Since the required currents and voltages are within the capability

Table G.1: Typical quiescent current drawn by DSP boards. The quiescent state is the condition when minimal processing is being performed by the board.

Board	Quiescent current
TMS320C6713 DSK	150 mA
OMAP-L138 Zoom Experimenter Kit	230 mA
LCDK	395 mA

of most USB-based external batteries, one possible solution is to either buy or assemble a cable that will connect such an external battery to the DSP board. Both options are described here.

Buy a cable: Look for a cable listed as a "USB 2.0 A to 5.5/2.5mm Barrel Connector Jack DC Power Cable" or something similar to that.

Assemble a cable: If you would rather build your own cable, follow these steps. We used two spare cables that we had on hand, and cut off the unneeded portion of the cables. The USB end of the cable to be assembled is shown in Figure G.1(a). The red and black wires correspond to the +5 volt DC and ground connection of the USB specification, respectively. The green and white wires are used for data transfer, and are therefore not used in this application. The DC end of the cable to be assembled is shown in Figure G.1(b). The red wire of the USB end needs to be soldered to whichever wire on the DC end connects to the center part of the DC power plug, and the black wire of the USB end needs to be soldered to the other wire on the DC end. Since color codes or stripes may not be consistent on such DC cables, we used an ohmmeter to verify the wiring of these two connections. After these two connections are soldered together, the exposed conductors need to be properly insulated. We used electrical tape for this purpose; alternatively, heat shrink tubing could have been used.

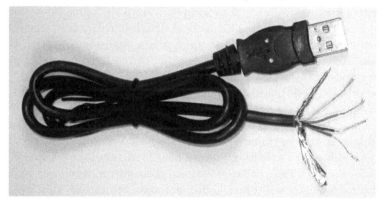

(a) The USB end of a cable to be assembled. This end will connect to the external battery.

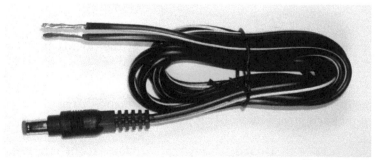

(b) The DC end of a cable to be assembled. This end will connect to the DSP board.

Figure G.1: The two ends of a cable for connecting a DSP board to a USB external battery.

Figure G.2: An example of a DSP board connected to an external USB battery. The board can operate with no connection to AC power.

G.3 Testing

G.3.1 Initial testing

After assembly, we connected the cable to our USB battery and observed the output voltage using an oscilloscope (a multimeter could also be used). This step verifies that you have the correct polarity and that your battery is actually providing about +5 volts DC as required. This initial check is highly recommended before connecting the cable to your DSP board.

G.3.2 Final testing

Once the cable is verified, connect the cable between the USB battery and the DSP board. If you are using the OMAP-L138 board, you will also need to power up the system by turning on the slide switch. A fully assembled and working system is shown in Figure G.2. The Hyperjuice 100 watt-hour (20 amp-hour) system is shown, which should power the OMAP-L138 board for about three days. We operated the system for more than a day without difficulty!

G.4 Conclusion

Using the method described in this appendix, you can gain increased portability of your DSP board, and also isolate it from the AC power systems. The cable can also power the DSP board from your computer's USB (type A) port, if desired. This allows you to eliminate one of the power cords needed for your real-time DSP development station.

Appendix H

Programming Perils and Pitfalls

PROGRAMMING in a real-time environment can be challenging even for experienced programmers. This appendix is intended to illustrate some of the common problems that are encountered in this environment, and present practical strategies for avoiding them.

H.1 Debug versus Release Builds

When a project is created in Code Composer Studio, there are two build configurations that are established: *Debug* and *Release*. The debug configuration will embed debugging information in the object file (information that links assembly instructions to the original source code), and also will not optimize the generated code so that there is a direct correspondence between a line of source code and the assembly language that is generated. These permit symbolic debugging, and ensure that the assembly code will execute in the order that the C code was written. The debug configuration is useful when developing software, but the generated code is often significantly slower than the release version. In the release configuration, the compiler attempts to optimize the generated code for best performance, using a number of transformations and algorithms. This means that there may no longer be a 1-to-1 correspondence between the source code and the assembly code; as functionality is moved and reordered, code is reused where possible, and redundancies are eliminated in order to maximize execution speed and/or minimize code size. Debugging the assembly code generated by a release build is a significant challenge for even seasoned programmers. The types and degrees of optimization employed can be controlled on a per-project and per-file basis; further information on this is available in the CCS documentation.

H.2 The Volatile Keyword

Two common situations in real-time DSP programming are variables that directly reference hardware, and variables that are used to communicate between interrupt service routines and the main program. Both of these situations require that the *volatile* keyword be used to control the compiler's optimization of memory references. In the first case, when a pointer variable is dereferenced to access a hardware register, the compiler's optimizer will assume that the transfer is being made to a standard read/write memory location. In the second case, the compiler will assume that the memory location will only change when it is written to in the function being compiled, and that no other access will be made concurrent with that function's execution. For example, suppose there is an integer pointer variable *mcbsp_spcr* that is used to read the McBSP1 receive register status bit as shown below, in order to wait until data is received by the McBSP.

```
unsigned int *mcbsp_spcr = (unsigned int *)McBSP1_SPCR;

while(!(*mcbsp_spcr & 0x00020000)) // wait for codec ready
    ;
```

In the debug build, the code executes as expected because no optimization is done. However, in the release build, the compiler identifies the expression **!(*mcbsp_spcr & 0x00020000)** to be loop-invariant code, and so pulls it out of the loop and only reads from that location once. While this is generally a very good optimization for true memory locations, in this case we are reading a peripheral register that may change; thus, it is NOT loop-invariant. To force the compiler to actually read the location represented by the variable in each loop iteration, we add the qualifier *volatile* to the variable declaration as shown below.

```
volatile unsigned int *mcbsp_spcr = (unsigned int *)McBSP1_SPCR;
```

The volatile keywords informs the compiler that it may not optimize out any accesses to this variable, so it generates code that actually reads the McBSP register in each iteration. A similar situation occurs when a variable is used to write repeatedly to a hardware register, in this case McBSP1's transmit data register, as illustrated below.

```
unsigned int *mcbsp_dxr = (unsigned int *)McBSP1_DXR;

*mcbsp_dxr = 1;
*mcbsp_dxr = 2;
*mcbsp_dxr = 3;
```

If this code is compiled under a release build, only a single write of the value 3 will occur. Declaring *mcbsp_dxr* to be volatile will force the compiler to perform the three separate write operations.

When using global variables to communicate between the main program and interrupt service routines (or between interrupt service routines), you should normally declare the global variables to be volatile as well, particularly if they are used in loops. Otherwise, the compiler may optimize out the variable references and you will miss any changes that occur to the variable during an interrupt.

H.3   Function Prototypes and Return Types

If a function is not declared before it is used, the C language requires that the compiler assume that function return type is *int*. This seemingly benign behavior has been observed as the cause of many programs that fail to work properly, because failing to declare a function in C is not an error and so it is not flagged as such. Consider the code below, noting that the `sinf` function was never declared.

```
float x;

x = sinf(0);
```

In the C6000 architecture, register A4 is used for the return of 32-bit or smaller values. The `sinf` function actually returns a single-precision floating-point number in A4. However, since the function was never declared, the compiler assumes that the return type is *int*. So, the compiler assumes A4 contains an integer, and adds code (specifically the INTSP instruction) to convert the value in it to a *float* before storing it in *x*. As can be imagined, taking a floating-point bit pattern and performing an integer to floating-point conversion on it produces meaningless values. To prevent this situation, it is important (and good programming practice) to declare all functions before use. In the code below, the `math.h` header has been included to ensure the proper declaration of the `sinf` function.

```
1 #include <math.h>
  float x;

3
  x = sinf(0);
```

Now knowing that the `sinf` function returns a float, the compiler will take the return value in register A4 and transfer it into the variable *x* directly, giving the correct result. Always ensuring that all functions are declared before use will avoid these situations. This can be quite difficult to debug because the code is otherwise correct.

H.4 Arithmetic Issues

A high-level language compiler typically supports a number of arithmetic operations. The compiler will guarantee correct results; however, in real-time software we are also concerned with how long it will take to do the calculation. For an operation that is supported in the processor (i.e., add), the compiler will generate code to use the hardware to perform the calculation. For operations that are not supported in the processor hardware, the compiler will generate software to accomplish the calculation. In general, the software calculations will be much slower than those performed in hardware.

The TMS320C6x DSPs do not have divider hardware, so division should be avoided whenever possible. In the code below, the calculations are numerically equivalent.

```
  float x = 100.0F;

2
  x = x / 10.0F;   // calculation A
4 x = x * 0.1F;    // calculation B
```

Calculation A specifies a division, so the compiler will insert a call to a subroutine to perform the calculation in software. Since the processor has a hardware multiplier, the calculation B can be accomplished much faster. Note that the "F" suffix on the numbers indicates that they are constants of type *float* — otherwise they would be interpreted as type double, requiring the promotion of *x* to type double before performing the calculation as a double-precision operation.

When using an array variable to implement circular buffering, the index needs to be "wrapped around" when the end of the buffer is reached. In the code sample below, a buffer and an index variable are allocated.

```
  #define BUFFER_SIZE 100
2 float x[BUFFER_SIZE] = {0.0F};
  int index = 0;
```

In the following examples, we will assume the index value is being incremented. A decrementing index would be handled in a similar fashion. Perhaps the most immediately intuitive way to accomplish index wraparound is to simply check the index value and set it back to 0 when it reaches the end of the buffer.

```
1 index++;
  if(index >= BUFFER_SIZE)
3     index = 0;
```

Note that this requires a comparison, and is limited to index increments of 1. If arbitrary increments are needed, we need another approach. The *modulus* operation (%) provides a seemingly simple fix.

```
1  index++;
   index = index % BUFFER_SIZE;
```

However, the modulus operator computes the remainder of the index value divided by BUFFER_SIZE, so we are implicitly invoking a division operation. As an alternative, note that if the increment is less than BUFFER_SIZE, we can obtain the remainder by subtracting BUFFER_SIZE whenever the index is greater than or equal to BUFFER_SIZE.

```
   index++;
2  if( index >= BUFFER_SIZE )
       index = index - BUFFER_SIZE;
```

This reduces the modulus calculation to a simple subtraction operation, which is supported in hardware. However, it still requires a comparison to see if the index needs to be wrapped around. In real-time code, we may find even this operation to be prohibitively expensive. To eliminate the comparison completely, the buffer size is set to 2^n. Then, the wraparound is accomplished with only a logical AND operation of the index with $2^n - 1$. If the index is less than BUFFER_SIZE, the AND operation will leave it unchanged. If the index is greater than or equal to BUFFER_SIZE, the AND operation will result in the same result as the modulus operation.

```
1  #define BUFFER_SIZE 512 // must be a power of 2
   float x[BUFFER_SIZE] = {0.0F};
3  int index = 0;

5  index++;
   index = index & (BUFFER_SIZE - 1);
```

Note that in this implementation the buffer size *must* be a power of 2. This is a classic software trade-off between size and speed, and is often seen in production code.

H.5   Controlling the Location of Variables in Memory

When declaring a variable in software, we normally do not concern ourselves with the actual variable location in memory. Rather, we simply refer to the variable by name. The compiler and linker are responsible for making sure that the correct memory location(s) are accessed. However, there are times when we will want to control where variables are placed in memory. To do that, we need to do two things:

1. instruct the linker where the physical memory is in our system, and

2. tell the compiler which variables we want placed in locations other than the default locations.

When our code is compiled, the compiler places the output into a number of predefined sections. Global variables are typically placed in the *.data* or *.bss* sections. The linker command file (i.e., lnk6748.cmd) lists the physical memory available in the system, and indicates which sections are placed into which memory areas. In the linker command files used throughout the text, all compiler output is placed into the DSP's on-chip memory (the *IRAM* area). This is a relatively small memory area, so if we want to have large data buffers we need to place them in the much larger off-chip memory. In the linker command file, this area is designated *SDRAM*; all compiler output in section *"CE0"* will be placed there.

To instruct the compiler to place a given variable into the *"CE0"* section, we use a compiler *pragma*. In general, pragmas are compiler-specific directives that permit detailed control over various aspects of the compiler's operation. To control the section into which a variable is placed, we can use the `DATA_SECTION` pragma. This instructs the compiler to place the variable named as the first parameter into the section named as the second parameter.

```
#pragma DATA_SECTION (buffer, "CE0"); // allocate buffer in SDRAM
volatile float buffer[BUFFER_LENGTH];
```

Further information on the various pragmas available in Code Composer Studio can be found in the online help and the C compiler user's manual.

H.6   Real-Time Schedule Failures

One of the most difficult challenges in writing real-time software is determining if the software will in fact be able to meet the real-time schedule. In particular, for an interrupt driven system, each interrupt service routine (ISR) must complete its processing before the next interrupt occurs, and the programmer must allow sufficient "slack time" to account for interrupt service overhead. One simple and effective way to measure the time that an ISR takes is to change the state of a logic signal on entering and leaving the ISR, and then monitor that signal with an oscilloscope. The `WriteDigitalOutputs()` function allows this to be done easily by setting the state of four digital signals on the DSKs, as shown below.

DSK type	Bit 3	Bit 2	Bit 1	Bit 0
C6713	LED3	LED2	LED1	LED0
OMAP	J6-9	J6-8	J6-7	J6-6

Example code is shown below.

Listing H.1: Checking for real-time schedule failure using the `WriteDigitalOutputs()` function.

```
interrupt void MyISR()
{
    WriteDigitalOutputs(1);      // set digital output bit 0 high
    // your ISR code here
    WriteDigitalOutputs(0);      // set digital output bit 0 low
}
```

The approximate percentage of CPU time spent in the ISR is then approximately the duty cycle of the digital signal. It is approximate because the time required to recognize the interrupt and start executing the ISR, and the time required to resume normal execution after the ISR, are not measurable this way.

As an alternative, the state of the interrupt flags register (IFR) can be examined at the end of the ISR. For most of the code in this book, hardware interrupt INT12 is used. If the 12th-bit of the IFR is a 1 at the end of the ISR, that means that another interrupt is pending before you finished servicing the current one, so the real-time schedule has not been met. Example code to implement this method is shown next.

Listing H.2: Checking for real-time schedule failure using the interrupt flags register.

```
Uint32 Overrun = 0;

interrupt void MyISR()
{
    // your ISR code here
    if(IFR & 0x00001000) {      // check if INT12 is pending
        Overrun++;              // if so, increment the count
    }
}
```

H.7   Variable Initialization

In the C programming language, declaring a variable does not automatically cause that variable to be initialized to a known value. In general, variables must always be set to a value before they are evaluated in a C program. This does not mean that they need to be initialized in the declaration, as long as they are written to in an assignment statement before they are evaluated. The code below implements a simple IIR filter. In this example, the variables x and y are intentionally (and incorrectly) left uninitialized.

Listing H.3: Example IIR filter code with incorrect variable initialization.

```
// static variables
float B[2] = {1.0, -1.0}; // numerator coefficients
float A[2] = {1.0, -0.9}; // denominator coefficients
float x[2];               // input
float y[2];               // output

// function code
x[0] = input;             // get input value
y[0] = -A[1]*y[1] + B[0]*x[0] + B[1]*x[1]; // calc. the output
x[1] = x[0];              // setup for the next input
y[1] = y[0];              // setup for the next input
output = y[0];            // send filter output
```

For x[0] and y[0], this oversight will not cause a problem. The variable element x[0] is assigned a value on line 8 before it is evaluated on lines 9 and 10. Similarly, y[0] is assigned a value on line 9 before it is evaluated on lines 11 and 12. However, it is not acceptable for x[1] and y[1], since they are both evaluated on line 9 before either has been assigned a value. Although this may seem minor, it is in fact a major problem. If either variable randomly has a large numeric value, that is equivalent to a large transient that may take a long time to decay. The worst case situation is if either x[1] or y[1] has a value of NaN (not a number). In that case, the result of the line 9 calculation with a NaN results in a value of NaN being assigned to y[0], which is then assigned to y[1] on line 11. This means that the line 9 assignment to y[0] thereafter will **always** be a NaN, so the filter will never function. To prevent this, the x and y variables should be initialized as shown below.

Listing H.4: Correct variable initialization.

```
float x[2] = {0.0, 0.0}; // input
float y[2] = {0.0, 0.0}; // output
```

H.8 Integer Data Sizes

The C programming language does not specify a fixed size for integer data types such as `int`, `short`, `long`, etc. Rather, the data type `int` is set to be the machine word size for a specific compiler target. In the C6000 DSPs, the registers are 32-bits, so the size of the `int` data type is 32-bits. Since we only are creating code for the C6000 family, this does not present a problem once you learn the sizes of the different data types. However, suppose you then wanted to reuse your code on a different architecture. The size of the integer data types might be different; if so, you would have to go through your code and change all of your variable declarations to be the correct size.

To make your code more portable across different architectures, a common technique is to define a set of data types that explicitly indicate the size of the variable. The C programming language supports defining new data types using the **typedef** compiler directive. An example is shown in Listing H.5 below. The **typedef** directive on line 1 tells the compiler that `Uint32` is a new name for the data type `unsigned int`. By coding with a set of explicitly sized types such as `Uint32` and `Int16`, it is easy for the programmer to select the required variable size.

Listing H.5: C6000 typedef directives.

```
  typedef unsigned int        Uint32;
2 typedef short               Int16;
```

We use names for our **typedef** directives that we hope are unambiguous to the reader. For example, `Uint32` is a 32-bit unsigned integer, `Int16` is a 16-bit signed integer, `Uint8` is an 8-bit unsigned integer, and so on.

When porting your code to a different architecture, the only change required is to include an appropriate set of **typedef** directives. For example, if you were porting code to a C5000 DSP architecture, the size of the `unsigned int` is 16-bits but the size of the `unsigned long` is 32-bits. Therefore, you would use the **typedef** directives shown in Listing H.6 below.

Listing H.6: C5000 typedef directives.

```
  typedef unsigned long       Uint32;
2 typedef short               Int16;
```

All the necessary **typedef** directives needed for projects in this book are contained in the `tistdtypes.h` file that you include in each project. Using conditional compilation, the correct set of **typedef** directives is automatically selected when you compile your code.

Appendix I

Comparison of DSP Boards

I.1 Introduction

WE are firm believers in the need for a working knowledge of real-time DSP to be part of a complete EE/ECE curriculum. Such a working knowledge cannot come only through books, lectures, or MATLAB demos; students need to use actual DSP hardware and get real-time applications to run successfully before they can acquire a practical working knowledge of real-time DSP. Throughout the years, we've used a number of boards in our labs for this purpose using both fixed- and floating-point Texas Instruments (TI) processors, such as the C50, C31, C6201, C6211, C6711, C6713, and most recently the multi-core OMAP-L138 (which includes both a C6748 core and an ARM926 core). Of these boards, several are now only of historical interest, while the boards based on the C6713 and the OMAP-L138 remain our primary targets of interest.

I.2 Three Boards

The Spectrum Digital C6713 DSK, the Logic PD OMAP-L138 Zoom Experimenters Kit (ZEK), and the newer Texas Instruments OMAP-L138 Low Cost Development Kit (LCDK) can all be used effectively with this book. How do these three boards compare? Table I.1 provides the most salient comparative details.

We provide support for the C6713 DSK in the latest edition of our book mainly for legacy purposes, as many universities have labs populated with these boards. For those just getting started, populating new labs, or for those wanting to upgrade existing labs, one of the two OMAP-L138 boards seems to make more sense. Using basic criteria such as price and available I/O, the new LCDK appears to be the better choice.[1] The only slight disadvantage to the LCDK is the need for an external XDS100 emulator, but this is a minor issue. After using both boards, we now prefer the LCDK. Beyond price and I/O, the comparison of OMAP boards gets a bit more interesting, if you start to consider more subtle issues.

For example, while both OMAP-L138 boards use the identical audio codec chip, the two manufacturers chose to integrate that codec into the overall board design in different ways. The ZEK only makes available line in and line out, whereas the LCDK also makes available an amplified microphone input (handy for commonly available non-powered microphones).

---

[1]The OMAP-L138 Experimenter Kit is no longer being manufactured, but many universities still use this board.

424 APPENDIX I. COMPARISON OF DSP BOARDS

Table I.1: A comparison of the three primary DSP boards that are supported by this book.

	Spectrum Digital/TI C6713 DSK	Logic PD OMAP-L138 Zoom Experimenter Kit	TI OMAP-L138 Low Cost Development Kit (LCDK)
Processor	C6713 DSP	OMAP-L138 dual core: C6748 VLIW DSP and ARM926 RISC GPP on a SOM	OMAP-L138 dual core: C6748 VLIW DSP and ARM926 RISC GPP
Processor Clock Freq.	225 MHz (fixed)	375 MHz (max)	456 MHz (max)
RAM	16 MB of SDRAM	128 MB mDDR SDRAM[a]	128 MB DDR2 SDRAM
Flash memory	512 KB	8 MB SPI-NOR Flash	128 MB NAND Flash
Audio codec	TLV320AIC23	TLV320AIC3106 (access to line in and line out only)	TLV320AIC3106 (access to line in, microphone in, and line out)
Other I/O	None, but an available HPI interface board from eDSP provides parallel port, USB, serial RS-232, and digital input/output ports as user selectable resources available to the DSK software	USB, SATA, Ethernet (RJ-45), MMC/SD card slot, serial (RS-232), Integrated (LCD, touch, and backlight) Connector for optional Zoom Display Kits, JTAG Note: XDS100 emulation is built into the board.	USB, SATA, Ethernet (RJ-45), MMC/SD card slot, Composite Video (NTSC/PAL) input, VGA output, Leopard Imaging Camera Sensor input, LCD Port (Beagleboard XM connectors) output, two user push button inputs, JTAG[b]
Price	$395	$495[c]	$195[d]

[a]Older boards shipped with 64 MB of mDDR SDRAM.

[b]Early versions of the LCDK included an Authentec fingerprint swipe sensor, but since Authentec subsequently discontinued production of this sensor, newer LCDKs do not include a fingerprint reader.

[c]No longer available.

[d]Note: to program the LCDK in C (using Code Composer Studio from TI), you will also need an inexpensive XDS100 emulator, since it isn't part of the main board. These are available at a suggested retail price of $79 from TI's e-store or from a variety of third-party vendors.

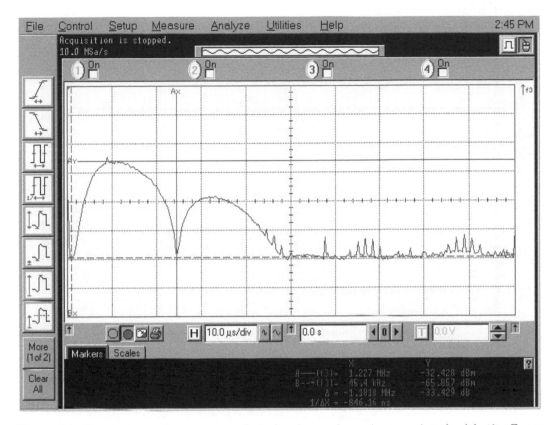

Figure I.1: Spectrum analyzer screen shot showing codec noise associated with the Zoom Experimemters Kit.

Furthermore, the power supply decoupling of the codec chip is very different between the two boards, and this is important to some applications.

It can be seen from the board schematics that the codec on the ZEK connects directly to the "noisy" switching DC power supply, whereas the LCDK uses LC filtering on the power connection. From a design standpoint, the better board is the LCDK, since power supply noise is not coupled into the codec as it is in the ZEK. One could argue that such power supply noise is well above the audio range intended for the audio codec, so why "waste" money on filter components? But such high-frequency noise can still be problematic in a laboratory setting where processed signals are routinely analyzed using traditional test and measurement equipment. This unnecessary high-frequency noise can be clearly seen in the screen capture of Figure I.1, which shows the average spectrum of the ZEK's audio codec output.

In this figure, the Bx marker (seen at the far left of the display) is placed at the first spectral null near 45 kHz, so the energy shown in Figure I.1 is all well above the audio frequencies. But it can still cause a problem. Often, the system's output is analyzed by test and measurement equipment (e.g., an oscilloscope, spectrum analyzer, or a vector signal analyzer) that is usually of the high-speed sampled type (e.g., a digital sampling oscilloscope or DSO). Such test equipment typically does not incorporate antialiasing filters in the front end, meaning that aliasing of this "out of the audio band energy" can end up in the audio range and become a huge problem for certain DSP applications. This problem could easily have been avoided by a more prudent circuit design. The design used in the LCDK clearly demonstrates this, as evidenced by its quieter code output.

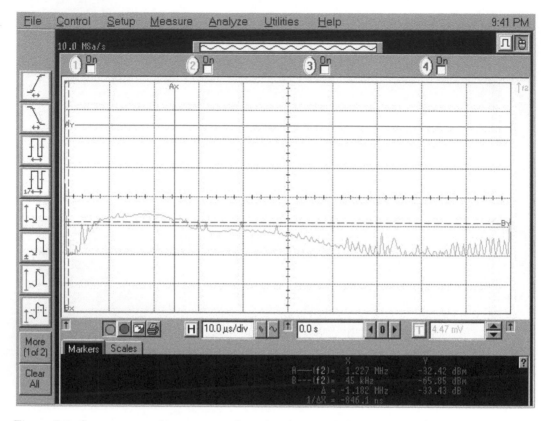

Figure I.2: Spectrum analyzer screen shot showing much lower levels of codec noise associated with the LCDK.

Figure I.2 shows the average spectrum of the LCDK's audio codec output. Compare this to the previous figure showing the ZEK codec output. The LCDK uses exactly the same AIC3106 codec chip that is used in the ZEK, and the sample frequency, scales, and markers for the two figures are as close to identical as we could get them. The figure of the LCDK's output clearly shows a substantial reduction (approximately 30 dB) in the "out of audio band noise" compared to the ZEK.

I.3   Conclusion

Based on price, available I/O, and the noise characteristics of the codec output, the better of the two OMAP-L138 boards seems to be the LCDK. That being said, this book fully supports all three boards: the Spectrum Digital C6713 DSK, the Logic PD Zoom OMAP-L138 Experimenters Kit (ZEK), and the Texas Instruments OMAP-L138 Low Cost Development Kit (LCDK).

Appendix J

Abbreviations, Acronyms, and Symbols

THIS is a partial list of abbreviations, acronyms, and symbols used in the text, provided in the hope that it will be helpful to some readers.

Symbols

( )	used for a continuous function.
[ ]	used for a discrete function.

Greek Letters

α	feedback coefficient for simple IIR filters, such as those used for a type of echo generation for guitar special effects.
λ	wavelength.
π	ratio of a circle circumference to diameter, 3.1415926535897932...
τ	time constant.
ω	radian frequency.

A

a	filter coefficient associated with an output term, y. When used in a transfer function, the a coefficients are associated with the denominator of the transfer function.
A	vector or array containing all of the a terms.
ADC	analog-to-digital converter.
AIC	analog interface circuit (see codec).
AGC	automatic gain control.
AM	amplitude modulation.
ANC	adaptive noise cancellation.
ARM	Advanced RISC Machine, a 32-bit reduced instruction set computer (RISC) instruction set architecture (ISA) developed by ARM Holdings.
AWGN	additive white Gaussian noise.

B

b	filter coefficient associated with an input term, x. When used in a transfer function, the b coefficients are associated with the numerator of the transfer function.
B	vector or array containing all of the b terms.
BW	bandwidth of a bandpass signal.
BP	bandpass.
BPF	bandpass filter.
BPSK	binary phase shift keying.

C

C	value of capacitance.
CCS	Texas Instruments' Code Composer Studio™.
CD-ROM	compact disk read-only memory.
CISC	complex instruction set computer.
codec	coder-decoder. An integrated circuit that contains both an ADC and a DAC.
CPU	central processing unit.

D

DAC	digital-to-analog converter.
DC	direct current (0 Hz).
DDS	direct digital synthesizer or direct digital synthesis.
DF-I	direct form I.
DF-II	direct form II.
DFT	discrete Fourier transform.
DMA	direct memory access.
DSK	DSP starter kit.
DSP	digital signal processing or digital signal processor.
DTFT	discrete-time Fourier transform.
DTMF	dual-tone, multiple-frequency signals as defined by telephone companies.

E

ECG	electrocardiogram.
EDMA	enhanced direct memory access.

F

FCC	Federal Communications Commission.
FIR	finite impulse response.
FFT	fast Fourier transform.
FT	Fourier transform.
$\mathcal{F}$	Fourier transform.

$\mathcal{F}^{-1}$	inverse Fourier transform.
f_h	highest or maximum frequency that is present in a signal.
F_s	sample frequency (samples/second) $= 1/T_s$.

G

GPP	general purpose processor.
GPU	graphics processing unit.

H

$H(e^{j\omega})$	discrete-time frequency response.
$H(j\omega)$	continuous-time frequency response.
$h[n]$	discrete-time impulse response or unit sample response.
$h[t]$	continuous-time impulse response.
$H(s)$	continuous-time transfer or system function.
$H(z)$	discrete-time transfer or system function.
HDTV	high-definition television.
HP	highpass.
HPF	highpass filter.
HPI	host port interface.
Hz	hertz (cycles per second).

I

IEEE 754	floating point number format.
IF	intermediate frequency.
IFFT	inverse fast Fourier transform.
IIR	infinite impulse response.
ISA	instruction set architecture.
ISR	interrupt service routine.

J

j	$\sqrt{-1}$; identifies the imaginary part of a complex number. Some authors use the letter i instead of the letter j.
JTAG	Joint Test Action Group, commonly used as the name of a debugging interface for printed circuit boards and IC chips. Formalized as IEEE Std 1149.1 in 1990.

L

$\mathcal{L}$	Laplace transform.
$\mathcal{L}^{-1}$	inverse Laplace transform.
L	value of inductance.
LCDK	Low Cost Development Kit.
LFSR	linear feedback shift register.

LP   lowpass.

LPCM   linear pulse code modulation.

LPF   lowpass filter.

LSB   lower sideband, also used for least significant bit.

$\boxed{\text{M}}$

M   the number of bands in a graphic equalizer.

MA   moving average.

McASP   multi-channel audio serial port.

McBSP   multi-channel buffer serial port.

ML   maximum likelihood.

$\boxed{\text{N}}$

n index or sample number.

N often used as filter order; in other contexts, it is used for the length of a sequence, or for the length of an FFT.

NCO   numerically controlled oscillator.

$\boxed{\text{O}}$

OMAP   Open Multimedia Application Platform, a family of proprietary multi-core system on chips (SoCs) by Texas Instruments.

$\boxed{\text{P}}$

PC   personal computer.

PCM   pulse code modulation.

PLL   phase-locked loop.

PN   pseudonoise.

PSK   phase shift keying.

$\boxed{\text{Q}}$

Q quality factor. Q = bandwidth of a BP filter divided by its center frequency. The higher the value of Q, the more selective the BP filter is.

QAM   quadrature amplitude modulation.

QPSK   quadrature phase shift keying.

$\boxed{\text{R}}$

r magnitude of a pole. This is a measure of how far the pole is from the origin.

R   value of resistance.

RC   resistor-capacitor.

RISC   reduced instruction set computer.

RF   radio frequency.

S

s	the Laplace transform independent variable, $s = \sigma + j\omega$.
SoC	system on chip.
SOS	second-order section.

T

τ	a dummy variable often used in convolution.
t	time.
T	period of a signal or function.
TED	timing error detector.
T_s	sample period $= 1/F_s$.
TI	Texas Instruments.

U

$u[n]$	discrete-time unit step function.
$u(t)$	unit step function.
U.S.	United States (of America).
USB	upper sideband; also used for Universal Serial Bus.

V

V	voltage in volts.
V_{in}	input voltage.
V_{out}	output voltage.
VLIW	very long instruction word; this is a type of architecture for DSPs.

W

winDSK	original Windows-based program for the C31 DSK, created by Mike Morrow.
winDSK6	Windows-based program, the follow-on to winDSK, for the C6x DSK series. It was created by Mike Morrow.
winDSK8	Windows-based program, the follow-on to winDSK6, for both OMAP-L138 multi-core boards and the C6713 DSK. It was created by Mike Morrow.

X

$X(j\omega)$	result of the Fourier transform $\mathcal{F}\{x(t)\}$; it shows the frequency content of $x(t)$.
$x[n]$	a discrete-time input signal.
$x(t)$	a continuous-time input signal.

Y

$Y(j\omega)$	result of the Fourier transform $\mathcal{F}\{y(t)\}$; it shows the frequency content of $y(t)$.
$y[n]$	a discrete-time output signal.

$y(t)$ a continuous-time output signal.

$\boxed{\mathbf{Z}}$

z the independent transform variable for discrete-time signals and systems.

z^{-1} a delay of 1 sample time.

Z_c impedance of a capacitor.

$\mathcal{Z}$ z-transform.

$\mathcal{Z}^{-1}$ inverse z-transform.

ZEK   Zoom Experimenter Kit

References

[1] B. Porat, *A Course in Digital Signal Processing*. John Wiley & Sons, 1997.

[2] A. V. Oppenheim and R. W. Schafer, *Discrete-Time Signal Processing*. Prentice Hall, 3rd ed., 2009.

[3] J. G. Proakis and D. G. Manolakis, *Digital Signal Processing*. Prentice Hall, 4th ed., 2007.

[4] S. K. Mitra, *Digital Signal Processing: A Computer-Based Approach*. McGraw-Hill, 4th ed., 2011.

[5] R. G. Lyons, *Understanding Digital Signal Processing*. Prentice Hall, 3rd ed., 2011.

[6] S. W. Smith, *Digital Signal Processing: A Practical Guide for Engineers and Scientists*. Newnes, 2003.

[7] R. G. Lyons, *Streamlining Digital Signal Processing: Tricks of the Trade Guidebook*. John Wiley & Sons, 2007.

[8] C. Marven and G. Ewers, *A Simple Approach to Digital Signal Processing*. John Wiley & Sons, 1996.

[9] J. H. McClellan, R. W. Schafer, and M. A. Yoder, *DSP First: A Multimedia Approach*. Prentice Hall, 1998.

[10] C. S. Burrus, "Teaching filter design using MATLAB," in *Proceedings of the IEEE International Conference on Acoustics, Speech, and Signal Processing*, pp. 20–30, Apr. 1993.

[11] C. J. McCormack, A. S. Ali, R. L. Haupt, and C. H. G. Wright, "Computer supplements to engineering labs," *ASEE Comput. Educ. J.*, vol. III, pp. 58–62, Apr. 1993.

[12] R. F. Kubichek, "Using MATLAB in a speech and signal processing class," in *Proceedings of the 1994 ASEE Annual Conference*, pp. 1207–1210, June 1994.

[13] R. G. Jacquot, J. C. Hamann, J. W. Pierre, and R. F. Kubichek, "Teaching digital filter design using symbolic and numeric features of MATLAB," *ASEE Comput. Educ. J.*, vol. VII, pp. 8–11, January–March 1997.

[14] M. A. Yoder, J. H. McClellan, and R. W. Schafer, "Experiences in teaching DSP first in the ECE curriculum," in *Proceedings of the 1997 ASEE Annual Conference*, June 1997. Paper 1220-06.

[15] C. H. G. Wright and T. B. Welch, "Teaching real-world DSP using MATLAB," *ASEE Comput. Educ. J.*, vol. IX, pp. 1–5, Jan–Mar 1999.

[16] T. B. Welch, B. Jenkins, and C. H. G. Wright, "Computer interfaces for teaching the Nintendo generation," in *Proceedings of the 1999 ASEE Annual Conference*, June 1999. Paper 3532-02.

[17] J. W. Pierre, R. F. Kubichek, and J. C. Hamann, "Reinforcing the understanding of signal processing concepts using audio exercises," in *Proceedings of the IEEE International Conference on Acoustics, Speech, and Signal Processing*, vol. 6, pp. 3577–3580, Mar. 1999.

[18] T. B. Welch, C. H. G. Wright, and M. G. Morrow, "Poles and zeroes and MATLAB, oh my!," *ASEE Comput. Educ. J.*, vol. X, pp. 70–72, Apr. 2000.

[19] T. B. Welch, M. G. Morrow, and C. H. G. Wright, "Teaching practical hands-on DSP with MATLAB and the C31 DSK," in *Proceedings of the 2000 ASEE Annual Conference*, June 2000. Paper 1320-03.

[20] C. H. G. Wright, T. B. Welch, D. M. Etter, and M. G. Morrow, "Teaching DSP: Bridging the gap from theory to real-time hardware," *ASEE Comput. Educ. J.*, vol. XIII, pp. 14–26, July 2003.

[21] T. B. Welch, C. H. G. Wright, and M. G. Morrow, "Caller ID: An opportunity to teach DSP-based demodulation," in *Proceedings of the IEEE International Conference on Acoustics, Speech, and Signal Processing*, vol. V, pp. 569–572, Mar. 2005. Paper 2887.

[22] C. H. G. Wright, M. G. Morrow, M. C. Allie, and T. B. Welch, "Using real-time DSP to enhance student retention and engineering outreach efforts," *ASEE Comput. Educ. J.*, vol. XVIII, pp. 64–73, Oct–Dec 2008.

[23] T. B. Welch, C. H. G. Wright, and M. G. Morrow, "The DSP of money," in *Proceedings of the IEEE International Conference on Acoustics, Speech, and Signal Processing*, pp. 2309–2312, Apr. 2009.

[24] T. B. Welch, C. H. G. Wright, and M. G. Morrow, "Software defined radio: Inexpensive hardware and software tools," in *Proceedings of the IEEE International Conference on Acoustics, Speech, and Signal Processing*, pp. 2934–2937, Mar. 2010.

[25] M. G. Morrow, C. H. G. Wright, and T. B. Welch, "Real-time DSP for adaptive filters: A teaching opportunity," in *Proceedings of the IEEE International Conference on Acoustics, Speech, and Signal Processing*, May 2013.

[26] C. H. G. Wright, T. B. Welch, and M. G. Morrow, "Leveraging student knowledge of DSP for optical engineering," in *Proceedings of the 2015 IEEE Signal Processing and Signal Processing Education Workshop*, pp. 148–153, Aug. 2015.

[27] S. D. Stearns, *Digital Signal Processing with Examples in MATLAB*. CRC Press, 2nd ed., 2012.

[28] V. K. Ingle and J. G. Proakis, *Digital Signal Processing Using MATLAB V.4*. Bookware Companion Series, PWS Publishing, 1997.

[29] J. H. McClellan, C. S. Burrus, A. V. Oppenheim, T. W. Parks, R. W. Schafer, and S. W. Schuessler, *Computer-Based Exercises for Signal Processing Using MATLAB 5*. MATLAB Curriculum Series, Prentice Hall, 1998.

[30] A. Ambardar and C. Borghesani, *Mastering DSP Concepts Using MATLAB*. Prentice Hall, 1998.

[31] D. C. Hanselman and B. L. Littlefield, *Mastering MATLAB 7*. Prentice Hall, 2005.

[32] D. M. Etter, *Engineering Problem Solving with MATLAB*. Prentice Hall, 2nd ed., 1997.

[33] D. M. Etter, *Introduction to MATLAB*. Prentice Hall, 2nd ed., 2011.

[34] H. V. Sorensen and J. Chen, *A Digital Signal Processing Laboratory Using the TMS320C30*. Prentice Hall, 1997.

[35] R. Chassaing, *DSP Applications Using C and the TMS320C6x DSK*. John Wiley & Sons, 2002.

[36] N. Kehtarnavaz, *Real-Time Digital Signal Processing Based on the TMS320C6000*. Elsevier, 2005.

[37] C. H. G. Wright and T. B. Welch, "Teaching DSP concepts using MATLAB and the TMS320C5X," in *Proceedings of the 1998 Texas Instruments DSP Educators and Third-Party Conference*, August 6–8, 1998.

[38] C. H. G. Wright and T. B. Welch, "Teaching DSP concepts using MATLAB and the TMS320C31 DSK," in *Proceedings of the IEEE International Conference on Acoustics, Speech, and Signal Processing*, Mar. 1999. Paper 1778.

[39] M. G. Morrow, T. B. Welch, and C. H. G. Wright, "An inexpensive software tool for teaching real-time DSP," in *Proceedings of the 1st IEEE DSP in Education Workshop*, IEEE Signal Processing Society, Oct. 2000.

[40] M. G. Morrow, T. B. Welch, C. H. G. Wright, and G. York, "Teaching real-time beamforming with the C6211 DSK and MATLAB," in *Proceedings of the 2000 Texas Instruments DSP Educators and Third-Party Conference*, August 2–4, 2000.

[41] C. H. G. Wright, T. B. Welch, and M. G. Morrow, "Teaching transfer functions with MATLAB and real-time DSP," in *Proceedings of the 2001 ASEE Annual Conference*, June 2001. Session 1320.

[42] M. G. Morrow, T. B. Welch, and C. H. Wright, "An introduction to hardware-based DSP using winDSK6," in *Proceedings of the 2001 ASEE Annual Conference*, June 2001. Session 1320.

[43] T. B. Welch, C. T. Field, and C. H. G. Wright, "A signal analyzer for teaching signals and systems," in *Proceedings of the 2001 ASEE Annual Conference*, June 2001. Session 2793.

[44] G. W. P. York, M. G. Morrow, T. B. Welch, and C. H. G. Wright, "Teaching real-time sonar with the C6711 DSK and MATLAB," in *Proceedings of the 2001 ASEE Annual Conference*, June 2001. Session 1320.

[45] M. G. Morrow, T. B. Welch, and C. H. G. Wright, "A tool for real-time DSP demonstration and experimentation," in *Proceedings of the 10th IEEE Digital Signal Processing Workshop*, Oct. 2002. Paper 4.8.

[46] T. B. Welch, D. M. Etter, C. H. G. Wright, M. G. Morrow, and G. J. Twohig, "Experiencing DSP hardware prior to a DSP course," in *Proceedings of the 10th IEEE Digital Signal Processing Workshop*, Oct. 2002. Paper 8.5.

[47] C. H. G. Wright, T. B. Welch, D. M. Etter, and M. G. Morrow, "A systematic model for teaching DSP," in *Proceedings of the IEEE International Conference on Acoustics, Speech, and Signal Processing*, vol. IV, pp. 4140–4143, May 2002. Paper 3243.

[48] C. H. G. Wright, T. B. Welch, D. M. Etter, and M. G. Morrow, "Teaching hardware-based DSP: Theory to practice," in *Proceedings of the IEEE International Conference on Acoustics, Speech, and Signal Processing*, vol. IV, pp. 4148–4151, May 2002. Paper 4024.

[49] C. H. G. Wright, T. B. Welch, D. M. Etter, and M. G. Morrow, "Teaching DSP: Bridging the gap from theory to real-time hardware," in *Proceedings of the 2002 ASEE Annual Conference*, June 2002.

[50] G. W. P. York, C. H. G. Wright, M. G. Morrow, and T. B. Welch, "Teaching real-time sonar with the C6711 DSK and MATLAB," *ASEE Comput. Educ. J.*, vol. XII, pp. 79–87, July 2002.

[51] T. B. Welch, R. W. Ives, M. G. Morrow, and C. H. G. Wright, "Using DSP hardware to teach modem design and analysis techniques," in *Proceedings of the IEEE International Conference on Acoustics, Speech, and Signal Processing*, vol. III, pp. 769–772, Apr. 2003.

[52] T. B. Welch, M. G. Morrow, C. H. G. Wright, and R. W. Ives, "commDSK: A tool for teaching modem design and analysis," in *Proceedings of the 2003 ASEE Annual Conference*, June 2003. Session 2420.

[53] C. H. G. Wright, T. B. Welch, and M. G. Morrow, "An inexpensive method to teach hands-on digital communications," in *Proceedings of the IEEE/ASEE Frontiers in Education Annual Conference*, Nov. 2003.

[54] T. B. Welch, M. G. Morrow, and C. H. G. Wright, "Using DSP hardware to control your world," in *Proceedings of the IEEE International Conference on Acoustics, Speech, and Signal Processing*, vol. V, pp. 1041–1044, May 2004. Paper 1146.

[55] T. B. Welch, M. G. Morrow, C. H. G. Wright, and R. W. Ives, "commDSK: A tool for teaching modem design and analysis," *ASEE Comput. Educ. J.*, vol. XIV, pp. 82–89, Apr. 2004.

[56] M. G. Morrow, T. B. Welch, and C. H. G. Wright, "Enhancing the TMS320C6713 DSK for DSP education," in *Proceedings of the 2005 ASEE Annual Conference*, June 2005.

[57] M. G. Morrow and T. B. Welch, "winDSK: A windows-based DSP demonstration and debugging program," in *Proceedings of the IEEE International Conference on Acoustics, Speech, and Signal Processing*, vol. 6, pp. 3510–3513, June 2000.

[58] M. G. Morrow, C. H. G. Wright, and T. B. Welch, "winDSK8: A user interface for the OMAP-L138 DSP board," in *Proceedings of the IEEE International Conference on Acoustics, Speech, and Signal Processing*, pp. 2884–2887, May 2011.

[59] M. G. Morrow, C. H. G. Wright, and T. B. Welch, "Old tricks for a new dog: An innovative software tool for teaching real-time DSP on a new hardware platform," in *Proceedings of the ASEE Annual Conference*, June 2011.

[60] Educational DSP (eDSP), L.L.C., "Accessible technology for education," 2016. http://www.educationaldsp.com/.

[61] The MathWorks, Inc., *MATLAB: The Language of Technical Computing*, 2016.

[62] S. M. Kuo and B. H. Lee, *Real-Time Digital Signal Processing: Implementations, Applications and Experiments for the TMS320C55x*. John Wiley & Sons, 2001.

[63] R. E. Ziemer and R. L. Peterson, *Introduction to Digital Communication*. Prentice Hall, 2nd ed., 2001.

[64] L. W. Couch II, *Digital and Analog Communication Systems*. Prentice Hall, 7th ed., 2007.

[65] B. Sklar, *Digital Communications: Fundamentals and Applications*. Prentice Hall, 2nd ed., 2001.

[66] M. Rice, *Digital Communications: A Discrete-Time Approach*. Prentice Hall, 2009.

[67] J. G. Proakis, *Digital Communications*. McGraw-Hill, 4th ed., 2001.

[68] R. C. Dixon, *Spread Spectrum Systems with Commercial Applications*. John Wiley & Sons, 3rd ed., 1994.

[69] New Wave Instruments, "Linear feedback shift registers: Implementation, m-sequence properties, and feedback tables," 2011. http://www.newwaveinstruments.com/resources/articles/m_sequence_linear_feedback_shift_register_lfsr.htm.

[70] K. C. Pohlmann, *Principles of Digital Audio*. Howard W. Sams & Co., 2nd ed., 1989.

[71] Texas Instruments, Inc., *TMS320C6000 DSP Peripherals Overview Reference Guide*, 2009. Literature Number: SPRU190Q. URL: http://www.ti.com/lit/ug/spru190q/spru190q.pdf.

[72] J. W. Cooley and J. W. Tukey, "An algorithm for the machine computation of complex fourier series," *Mathematics of Computation*, vol. 19, pp. 297–301, Apr. 1965.

[73] S. M. Kay, *Modern Spectral Analysis: Theory and Application*. Prentice Hall, 1988.

[74] S. M. Kay, *Fundmentals of Statistical Signal Processing: Estimation Theory*, vol. 1. Prentice Hall, 1993.

[75] D. G. Manolakis, V. K. Ingle, and S. M. Kogon, *Statistical and Adaptive Signal Processing: Spectral Estimation, Signal Modeling, Adaptive Filtering, and Array Processing*. McGraw-Hill, 2000.

[76] M. R. Schroeder, "Natural sounding artificial reverberation," *Journal of the Audio Engineering Society*, vol. 10, pp. 219–223, 1962.

[77] S. J. Orfanidis, *Introduction to Signal Processing*. Prentice Hall, 1996.

[78] H. Chamberlin, *Musical Applications of Microprocessors*. Hayden Book Company, 2nd ed., 1985.

[79] R. M. Rangayyan, *Biomedical Signal Analysis: A Case-Study Approach.* John Wiley & Sons, 2nd ed., 2015.

[80] C. F. N. Cowan and P. M. Grant, eds., *Adaptive Filters.* Prentice-Hall, 1985.

[81] S. Haykin, *Adaptive Filter Theory.* Prentice Hall, 1996.

[82] S. D. Stearns, *Digital Signal Processing with Examples in MATLAB.* CRC Press, 2003.

[83] A. D. Poularikas and Z. M. Ramadan, *Adaptive Filtering Primer with MATLAB.* CRC Press, 2006.

[84] B. Widrow, J. R. Glover, Jr., J. M. McCool, J. Kaunitz, C. S. Williams, R. H. Hearn, J. R. Zeidler, E. Dong, Jr., and R. C. Goodlin, "Adaptive noise cancelling: Principles and applications," *Proceedings of the IEEE*, vol. 63, no. 12, pp. 1692–1716, 1975.

[85] A. B. Carlson, P. B. Crilly, and J. C. Rutledge, *Communication Systems.* McGraw-Hill, 4th ed., 2002.

[86] M. E. Frerking, *Digital Signal Processing in Communication Systems.* Van Nostrand Reinhold, 1994. 7th printing by Kluwer Academic Publishers, 2000.

[87] S. A. Tretter, *Communications System Design Using DSP Algorithms: With Laboratory Experiments for the TMS320C30.* Plenum Press, 1995.

[88] S. A. Tretter, *Communications System Design Using DSP Algorithms: With Laboratory Experiments for the TMS320C6701 and TMS320C6711.* Kluwer Academic Publishers (Plenum Press), 2003.

[89] U. Mengali and A. N. D'Andrea, *Synchronization Techniques for Digital Receivers.* Plenum Press, 1997.

[90] M. M. Mano and M. D. Ciletti, *Digital Design.* Prentice Hall, 4th ed., 2007.

[91] R. W. Hamming, *Coding and Information Theory.* Prentice Hall, 2nd ed., 1986.

[92] J. Kurzweil, *An Introduction to Digital Communications.* John Wiley & Sons, 2000.

[93] Texas Instruments, Inc., *TMS320 DSP/BIOS v 5.42 User's Guide*, 2012. Literature Number: SPRU423I. URL: http://www.ti.com/lit/ug/spru423i/spru423i.pdf.

[94] Texas Instruments, Inc., *TMS320C6000 DSP/BIOS 5.x Application Programming Interface (API) Reference Guide*, 2012. Literature Number: SPRU403S. URL: http://www.ti.com/lit/ug/spru403s/spru403s.pdf.

[95] Institute of Electrical and Electronics Engineers (IEEE), "IEEE standard for floating-point arithmetic: IEEE 754-2008," 2008. Identical content international standard is ISO/IEC/IEEE 60559:2011.

[96] R. W. Hamming, *Numerical Methods for Scientists and Engineers.* McGraw-Hill, 2nd ed., 1973.

[97] S. S. Rao, *Applied Numerical Methods for Engineers and Scientists.* Prentice Hall, 2002.

[98] Texas Instruments, Inc., *TMS320C6000 CPU and Instruction Set Reference Guide*, 2006. Literature Number: SPRU189G. URL: http://www.ti.com/lit/ug/spru189g/spru189g.pdf.

[99] J. L. Hennessy and D. A. Patterson, *Computer Architecture: A Quantitative Approach*. Morgan Kaufmann Publishers, 4th ed., 2007.

[100] J. A. Fisher, P. Faraboschi, and C. Young, *Embedded Computing: A VLIW Approach to Architecture, Compilers and Tools*. Morgan Kaufmann Publishers, 2004.

[101] Texas Instruments, Inc., *OMAP-L138 C6-Integra DSP+ARM Processor*, 2014. Literature Number: SPRS586I. URL: http://focus.ti.com/lit/ds/symlink/omap-l138.pdf.

Index